The

# Urban Labor Market

and

# Income Distribution

A World Bank Research Publication

The

# Urban Labor Market
and
# Income Distribution

A Study of Malaysia

*Dipak Mazumdar*

Published for the World Bank
Oxford University Press

Oxford University Press

NEW YORK OXFORD LONDON GLASGOW
TORONTO MELBOURNE WELLINGTON HONG KONG
TOKYO KUALA LUMPUR SINGAPORE JAKARTA
DELHI BOMBAY CALCUTTA MADRAS KARACHI
NAIROBI DAR ES SALAAM CAPE TOWN

© 1981 by the International Bank
for Reconstruction and Development / The World Bank
1818 H Street, N.W., Washington, D.C. 20433 U.S.A.

The views and interpretations in this book are the
author's and should not be attributed to the World
Bank, to its affiliated organizations, or to any
individual acting in their behalf.

*Library of Congress Cataloging in Publication Data*

Mazumdar, Dipak, 1932–
   The urban labor market and income distribution.
   (A World Bank research publication)
   Includes bibliographical references and index.
   1.   Labor supply—Malaysia.   2.   Income distribution
—Malaysia.   I.   International Bank for Reconstruction
and Development.   II.   Title.   III.   Series: World Bank
research publication.
HD5822.6.A6M39          331.12'09595          80-24413
ISBN  0-19-520213-9
ISBN  0-19-520214-7 (pbk.)

# Contents

## Part III.  Unemployment

## Part IV.  Summary of Findings

# Figures

# Tables

# Preface

THIS BOOK HAS ITS ORIGIN in the concern of development economists in the World Bank and elsewhere with the unemployment of young people—particularly the more educated among them—in the urban labor markets of developing countries. Since the government of Malaysia shared a strong interest in research on this problem, it was decided to mount a comprehensive study in Malaysia which would cover most of the salient aspects of urban labor markets and income distribution in a developing country. When I came to take charge of this research project, I was already involved in studies of the working of such markets, especially the relation between the formal and informal sectors.

The original surveys on which this work is based were organized by the Bank and undertaken in 1973–75. Although preliminary reports were available soon after and were discussed with officials in Malaysia in early 1975, it has been a lengthy process to integrate all the material into a full-length book and then to edit and publish it. The labor market scene in Malaysia has changed substantially since the early 1970s. As the book goes to press I am inclined to speculate hopefully that some other researchers will be interested in studying the impact of economic growth in Malaysia on several of the large issues discussed here. A second look at the labor market, say, ten years after the benchmark study would, it seems to me, yield rich results for our understanding of labor market processes in developing countries. Examples of the more important topics would include: the decline in the rate of youth unemployment, the impact of accelerated industrialization on the relation between the formal and informal sectors, changes in the rates of returns to human capital factors, and trends in racial earnings differentials.

The major theme of the book is the perennial one: what causes low earnings? The nature and extent of the problem have been delineated, particularly in Part I of the book, but some of the favorite explanations such as labor market segmentation and discrimination are seen in Part II to account at best for only a portion of the problem. The search for socioeconomic explanations of low earnings must go on. Comparative studies, some already under way, of labor markets in other developing countries will shed further light.

It remains for me to thank a group of institutions and persons who have been particularly helpful. The School Leavers Survey could not have been undertaken without the enthusiastic cooperation of the Ministry of Labor (Information) of the government of Malaysia. The Economic Planning Unit of the prime minister's secretariat provided a valuable umbrella and much needed help at crucial points. The staff of the Statistics Department were always ready to oblige with their time and their data files.

Several research assistants have worked with me on the project over the years. Shigeko Asher (now a staff member of the Bank) administered the School Leavers Survey in Malaysia and did a very competent job in the field. Parita Suebsaeng and Masood Ahmed (also now a staff member of the Bank) were primarily responsible for helping me with the analysis of the data at the World Bank and at the London School of Economics, respectively. Their contributions often went beyond the normal requirements of a competent research assistant.

Peter Bocock edited the manuscript, and Jane H. Carroll and Christine Houle prepared the book for publication and supervised production. Raphael Blow prepared the figures, Chris Jerome read and corrected proof of the book, and Ralph Ward and James Silvan prepared the index.

The
# Urban Labor Market
and
# Income Distribution

A Study of Malaysia

# CHAPTER I

# Overview

THIS BOOK IS A DETAILED CASE STUDY of the working of the labor market in the urban sector of Peninsular Malaysia[1] and of the factors which affect the distribution of income in the sector. Because its primary focus is on income distribution at the lower end of the earnings scale and on the determinants of poverty, the discussion is, for the most part, confined to labor earnings. It does not deal with the distribution of unearned incomes which is unlikely to be significant for the relatively poor households with which the book is principally concerned. The main sources from which the book's analysis is derived are two surveys conducted by the World Bank in 1973 and 1975.[2] The information obtained from these surveys has been supplemented for the purpose of the analysis by a range of published Malaysian government statistics, including in particular the Post Enumeration Survey (PES) of 1970.

At first sight, a case study of income distribution in Malaysia might seem to be of relatively limited application to the problems of the developing world as a whole. Malaysia is a member of the middle-income group of developing countries. Its resources include a number of reasonably successful cash crops and a quite extensive education system. Absolute poverty is thus less pervasive in Malaysia than in some Asian or African countries. At the same time, however, the relative poverty of the main racial group in the country, the Malays, is a problem of real political and social significance. This problem is by no means unique to Malaysia. Systematic variations in income by race, by tribe, or by language group exist in many other developing countries; an

1. Peninsular Malaysia consists of the territory of Malaysia, excluding the provinces of Sarawak and Sabah or Borneo.
2. These were a 1973 tracer study, known as the School Leavers Survey (SLS), and a 1975 household survey, known as the Migration and Employment Survey (MES).

3

analysis of the causes of these differences in Malaysia, and of the government's efforts to reduce them, is of wide general relevance. In addition, despite the country's relatively high level of per capita income and its reasonably good resource base, Malaysia's urban sector has a number of fundamental economic features in common with those poorer developing countries. The importance of rural-urban migration in the process of urbanization, the coexistence in the urban labor market of modern and traditional sectors, and the positive relation between formal educational qualifications and urban earnings and employment opportunities are examples of such common features.

The present study concentrates on labor market issues in the urban sector, because the factors affecting labor earnings can be isolated and examined rather more easily in an urban context than in a rural one. Although self-employment represents a substantial part of total urban employment in Malaysia (around 26 percent), it is much less important in the cities than it is in the rural areas. Consequently, an analysis that emphasizes the factors determining wage income—as opposed to one that considers the distribution of total assets—can more appropriately be drawn from and applied to urban income distribution data.

The ultimate concern of this book is the distribution of income among households. A household's standard of living is broadly the product of the income per earning member and the ratio of dependents to earners in the household (sometimes known as the "dependency ratio"). Put more fully, a household's earned income per capita (or per adult equivalent unit) will be determined by several factors: the number of dependents who are demographically determined, that is, the number of children outside working age; the number of potential earners among the adults in the household; the proportion of potential earners who were actually earning—the household employment rate—which is partly an economic variable; and the individual earnings of the members of the household who are in fact employed.

The relative importance of these various factors in the urban economy of Malaysia is the subject of Part I of this book. Households are divided into four classes according to their income level per adult equivalent unit, and the differences between the classes are studied with regard to their household earnings and dependency ratios. Chapter 3 is largely descriptive, setting out the basic characteristics of the different classes of household. The data presented suggest that relatively poor households suffer from a relatively high burden of dependency, which includes adult as well as child dependents. This state of affairs is not due to the prevalence of joint[3] rather than nuclear families—extended families, in fact, have a relatively low incidence of poverty. Nor is the high adult dependency ratio among poor households a consequence of the age of the head of the family (or the principal household earner). The economic causes of this phenomenon are analyzed in Chapter 4, which contains a discussion on the factors affecting the variations in employment rates (the obverse of the dependency ratios) among adults in different household income classes.

Given that a relatively high burden of dependency is one of the causes of household poverty, it is important to establish its quantitative effect in generating low standards of living compared with that of income per earner. Chapter 5 breaks down household income per adult equivalent unit into its three components—the number of household members, the proportion who are earners, and the average income per earner—and shows that levels of income are much more strongly affected by average income per earner than by the burden of dependency in the household. A policy conclusion of some importance emerges from this finding. Efforts to reduce the burden of dependency among poor households, either through family planning programs or through policies to increase the employment opportunities of females and nonprime-age males, may help to alleviate relative poverty; the principal objective of policy, however, should be to tackle problems associated with low individual earnings.

This conclusion is given added strength when the analysis moves from a description of the actual magnitudes of dependency ratios and earnings to a detailed examination of the predicted values of these variables based on simple functions of employment and earnings according to the personal characteristics (such as education and age) of members of the household. The predicted values of earnings that represent the average expectations of a particular class based on the characteristics of its earners are, as is shown in Chapter 5, substantially above the actual earnings of the poor households and substantially below those of the rich households. The poor are poor, not only because their earning members have fewer human capital endowments (experience and education) than the rich, but also because they earn substantially less than what they might have expected to earn on the basis of the average

---

3. For the purpose of this study a joint family is defined as any family living in a single residence with working family members from two or more generations.

return to their levels of education and experience. Exactly the opposite is true, of course, for the rich households.

The unequal distribution of income among households is then largely a consequence of differences in the individual earnings of members of rich and poor households. Part II of this book is concerned with the analysis of individual earnings. It has already been noted that about 26 percent of urban income earners in Malaysia are self-employed. Unfortunately, the data on which this book is based can support only a limited discussion of the determination of the earnings of the self-employed. A full examination of this issue would need to analyze the distribution of physical assets among the self-employed and the history of their acquisition of assets. This area is well worth investigating but requires a type of field survey which could not be undertaken. Chapter 7 does, however, present a comparative outline of the patterns of earnings of employees and the self-employed. The comparison clearly shows the heterogeneous character of the earnings of the self-employed and suggests that no simple generalization can be made about the difference in earnings between the two groups. This point is important because some popular discussions have equated low earnings with the informal sector of the urban labor market and have associated the self-employed with the informal sector.

The rest of Part II discusses a number of specific factors that affect the earnings of employees. Chapter 8 presents a full analysis of the earnings of male employees in reference to the human capital model. This model—and, in particular, its education component—explains a substantial proportion of the variance in earnings by household. The model's explanatory power is much greater for the Malaysian sample studied in this book than it is for developed countries. This is partly because of the relative importance of the public sector (in which formal education and seniority rules are key determinants of earnings), and partly because occupational differentials in earnings are so much greater in Malaysia and other developing countries than in developed countries. The human capital model, however, substantially overestimates earnings at the lower end of the distribution and underpredicts them at the upper end. Is it possible to isolate other factors that will throw more light on differences in earnings between individuals?

Chapter 9 analyzes the widely discussed hypothesis of the dichotomy between formal and informal sector or modern and traditional employment in the urban labor market. The analysis attempts to clarify the meaning of the dichotomy and to assess its quantitative importance in the Malaysian context. Chapter 10 examines the crucial issue of racial differences in earnings in Malaysia. Is race itself a factor in the determination of income levels, over and above the general explanation provided by human capital elements? Do earnings correspond to levels of formal education and experience in the same way for members of both the disadvantaged and the better-off races? Chapter 11 turns to the phenomenon of migration into the cities covered by the sample and seeks to assess the link between migration and low incomes.

Many of the issues discussed in Chapters 8 to 11 implicitly deal not only with the earnings of an individual at a point of time, but also with the profile of his or her lifetime earnings. The earnings function analysis which is used extensively in this book seeks to throw light on the lifetime profiles by putting together cross-section data on the earnings of individuals at different ages. The questionnaire used in the World Bank Migration and Employment Survey (MES) collected a limited amount of information from respondents about their work history. This material is analyzed in Chapter 12 to throw some light on the nature and extent of mobility within the urban labor market and its implications for changes in earnings over the lifetime of a worker.

In many economies, particularly in industrialized countries, unemployment is one of the basic causes of poverty. Part III of the book shows that although open unemployment is very high in Peninsular Malaysia, its nature is very different from that in developed countries. The problem is not so much one of chronic or recurrent unemployment among adult males, as one of lack of employment among youths, especially those with secondary education. Thus, there is only a limited direct relationship between poverty and unemployment in Malaysia, but unemployment among the young affects household standards of living by increasing the dependency ratio.

The Malaysian unemployment problem is of general interest for urban labor market analysis in developing countries for two reasons. First, it presents a paradoxical picture of high rates of unemployment in an economy which is relatively well-off by developing country standards and has had (as will be shown in the next section) very respectable rates of growth in the past. Second, there appears to be a close connection between government policies relating to income and education, which are intended to ameliorate conditions of poverty (particularly among the disadvantaged racial group) and the problem of unemployment. It is important for Malaysia and for other similarly placed developing countries to be fully aware of this connection.

Because of the importance of the problems of urban employment and income distribution, the World Bank undertook a special School

Leavers Survey (sls) in 1973 with the full cooperation of the Malaysian government. The data gathered in this survey provide the basis of much of the analysis of open unemployment in Malaysia in Part III of the book. The introduction to Part III presents a framework for the survey's findings, putting the analysis into the context of current theories of the determination of wages. Chapter 14 puts the Malaysian problem in an international context, and Chapters 15, 16, and 17 complete the study with discussions of a number of special issues arising from the survey's findings.

Each of the three sections of the book—dealing with households, individual earnings, and unemployment—begins with an introductory discussion of the theoretical framework underlying the subsequent analysis; references are provided to relevant discussions in the literature on the subject. The book concludes with a brief (and hence necessarily selective) summary of the major conclusions of the study as a whole.

## The Economy of Peninsular Malaysia

This section presents an overview of the major features of the Malaysian economy that are relevant to the issues discussed in the rest of the book.

Urbanization is an important component of economic development in Malaysia. The data in Table 1-1, calculated by Professor Suresh Narayanan from successive censuses, give an idea of the process of urbanization over time. Urban areas in Malaysia are defined demographically

Table 1-1. Urban Population Growth in Peninsular Malaysia

| Census | Urban population as percent of total | Number of urban centers | Average annual growth rate of population (percent) | |
|--------|--------|--------|--------|--------|
| | | | Urban | Rural |
| 1921 | 14.0 | 11 | — | — |
| 1931 | 15.0 | 16 | 3.38 | 2.52 |
| 1947 | 18.9 | 22 | 3.05 | 1.33 |
| 1957 | 26.6 | 38 | 5.84 | 1.45 |
| 1970 | 28.7 | 49 | 5.21 | 2.40 |

*Source:* Suresh Narayanan, "Urban In-Migration and Urban Labor Absorption: A Study of Metropolitan Urban Selangor" (thesis submitted to the Faculty of Economics and Administration, University of Malaya, February 1975), tables II.1 and II.2, pp. 26 and 28.

Table 1-2. Urban Population by City Size, 1957–70

| Population | Percentage of urban population in the size group | | Annual growth rate (percent), 1957–70 |
|---|---|---|---|
| | 1957 | 1970 | |
| More than 100,000 | 49.0 | 50.7 | 3.51 |
| 50–100,000 | 24.0 | 26.1 | 3.91 |
| 20–50,000 | 13.8 | 12.2 | 2.33 |
| 10–20,000 | 13.3 | 11.0 | 1.79 |
| Total | 100.0 | 100.0 | 3.20 |

Source: Narayanan, "Urban In-Migration," table II.6.

as having a minimum population of 10,000—a relatively high figure compared with those used in other countries' definitions. Notwithstanding this rather stringent definition of urban areas, the figures show substantial rates of growth for the urban population compared with the rates shown for those living in rural areas. The recent apparent reduction in the urban growth rate suggested by a simple comparison of the 1957 and 1970 figures reflects special factors associated with the very large increases in urban population between 1947 and 1957—notably the postwar disturbances and the resettlement of the Chinese population in "new villages."[4]

Narayanan also compiled figures for urban growth rates broken down by size of urban center between the census years 1957 and 1970. Table 1-2 reproduces his data. Overall, the picture is one of growing concentration of population in cities with populations of more than 50,000, with the most notable increase taking place in medium to large cities of from 50,000 to 100,000 people.

As in urban areas in many other developing countries, about a third of the labor force in Malaysian towns is engaged in manufacturing activities and another third in sales and services. White-collar workers comprise just under a fifth of the labor force in smaller towns, rising to about a quarter in the larger ones (see Table 1-3).

4. Narayanan makes the point that whereas most new villages in the country had populations of less than 10,000 and were therefore nonurban by definition, the general disruptions contributed to urban drift. Also the expanded security forces were mostly urban based.

Table 1-3. Percentage Distribution of Labor Force by Occupation and Residence, Peninsular Malaysia, 1970

| | Towns | | Rural areas | |
| --- | --- | --- | --- | --- |
| Occupation | More than 75,000 | 10,000– 75,000 | 1,000– 10,000 | Less than 1,000 |
| Professional | 8.4 | 9.7 | 5.5 | 2.4 |
| Administrative or managerial | 1.9 | 1.2 | 0.7 | 0.2 |
| Clerical | 13.4 | 7.7 | 3.6 | 1.8 |
| Sales | 15.2 | 15.6 | 12.0 | 4.1 |
| Services | 16.8 | 12.9 | 9.4 | 4.0 |
| Agriculture | 2.6 | 13.4 | 38.6 | 66.0 |
| Production workers | 31.9 | 30.2 | 21.6 | 12.6 |
| Total labor force (thousands)[a] | 494.4 | 309.2 | 351.3 | 1,716.1 |

a. Includes unemployed and those not elsewhere classified.
*Source:* 1970 Population Census of Malaysia, vol. 2.

### Rural-Urban Income Differences

One of the features of urbanization is the maintenance or exacerbation of substantial income differentials between the rural and the urban sectors. This rural-urban income gap is typically accompanied by, and tends to contribute to, sizable inequalities of income within the urban sector. Malaysia is no exception to this general pattern.

Sudhir Anand has compiled a comprehensive picture of the distribution of income in Peninsular Malaysia from the data collected by the Post-Enumeration Survey (PES) of 1970.[5] He considers the distribution of individuals in terms of the per capita income and location of their households, in order to focus attention on the variations by location in standards of living enjoyed by individuals who presumably share equally in the total income accruing to the household. It should be clearly understood that this analysis of the distribution of income will be different from that of the distribution of personal earnings. Anand's fig-

5. Sudhir Anand, *Inequality and Poverty in Malaysia: Measurement and Decomposition* (New York: Oxford University Press, forthcoming).

ures for the differences in per capita income and its distribution between the urban and the rural sectors are as follows:[6]

| | Metropolitan towns | Other urban towns | Rural | Total |
|---|---|---|---|---|
| Mean income (Malaysian dollars per month) | 92 | 62 | 38 | 50 |
| Gini coefficient | 0.5082 | 0.4582 | 0.4505 | 0.4980 |
| Theil index | 0.5214 | 0.4173 | 0.4135 | 0.5161 |

Along with an increase in the per capita income as one moves from the rural to the urban and to the metropolitan areas, there is an increase in the inequality in the distribution of income by either of the two indexes used.

The size of the overall gap between rural and urban incomes should not, however, obscure the extent of the inequality in the distribution of income within each sector. A quantitative idea of the two components of inequality may be formed by decomposing the overall index into the portions of it represented by inequalities within a given group and inequalities between that group and the others being considered. The Theil index of inequality calculated by Anand lends itself to algebraic decomposition into the two components.[7] It appears from his figures that only 13.7 percent of the inequality measured by the Theil index can be ascribed to the differences in mean incomes between rural, urban, and metropolitan towns.[8]

It would have been useful to place the Malaysian rural-urban income differentials in an international perspective, but there are currently insufficient comparative data for different economies, partly no doubt because of varying national definitions of the urban sector. Data have, however, been collected for many countries on differences between agricultural and nonagricultural incomes—the so-called Kuznets ratio—which is obviously related to the rural-urban income gap. Kuznets presented data on interindustry differences in product per worker for countries at different levels of development (the figures broadly relate to about 1960). His conclusion was that "per worker product in the non-agricultural sectors is from 4 to 1.5 times as high as that in the

6. Ibid., table 3.11, chap. 3. The Malaysian dollar, also known as ringgit after 1971, equaled US$0.33 through 1971. According to the PES, metropolitan towns were Johore Bahru, Malacca, Kuala Lumpur, Klang, Ipoh, and Georgetown. Towns of more than 10,000 population are considered urban.

7. Ibid., appendix.

8. Ibid., chap. 3.

agricultural sector . . . and perhaps most significant, the intersectoral difference in product per worker between the agricultural and the other sector narrows steadily as we move from the low to high per capita product countries."[9] This conclusion was revised by Chenery and Syrquin for a sample of a larger number of countries (figures relating to about 1965). They found that "relative labor productivity in the primary sector falls from about 70 percent to 50 percent at an income level of $500 and then gradually rises as agricultural technology is modernized and the surplus agricultural labor is absorbed by the rest of the economy."[10] Chenery and Syrquin do not discuss in detail the reasons for the observed U-shaped pattern of productivity difference. The thrust of their argument seems to be that accumulation and technological advance are concentrated in industry and public utilities. This situation creates a demand for labor which can be met only by migration from the rural areas, but the rate of growth of the labor force in recent years has been substantially above the excess demand from the urban or developing sector. "Equalization of factor returns is hampered by immobility and unequal access to capital, land, and other complementary factors."[11] There is then an accumulation of surplus labor, in some sense, in the primary rural sector as income begins to rise from a low base.

Chenery and Syrquin present a graph (reproduced in Figure 1-1) showing the scatter of points depicting the relative productivity of the primary sector of a country and its per capita gross national product (GNP). The position of Malaysia on the graph fitted to the scatter reveals two points of interest: (1) Although Malaysia has one of the highest per capita income levels in Asia its position is still on the left branch of the U-shaped curve. That is, if the international cross-section perspective were to depict some kind of a norm, the expectation would be for a further decline in the relative productivity of the primary sector with economic development in Malaysia. (2) The point for Malaysia is significantly above the graph fitted to the scatter, which suggests that Malaysia has a high-productivity primary sector compared with those of other countries at a similar stage of economic develop-

9. Simon Kuznets, *Economic Growth of Nations: Total Output and Production Structure* (Cambridge: Belknap Press of Harvard University Press, 1971), p. 211; see also table 31, pp. 209–11.

10. Hollis Chenery and Moises Syrquin, *Patterns of Development, 1950–1970* (Oxford: Oxford University Press, 1975), p. 53.

11. Ibid., p. 48.

Figure 1-1. Labor Productivity Indexes: Scatter for Primary Sector
of Thirty-nine Countries, 1965

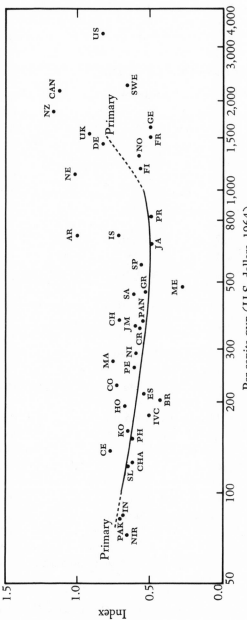

Per capita GNP (U.S. dollars, 1964)

*Key:* AR-Argentina; BR-Brazil; CAN-Canada; CE-Ceylon (Sri Lanka); CH-Chile; CHA-China; CO-Colombia; CR-Costa Rica;
DE-Denmark; ES-El Salvador; FI-Finland; FR-France; GE-Germany, Federal Republic of; GR-Greece; HO-Honduras; IN-India;
IS-Israel; IVC-Ivory Coast; JA-Japan; JM-Jamaica; KO-Korea, South; MA-Malaysia; ME-Mexico; NE-Netherlands; NI-Nicaragua;
NIR-Niger; NO-Norway; NZ-New Zealand; PAK-Pakistan; PE-Peru; PH-Philippines; PR-Puerto Rico; SA-South
Africa; SL-Sierra Leone; SP-Spain; SWE-Sweden; UK-United Kingdom; US-United States.

*Source:* Hollis Chenery and Moises Syrquin, *Patterns of Development, 1950–1970* (Oxford: Oxford University Press,
1975), fig. 9, p. 52.

ment, as measured by GNP per capita. In the light of this last point, it is worth examining the structure of the primary sector of Malaysia and the coexistence of the estate and traditional subsectors within it.

### Dualism in the Primary Sector of Malaysia

Table 1-4 gives the percentage distribution of value added and of employment in the principal sectors of the economy of Peninsular Malaysia in 1970. With regard to the distribution of the labor force, Malaysia was almost in the same position as Korea and the Philippines at about this date, with about half its total employment in agriculture. Korea had a slightly higher percentage of the labor force (by about 2 percentage points) in manufacturing,[12] but considering the differences in income levels the sectoral employment pattern was remarkably similar in the three economies. Specifically, although Malaysia had a per capita GDP of perhaps 50 percent above the level of the Philippines and a third above that of Korea, it did not have, as might have been expected, a smaller agricultural labor force and a larger proportion of total employment in the secondary or tertiary sectors.

To some extent, Malaysia's combination of high GDP and largely agriculture-based employment reflects the fact that the country's agricultural sector includes high-productivity estates as well as traditional low-income agriculture. Without the estate sector the GDP per capita of Malaysia would have been substantially lower—nearer, perhaps, to that of a country such as the Philippines which supports half its labor force in agriculture.

With regard to the U-shaped relationship observed by Chenery and Syrquin, it might be expected that the disparity in levels of productivity between traditional agriculture and the rest of the economy would be much larger in high-income economies such as Malaysia and Korea than it would be in, say, the Philippines—which has a similar intersectoral division of the labor force but a significantly lower level of national income. This is indeed true for agricultural productivity in Malaysia if the estate sector is excluded. With an index of productivity per worker of 1.00 for the whole economy (around 1970), Peninsular Malaysia showed a productivity of 0.44 for traditional agriculture. This com-

12. For comparable data on Korea see Parvez Hasan, *Korea* (Baltimore: Johns Hopkins University Press, 1976), p. 48; and on the Philippines, see the International Labour Organisation (ILO) Mission Report (Geneva, 1974), p. 12.

Table 1-4. Employment and Output in Peninsular Malaysia

| Sector | Labor force (thousands) (1) | Value added (millions of Malaysian dollars) (2) | Percentage of total GDP (3) | Percentage of total employment (4) | Productivity (3) ÷ (4) |
|---|---|---|---|---|---|
| Agriculture | 1,454 | 2,517 | 29.7 | 49.0 | 0.61 |
| Estates | 270 | 797 | 9.4 | 9.1 | 1.01 |
| Small-scale | 1,076 | 1,353 | 16.0 | 36.3 | 0.44 |
| Forestry and fishing | 108 | 367 | 4.3 | 3.6 | 1.20 |
| Mining and manufacturing | 366 | 1,802 | 21.3 | 12.3 | 1.73 |
| All services | 1,144 | 4,147 | 49.0 | 38.7 | 1.27 |
| Social overhead[a] | 232 | 871 | 10.3 | 7.8 | 1.32 |
| Other services | 912 | 3,276 | 38.7 | 31.1 | 1.24 |
| Total employment GDP at factor cost | 2,964 | 8,466 | 100.0 | 100.0 | 1.00 |

a. Includes construction, electricity, water and sanitary services, and transport and communication.
Source: Government of Malaysia, Department of Statistics.

pares with 0.50 and 0.72 for all agriculture in Korea and the Philippines, respectively, where the importance of estates is small. In contrast, including estates brings up the relative productivity index for all agriculture in Malaysia to 0.61 (the estates by themselves have a relative productivity of 1.01).

The existence of a large gap in labor productivity between traditional agriculture and the nonagricultural sectors—and by implication between the bulk of the rural areas and the urban economy—has an important effect on the distribution of income in the urban areas in Malaysia; generally speaking, an economy characterized by a large rural-urban income gap will tend to have a relatively unequal distribution of incomes within the urban sector. In the Malaysian context the position is further complicated by the significantly different racial composition of the rural and urban labor forces; the racial disparities in income exacerbates the problem of rural-urban inequality.

*Racial Imbalance*

The population of Malaysia is made up of three principal racial groups—Malays, Chinese, and Indians. Of the three groups, the Malays are the least urbanized, in the sense that the proportion of the Malay population living in urban areas is smaller than that of the two non-Malay groups. This low degree of Malay urbanization is often considered to be a cause of the relatively low levels of income among Malays compared with the other two communities (particularly the Chinese). Racial differences in urbanization over time are presented in Table 1-5, compiled by Narayanan. The Malay share in the urban

Table 1-5. Racial Differences in Urbanization, 1931–70

| | Percentage of population in urban areas | | | | Percentage of urban population by race | | | |
| --- | --- | --- | --- | --- | --- | --- | --- | --- |
| Year | Malay | Chinese | Indian | Total | Malay | Chinese | Indian | Other |
| 1931 | 5.3 | 24.0 | 17.5 | 15.1 | 17.3 | 54.0 | 17.5 | 11.2 |
| 1947 | 7.3 | 31.1 | 25.8 | 18.9 | 19.0 | 63.1 | 14.7 | 3.2 |
| 1957 | 11.2 | 44.7 | 30.6 | 26.6 | 21.0 | 62.6 | 12.8 | 3.6 |
| 1970 | 14.9 | 47.4 | 34.7 | 28.7 | 27.6 | 58.4 | 12.7 | 3.1 |

*Source:* Suresh Narayanan, "Urban In-Migration and Urban Labor Absorption," tables II.7 and II.8.

population has been increasing rather more rapidly in the last intercensal period, but even in 1970 only a small proportion of the Malay population was living in urban areas.

Summary data on differences between Malay and Chinese earnings in Table 1-6 show that these variations are not confined to urbanized groups; the rural-urban income differential also seems to be larger for the Malays. Not only do the Chinese participate more in the lucrative

Table 1-6. Mean Earnings by Race and Residence, 1970
(Malaysian dollars per month)

| Race | Metropolitan | Towns | Rural | Malaysia |
| --- | --- | --- | --- | --- |
| Malay | 243 | 170 | 104 | 118 |
| Chinese | 256 | 214 | 177 | 209 |
| All | 267 | 201 | 128 | 163 |

*Source:* Sudhir Anand, *Inequality and Poverty in Malaysia,* table 6-5.

urban economy, but those Chinese who live in rural areas seem to be markedly better off, on average, than the Malays. The evidence suggests that there is a much sharper difference between rural and urban incomes among Malays than among Chinese; that is, rural-urban migration succeeds in equalizing income between strata to a significantly lesser extent for the Malays. This may be partly because of the relatively low rate of Malay migration. It may also be a consequence of specific patterns of migration, which may leave a larger proportion of the Malays in especially low-income localities within rural areas.

## Trends in Employment

Much of the discussion in this book of the problems of income distribution and labor markets in urban Malaysia refers to the years from 1973 to 1975, during which the World Bank surveys were undertaken. It may, therefore, be useful to conclude this introduction with some background information about the trends in employment in Peninsular Malaysia over the decade or so leading up to those years, when the patterns underlying many of the problems to be discussed in this book were established. Reasonably firm estimates of the growth and absorption of the labor force are available for the period between the two most recent censuses of 1957 and 1970; the discussion which follows outlines some of the principal trends during this period and concludes with a brief summary of a few of the more salient features of changes since 1970.

### Growth and Absorption of the Labor Force, 1957–70

The adjusted "best estimates" for Malaysia's labor force in 1957 and 1970 are:[13]

|         | Labor force (thousands) | |
|---------|------|------|
|         | 1957 | 1970 |
| Males   | 1,546 | 2,016 |
| Females | 661 | 914 |
| Total   | 2,207 | 2,930 |

13. D. R. Snodgrass, "The Growth and Utilization of Labor Supply in West Malaysia" (Kuala Lumpur: Economic Planning Unit, February 1972; processed). The 1957 figure for females has been adjusted for the undernumeration of female workers in the census (O. J. McDiarmid, "Employment and the Labor Situation," World Bank, 1975). The 1970 census figures were limited to the experienced labor force. They were raised 12 percent to obtain the total labor force.

Table 1-7. Structure of Employment, 1957–70

| Sector | 1957 | | 1970 | | Change 1957–70 | |
| --- | --- | --- | --- | --- | --- | --- |
| | Thousands | Percent | Thousands | Percent | Thousands | Percent of increment |
| Agriculture | 1,223 | 56.9 | 1,443 | 48.8 | 220 | 27.2 |
| Secondary (mining, manufacturing, and construction) | 288 | 13.4 | 469 | 15.9 | 181 | 22.4 |
| Public administration and defense | 167 | 7.8 | 240 | 8.1 | 73 | 9.0 |
| Tertiary (service) | 471 | 21.9 | 806 | 27.2 | 335 | 41.4 |
| Total employed | 2,149 | 100.0 | 2,958 | 100.0 | 809 | 100.0 |

*Source:* D. R. Snodgrass, "The Growth and Utilization of Labor Supply in West Malaysia," for 1957; Economic Planning Unit (EPU), Manpower Section, "Indicators of the 1970 Employment Position," November 25, 1970.

The growth in the labor force during the period (at 2.8 percent a year) was substantially above that in the decade from 1947 to 1957. The shape of the population pyramid in 1947 was heavily influenced by the high deathrates of the 1930s and 1940s and also by the fact that the birthrate was low, to some extent because of the abnormally high ratio of males to females up to this time. Thus, the biological potential for growth in the adult population was low in the decade between 1947 and 1957, regardless of birthrates and the rates of child survival. During the decade between 1957 and 1967, however, postwar demographic trends led to a rapid acceleration in the growth of the adult population.[14]

The rate of participation of the adult population in the labor force fell somewhat (probably as a consequence of urbanization and the larger proportion of teenagers in schools), but the change was small: as a percentage of the population aged 15 to 64, the rate fell from 65.8 in 1957 to 64.0 in 1967. There is some evidence (from a census midpoint labor force survey in 1962) that the rate of growth of labor supply probably accelerated in the latter half of the decade.

In Table 1-7 total employment was estimated by adding the employment totals for individual industries. The rate of growth in employment over the period is somewhat lower than the rate of growth of the labor force between 1957 and 1967 (2.5 percent a year against 2.8 percent). This may be because the primary sources used for the two sets of data are different, but at least part of the gap is probably due to an increase in unemployment over the period. Unfortunately, no firm conclusion can be reached on this point because the earliest data on the unemployment rate come from the 1962 sample survey. Although small differences in unemployment rates measured by different sample surveys are not very reliable, for what they are worth, the rates were 6.1 percent in 1962, 6.8 percent in 1967, and 7.9 percent in 1971.

The data in Table 1-7 show some interesting changes in the structure of employment. Malaysia's rate of growth of employment in manufacturing has been quite high by developing countries' standards, but in 1970 the manufacturing sector as a whole still accounted for a relatively small proportion of total employment. The most significant features of the table are the slow rate of growth of employment in agriculture and the remarkably high rate of growth of employment in the tertiary (service) sector. Over the period, this sector, together with

14. The average percentage rates of increase for population from the age of 15 to 64 were as follows: 1.7 percent from 1947 to 1957, and 3.0 percent from 1957 to 1967.

public administration and defense, accounted for more than half the increase in total employment.

Employment growth in a given sector is determined by the rate of growth of output in the sector on the one hand, and the rate of growth of labor productivity on the other. In the case of the tertiary sector, it is very difficult to separate the factors affecting employment growth into these two components because the only measure of output in much of the sector is the income accruing to those employed there. In the case of agriculture, however, output and productivity trends can usefully be examined to see what light they throw on the reasons for the slow growth of agricultural employment. The relevant material is presented in Table 1-8.

Table 1-8. Annual Percentage Changes in Value Added
and Productivity, 1957–67

| Item | Value added (1964 prices) | Employment | Value added per worker (1964 prices) | Value added per worker (current prices) |
|---|---|---|---|---|
| All agriculture, forestry, and fishing | 4.1 | 1.3 | 2.8 | 1.1 |
| Modern agriculture | 4.0 | −0.3 | 4.0 | 1.0 |
| Traditional agriculture | 4.2 | 1.8 | 2.4 | 1.5 |
| Total economy | 4.9 | 2.4 | 2.5 | 3.4 |

Source: D. R. Snodgrass, "The Growth and Utilization of Labor Supply in West Malaysia."

The format of this table is an attempt to separate the experience of the modern and traditional sectors of agriculture. Employment in the modern sector consists mainly of wage earners working on the estates. This sector also includes land development by the government, involving clearing of forests and settlement of families in the newly vested land for cultivation. Even though some form of peasant proprietorship prevails in some of the more recent land development schemes, however, this type of employment is analogous to a wage-earning situation since the number of families to be settled per unit of land is predetermined by government policy. Traditional agriculture is, by contrast, essentially characterized by self-employment.

The figures in Table 1-8 suggest that the employment lag in agriculture during the decade was not caused by a slow absolute rate of growth of physical output. Although value added in both sectors of the agricultural economy rose in constant prices at a rather lower rate than real national income as a whole, the rate for agriculture was nevertheless substantial.

The figures for the change in value added per worker at constant prices could be thought to show that the incomes of those working in agriculture as a whole rose faster than incomes in the rest of the economy, and that income per worker in the traditional agricultural sector at least kept pace with the trend in the rest of the economy. Such a conclusion would be wrong, because it ignores the fact that the internal terms of trade turned strongly against agriculture during this period (in other words, the prices of agricultural products fell in relation to other prices in the economy).

The prices of Malaysia's agricultural products, and rubber prices in particular, tend to fluctuate substantially from year to year, and the relationship between those prices and those of imports and other domestically produced goods can change markedly over time. If the price of rubber falls sharply, the consequent fall in Malaysia's external terms of trade means that some of the country's potential real income growth is lost to the rest of the world. This change in relative prices will also affect the distribution of income within the Malaysian economy, to the extent that the value of rubber exports as a proportion of the total national product of Malaysia differs from the contribution of rubber to the income of producers in the agricultural sector.

In 1960 total exports of goods and nonfactor services accounted for about 55 percent of Malaysia's GDP. This proportion declined gradually over the first five-year-plan period to a level of 48 percent in 1965.[15] The percentage share of rubber in the total value of exports fluctuates from year to year. Annual figures for the years between 1960 and 1964 were 52, 40, 37, and 35 percent respectively; rubber prices were exceptionally high in 1960.[16] Rubber in Malaysia is produced partly on estates using wage labor and partly by peasant smallholders who grow

15. First Malaysia Plan, 1966–70 (Kuala Lumpur, 1965), table 2.3, p. 24.
16. First Malaysia Plan, tables 2.2 and 2.3, pp. 23–24.

rubber as a cash crop along with other crops such as paddy. The share of rubber in the peasant economy was:[17]

|  | 1957 | 1962 | 1967 |
|---|---|---|---|
| Percentage of rubber produced by smallholders | 42 | 41 | 43 |
| Percentage of total income in traditional agriculture contributed by rubber | 33 | 31 | 23 |

The declining importance of rubber in the smallholding sector during the decade from 1957 to 1967 reflects the peasants' rational response to falling rubber prices. The figures nevertheless show that, over much of the period, rubber contributed a good deal more to the income of the peasant sector than it did to Malaysia's national income. The importance of rubber in the smallholder sector becomes even greater if consideration is limited to the peasants' cash crops (that is, if subsistence production is excluded from calculations of their income). A decline in the price of rubber relative to other prices will consequently lead to a redistribution of income away from the peasant sector; the same situation will, of course, apply to the estate sector of agriculture.

Smallholders both produce and consume paddy (the other main peasant crop), and a net production surplus is sold to consumers outside the sector. Since Malaysia had to import paddy to meet its total consumption requirements in the 1960s, a relative fall in the price of paddy would help the domestic economy, but largely in the nonpeasant sector. It would mean a net redistribution of income away from the peasant sector as a whole to the nonagricultural (and urban) sector.

In Table 1-8, the difference between the figures in the third and fourth columns represents the annual percentage change in prices over the decade. The table shows that prices increased at an average rate of 0.9 percent a year for the economy as a whole, but that agricultural prices fell, and much more sharply. The fall in the price of rubber, which accounted for much but not all of the decline, had a particularly marked effect on the modern agricultural sector. Value added per worker increased at only 1 percent a year at current prices, although the rate of increase at constant prices was as high as 4 percent a year. The traditional agricultural sector was also significantly affected; at

17. Derived from figures presented by D. R. Snodgrass, "Growth and Utilization of Labor Supply in West Malaysia," table 6, p. 21.

current prices, value added per worker in this sector grew at less than half the rate of growth of the economy as a whole.

This relative deterioration of agricultural incomes may partly account for the observed movement of labor out of agriculture. In the case of estate labor such a movement was, of course, involuntary. Faced with the problem of falling prices, employers in the estate sector responded by economizing on labor; during the 1960s employment actually decreased at a rate of 1.7 percent a year while physical output was increasing. Outside the estate sector total employment remained steady, but the fall in relative income induced large numbers of persons who might have gone to work in agriculture to seek employment elsewhere. To some extent, the large increase in employment in the tertiary sector represents a consequence of this state of affairs. Workers who left the agricultural sector because of its poor income opportunities probably moved into the poorer end of the service sector.

This view of the way Malaysia's employment structure changed during the 1960s is consistent with other observed trends over the period. Some indication of an increase in the rate of measured unemployment over the period has already been noted. Data on wage rates or earnings are very sparse in Malaysia, but a few series which could be constructed from the files of the Ministry of Labor are shown in Table 1-9. They are of limited value since they do not specifically reflect the experiences of the informal sector of the economy. They do, however, suggest—if they represent general trends in the economy—that wages probably increased by about 20 to 25 percent over the ten-year period, or around 2 percent a year. Malaysia had "a remarkable record of price stability during the 1960s and up to 1971."[18] Real wages in the organized sector thus maintained a rate of increase somewhat lower than the real rate of growth of productivity in traditional agriculture, although the former was a third higher than the latter at current prices. The decline in the terms of trade of agriculture meant that a substantial part of the sector's real growth was lost—much of it to the rest of the world. Within the Malaysian economy, agriculture lost by comparison with the nonagricultural sector, so that urban workers' incomes improved at the expense of those of producers in agriculture. Wage earners in the formal urban sector accounted for part of this gain, and their income increased at a higher rate than that of the peasant farmers. Urban workers in the informal sector probably did less well, although no evidence is available on this point.

18. Midterm Review of the Second Malaysia Plan, p. 111.

Table 1-9. Trends in Wages in Selected Occupations
(Malaysian dollars)

| Occupation | 1960 | 1961 | 1962 | 1963 | 1964 | 1965 | 1966 | 1967 | 1968 | 1969 |
|---|---|---|---|---|---|---|---|---|---|---|
| *Rubber estates* | | | | | | | | | | |
| Tappers | | | | | | | | | | |
| Male daily rate (time rated only) | 3.40 | 2.80 | 2.80 | 2.80 | 3.15 | n.a. | 3.75 | 3.40 | 3.70 | 4.00 |
| Average monthly earnings (all) | 94.00 | 86.00 | 86.00 | 85.00 | 91.00 | n.a. | 94.00 | 97.00 | 99.00 | 116.00 |
| Weeders (women daily rates) | 2.70 | 2.30 | 2.40 | 2.20 | 2.40 | n.a. | 2.50 | n.a. | 2.60 | 2.70 |
| *Oil palm estates* | | | | | | | | | | |
| Harvesters (daily rate) | 3.35 | 3.20 | 3.20 | 3.80 | 4.00 | n.a. | 4.60 | 3.45 | 3.45 | 4.70 |
| Weeders (women daily rates, directly employed) | 2.85 | 2.07 | 2.25 | 2.40 | 2.40 | n.a. | 2.50 | 2.50 | 2.60 | 2.70 |
| *Tin dredges (workshop)* | | | | | | | | | | |
| Skilled | 6.80 | 6.95 | 7.90 | 8.10 | 8.50 | n.a. | 8.60 | 9.00 | 9.10 | 8.80 |
| Semiskilled | 4.95 | 5.05 | 5.80 | 5.50 | 6.00 | n.a. | 6.50 | 6.40 | 7.00 | 6.70 |
| Unskilled | 4.25 | 4.30 | 4.70 | 4.50 | 5.00 | n.a. | 4.90 | 5.40 | 5.20 | 5.20 |
| *Bus companies* | | | | | | | | | | |
| Skilled workshop staff | 5.70 | 6.00 | 6.20 | 6.35 | 6.50 | n.a. | 6.90 | 7.60 | 8.20 | 7.70 |
| Semiskilled workshop staff | 3.95 | 3.90 | 3.75 | 4.05 | 4.25 | n.a. | 5.70 | 5.70 | 5.65 | 5.75 |
| General laborers (men) | 3.25 | 3.90 | 3.60 | 3.60 | 3.90 | n.a. | 4.00 | 4.80 | 5.10 | 4.80 |
| Clerks and storekeepers (monthly rate) | 247 | 216 | 220 | 224 | 229 | n.a. | 236 | 243 | 231 | 219 |

n.a. Not available.
*Source:* Ministry of Labor.

*Recent Trends, 1970–75*

The Third Malaysia Plan, published in 1976, reviewed trends in employment during the second plan period (1970–75). In the absence of large-scale national surveys of earnings and employment, conclusions about trends in the labor market must remain very tentative. But the figures given in the plan suggest that there was little change during this period in the contribution of broad sectors of the economy to employment growth. "The commercial and services sectors contributed 43.6 percent of total new employment, while the agriculture and the manufacturing sectors accounted for 25.5 percent and 18.4 percent, respectively." These orders of magnitude are much the same as those indicated in Table 1-8. With respect to annual growth rates, "the manufacturing sector set the pace for employment creation with a rate of 6.6 percent per annum." Employment in agriculture grew at a mere 1.6 percent a year, while the growth rates in the trades and services sector ranged between 4.5 and 5.0 percent. The plan document concluded that there had been a net improvement in the employment situation. "The economy achieved an employment growth rate of 3.3 percent per annum resulting in a net increase of 588,000 new jobs, as compared to 618,200 new entrants to the labor force . . . The rate of job creation had the positive effect of reducing the unemployment rate of 7.4 percent in 1970 to 7.0 percent in 1975."[19]

Whether or not the balance between job seekers and job creations has changed significantly in the recent past, the substantial developments in the Malaysian economy during the second plan period were caused by price movements. As noted above, the movement of the terms of trade against agriculture, especially the decline in the price of rubber, was a major factor contributing to the pressure on the labor market in the 1960s. This adverse movement of the terms of trade took place in a general environment of price stability in the economy as a whole. By contrast, "the general level of prices in Malaysia rose dramatically during 1971–75 as world inflation gathered strength."[20] The increase in prices started to gather strength in 1972, accelerated sharply in 1973 and 1974, and slowed down in 1975. The unit values of Malaysia's major primary exports, including rubber and palm oil, followed the same cyclical pattern—falling somewhat during 1970–72, rising appre-

19. Third Malaysia Plan (Kuala Lumpur, 1976), p. 140 and table 8.1.
20. Ibid., p. 125.

ciably in 1973–74, and then declining significantly in 1975. Over the period as a whole, however, export prices rose—the price of rubber, for example, registered an annual average increase of 1.8 percent between 1970 and 1975. The unit price of palm oil exports increased at a much higher annual average rate of 8.6 percent.[21] Import prices, of course, increased at an even faster rate, so that the external terms of trade declined for the Malaysian economy as a whole.

The 1970–75 decline in the external terms of trade during a period of inflation had a quite different effect on the terms of trade of the agricultural sector than had the previous decline of the 1960s, when the overall price level had been relatively stable. In the more recent period, the nonagricultural sector probably bore the brunt of the increases in the prices of rice and other cereals; these increases, at an annual average rate of 12.1 percent, were bound to have more of an adverse effect on the nonagricultural sectors than on the smallholders, many of whom were net sellers of rice. Thus, although there are no precise price indexes to prove the point conclusively, it is highly probable that the relative economic position of agricultural workers improved in the first half of the 1970s because of price trends which favored them over workers in other sectors. (The real rate of growth of agricultural output from 1971 to 1975 was 4.3 percent a year, a little higher than in the 1960s.[22]) This state of affairs in turn probably reduced the pressure to seek gainful employment outside agriculture during the period.

21. Ibid., table 7.1, p. 127.
22. Ibid., table 4.11, p. 69.

# Part I

# *The Household*

CHAPTER 2

# Introduction to Part I

PART I OF THIS BOOK discusses the economics of the household in urban Malaysia, in order to throw light on the major determinants of the household standard of living of the population. The next two chapters make extensive use of two sources of empirical data. In the first of these, the World Bank Migration and Employment Survey (MES) of 1975, basic information was collected on all persons residing in the households surveyed for a limited number of variables, while some respondents from each household provided more detailed information on a much larger number of variables. The analysis which follows presents data from the basic household questionnaires administered to all respondents; parts of the analysis will present data separately for Kuala Lumpur and two large East Coast towns,[1] to provide points of comparison between the metropolis and the newer urban labor markets.

The other principal source of data used in the pages which follow is the Post-Enumeration Survey of 1970 (PES), which provided information on a more limited number of topics for households in urban Malaysia. Chapter 3 begins with an analysis of a portion of the PES data set, which provides an overall picture of the urban household—its size, composition, and the dependency ratio. Households are divided into four classes according to the level of *earned* income per adult equivalent unit, hereafter called YCON. No information was collected on nonwage income accruing to the household, so that household income refers only to the aggregate of the earnings of all household members. Adult equivalent units for each household were calculated by assigning weights to members of the household according to their age.[2] The distribution

1. Kuantan and Kota Bharu.
2. In the PES data set the weights used were: 0.1 for babies, 0.3 for children aged 1–6, 0.6 for those aged 7–15, and 1.0 for all adults. In the MES data set, because of more limited information on age, a weight of 0.5 was assigned to all persons under 15 and 1.0 to all persons older than 15.

of all households by their individual YCON values was obtained, and the total was broken down into four groups. The poor households are the 30 percent of the total starting from the bottom end of the YCON distribution; the next 40 percent are the low-income households; the next 20 percent are the middle group; and the remaining 10 percent are the rich. The principal features of the characteristics of the households and those of the earning members of the households are studied for each of the four separate groups.

One of the major features of household behavior—a feature, in fact, that substantially affects disparities in standards of living—is the ratio of *potential* earners to those who *actually* work in the labor market. Following the descriptive analysis of household composition, Chapter 4 presents a systematic analysis of the determinants of employment rates and attempts to unravel some of the causal factors underlying the variations between different households' dependency ratios.

The material in Chapters 3 and 4, while of interest in itself, is preliminary to Chapter 5, which provides a formal treatment of the components of the household's standard of living as measured by YCON. The purpose of this exercise is to decompose the factors affecting YCON—the demographic ones determining the potential dependency ratio, and the economic ones determining the actual employment rates of potential earners and the earning per worker. This discussion is followed by an assessment of the relative importance of each of these factors, which produce differences between the mean YCON values of the households in the four economic classes.

# CHAPTER 3

# The Household in Urban Malaysia: Dependency, Participation, and Family Size

THE POST-ENUMERATION SURVEY (PES) data are used in this chapter to present an overview of households in urban Malaysia by the four levels of living standards, in terms of earned income per adult equivalent unit (YCON), described in the introduction. Under the PES definition, the term "household" covered all persons living under a single roof, but the present analysis excludes boarders, visitors, and live-in servants from the household unit. One-person households were also excluded, in order to minimize the possible misleading effect on the overall picture of the inclusion of temporary households.

## Size of the Household

The frequency distribution of households by size is shown in Figure 3-1 for each of the four economic classes. The figure shows that the poor households come close to having a normal distribution, and that the distribution becomes more skewed to the right with increases in the standard of living. The graph suggests that small families may help to raise the standard of living of household members. This preliminary demographic finding will be subject to more thorough investigation in the next chapter, which will show that this first impression needs to be revised in some important respects. Table 3-1 presents summary statistics about the size of the household by YCON class.

The question of racially determined differences in poverty levels is a source of much concern in Malaysia. The PES sample was broken down by race and YCON class to throw light on this issue. Table 3-2 shows a clear difference between the two main racial groups. A much higher proportion of Malay households than of Chinese is found in the poor class, and this difference is more or less counterbalanced by the fact

Figure 3–1. Distribution of Size of Households

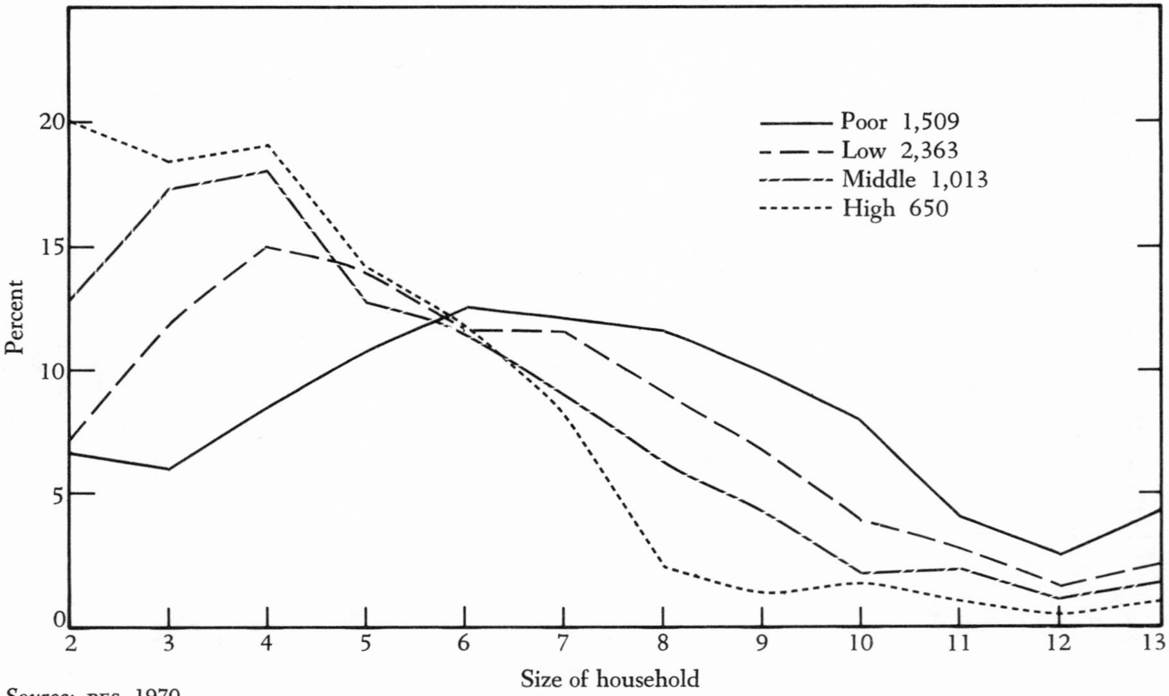

Poor 1,509
Low 2,363
Middle 1,013
High 650

Percent

Size of household

*Source:* PES, 1970.

Table 3-1. Summary Statistics of Household Size by YCON Class

| Statistic | Poor | Low | Middle | High | All |
|---|---|---|---|---|---|
| Mean | 7.09 | 6.07 | 5.26 | 4.51 | 6.00 |
| Standard deviation | 3.11 | 2.88 | 2.71 | 2.39 | 2.98 |
| First quartile | 4.84 | 3.88 | 3.21 | 2.77 | 3.73 |
| Median | 6.90 | 5.62 | 4.65 | 4.10 | 5.57 |
| Third quartile | 9.05 | 7.81 | 6.75 | 5.75 | 7.81 |

Source: PES, 1970.

that the percentage of Chinese households in the high-income class is twice that of Malay households in this class. The mean size of Chinese households in the poor class is significantly higher than that of the Malays in this class (by almost 15 percent), although the difference between the size of households of the two races is not significant for the sample as a whole or for the other YCON classes. This suggests that demographic factors may represent the principal cause of poverty among Chinese families, and that without the pressure of large family size an even smaller percentage of Chinese households would be found in the bottom YCON class.

The importance of this finding prompted an examination of the data from the 1975 World Bank Migration and Employment Survey (MES)

Table 3-2. Number and Size of Households by YCON Class and Race

| Race | Poor | Low | Middle | High | All |
|---|---|---|---|---|---|
| Malay | | | | | |
| Mean size | 6.40 | 6.02 | 4.88 | 4.43 | 5.85 |
| Standard deviation | 2.97 | 2.88 | 2.58 | 2.42 | 2.90 |
| Number | 538 | 649 | 253 | 97 | 1,537 |
| Percent | 35.0 | 42.0 | 16.5 | 6.3 | 100.0 |
| Chinese | | | | | |
| Mean size | 7.38 | 6.13 | 5.43 | 4.59 | 6.05 |
| Standard deviation | 3.09 | 2.87 | 2.79 | 2.41 | 2.97 |
| Number | 676 | 1,430 | 622 | 409 | 3,137 |
| Percent | 21.6 | 45.6 | 19.8 | 13.0 | 100.0 |
| Indian | | | | | |
| Mean size | 7.63 | 5.79 | 5.05 | 4.50 | 6.15 |
| Standard deviation | 3.20 | 2.89 | 2.41 | 2.50 | 3.11 |
| Number | 284 | 277 | 129 | 104 | 794 |
| Percent | 35.8 | 34.9 | 16.3 | 13.1 | 100.0 |

Source: PES, 1970.

Table 3-3. Percentage Distribution of Households
by YCON Class and Race

| Area and race | Percent | | | | Total number |
|---|---|---|---|---|---|
| | Poor | Low | Middle | High | |
| Kuala Lumpur | | | | | |
| Malay | 30 | 28 | 29 | 13 | 382 |
| Chinese | 31 | 32 | 24 | 14 | 607 |
| East Coast | | | | | |
| Malay | 42 | 31 | 19 | 8 | 544 |
| Chinese | 6 | 26 | 41 | 27 | 224 |

Source: MES, 1975.

to see if the finding for all urban Malaysia was also valid for Kuala Lumpur and the two East Coast towns. The percentages of Malay and Chinese households in the four YCON classes (see Table 3-3) indicate that the East Coast towns follow roughly the pattern for all urban Malaysia given in the PES data set, but that in Kuala Lumpur, the metropolis, the percentage distribution of Malay households in the four YCON classes is remarkably similar to that of the Chinese.[1] Nevertheless, the finding derived from the PES data set that poverty among Chinese households seems to be strongly correlated with family size remains valid for the sample in Kuala Lumpur as well. The average size of poor Chinese households was 7.95 compared with 6.45 for the Malays; in the low YCON class, the Chinese household size was 6.60 compared with 5.14 for the Malays. (Both differences in mean are statistically significant.)

## Earners and Dependents

The larger, relatively poor households have more children as well as more adults per household. Figures derived from the PES data set showing the composition of households by race and YCON are presented in Table 3-4. The larger number of adults found in households of lower YCON classes does not increase the number of earners in these house-

1. It will be recalled that the calculation of YCON levels was slightly different for the households covered by the MES.

Table 3-4. Composition of Households by Race
and YCON Class
(number)

| Race | Poor | Low | Middle | High |
|---|---|---|---|---|
| Malay | | | | |
| Total size | 6.40 | 6.02 | 4.88 | 4.43 |
| Children under 6 | 1.10 | 1.16 | 0.93 | 0.70 |
| Children, 6–14 | 2.00 | 1.59 | 0.93 | 0.93 |
| Adults | 3.30 | 3.27 | 3.02 | 2.80 |
| Chinese | | | | |
| Total size | 7.38 | 6.13 | 5.43 | 4.59 |
| Children under 6 | 1.11 | 1.60 | 0.88 | 0.69 |
| Children, 6–14 | 2.47 | 1.60 | 1.05 | 0.81 |
| Adults | 3.83 | 3.44 | 3.50 | 3.09 |

Source: PES, 1970.

holds; in fact, the mean number of earners remains roughly constant from one YCON class to another for both racial groups, although it becomes smaller at the lower YCON levels.

The demographic characteristics of the family and the participation rates of adults in employment can be combined to compute dependency ratios expressing the ratio of nonearners to earners in each household. These can be further broken down to give the child dependency and adult dependency ratios separately, using dependent children and adults respectively as the numerator (Table 3-5). Both types of dependency ratios fall systematically with increases in YCON, but the ratio for children falls faster than that for adults. It might be thought that the proportionately and absolutely higher child dependency ratio in poor families is a consequence of overrepresentation of young families in this group, and that the observed relationship could, therefore, be partly spurious. This hypothesis can be checked by examining the variations in the dependency ratio according to the age of the principal earner.[2] The findings for each YCON class are plotted in Figure 3-2.

2. The principal earner was defined as the person with the highest earnings in the household. The age of the principal earner, rather than that of the head of the household, was used to indicate the life cycle of the household, because in the Malaysian situation the formal head of the household would often be described as the aged retired member.

Table 3-5. Dependency Ratios and Components by YCON Class

| YCON class | Total dependency ratio | Proportion of total contributed by adult dependency | Proportion of total contributed by child dependency |
|---|---|---|---|
| Poor | 3.975 (2.670) N = 1,515 | 35.4 | 64.6 |
| Low | 3.080 (2.183) N = 2,377 | 37.0 | 63.0 |
| Middle | 2.396 (1.989) N = 1,019 | 43.5 | 56.5 |
| High | 1.950 (1.742) N = 655 | 45.6 | 54.4 |

*Note:* Standard deviations are given in parentheses.
*Source:* PES, 1970.

The dependency burden by the age of the principal earner is very much the same for households of different classes except in the case of the youngest groups of principal earners, in which the richer households have more dependents. Otherwise the level of dependency is absolutely higher for the poorer YCON classes whatever the age of the principal earner.

The level of poverty in a community may, nevertheless, be linked to the presence in it of a significant proportion of families whose principal earners are in the older age groups in which the burden of dependency is high. Information on the age distribution of principal earners by YCON class is given for the PES sample in Table 3-6 and is portrayed in Figure 3-3. The graphs of the distributions show quite clearly that the poorer YCON households have larger percentages of principal earners who are relatively old. For the rich, middle- and low-income groups, the percentage of principal earners peaks in the 30–39 age group. However, about 45 percent of rich and middle YCON principal earners are above the age of 40, while the corresponding proportion for low YCON families is about 50 percent and reaches over 60 percent among poor families. Thus the higher relative age of the principal earner must be considered to be one of the characteristics of poor families in urban Malaysia.

Figure 3–2. Dependency Ratios by YCON Class and
Age of Principal Earner

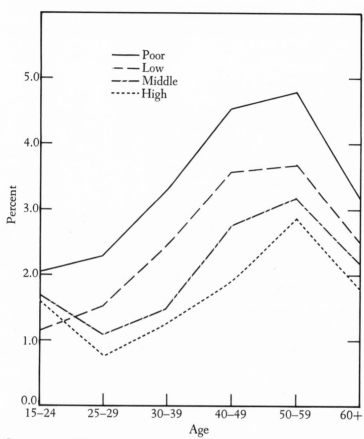

Source: PES, 1970.

## Principal Earners

The educational attainments of principal earners in the different
YCON classes are shown in Table 3-7. Only a few of the principal earners
in the three lower YCON classes are likely to have progressed beyond a
certain level: complete primary for the poor class, incomplete lower
secondary for the low, and complete middle secondary for the middle
and high YCON classes. At the same time, however, there is a consider-

Table 3-6. Age Distribution of Principal Earners by Household Type

| Age of principal earner | Poor | Low | Middle | High | Total |
|---|---|---|---|---|---|
| 15–19 | | | | | |
| Percent | 2.0 | 1.0 | 1.2 | 0.5 | 1.3 |
| Number | 31 | 24 | 12 | 3 | 70 |
| 20–24 | | | | | |
| Percent | 5.5 | 5.5 | 6.6 | 2.8 | 5.4 |
| Number | 83 | 131 | 67 | 18 | 299 |
| 25–29 | | | | | |
| Percent | 6.1 | 12.0 | 16.7 | 14.4 | 11.5 |
| Number | 93 | 285 | 170 | 94 | 642 |
| 30–39 | | | | | |
| Percent | 25.3 | 31.1 | 32.7 | 35.0 | 30.3 |
| Number | 383 | 738 | 333 | 229 | 1,683 |
| 40–49 | | | | | |
| Percent | 32.0 | 25.2 | 19.5 | 20.2 | 25.4 |
| Number | 484 | 598 | 199 | 132 | 1,413 |
| 50–98 | | | | | |
| Percent | 29.0 | 25.2 | 23.3 | 27.2 | 26.1 |
| Number | 439 | 598 | 237 | 178 | 1,452 |
| Total number | 1,513 | 2,374 | 1,018 | 654 | 5,559 |

*Source:* PES, 1970.

Table 3-7. Educational Attainment of Principal Earners
by YCON Class
(percent)

| Educational attainment | Poor | Low | Middle | High | Total |
|---|---|---|---|---|---|
| No schooling | 31.5 | 19.4 | 11.5 | 5.2 | 19.8 |
| Incomplete primary | 37.5 | 35.4 | 19.0 | 9.7 | 29.9 |
| Complete primary | 20.9 | 23.3 | 16.3 | 6.3 | 19.4 |
| Incomplete lower secondary | 5.6 | 10.8 | 14.6 | 9.5 | 9.9 |
| Complete lower secondary | 1.4 | 2.7 | 4.6 | 2.3 | 2.6 |
| Incomplete upper secondary | 1.9 | 4.3 | 15.6 | 17.2 | 7.2 |
| Complete upper secondary | 1.0 | 3.5 | 15.7 | 32.2 | 8.4 |
| Incomplete higher school | 0.1 | 0.4 | −0.1 | 3.7 | 0.8 |
| Higher school and above | 0.1 | 0.2 | 1.6 | 14.0 | 2.0 |
| Total number | 1,511 | 2,374 | 1,018 | 652 | 5,598 |
| Mean | 2.19 | 2.72 | 4.07 | 5.77 | 3.18 |
| Standard deviation | 1.22 | 1.55 | 2.15 | 2.35 | 1.66 |

*Note:* The educational system of Malaysia is described in the appendix to Chapter 8.
*Source:* PES, 1970.

Figure 3–3. Age Distribution of Principal Earner

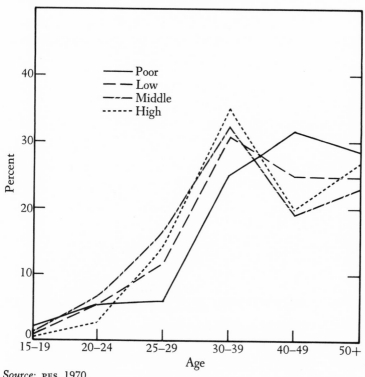

Source: PES, 1970.

able degree of overlapping in the educational attainments of the different income classes. The wide spread in the educational attainments of the high YCON principal earners is particularly noticeable.

The occupational distribution of principal earners, derived from MES data, is given in Table 3-8. As with the educational distribution, which breaks down the information by region, there is an overlap between the income classes. Predictably, however, the proportion of production workers decreases and that of white-collar workers increases with higher YCON. Sales and service occupations are by no means restricted to the poor, which suggests that these occupations are not necessarily informal sector jobs held by individuals who have either failed to find work in the modern sector or are marking time while they try to enter it. In fact, the percentage of workers employed in sales and services actually increases with income levels for the East Coast region.

Table 3-8. Occupational Distribution of Principal Earners by YCON Class and Region (percent)

| Occupation | Kuala Lumpur | | | | East Coast | | | |
|---|---|---|---|---|---|---|---|---|
| | *Poor* | *Low* | *Middle* | *High* | *Poor* | *Low* | *Middle* | *High* |
| Professional and technical | 4.0 | 9.5 | 13.6 | 33.2 | 2.8 | 6.8 | 12.6 | 29.2 |
| Administrative and managerial | 1.2 | 2.0 | 5.6 | 13.6 | 0.8 | 3.0 | 3.2 | 10.0 |
| Clerical and white collar | 7.6 | 14.3 | 22.0 | 16.3 | 4.1 | 8.0 | 13.1 | 14.2 |
| Sales | 16.7 | 15.2 | 10.9 | 15.2 | 18.1 | 18.1 | 24.3 | 23.3 |
| Services | 9.4 | 10.1 | 13.4 | 9.8 | 9.9 | 13.9 | 7.7 | 11.7 |
| Agricultural | 7.3 | 3.1 | 2.2 | 2.2 | 8.2 | 2.1 | 1.8 | 1.7 |
| Production and manufacturing | 53.7 | 45.9 | 32.3 | 9.7 | 56.0 | 48.0 | 37.5 | 10.0 |

*Source:* MES, 1975.

Self-employment, however, appears to be linked to relatively low household income levels. This fact emerges from Table 3-9, which tabulates the employment status of principal earners by household income levels. For both regions, the proportions of self-employed decrease quite significantly with increases in income. Among employees, a greater proportion of high-income earners work in larger plants. If plant size is used as a proxy for the degree of organization of the labor market, there appears to be a correlation between the household's income classification and the probability of its principal earner being employed in what might be called the more formal or organized sector of the urban labor market.

## The Role of Secondary Earners: Nuclear and Joint Families

An examination of household standards of living needs to take into account the contribution of secondary earners to household income. The role of secondary earnings in raising some households above the poverty line is well known in the economies of developed countries. A recent study in the United Kingdom, for example, reached the conclusion that "even among husbands on earnings under 70 pence an hour, only 19 percent of families were poor if the wife worked, compared with 76 percent if the wife did not work."[3]

In less developed countries the issue is not predominantly the participation of the wife in labor market activities. "Joint families," in which not only the wife but also the children of the principal earner or other relatives contribute to household income, are common in these countries; the relevant question is whether the formation of joint households helps to mitigate poverty.

The analysis of household data from the MES defined a joint household as one which contained members other than the household head, his spouse, and his children or a household which supported non-earning dependent parents. In other words, as long as the children of the head of the household are dependents or secondary earners, the household will be considered a nuclear one—provided that other members of the family do not reside in the household—but if the children of the head of the household are the principal earners, the household is considered to be a joint one.

3. Royal Commission on the Distribution of Income and Wealth, "The Causes of Poverty," Background Paper no. 5 (London, 1978), p. 25.

Table 3-9. Employment Status of Principal Earners by YCON Class and Region (percent)

| Employment | Kuala Lumpur | | | | East Coast | | | |
|---|---|---|---|---|---|---|---|---|
| | Poor | Low | Middle | High | Poor | Low | Middle | High |
| Size of work place | | | | | | | | |
| 0–9 employees | 13.7 | 13.2 | 5.6 | 6.0 | 18.9 | 16.9 | 14.4 | 6.7 |
| 10–99 employees | 28.7 | 25.6 | 30.4 | 19.0 | 25.9 | 32.1 | 28.8 | 41.7 |
| More than 100 employees | 32.2 | 36.6 | 46.3 | 58.2 | 13.2 | 18.6 | 21.6 | 25.8 |
| Unspecified number of employees | 2.3 | 2.2 | 2.2 | 1.1 | 0.8 | 1.3 | 0.5 | 0.0 |
| Self-employed | 22.2 | 21.3 | 15.2 | 15.2 | 41.2 | 31.2 | 34.7 | 25.8 |

Source: MES, 1975.

The analysis also tried to identify households which consisted only of single persons or which were made up of unrelated males (so-called chummeries). But these types of households, which are common in some urban areas of Asia (notably in Indian urban centers), are rare in the three Malaysian cities surveyed. They accounted for 3.2 percent and 2.9 percent of the total number of households in the sample. It therefore appears to be reasonable to confine the discussion that follows to nuclear and joint households. According to data taken from PES, 1970, the percentage distribution of the two types of households among the four YCON classes was:

| Type of household | Poor | Low | Middle | High | Total |
|---|---|---|---|---|---|
| Nuclear | 35.7 | 42.6 | 15.1 | 6.6 | 51.7 |
| Joint | 28.1 | 41.0 | 20.7 | 10.2 | 41.4 |
| All households | 30.5 | 40.3 | 19.9 | 9.3 | 100.0 |

The figures suggest that joint families have a smaller incidence of poverty than nuclear ones. Joint families do not necessarily, however, have a greater earning capacity in terms of the ratio of earners to dependents. Wide variations in earning capacity and levels exist in both types of family structure. Table 3-10 shows the distribution of joint and nuclear households by the percentage of total income contributed by the principal earner, for all households in the sample and for the subset of poor households. The figures bear out the logical assumption that the formation of joint families has the net effect of mitigating poverty. Joint families appear to be more likely to receive income from secondary earners (65 percent of joint households have secondary

Table 3-10. Percentage Distribution of Households by Percentage of Total Income Contributed by the Principal Earner in Joint and Nuclear Households

| Household type | Percentage of total income contributed | | | | |
| | Less than 25 | 25–50 | 50–75 | 75–99 | 100 |
|---|---|---|---|---|---|
| All households | | | | | |
| Joint | 13.7 | 23.5 | 28.4 | 5.0 | 29.5 |
| Nuclear | 1.7 | 7.0 | 17.8 | 4.1 | 69.4 |
| Poor households | | | | | |
| Joint | 12.2 | 9.5 | 20.8 | 2.7 | 54.7 |
| Nuclear | . . . | 4.0 | 12.5 | 2.6 | 79.9 |

. . . Zero or negligible.
Source: PES, 1970.

Figure 3-4. Distribution of Poor Households by Different Family Types

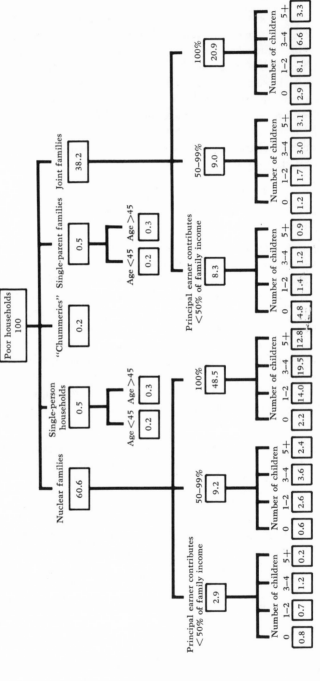

*Note:* The numbers in the boxes are percentages of the total number of poor households.

*Source:* MES, 1975.

44

earners who contribute at least a quarter of the family income, as against only 27 percent of nuclear families). Moreover, the incidence of poverty appears to be lower among joint families with more than one earner. More than half the joint families in the poor subgroup are those whose only source of earnings is the principal earner.

The next chapter contains a more detailed examination of the characteristics of secondary earners; meanwhile, it is worth briefly examining the concept of the "poverty tree," which shows the contribution of secondary earners to household income and the burden on households of child dependency. The poverty tree for poor households in the MES sample is shown in Figure 3-4. The incidence of poverty, as might be expected, increases in both nuclear and joint households with the proportion of household income contributed by the principal earner and with the number of children. The figure shows the proportion of poor households in the different categories represented by individual boxes. The largest subsets in the total poor group are those in which the principal earner is the sole source of household income and the household has dependent children. An interesting point, however, is that while as many as 70 percent of poor households (nuclear and joint together) have only one earner, such families with five or more children constitute only 16 percent of the total.

# CHAPTER 4

# Determinants of Employment Rates

IT WAS SUGGESTED IN THE PREVIOUS CHAPTER that one of the main factors associated with (and affecting) variations in household standards of living is the proportion of adults in the household who are earners. In Table 3-5 it was shown that adult dependency contributed significantly to the overall burden of dependency in the four household income classes in both regions. The factors determining the rates of employment of different groups of adults therefore warrant careful study as part of any overall consideration of the causes of household poverty.

## Variations in Employment Rates

The following paragraphs describe the differences in employment rates by income class, age, and marital status for both men and women.

### By Income Class

Table 4-1 shows the structure of employment rates by income class for three groups of adults (those over 15): all males, married women, and unmarried women. Employment rates are consistently higher in the better-off households for all three types of adults in both regions, with the interesting exception of men in Kuala Lumpur, where there is an increase between the poor and the low YCON classes but not thereafter. The progression is quantitatively most important for married women in both regions—but more so in Kuala Lumpur.

### By Age Group

Male and female employment rates by age and marital status are given for all income classes together in Table 4-2. There are some marked differences in employment rates between the metropolitan labor market of Kuala Lumpur and the smaller towns of the East Coast.

Table 4-1. Overall Employment Rates

| YCON class | Kuala Lumpur | | | East Coast | | |
|---|---|---|---|---|---|---|
| | Men | Married women | Unmarried women | Men | Married women | Unmarried women |
| Poor | 0.807 | 0.038 | 0.444 | 0.742 | 0.07 | 0.24 |
| Low | 0.865 | 0.143 | 0.541 | 0.823 | 0.08 | 0.16 |
| Middle | 0.870 | 0.191 | 0.557 | 0.836 | 0.12 | 0.35 |
| High | 0.866 | 0.461 | 0.566 | 0.907 | 0.25 | 0.41 |
| All men or all women | 0.8380 | 0.3315 | | 0.7858 | 0.1731 | |

Source: MES, 1975.

Female employment rates, for both married and single women, are higher for all age groups up to age 40 in Kuala Lumpur, as are the rates for young unmarried males under 25. In addition, the pattern of female employment rates by age groups shows an interesting difference between the two types of labor markets.

In Kuala Lumpur, the employment rates for married females increase sharply up to the age of 30, and then fall off equally sharply through the succeeding age groups. Employment rates for single women are naturally higher for each age group, but they show a similar pattern —though the variations are not as sharp. Since the proportion of women who marry increases quite sharply in the earlier years (so that only about 4.5 percent are unmarried in the 31–40 age group), for females as a whole, the employment rate increases with age to a maximum level in the 26–30 age group and then declines continuously with age. This pattern is very similar to that of female employment in advanced industrial countries, such as the United States, until before World War II, although the peak in participation rates shown in the censuses up to 1940 occurred at a slightly younger age (20–24).[1] More recently the

1. See V. K. Oppenheimer, The Female Labor Force in the United States, Population Monograph Series no. 5 (Berkeley: University of California Press, 1970), table 1.3 and chart 1.1, pp. 8–9. Note that the U.S. material is on participation rather than employment rates, that is, it includes in the denominator persons declaring themselves to be unemployed. In the survey data set for Malaysia the returns on unemployment were not used because it was felt that data on unemployment obtained from a household survey (without specific instructions on unemployment) would not be very accurate. Differences between employment and participation rates would be more important for the younger age groups.

Table 4-2. Employment Rates by Age, Sex, Marital Status, and Region

| | | | | | Age | | | | Total number of workers |
|---|---|---|---|---|---|---|---|---|---|
| Region | Under 16 | 16–20 | 21–25 | 26–30 | 31–40 | 41–50 | 51–60 | 61 and over | |
| Kuala Lumpur | | | | | | | | | |
| Married men | 100[a] | 66.7[a] | 93.1 | 98.3 | 97.9 | 99.6 | 69.0 | 24.1 | 1,123 |
| Single men | 27.8 | 55.2 | 91.0 | 94.5 | 92.5 | 50.0[a] | 50.0[a] | — | 1,042 |
| Divorced or widowed men | — | — | 100[a] | 100[a] | 75.0[a] | 87.7 | 0.0[a] | 8.7 | 1,042 |
| Married women | 0.0[a] | 13.2 | 22.9 | 30.1 | 18.0 | 14.5 | 6.1 | 4.8 | 1,104 |
| Single women | 25.5 | 39.3 | 70.7 | 78.6 | 75.0 | 33.3[a] | 0.0[a] | 0.0[a] | 679 |
| Divorced or widowed women | 0.0[a] | 50.0[a] | 66.7[a] | 50.0[a] | 50.0 | 15.6 | 7.7 | 5.1 | 169 |
| Percent of men who are married or divorced | 4.0 | 0.07 | 16.2 | 61.7 | 87.9 | 98.3 | 97.8 | 100.0 | |
| Percent of women who are married or divorced | 6.0 | 10.8 | 52.3 | 86.2 | 96.4 | 98.5 | 99.1 | 99.3 | |

*Kuantan and Kota Bharu*

| | | | | | | | | | |
|---|---|---|---|---|---|---|---|---|---|
| Married men | — | 100[a] | 98.7 | 99.4 | 99.3 | 98.5 | 64.3 | 38.0 | 857 |
| Single men | 5.5 | 34.2 | 84.3 | 98.4 | 94.4 | 80.0 | 50.0[a] | 50.0[a] | 576 |
| Divorced or widowed men | — | 100[a] | — | 100[a] | 100 | 100 | 66.7 | 0.0 | 36 |
| Married women | — | 3.6 | 17.2 | 14.4 | 15.4 | 18.8 | 2.4 | 5.0 | 824 |
| Single women | 2.4 | 16.3 | 41.7 | 52.4 | 57.1 | 0.0[a] | — | — | 370 |
| Divorced or widowed women | — | — | 0.0[a] | 100[a] | 28.6 | 13.0 | 11.1 | 0.0 | 112 |
| Percent of men who are married or divorced | 0.0 | 1.2 | 28.2 | 72.1 | 94.5 | 97.6 | 97.4 | 97.0 | |
| Percent of women who are married or divorced | 0.0 | 26.8 | 68.1 | 89.7 | 97.4 | 98.4 | 100.0 | 100.0 | |

— Not applicable.
*Note:* The employment rate for each group is calculated as "the number of people in that group who work in either their own or family business, or for someone else, divided by the total number of people in that group."
a. The total number of people in the group is less than five.
*Source:* MES, 1975.

distribution of employment rates by age has become bimodal in developed countries; a second peak has emerged in the 40–49 age group, representing the widespread post–World War II phenomenon of married women returning to work (or entering the labor force for the first time) after their children have grown up. This latter development has not yet emerged in Kuala Lumpur.

In the East Coast towns, employment rates for married women are generally lower at all ages, as has already been noted; moreover, employment among this group does not reach a peak in the 26–30 age group as was the case in Kuala Lumpur. By and large, the employment rates for married women show little significant change between the ages of 21 and 50; in fact, the highest rate was registered for the 41–50 age group (18.8 percent). For married and unmarried females together, the employment rate peaks in the 31–40 age group, but this reflects the very high employment rate of single women in this age group. By contrast, the Kuala Lumpur peak for females aged 26–30 could be ascribed to the peak in the employment rate for married women in this age group.

## Analysis

In the sections which follow the determinants of employment rates are analyzed for the different types of adults separately in the two regions. Because the marital status of women is a key factor in their employment decisions, two female groups are examined—married and single, regardless of age. For the male groups, because variations in employment rates will be most apparent among the youngest and oldest age cohorts, it was decided to study men in the 15–25 age group and those aged 45 or over, regardless of marital status.

The methodology adopted in each case is that of single equation ordinary least squares (OLS). The dependent variable measures work status, taking a value of one if the person is working and zero otherwise. It was decided to use this methodology rather than more sophisticated analytical techniques because the extra cost (in time and money) of such techniques would not be justified by the marginal gains in the efficiency of the estimation.[2] The single equation approach for each

2. There are some problems in applying the ordinary least squares (OLS) method of estimating regression equations when the dependent variable is binary, that is, can take only one of two values: zero or one. In particular, the estimates

class of adults treated separately does not, however, allow for joint decisionmaking within the household. One of the explanatory variables used in each of the equations is the income adequacy of the household.[3] The implication of this method is that each class of adults within a household makes the decision as to whether to participate, separately and one at a time. The nature of the bias introduced by this piecemeal view of decisionmaking cannot be established without a more complex model of the household. It is, however, doubtful if the data base used in this study can support such complex models, which have only rarely been used, in most instances by researchers with much larger and more elaborate data sets, such as those available for the United States. It is most important to emphasize another limitation of the data base used here, which is the unavailability of information on nonlabor income accruing to the household. This undoubtedly affects the income adequacy variable which should, in principle, include nonlabor income in addition to the earnings of "other" household members.

## Married Women

The variables used to explain the employment rates of married women are education (in seven categories), age (in five categories), race (in three categories), income adequacy, number of adult females in the household (in four categories), and the presence of children under 6 in the household. Income adequacy is the only noncategoric variable entered in the regression model. It is measured by taking the earnings of all other members per adult equivalent unit in the household. The logarithm of the variable is used in the regression to reduce its variance.

In American studies of employment rates of married women, the presence of small children has been found to be an important determinant of the ability (or decision) of married women to seek gainful

---

would tend to be inefficient insofar as there is the possibility of predicting values outside the zero-one range. It has been shown, however, that the OLS estimates do not generally tend to cluster around either zero or one. After a careful study of the costs and benefits associated with the use of alternative estimation procedures such as LOGIT or PROBIT analysis, it was decided that the disadvantages of using OLS were outweighed by the saving of both computer and project time, since the inefficiency in the estimates was likely to be slight.

3. Income adequacy is measured by summing the earnings of all the household members other than the class whose participation rate is being studied in the particular equation.

employment.[4] The existence of extended families in Asian countries such as Malaysia leads one to doubt the importance of this particular factor in household decisionmaking. As has already been noted, many households contain more than one adult female. It can be hypothesized that the decision of a married woman to participate in the labor market would be strongly influenced by the availability of another adult woman to do the household work, including the care of the children. The larger the number of adult females in the household, the higher the probability that a married woman could be released from household pressures and could work in the marketplace. Of course, the choice between household work and market activity is a joint decision affecting all women of working age in the household, whether married or not. With a single equation analysis of the participation of different types of potential earners, however, the total number of adult females in the household can be expected to be a significant explanatory variable for the married and unmarried females taken separately.

KUALA LUMPUR. In the model for Kuala Lumpur there is the possibility of multicollinearity in the explanatory variables. Intercorrelation is most likely between income adequacy on the one hand, and education together with the number of adult females in the household, on the other. The simple correlation coefficients of income adequacy with these other two variables are:[5]

| ED2 | ED3 | ED4 | ED5 | ED6 | ED7 | FEM2 | FEM3 | FEM4 |
|------|------|------|------|------|------|------|------|------|
| −0.16 | 0.07 | 0.23 | 0.08 | 0.15 | 0.14 | 0.01 | 0.07 | −0.02 |

There appears to be some correlation between income adequacy and education levels 4, 6, and 7, but the values are not high. An inspection of the correlation matrix showed that intercorrelation was not important anywhere else in the model.

The estimated employment function for married women in Kuala Lumpur is presented in Table 4-3. The age variables are missing since none of the five age categories turned out to be of any significance in the model. It was noted in the previous section that the employment rates of married women in the Kuala Lumpur sample did vary with age, rising to a peak in the 26–30 age group, but then dropping to a lower level for those in their thirties and forties. The age-related variations in

---

4. James A. Sweet, *Women in the Labor Force* (New York: Seminar Press, 1973), chap. 4.
5. For the definition of these variables, see Table 4–3.

Table 4-3. Employment Function of Married Women, Kuala Lumpur

| Variable | Value of coefficient | t-ratio | Step number | Proportion or mean value |
|---|---|---|---|---|
| *Education* | | | | |
| Primary (ED2) | . . . | . . . | | 0.47 |
| Some secondary (ED3) | 0.18 | 6.79 | 4 | 0.15 |
| School certificate (ED4) | 0.47 | 12.32 | 1 | 0.07 |
| Higher school certificate (ED5) | 0.74 | 6.46 | 3 | 0.01 |
| Diploma (ED6) | 0.64 | 5.84 | 5 | 0.01 |
| Degree (ED7) | 0.32 | 4.83 | 6 | 0.02 |
| No schooling (base) | — | — | | 0.27 |
| Log of income adequacy | 0.038 | 4.07 | 2 | 4.8216 (1.0376) |
| *Race* | | | | |
| Chinese | −0.050 | −2.31 | 9 | 0.63 |
| Indian and others | −0.089 | −2.65 | 8 | 0.10 |
| Malay (base) | — | — | | 0.27 |
| *Number of adult females* | | | | |
| Two (FEM2) | . . . | . . . | | 0.28 |
| Three (FEM3) | 0.10 | 3.80 | 7 | 0.16 |
| More than three (FEM4) | 0.069 | 2.45 | 10 | 0.15 |
| One (base) | — | — | | 0.31 |
| Constant | . . . | . . . | | |
| N = 1,380 | | | | |
| R² = 0.22 | | | | |
| F = 35.166 | | | | |

. . . Not significant.
— Not applicable.
Note: The figure in parentheses is the standard deviation; N = sample size.
Source: MES, 1975.

employment rates appear, however, to be overshadowed by other, more important factors in the model.

The education and income adequacy variables, which enter the equation in the first six steps, account for as much as 20.7 percent of the 22 percent of the variation which the model was successful in explaining. The influence of education on the employment of married women becomes really important only after they have received a school certificate. Indeed, this category of education (ED4), which was attained by 7 percent of the sample, is the single most important explanatory factor for the employment rates of married women. Entering at the first step of the stepwise model, it accounted for no less than 10.3 percent of the variations. Higher educational categories also had significant and large coefficients. By contrast, married women with primary education had the same employment rates as those with no schooling, and the coefficient for those with some secondary education (less than school certificate) was significant but of a much lower value than were the coefficients of the higher educational categories.

Income adequacy is also an important explanatory variable. Entering the model at step 2, it accounts for another 3 percent of the variation in employment rates. The importance of this variable may be underestimated by comparison with the other factors analyzed in this chapter because income adequacy is the only variable not used in grouped categories. An idea of its quantitative importance can be conveyed by considering an increase in the log value of income adequacy from a level one standard deviation below its mean to one deviation above the mean—roughly a position from a low- to a middle-income household. In terms of the present model, other things remaining equal, this would lead to an increase of 8 percent in the employment rate of married women.

The observed positive association of income adequacy with employment rates warrants some discussion. In studies of employment patterns among married women in the United States, this association is usually stated to be negative.[6] A negative association between the two variables is also predicted by standard economic theory. A married woman's decision to participate in market activity in preference to leisure or household work will be positively related to age and education, but negatively related to income adequacy as long as leisure or "home goods" are normal goods with a positive income elasticity.[7] Insofar as the standard economic prediction about the effect of income adequacy is violated in the Malaysian case, it must be concluded either that the benefits of leisure or domestic life are not greatly valued in Malaysia or that the observed behavior is not so much the outcome of a choice between alternatives in the *supply* side of the market as of an economic environment which limits *demand* for female labor to those who are relatively well-off. This latter conclusion may well be the real reason for the positive

6. Sweet, *Women in the Labor Force*, found the association to be negative for white women, but weak and indeterminate for black married women.

7. Higher age and education increases the potential wage the woman can command in the market and hence induces a substitution away from leisure and household work. An increase in income adequacy, however, leads to an increase in demand for leisure and goods produced in the household.

association between income adequacy and participation in Kuala Lumpur (and perhaps in many other urban labor markets in developing countries). Married women from relatively well-off families have employment opportunities which are not fully accounted for by the fact that they are better educated than poorer women. Sociological factors—attitudes toward female employment and the ability to employ servants—may also contribute to the positive relationship between relative affluence and employment among females in the sample.

The next explanatory variable which entered significantly into the regression equation after education and income adequacy was the number of adult females in the households. As might be expected, the employment value of married women increased with the presence of more than one adult female in the household. This effect was observed to be significant, not only for households having two adult females, but for those with three and (to a lesser extent) more than three adult females. A possible explanation (which is no more than a surmise) is that the second female adult in many two-female-adult households might be elderly or infirm, and a third female would be needed to take care of the marketing and domestic activities before the married woman could go out to work.

Race is also a significant explanatory variable in the model. Other things being equal, both Chinese and Indian married women are less likely to go out to work than Malay women. This finding contradicts the popular view that Moslem women are more homebound. Since observed employment rates are determined by both supply and demand factors, however, opportunities for employment of Chinese women could conceivably be low in Kuala Lumpur.

To sum up, education and household income adequacy are the most significant determinants of the employment rate of married women in the metropolitan labor market. The other significant variables—the number of adult females in the household and race—have lower explanatory power and have much smaller coefficients than the first two. The observed sharp increases in employment rates of married women with increases in household income (YCON) is partly owing to the direct positive effect of income adequacy, and partly owing to the higher educational attainments of the women in the richer households.

EAST COAST. The regression model performed much less satisfactorily for married women in the East Coast than in Kuala Lumpur, explaining only 7 percent of the variations as against 22 percent. As shown in Table 4-4, education was again the most significant variable; as in Kuala

Table 4-4. Employment Function of Married Women, East Coast

| Variable | β | t-ratio | Step number | Proportion in sample |
|---|---|---|---|---|
| *Education* | | | | |
| Primary (ED2) | . . . | . . . | | 0.49 |
| Some secondary (ED3) | 0.11 | 3.18 | 3 | 0.10 |
| School certificate (ED4) | 0.33 | 6.49 | 1 | 0.04 |
| Higher school certificate (ED5) | . . . | — | | 0.001 |
| Diploma (ED6) | 0.53 | 3.90 | 2 | 0.005 |
| Degree (ED7) | None | — | | None |
| No schooling (base) | — | — | | |
| *Age* | | | | |
| 30–49 | 0.041 | 2.04 | 4 | 0.48 |
| 50 and over (base) | — | — | | 0.12 |
| *Number of adult females* | | | | |
| Two (FEM2) | 0.047 | 2.00 | 5 | 0.25 |
| Three (FEM3) | 0.040 | 1.47 | 6 | 0.17 |
| One (base) | — | — | | 0.48 |
| Constant | 0.045 | 2.73 | | |
| N = 941 | | | | |
| R² = 0.07 | | | | |
| F = 11.67 | | | | |

. . . Not significant.
— Not applicable.
*Source:* MES, 1975.

Lumpur, the positive effect began to appear at the post-primary level, becoming substantially greater for school certificate holders and above. The number of adult females in the household was again significant. Married women in the 30–40 age group had somewhat higher participation rates than those aged 50 and over. In contrast to the Kuala Lumpur situation, however, neither income adequacy nor race seemed to have significant explanatory power.

As noted earlier, the participation rate for married women was much lower in the East Coast towns than in the metropolis, although the rate increased with income level in much the same way as in Kuala Lumpur. Moreover, self-employment in a worker's own or family business accounted for a much larger proportion of female employment in the East Coast than in Kuala Lumpur; this phenomenon may partially explain the relatively poor performance of the model in the East Coast labor market.

## Unmarried Women

The incidence of marriage is high in both Kuala Lumpur and the East Coast towns. In Kuala Lumpur, only 14 percent of women in the 26–30 age group were unmarried; in the East Coast towns, only 10 percent were unmarried. After the age of 30 the percentage of unmarried women dropped to very low levels. For the purpose of the present analysis, it was decided to include the widowed and divorced in the sample of unmarried women, on the plausible assumption that the employment patterns of the groups would be influenced by similar factors and that these factors would differ from those affecting the employment of married women. The decision had the added advantage of increasing the numbers in the sample in the over-30 age groups. The overall employment rate of the combined sample as described was 53 percent in Kuala Lumpur and 28 percent in the East Coast towns.

The results of the regression models are given in Table 4-5 for both regions. A basic difference between these results and those for married women is at once evident. Although in both regions the employment rates of married women were significantly affected by education, and not all by age, for the unmarried women the situation is exactly the opposite. In both regions age is the predominant explanatory variable; education, though not entirely without significance, is a very weak predictor. This difference is not caused by the absence from the sample of significant numbers of married women in the younger age groups (see Table 4-2). It is clear that youth itself has a significant positive effect on the employment rate of unmarried women, but not that of married women, in both the Kuala Lumpur and East Coast labor markets.

The age effect is seen to be stronger in Kuala Lumpur. All four age groups enter the explanatory model in the first four steps, and contribute as much as 23 points of the 26 percent of the variation explained. The 20–24 and 25–29 age groups are the most important and together contribute 15.5 percent of the explained variation. These two age groups also contribute the greatest explanatory weight in the East Coast towns, though they have somewhat lower coefficients and a lower explanatory power of 12.8 percent. In the East Coast, moreover, there is one exception to the entry of the age groups as significant variables in the first stages of the stepwise regression. Race enters the equation at the third step, relegating the 39–45 age group to the fifth—whereas in Kuala Lumpur it is race which enters the model at the fifth step, *after* all the age groups have been considered.

The sign of the coefficient of the race variable in Table 4-5 requires special attention. It was noted earlier that being Chinese had a significantly *negative* employment effect among married women in Kuala Lumpur but was not significant in the East Coast. In the case of unmarried women, the reverse situation is observed. Chinese women have *higher* employment rates—and relatively more so in the East Coast. It is tempting to speculate on a possible sociological explanation in terms of the effect of marriage on the labor market activity of Chinese women.

### Young Males Aged 16 to 25

The pattern of young male employment can be simply explained. The employment rate is related positively to age, grouped in two-year intervals starting with the 16–17 base group, and it varies inversely with education. This pattern is predictable; more education means later entry into the labor market, and higher age is a proxy for a longer period of search. This explanation is reasonable and applicable to all societies; nevertheless, the specific variables used in the regression model illustrated in Table 4-6 and the pattern of the coefficients reflect quite strongly the peculiarities of Malaysian labor markets.

The school certificate examination would typically be passed in the sixteenth year. If absorption in the labor force were prompt, there should be no significant negative coefficients of the kind shown in the table for the "some secondary" and "school certificate" education categories. Similarly, if new entrants into the labor market found jobs relatively early, there would not be large positive coefficients for ages above 16–17. Thus, the results reflect two features of the labor market in Malaysia: the relatively late age at which young people seem to obtain employment and, if age is held constant, the long period taken by secondary school leavers to get jobs.

These features will reappear in several contexts in later parts of this book. The long period of waiting before getting work which the school leaver has to face—lengthy by comparison with the situation in many other developing countries, let alone in developed countries—is an important and puzzling aspect of unemployment in Malaysia. The phenomenon is verified and discussed in Part III of the book, which uses independent data obtained from special surveys of unemployment.

The data in Table 4-6 suggest some contrasts between the Kuala Lumpur and East Coast labor markets. The mean employment rate of the sample is substantially higher in Kuala Lumpur (72 percent as against 52 percent in the East Coast towns). A major factor contributing to this difference seems to be the significantly higher proportion of people in the East Coast aged 16–17, the age group whose employment rate is lowest.

The other interesting interregional difference relates to the effect of race on participation in the labor market. If other factors are controlled, Malays have a higher employment rate in the labor market in the East Coast, but the pattern is reversed for Kuala Lumpur. It is arguable that the Malay private sector is relatively more important in the East Coast towns and thus provides better employment opportunities for young Malay males. Conversely, public employment, which favors Malays, is more important in Kuala Lumpur. Presumably, however, the waiting period for a young person wishing to obtain a public sector job is substantial—a factor that will tend to lower the overall employment rate for groups seeking such jobs. In any case, the race variable is introduced only toward the end of the stepwise regression model, suggesting its relatively minor role in the explanatory framework.

### Older Males Aged 45 and Over

The last group whose employment rate was examined is that of males aged 45 and over. The results of the regression model for the two regions are given in Table 4-7 and can be simply summarized. In Kuala Lumpur, only three variables turned out to be significant: these were (in order of significance) age 55 and over, income adequacy, and age 50–54. In the East Coast, the same variables came into the model in the first three steps in exactly the same order, but a few others were also significant.

The significant and negative coefficients of the higher age groups compared with the base group of those aged 45–49 are obvious and to be expected. But the significant and positive coefficient of the income adequacy variable is not an intuitively obvious finding. The results strongly suggest that—as was noted earlier with regard to married women in Kuala Lumpur—employment rates of older men are not determined by leisure preferences. Older men are more likely to stay on at work if they are from households with higher income adequacy, either because they suffer less age-related disability than those from households with inadequate incomes or because their employment opportunities and working environments are relatively attractive. The coefficient of this variable is higher than that of married women in Kuala Lumpur. Although this variable is introduced in the model at the second step in both regions, the value of the coefficient is twice as much

Table 4-5. Employment Function of Unmarried Women (Including Widowed and Divorced), Kuala Lumpur and East Coast

| Variable | Kuala Lumpur | | | East Coast | | | Proportion in sample | |
|---|---|---|---|---|---|---|---|---|
| | β | t-ratio | Step number | β | t-ratio | Step number | Kuala Lumpur | East Coast |
| *Age* | | | | | | | | |
| 15–19 | 0.38 | 7.95 | 3 | 0.16 | 3.27 | 4 | 0.34 | 0.46 |
| 20–24 | 0.63 | 13.42 | 1 | 0.47 | 8.43 | 1 | 0.33 | 0.22 |
| 25–29 | 0.67 | 11.59 | 2 | 0.43 | 5.36 | 2 | 0.10 | 0.06 |
| 30–49 | 0.37 | 6.09 | 4 | 0.24 | 3.23 | 5 | 0.07 | 0.08 |
| 50 and over (base) | — | — | | — | — | | 0.16 | 0.18 |
| *Education* | | | | | | | | |
| Primary (ED2) | 0.11 | 2.53 | 8 | ... | ... | | 0.30 | 0.26 |
| Some secondary (ED3) | ... | ... | 5 | ... | ... | | 0.32 | 0.38 |
| School certificate (ED4) | 0.10 | 2.01 | 9 | ... | ... | | 0.16 | 0.12 |
| Higher school certificate (ED5) | ... | ... | | −0.28 | −2.01 | 6 | 0.02 | 0.02 |
| Diploma (ED6) | ... | ... | | ... | ... | | 0.01 | 0.002 |

| | | | | | | | None |
|---|---|---|---|---|---|---|---|
| Degree (ED7) | ... | ... | | ... | ... | | 0.01 | |
| No schooling (base) | — | — | | — | — | | 0.18 | 0.22 |
| *Race* | | | | | | | | |
| Chinese | 0.079 | 2.76 | 6 | 0.16 | 4.41 | 3 | 0.68 | 0.34 |
| Indian and others | ... | ... | | ... | ... | | 0.10 | 0.06 |
| Malay (base) | — | — | | — | — | | 0.22 | 0.60 |
| *Number of adult females* | | | | | | | | |
| Two (FEM2) | −0.084 | −2.74 | 7 | ... | ... | | 0.26 | 0.35 |
| Three (FEM3) | ... | ... | | ... | ... | | 0.31 | 0.32 |
| More than three (FEM4) | ... | ... | | ... | ... | | 0.39 | 0.30 |
| One (base) | — | — | | — | — | | 0.04 | 0.03 |
| Constant | ... | | | ... | | | | |
| N | 1,092 | | | 573 | | | | |
| R² | 0.26 | | | 0.18 | | | | |
| F | 41.73 | | | 20.62 | | | | |

... Not significant.
— Not applicable.
*Source:* MES, 1975.

Table 4-6. Employment Regression on Males Aged 16-25, Kuala Lumpur and East Coast

| Variable | Kuala Lumpur | | | East Coast | | | Sample proportions | |
|---|---|---|---|---|---|---|---|---|
| | β | t-ratio | Step number | β | t-ratio | Step number | Kuala Lumpur | East Coast |
| Education | | | | | | | | |
| No schooling | ... | ... | | 0.194 | 1.41 | 11 | 0.01 | 0.02 |
| Primary (base) | — | — | | — | | | 0.04 | 0.24 |
| Some secondary | −0.227 | −7.07 | 3 | −0.278 | −5.88 | 7 | 0.51 | 0.54 |
| School certificate | −0.468 | −11.52 | 2 | −0.353 | −5.76 | 6 | 0.19 | 0.16 |
| Higher school certificate or above | −0.415 | −6.30 | 6 | −0.685 | −6.35 | 5 | 0.25 | 0.04 |
| Age | | | | | | | | |
| 16–17 (base) | — | | | — | | | 0.25 | 0.35 |
| 18–19 | 0.211 | 5.71 | 7 | 0.214 | 4.21 | 4 | 0.27 | 0.26 |
| 20–21 | 0.352 | 8.73 | 4 | 0.483 | 8.38 | 2 | 0.19 | 0.17 |
| 22–23 | 0.305 | 7.87 | 5 | 0.413 | 7.07 | 3 | 0.17 | 0.17 |
| 24–25 | 0.403 | 10.82 | 1 | 0.421 | 6.95 | 1 | 0.22 | 0.15 |

| | | | | | | | | |
|---|---|---|---|---|---|---|---|---|
| *Race* | | | | | | | | |
| Chinese | −0.094 | −3.21 | 8 | 0.211 | 4.83 | 8 | 0.60 | 0.28 |
| Indian and others | −0.133 | −2.27 | 9 | 0.259 | 2.49 | 9 | 0.09 | 0.04 |
| *Married* | ... | ... | | 0.199 | 2.16 | 10 | 0.02 | 0.05 |
| *Income adequacy* | ... | ... | | ... | ... | | 4.76 | 4.21 |
| Constant | 0.74 | 17.82 | | 0.40 | 7.98 | | — | — |
| $R^2$ | 0.295 | | | 0.402 | | | | |
| F | 38.41 | | | 25.96 | | | | |
| N | 838 | | | 437 | | | | |
| Mean of dependent variable | 0.720 | | | 0.524 | | | | |

... Not significant.
— Not applicable.
*Note:* Dependent variable = 1 if working, 0 otherwise.
*Source:* MES, 1975.

Table 4-7. Employment Rates of Males Aged 45 and Over

| Variable | Kuala Lumpur | | | East Coast | | | Proportions or mean | |
|---|---|---|---|---|---|---|---|---|
| | β | t-ratio | Step number | β | t-ratio | Step number | Kuala Lumpur | East Coast |
| *Age* | | | | | | | | |
| 45–49 | — | — | | — | — | | 0.11 | 0.12 |
| 50–54 | -0.262 | -2.76 | 3 | -0.36 | -3.14 | 3 | 0.15 | 0.22 |
| 55 and over | -0.750 | -9.62 | 3 | -0.62 | -6.18 | 1 | 0.74 | 0.66 |
| Income adequacy | 0.050 | 2.79 | 2 | 0.10 | 4.23 | 2 | 4.89 (1.36) | 4.28 (1.44) |
| *Race* | | | | | | | | |
| Malay (base) | — | — | | — | — | | 0.11 | 0.60 |
| Chinese | ... | ... | | -0.25 | -3.34 | 4 | 0.81 | 0.35 |
| Indian | ... | ... | | -0.30 | -1.99 | 6 | 0.08 | 0.05 |
| *Education* | | | | | | | | |
| No schooling (base) | — | — | | — | — | | 0.34 | 0.58 |
| Primary | ... | ... | | ... | ... | | 0.46 | 0.36 |
| Some secondary | ... | ... | | 0.379 | 2.36 | 5 | 0.09 | 0.04 |
| Constant | 0.741 | 6.30 | | 0.584 | 4.52 | | — | — |
| N | 178 | | | 181 | | | | |
| R² | 0.346 | | | 0.297 | | | | |
| F | 48.406 | | | 12.236 | | | | |
| Mean of employment rate | 0.389 | | | 0.437 | | | | |

... Not significant.
— Not applicable.
*Note:* Standard deviations in parentheses.
*Source:* MES, 1975.

for the East Coast as for Kuala Lumpur, and the increase in $R^2$ because of this variable is 5 percent in the East Coast as against 2 percent in Kuala Lumpur. Older men coming from households with income adequacy levels of one standard deviation above the mean have an employment rate 14 percent higher in Kuala Lumpur and 30 percent higher in the East Coast than that of the older men coming from households with income adequacy one standard deviation below the mean.

The age and income adequacy variables together explain 23 percent of the variations in employment rates for older men in the East Coast towns, and a high figure of 35 percent in Kuala Lumpur. Although in the metropolis no other variable was found to be significant, three others had significant coefficients in the East Coast, adding another 6 percent to the explained variation. These included two variables related to race —both the Chinese and the Indians had significantly lower employment rates—and one educational factor, that of some secondary schooling.

## Summary

The regression models on employment rates of different groups of adults pinpoint one of the major reasons for the observed inverse relation between the adult dependency ratio and the household standard of living. Two of the four groups studied—married women and older men over 45—show a clear positive association of participation rates with income adequacy. In the case of married women, moreover, the positive effect of education on employment rates tends to raise participation rates for the richer households. The variations in employment rates across income classes for young males aged 16–25 and for unmarried women are less easily explained. For young males, the inactivity of those from poorer households tends to be offset to some extent by the inverse relation between educational levels and employment rates. The fact that employment rates of unmarried women increase in the higher household income classes could be largely due to the higher proportion of younger women in the richer households; in the regression analysis education effects were seen to be of little importance for this group.

# CHAPTER 5

# Determinants of Household Standards of Living

IN THIS CHAPTER some of the major determinants of the economic well-being of households in the Kuala Lumpur and East Coast regions are analyzed, using the index of economic welfare, YCON (income per adult equivalent unit). The approach used is to break YCON down into its component elements and to see how well these individual components can be "predicted" from the total sample of households.

## Decomposition of YCON

YCON is defined as:

$$Y/N = L/N \cdot P/L \cdot E/P$$

where  $Y$ = income of the household

$N$ = number of adult equivalent units in the household

$L$ = number of potential earners in the household

$P$ = number of actual workers participating in market activity

$E$ = earned income of the participants.

This identity draws attention to the three separate elements that define the household's standard of living:

1. The ratio $L/N$ gives the number of adults as a proportion of the total adult equivalent unit value in a household, if all adults above, say, age 15 are considered as potential earners and all nonadults as nonearners. This ratio is determined by demographic factors (birthrates and deathrates) and by factors influencing the type of household formed (for example, nuclear or extended).

2. The ratio $P/L$ defines the proportion of the potential earners in a household which actually participates in the labor market. This ratio is partly determined by economic factors of the kind studied in the pre-

vious chapter, which influence the decisionmaking of different groups of earners.

3. The ratio $E/P$, which measures the earning strength of the household members who in fact participate in the market, will be broadly determined by the human capital characteristics of the participants, such as their age, sex, and education.

Some aspects of the participation and earnings functions of various groups of workers in the Malaysian economy have been examined in other chapters. This chapter will attempt to establish how well estimated functions can explain differences in household standards of living (YCON) for the four household income classes defined in the introduction to Part I. Before turning to the details of the procedure to be used, it will be useful to look at the quantitative importance of the individual components defining YCON in the two regions to be examined. For this purpose, the identity for YCON is simplified into a product with only two terms—the ratio of actual earners to the number of adult equivalent units, and the earnings per worker:

$$Y/N = P/N \cdot E/P.$$

This expression is linear in logarithms. Hence the variance in YCON can be expressed as:

$$\text{var} \ln (Y/N) = \text{var} \ln (P/N) + \text{var} \ln (E/P) + 2 \text{ cov} \ln (P/N) \cdot (E/P)$$

The values of the terms in this expression (derived from MES, 1975) are:

| Region | $Var \ln(Y/N)$ | $Var \ln(P/N)$ | $Var \ln(E/P)$ | $Cov \ln(P/N \cdot E/P)$ |
|---|---|---|---|---|
| Kuala Lumpur | 1.0968 | 0.2617 | 0.8519 | −0.0245 |
| East Coast | 0.9721 | 0.2844 | 0.7829 | −0.0478 |

The log variance of YCON is rather higher in Kuala Lumpur, suggesting a greater degree of inequality in household income distribution in the metropolis. In both regions, the variance in YCON is primarily accounted for by the variance in earnings—and the importance of earnings inequality is significantly higher in Kuala Lumpur. The covariance term is small in both regions. (The negative correlation between $P/N$ and $E/P$ is not very strong in either region.) The variance in the log of YCON accounted for by the covariance of these two ratios is around 5 percent in Kuala Lumpur and 10 percent in the East Coast.

The finding that the log variance in earnings is about three times that of the log variance in participation ratios in both regions is of great importance. If inequality of earnings accounts for so much more of the inequality in household standards of living than do the variations in earner-dependent ratios, then low earnings as such ought to be quantitatively more important than an unfavorable demographic structure in explaining low standards of living. This point will be discussed in greater detail later.

## Statistical Procedure

This section introduces the statistical procedure used to assess the relative importance of factors affecting employment and earnings of household members in the four YCON classes. The factors governing the value of $L/N$ are taken as being outside the scope of the analysis. In other words, the mean number of adult equivalent units per household and the number of adults per household at the different standards of living are taken as given, and the analysis concentrates on the impact on the total earnings of the different household classes of (1) the factors determining employment and (2) the factors determining the earnings of an employed member.

A problem arises in any attempt to distinguish the employment and earnings functions separately. As shown in Figure 5-1, there is an interlocking relationship between the significant variables involved; participation and earnings are jointly determined in the process of decision-making, given the accumulation of human capital of the household in question. More specifically, if the earnings function is written as:

$$\log Y = \alpha_1 + \beta_1 \text{ AGE} + \gamma_1 \text{ED} + \mu_1,$$

and the participation function as:

$$P = \alpha_2 + \beta_2 \text{ AGE} + \gamma_2 \text{ED} + \mu_2,$$

it is implicitly admitted that the same variables are determining both earnings and participation. If, in fact, the influence of the human capital variables on participation were entirely through their influence on potential earnings, then the estimated values of $\beta_1$ and $\gamma_1$ could be substituted in the participation equation to obtain an employment prediction. In reality, however, the influence of the age and education variables on participation may to some extent operate independently of the effect through earnings; moreover, some factors other than age and education could enter the participation function.

The present analysis does not seek to disentangle the complicated interrelation of equations in this system; instead, it follows the simplistic procedure of estimating single-equation functions for different classes of individuals. The following steps are involved:

Figure 5–1. Interrelation of Factors Affecting
Employment and Earnings

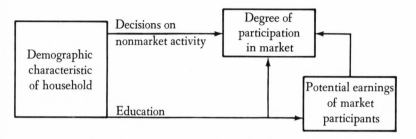

1. For the sample as a whole, functions determining employment are estimated for three classes of household members: adult males who are not principal earners, married adult females, and unmarried adult females. The principal earner is defined as the person contributing the most to household earnings, and the few cases of households in which the principal earner turned out to be female have been excluded from the analysis. Earnings functions are also calculated for two groups: adult males (lumping principal and secondary males together) and adult females (including both married and unmarried).

2. The mean values of the explanatory variables used in these functions are obtained for the households in the four YCON classes and, multiplying the coefficients by these values, a set of predictions is obtained for employment rates and earnings per participant for each type of household member. Since the number of each type of member in the households in the four classes can be established, it is possible to obtain the predicted YCON for each class. The relative importance of employment and earnings with predicted values of YCON will be observed from these results.

3. The comparison of actual and predicted values is made at each stage and serves two purposes. First, it makes it possible to factorize the causes of the difference between the actual and predicted values of household income into its two components—one stemming from the difference between employment pattern of each household class and that of the sample as a whole, and the other attributable to the difference between the actual level of earnings and the level suggested by the earnings functions. Second, and perhaps more important, the comparison will determine whether there are any systematic differences between actual and predicted values for the four household classes.

This last point needs some elaboration. In Figure 5-2A the earnings function of a particular class of workers is used as an example, and the vector of characteristics entering the earnings function is represented by a single variable in the X axis. With no systematic bias in the performance of the predictors between members of low- and high-income groups, the scatter of actual points in the plane would lie randomly on both sides of the fitted regression function. The actual values of earnings at different points of the X axis may differ from the predicted values depending on the closeness of the fit, but the differences between the two ought not to vary in any systematic way with X. (Although a linear function is shown in the graph, nonlinearities are taken care of in the estimated functions by the use of dummy variables.)

If the estimated function performs better for the middle values of X than for the extreme ones (because of explanatory variables not included in the function), then the predicted function will tilt around the cluster at the midpoint for which it predicts best, producing a difference between actual and predicted values for more extreme ranges of X. But there is no a priori reason why the tilt should be one way or the other—and so it is not possible to say whether the divergence between predicted and actual values will be positive or negative for low-income families. In Figure 5-2B the actual income of low earners is higher than that predicted for the sample as a whole, and the opposite holds true for the high earners. The nature of the relationship in any particular case is a matter of empirical investigation.

## Results

In this section the predicted earnings and employment rates of the main types of household members are examined for each class. The predicted household earnings are then built up by applying these values to the number of members of each type in an average household in each class.

### Earnings

The two earnings functions used in each region refer to all male earners and all female earners, respectively.[1] It is assumed that all male

---

1. In each case the log of earnings is estimated as a function of education, age, race, and type of enterprise. As will be shown in detail in Part II, these are the most important variables determining earnings in Malaysia.

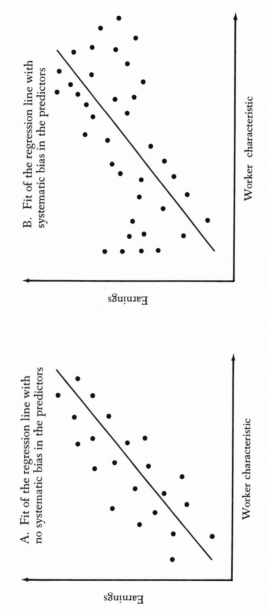

Figure 5–2. Examples of Actual and Predicted Earnings for One Class of Workers

A. Fit of the regression line with no systematic bias in the predictors

B. Fit of the regression line with systematic bias in the predictors

Earnings

Earnings

Worker characteristic

Worker characteristic

earners have the same earnings function, whether or not they are the
household's principal earners; for women, it is similarly assumed that
they have the same earnings function regardless of marital status. Separate predictions are, however, made for the expected earnings of
principal and secondary male earners, taking into account their different
characteristics in the four income classes. Predictions are also made
separately for female earners in each of the four classes. (For the purposes of this exercise, the few households with female principal earners
were excluded.) The actual mean earnings for the three types of earners
are computed for each income class, and those figures together with the
ratios of predicted to actual earnings are set out in Table 5-1.

Table 5-1. Actual Values, and Ratio of Predicted to Actual Values,
of Mean Earnings by Earner Status and YCON Class, 1974

| Region and earner status | Poor | Low | Middle | High |
|---|---|---|---|---|
| *Kuala Lumpur* | | | | |
| Principal males | 203 | 280 | 384 | 1,015 |
| Ratio | 1.22 | 0.93 | 0.80 | 0.60 |
| Secondary males | 106 | 136 | 185 | 328 |
| Ratio | 1.61 | 1.37 | 1.22 | 0.94 |
| Secondary females | 83 | 114 | 168 | 309 |
| Ratio | 1.33 | 1.19 | 1.01 | 0.89 |
| | | | | |
| *East Coast* | | | | |
| Principal males | 122 | 204 | 298 | 574 |
| Ratio | 1.23 | 0.91 | 0.91 | 0.75 |
| Secondary males | 61 | 112 | 145 | 225 |
| Ratio | 1.92 | 1.36 | 1.27 | 1.08 |
| Secondary females | 44 | 72 | 126 | 241 |
| Ratio | 1.59 | 1.25 | 0.95 | 0.85 |

Note: The first line of each category gives the actual mean earnings in Malaysian
dollars per month. The second line gives the ratio of predicted to actual earnings.
Source: MES, 1975.

The relation between predicted and actual earnings is similar for all
three types of earners considered in both regions. In all cases the earnings functions predict higher values than those actually recorded for the
lower income classes, and lower values than the actual earnings of the
higher income classes. The YCON class for which the function provides

the closest match between predicted and observed values varies from one type of earner to another for the two regions:

|  | Kuala Lumpur | East Coast |
|---|---|---|
| Principal males | Low | Low–middle |
| Secondary males | Middle–high | High |
| Secondary females | Middle | Middle |

This finding suggests that the overprediction of earnings for the poor YCON earners is likely to be greater for secondary earners—both male and female—and this is in fact what is shown in Table 5-1. The size of the difference between actual and predicted earnings of male principal earners is similar in the two regions, but the overprediction of earnings for the two bottom classes is substantially larger for secondary earners in the East Coast.

Both these points have a bearing on the possible cause of the underprediction of earnings for the workers in the low YCON classes. The earnings function took into account the influence on earnings of education, age, race, and type of enterprise in which earners worked. Apparently, however, these explanatory variables are not able to account for differences in average earnings between the four YCON classes, so that earners in the lower YCON groups perform worse than might be expected. The labor market factors causing this underprediction may be on the supply side (such as a failure of the direct human capital variable to represent the quality of labor accurately) or on the demand side (such as discrimination or monopsony). In either case, they could be expected to affect secondary earners more than principal ones, and to have a more pronounced effect on members of the former group working in smaller cities than on those in the more integrated labor market of the metropolis. This is just what the data in the table show.

## Employment

The same procedure was followed in the case of variations in employment rates for different groups of adults in the four YCON classes. The principal earner in the household is employed by definition. The analysis of employment rates therefore covers three other types of adults: secondary males (that is, those other than the principal earner), married females, and unmarried females. It is expected that labor market activity will be different for these three groups. The employment functions used were those described earlier for each group.[2]

2. See Chapter 4 for an extended discussion of the employment functions.

As with earnings, the expected and actual employment rates are estimated for the three groups in each YCON class. The results, and the ratios of predicted and actual rates, are set out in Table 5-2, which shows that the employment functions are much more accurate predictors than the earnings functions were. Whereas the earnings functions had systematically overpredicted the earnings of all classes of workers in the bottom YCON classes, the employment function overpredicts only in the

Table 5-2. Employment Rates of Adults by Earner Type and YCON Class

| Region and earner status | Poor | Low | Middle | High |
|---|---|---|---|---|
| *Kuala Lumpur* | | | | |
| Secondary males | 0.579 | 0.720 | 0.755 | 0.759 |
| Ratio[a] | 1.06 | 0.97 | 0.98 | 0.95 |
| Married females | 0.04 | 0.14 | 0.19 | 0.46 |
| Ratio[a] | 3.74 | 1.36 | 1.42 | 1.02 |
| Unmarried females | 0.44 | 0.54 | 0.56 | 0.57 |
| Ratio[a] | 1.02 | 0.92 | 0.95 | 0.95 |
| *East Coast* | | | | |
| Secondary males | 0.394 | 0.582 | 0.622 | 0.805 |
| Ratio[a] | 1.14 | 0.97 | 1.01 | 0.93 |
| Married females | 0.07 | 0.08 | 0.12 | 0.25 |
| Ratio[a] | 1.29 | 1.13 | 1.05 | 0.73 |
| Unmarried females | 0.24 | 0.16 | 0.35 | 0.41 |
| Ratio[a] | 0.91 | 1.55 | 0.98 | 0.77 |

*Note:* The first line of each category gives the actual employment rate.
a. The ratio of predicted to actual employment rates.
*Source:* MES, 1975.

case of married females. The predicted rates are very near to the actual one for nonprincipal males in both regions and for unmarried females in Kuala Lumpur. Only in the case of married females in both regions and, to a lesser extent, unmarried females in the East Coast does a pattern emerge similar to that observed with the earnings function, with overprediction of employment rates for the lower YCON classes and underprediction for the higher ones. These findings suggest that most potential earners in the lower YCON classes (with the exception of married women) are probably at less of a disadvantage with respect to employment possibilities than with respect to earnings.

## Household Income

The examination of total household income takes into account the contributions of the different types of earners and compares the predicted values derived from the earnings and employment functions with the actual levels of household income in the four classes. Table 5-3 gives a breakdown of the structure of income of an "average" household in each of the four income classes for the two regions. The income of the principal earner is reported first, followed by the mean number of each type of secondary earner in the household and the mean income contributed by him or her. It was noted in the previous chapter that the secondary earners' contribution to household income is relatively small in the case of the poor YCON class but is more substantial for the higher income groups. In Kuala Lumpur, the principal earner contributes, on average, 85 percent of the income of poor households compared with an average of around 70 percent for the households in the other income classes. In the East Coast, the relative contribution of the principal earner is generally greater for all classes except the highest: it decreases monotonically from a high of 90 percent for the poor to 70 percent for the rich.

The data presented in the table illustrate the relative importance of the contribution of different types of secondary earners. The mean number of each type of secondary earner generally increases with the YCON class. It has already been shown, however, that the employment functions predict the *rate* of employment for different classes of secondary earners fairly accurately, except in the case of married women. Thus the larger *numbers* of secondary male and unmarried female earners found in the higher income classes must be owing to a favorable distribution of the characteristics of household members (in terms of the variables which have significant weight in the estimated participation functions).

An examination of the composition of the sample in the different YCON classes (not reported here) helps to explain this phenomenon. The poorer households have a smaller number of male secondary earners as a result of these households' high proportion of older male members, relatively poor education levels, and low levels of income adequacy. Conversely, there appear to be more unmarried female secondary earners in the higher YCON groups, entirely as a consequence of

Table 5-3. Composition of Household Income by Earner Type and YCON Class

| Region and earner status | Poor | | Low | | Middle | | High | |
|---|---|---|---|---|---|---|---|---|
| | Mean number | Income[a] | Mean number | Income[a] | Mean number | Income[a] | Mean number | Income[a] |
| *Kuala Lumpur* | | | | | | | | |
| Principal males | | 212.5 | | 320.8 | | 487.6 | | 1,071.0 |
| Secondary males | 0.20 | 23.7 | 0.54 | 80.4 | 0.77 | 155.8 | 0.45 | 193.3 |
| Secondary married females | 0.02 | 2.6 | 0.13 | 17.7 | 0.15 | 38.2 | 0.32 | 175.8 |
| Secondary unmarried females | 0.16 | 14.3 | 0.28 | 34.6 | 0.40 | 68.5 | 0.33 | 99.3 |
| Total income | | 253.1 | | 453.5 | | 750.1 | | 1,539.4 |
| Adult equivalent unit (AEU) | | 5.26 | | 4.59 | | 4.13 | | 3.0 |
| Income per AEU | | 48.12 | | 98.80 | | 181.62 | | 386.78 |
| *East Coast* | | | | | | | | |
| Principal males | | 126.2 | | 233.9 | | 374.6 | | 619.2 |
| Secondary males | 0.14 | 9.62 | 0.32 | 40.2 | 0.48 | 77.3 | 0.45 | 116.6 |
| Secondary married females | 0.05 | 2.1 | 0.07 | 6.0 | 0.11 | 17.7 | 0.16 | 59.6 |
| Secondary unmarried females | 0.05 | 2.8 | 0.07 | 5.8 | 0.18 | 22.9 | 0.18 | 41.7 |
| Total income | | 140.7 | | 285.9 | | 492.5 | | 909.1 |
| AEU | | 4.91 | | 4.54 | | 4.06 | | 3.63 |
| Income per AEU | | 28.66 | | 62.97 | | 121.31 | | 250.44 |

a. Mean income in Malaysian dollars per month.
*Source:* MES, 1975.

the influence of the education variable. The table shows one exception to this pattern: there are fewer secondary males and unmarried females in the highest YCON class and thus these groups' participation levels are reduced for this YCON class. There is no such deviation from the trend for married females, who contribute a consistently larger number of secondary earners per household with increasing YCON. As already noted, married women in the richer households participate in labor market activity at levels higher than that predicted by the positive coefficient of the income adequacy variable in the equation for the whole sample's participation rate.

The data in Table 5-3 indicate that male secondary earners account for the bulk of the total secondary earners' contribution to household income in both regions. Married female earners are of minor importance except in the highest YCON class in Kuala Lumpur. The greater participation levels of secondary adults represent only a partial explanation of the higher incomes of households in the upper YCON classes. In general, the earners in a given household can be expected to contribute more to family income in the higher YCON classes as a consequence of their superior human capital attributes, such as education and skill. It has already been noted that the earnings functions for both males and females for the sample as a whole systematically understate the actual earnings of those in the higher YCON classes and overstate the earnings in the poor class. The quantitative importance of these two tendencies can be examined as part of the analysis of the factors underlying the differences in mean household income in the four classes. This is best done by computing the contribution of each type of earner to the household income as a product of the mean number of earners for each household of that type and his or her predicted earnings (derived from the relevant earnings function).

The calculations are presented in Table 5-4. The divergence in earnings across YCON classes in the table are caused by the different number of earners of each type per household and by the different human capital attributes of the average earner of each type in the relevant YCON class. A comparison of these figures with the actual earnings data shown in Table 5-3 illustrates the extent of the under- or overprediction involved. The differences between the two sets of figures represent the size of the gap between observed data and what the regression models of participation and earnings could "explain" (ignoring the underprediction of the rate of participation of married women in the higher YCON classes as being quantitatively of minor importance). The differences between actual and predicted incomes are shown in Table 5-5.

Table 5-4. Predicted Household Income: Number
of Earners Times Predicted Earnings
(Malaysian dollars per month)

| Region and earner status | Poor | Low | Middle | High |
|---|---|---|---|---|
| Kuala Lumpur | | | | |
| Principal males | 239.5 | 279.0 | 337.6 | 493.5 |
| Secondary males | 34.2 | 100.4 | 174.0 | 138.6 |
| Secondary married females | 2.2 | 17.8 | 25.5 | 88.7 |
| Secondary unmarried females | 17.6 | 38.4 | 68.0 | 90.8 |
| Total household income | 293.5 | 435.6 | 605.1 | 811.6 |
| Income per adult equivalent unit (AEU) | 55.8 | 94.9 | 181.6 | 203.9 |
| East Coast | | | | |
| Principal males | 140.2 | 189.8 | 284.1 | 420.5 |
| Secondary males | 16.4 | 6.3 | 13.2 | 32.8 |
| Secondary married females | 3.5 | 6.3 | 13.2 | 32.8 |
| Secondary unmarried females | 3.5 | 6.3 | 21.6 | 36.9 |
| Total household income | 163.6 | 251.0 | 407.2 | 599.6 |
| Income per AEU | 33.3 | 55.3 | 100.3 | 165.2 |

Source: MES, 1975.

### Conclusions on Differences in Standards of Living

The data presented in Table 5-5 emphasize the importance of "unexplained" differences in the levels of earnings of workers in different YCON classes. The relative excess of actual overpredicted earnings is greater for Kuala Lumpur than for the East Coast. It is greatest for the high YCON class but is also substantial for the middle group. The table also shows that except in the case of the high YCON group in Kuala Lumpur, virtually all the difference between the predicted and the actual values of household income is accounted for by the figures for the principal earner.

The importance of the unexplained earnings factor can be shown by relating the predicted income differences between classes in Table 5-4 to the actuals in Table 5-3. If the earnings of men and women had behaved as described by the earnings function, then—allowing for increases with YCON levels in the numbers of earners and the human capital attributes of each worker, and with the base for the poor equal to 100—the household income relatives for Kuala Lumpur would be:

| Poor | Low | Middle | High |
|---|---|---|---|
| 100 | 148 | 206 | 277 |

By way of contrast, the actual income relatives for the classes were:

| Poor | Low | Middle | High |
|------|-----|--------|------|
| 100 | 179 | 296 | 608 |

The differences in real standards of living between classes are, of course, wider than these indexes suggest because the higher income households have fewer adult equivalent units. The relatives for actual income per adult equivalent unit are:

| Poor | Low | Middle | High |
|------|-----|--------|------|
| 100 | 205 | 377 | 804 |

A comparison of the three sets of relatives given indicates that the earnings factor is quantitatively much more important than the demographic factors in accounting for differences in standards of living. For example, correcting the underprediction of earnings by the earnings function with actual earnings data more than doubles the ratio of the household income of the high to that of the poor YCON class. The

Table 5-5. Difference between Actual and Predicted Income
(Malaysian dollars per month)

| Region and earner status | Poor | Low | Middle | High |
|--------------------------|------|-----|--------|------|
| *Kuala Lumpur* | | | | |
| Principal earner | −27.0 | 41.8 | 150.0 | 577.5 |
| Secondary males | −10.5 | −20.0 | −18.2 | 54.7 |
| Secondary married females | 0.4 | 0.1 | 12.6 | 87.1 |
| Secondary unmarried females | −3.3 | −3.8 | 0.5 | 8.3 |
| Total household income | −40.4 | 17.9 | 145.0 | 727.8 |
| Percentage deviation from actual household income | −16.1 | 0.04 | 19.3 | 47.2 |
| *East Coast* | | | | |
| Principal earner | −14.0 | 44.1 | 90.5 | 198.7 |
| Secondary males | −6.8 | −8.4 | −11.0 | 7.2 |
| Secondary married females | −1.4 | −0.3 | 4.5 | 26.8 |
| Secondary unmarried females | −0.7 | −0.5 | 1.3 | 4.2 |
| Total household income | −22.9 | 34.9 | 85.3 | 309.5 |
| Percentage deviation from actual household income | −16.3 | 12.2 | 17.3 | 34.0 |

Source: Tables 5-3 and 5-4.

smaller number of adult equivalent units in the high YCON families, however, increases the ratio by only another 30 percent. Similar results (not reported here) could be obtained from the figures for the East Coast though the effect of the earnings factor would not be as great.

# Part II

# Personal Earnings

# CHAPTER 6

# Introduction to Part II

THE NEXT SIX CHAPTERS, which make up Part II of this study, are devoted to the analysis of individual earnings. Although there is some discussion in Chapter 7 of the earnings of the self-employed, most of the analysis relates to the determinants of the earnings of employees—and for the most part those of males. This limitation was dictated partly by reasons of space, and partly by the unavailability from survey data of the type of information necessary for an adequate examination of the determinants of the earnings of the self-employed, such as data on the growth rates of small businesses.

The starting point of the analysis of labor earnings is the human capital model. It was noted in Part I that predictions of earnings of household members based on their human capital attributes led to an overestimation of household income at the lower end of the distribution, and a more substantial underestimation at the upper end. This issue is discussed more fully in Chapter 8.

## The Human Capital Model

In some ways, the prediction of earnings from a multiple regression analysis of age and education factors is no more than an accounting procedure. Mean earnings are computed for each combination of education and age groups much as they would be in a table of cross-classifications—except that estimates are made of the "most probable" earnings for each cell, rather than of a straightforward statistical mean. No causal significance can or need be attributed to the analysis at this stage. An accounting framework of this kind is nevertheless of real descriptive value for an analysis of the earnings structure in Malaysia's urban labor market, for the simple reason that it accounts for a large part of the variance in earnings. Comparative data presented in Chapter 8 will show that the log variance of earnings "explained" by the simplest human capital model is much greater in Malaysia than in developed countries. In particular, the explanatory power of formal education seems to be much greater in the Malaysian context. This finding is related to the general tendency, noted in Chapter 7, for interoccupational differences in earnings to be relatively wide in less developed countries.

The transition from the demonstration of an *association* between education and earnings to a *causal connection* between them is a difficult one. If education can be shown statistically to be the single most important determinant of earnings, does it follow that giving more education to the poor is the best way of lifting them out of poverty? The question raises several underlying issues which warrant discussion.

First, the human capital model may approximate more closely to the actual earnings distribution at the upper than at the lower end of the distribution. Factors other than the ones incorporated into the model may be responsible to a more significant extent for low incomes than for high ones.

Second, the rate of return to education may vary with its level, providing substantially higher returns to individuals who progress further up the education ladder than to those with lower attainments.

Third, the association of higher earnings with more education may reflect not only straightforward supply-and-demand relationships in the labor market, but also the phenomenon of "credentialism" (a relatively inflexible pay structure that fixes levels of pay largely on the basis of formal qualifications). The importance in urban Malaysia of the public sector (which typically follows rigid rules about educational qualifications and seniority) makes an examination of the influence of credentialism on the human capital explanation of earnings especially relevant. If, in fact, a great deal of the observed association between education and earnings is caused by credentialism, an expansion in education is as likely to lead to unemployment as to higher earnings.

Fourth, the earnings function estimated on the basis of cross-section data describes the overall experience of several generations represented in the current labor market. The pattern of the rates of return to education of recent graduates from the education system may be radically different from that of the sample as a whole.

The empirical inquiry which follows is intended to shed some light on these questions. The problem of unemployment, for which the expansion of secondary education has been partly responsible, is the subject of a separate and extended discussion in Part III of the book, which presents a full analysis of the ways in which the labor market has adjusted in response to changes in the supply-and-demand situa-

ortions of Part III, particularly
er 8.

an labor markets in developing
otheses about the existence of
e same quality in different parts
are differentiated by the terms
d unorganized," "modern and
l that if the quality of labor is
xperience, an additional factor—
ed to explain variations in labor
an capital factors.
gh- and low-wage sectors of the
nployment in the formal sector
so that wage levels and work-
ilable, in general, to job seekers
unless they manage somehow to cross that protective barrier. This kind
of protection may arise from the action of trade unions, of governments,
or of both acting together. Examples of such institutional practices are
widespread in the less developed world. In many cases the main influence of such institutional distortions would be on fringe payments and
working conditions rather than on basic wage levels.

The development of protection for certain categories of labor in the
recent history of many developing countries is quite closely linked to
the implementation of import substitution programs as elements of
policies to foster industrialization. The protection from foreign competition granted to manufacturing in many countries has led to an inflation
of profits in this industry; the additional profits have in turn had to be
shared with labor to a varying extent on grounds of both equity and
political stability.

In the Malaysian context the role assigned to the public sector by
the government represents a second and probably more important protective element. One of the objectives of government policy in Malaysia
is to increase Malay participation in the higher-income urban sectors.

1. Arnold S. Harberger, "On the Social Opportunity Cost of Labor," *International Labor Review*, vol. 103 (1971), pp. 559–79.

This goal is partially pursued by maintaining a reasonably high proportion of Malays in public employment and by setting public sector wages at a relatively high level. The quantitative importance of the public sector in the urban labor market of Malaysia is discussed more fully below.

It should be stressed, however, that the free play of market forces, rather than institutional distortions of them, could itself lead to the growth of a protected sector in the urban labor market. This state of affairs can occur as a consequence of the correlation between worker efficiency and the wage level.[2] Up to a certain point, an increase in the wage per worker increases efficiency more than proportionately to the increase in the wage, so that the wage cost per unit of output falls. After a point, of course, the wage increase will lead to a less than proportionate increase in efficiency, and there will be no incentive for management to raise the wage level further. Even the existence of an excess supply of labor, however, will not induce management to reduce the wage to the lowest level possible; the established wage will be that which ensures the minimum wage cost per unit of existing employee output.

Why does this mechanism not apply to all firms in the urban economy? First, the strength of the functional correlation between wage and efficiency tends to be more important for enterprises which use modern technology and employ a large number of workers. Second, the type of wage policy described above is only appropriate to an enterprise with a stable labor force; in sectors of the urban labor market which have a high turnover, the stability of the correlation between given levels of efficiency and wages is lost. In fact, some firms may have to pursue a high-wage policy to build up a stable labor force; and, once stability is achieved, further wage increases may be forthcoming as the link between wage levels and efficiency becomes more firmly established.

Thus, even under free market conditions the wage level in some types of enterprises will be established at a level higher than that in other sectors of the same market. This wage level is a protected one, in the sense that job seekers who might wish to obtain employment cannot do so by bidding down the wage, since employment in the sector depends on a process of selection involving aptitude tests as well as competition for the limited number of available job openings.

2. See Harvey G. Liebenstein, "The Theory of Underemployment in Backward Economies," *Journal of Political Economy*, vol. 65 (1957), pp. 91–103; and Dipak Mazumdar, "The Marginal Productivity Theory of Wages and Disguised Unemployment," *Review of Economic Studies*, vol. 26 (1959), pp. 190–97.

A specific example of this type of labor market behavior is the Bombay textile industry.[3] Alongside a stable core of workers, with a relatively high wage, the industry employed a sizable proportion of its workforce on casual day-to-day contracts, providing it with a pool of potential recruits. The historical data developed in the course of the research showed conclusively that this two-tier labor market was established well before the era of trade unions and government intervention; the existence of this pool of less well-paid, available labor did not result in a reduction in the wage level for the core group of full-time employees.

The arguments of the last few paragraphs suggest another hypothesis about the characteristic nature of the formal sector, in addition to that of protection. The discussion above of both institutionally based and market-based protection has referred to firms employing modern technology and achieving the high labor productivity associated with it. Such firms typically also have much more formal work arrangements for their employees than other sources of labor market earnings. This leads to a distinction between the formal and informal sectors based on the belief that workers in firms using modern technology enjoy a protection that is qualitatively different from the protected market structure which hawkers, peddlers, and other groups in the informal sector of the market are sometimes said to evolve.[4] It may be that this special type of formal sector protection will have a relatively great quantitative impact on earnings in the sector.

To test this hypothesis, it is necessary to define clear-cut variables which will distinguish between the formal and informal sectors. The contractual and organizational difference between self-employment and wage employment has been suggested as one possible basis for making the distinction; another has been the type of employment activity—with the service industry described as a repository of labor which cannot find employment in the high-wage manufacturing sector. Both these approaches leave much to be desired. The wide spread of earnings *within* each segment of the labor market, documented in Chapter 7, suggests that each contains a labor force too heterogeneous for any differences in average earnings between the segments to be meaningful.

---

3. Dipak Mazumdar, "Labor Supply in Family Industrialization: The Case of the Bombay Textile Industry," *Economic History Review*, vol. 26 (1973), pp. 477–96.

4. See Lisa Pettie, "The Informal Sector: A Few Comments from Bogota," working draft, Department of Labor Studies and Planning, Massachusetts Institute of Technology.

It might be more appropriate to examine only wage employment and to look for characteristics of the various employers and enterprises which might lead to evident labor market segmentation. It is necessary to use proxies to isolate the type of enterprise which requires a relatively skilled or disciplined work force and in which a higher wage will constantly prevail. The size of the plant (that is, the number of workers employed) comes immediately to mind as one such proxy. It is plausible to maintain that the larger the plant, the more formally structured the work force will tend to be. To a lesser extent, the size of the plant will also be positively correlated with the greater use of modern technology. Other proxies for the varying levels of organization and technology used in different enterprises are conceivable and might even work better; the dichotomy of the public and private sectors is high on the list of possibilities.

## Segmentation and Human Capital Theory

The theory of labor market segmentation suggests that factors in the market produce differences in earnings over and above those produced by differences in earners' endowments. Two hypotheses about the way segmentation produces these earnings differentials are probably at work simultaneously.

According to the first hypothesis, labor market segmentation factors introduce an element of differentiation in earnings in addition to that produced by variations in the human capital attributes of the workers concerned. There will clearly be an overlap between the factors of human capital and segmentation. If the segmentation factors producing a high-wage sector are economic forces, employers can be expected to set wages at levels high enough to attract "superior" labor with better human capital attributes. But if the segmentation factors determining the higher wage are institutional, there will be an adjustment in the quality of labor attracted to the high-wage sector, with superior labor predominating over the long run. It is, of course, arguable that measurable human capital attributes (education and experience) do not fully reflect the quality of labor; nevertheless, there should be at least some correlation between the education and experience variables and the market segmentation variables. If the latter are strong, however, they will have an effect over and above education and experience variables.

The second hypothesis about market segmentation is that it influences the rate of return to the education and experience variables. This will happen if firms in the formal sector pursue wage policies which put a premium on formal education and seniority in employment. At this point the argument needs to take account of the debate between those who think of human capital attributes as enhancing the productivity of workers themselves and those who think of them as primarily screening devices. The observed rates of return to education and experience are viewed by some analysts as returns to a particular job selection mechanism rather than as investments in improvements in the quality of the labor force. The relevance of labor market segmentation to this screening hypothesis is that the effect of using human capital factors to screen job applicants will lead to a very sharp differentiation of incomes in the formal sector.

A formal sector employer may attach special importance to education or experience itself as a consequence of institutional factors in the wage determination process (for example, in the public sector) which are themselves consequences of economic factors not immediately apparent. Certain firms in the formal sector might place a high value on the particular characteristics imparted by the process of formal education—be it self-reliance, achievement-orientation, or merely amenability to a system of rules. In this interpretation, a selection process that favors formal education is really economizing on the search and information costs of gathering data on intangible but desirable attributes of the candidates. By a similar process, the hierarchical organization structures of formal sector firms institutionalize wage structures which ensure the automatic correlation of earnings with experience.

This discussion has suggested that it is impossible to examine the formal-informal sector variables contributing to differences in earnings separately from standard human capital factors, although the formal-informal sector variables can produce earnings differences over and above those caused by education and experience variables and can increase the quantitative importance of human capital factors in certain cases. An analysis of the impact of both sets of factors on earnings differences is undertaken in Chapter 9.

## Race and Differences in Earnings

Another important and conceptually distinctive variable which might cause differences in earnings between individuals with similar human capital attributes is race. The clear differences in income levels between the two major races, the Malays and the Chinese, are partly a result of historical trends that led to a disproportionate concentration of the Chinese population in urban areas, which have higher income levels than rural areas. Quite apart from the different racial composition of the urban and rural populations, however, the earnings levels of Malays and Chinese differ within the urban sector. Figure 6-1 shows the earnings distribution for the two races; the frequency distribution of earnings for the Chinese lies well to the right of that for the Malays. In particular, a substantially larger percentage of Chinese earns more than M$250 a month.

Sample data from the World Bank's 1975 Migration and Employment Survey (MES) indicate that the difference in earnings between the

Figure 6–1. Distribution of Male Earnings by Race

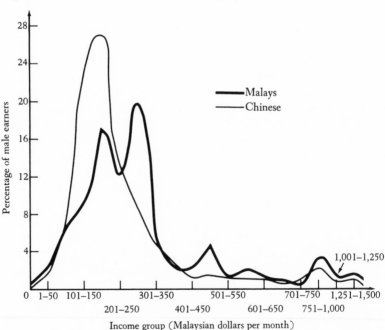

Income group (Malaysian dollars per month)

Source: MES, 1975.

races is greater in the smaller East Coast towns than in Kuala Lumpur. In the capital the mean earnings of Chinese male employees are only 10 percent higher than those of Malays; in the East Coast towns they are 33 percent higher. These figures are consistent with Anand's finding, based on the PES data set, that the interracial earnings gap was larger in other urban towns than in the metropolitan towns.

Having established the existence of an earnings gap, it is necessary to ask what has caused it. There are at least three aspects to the question: How much of the gap in earnings can be ascribed to differences in human capital attributes of the workers concerned, that is, their levels of schooling or experience or age? Given the same levels of age and education, do the Malays still earn less (in other words, is there a difference in the earnings functions for the two races which can be represented by a shift parameter)? Do the different returns to experience and education for the two races produce an earnings gap which is more marked at, say, the upper end of the educational ladder than at the lower?

The empirical inquiry undertaken in Chapter 10 addresses these questions. The problem of racial difference in earnings has been heavily researched by labor economists because of the importance of the problem in the United States, where poverty and racial discrimination are closely intertwined.[5] As well as asking empirical questions such as those in the preceding paragraph, the literature attempts to tackle a basic theoretical issue: why should profit maximizing employers pay workers with equivalent skills at different rates simply because they belong to a different race?

The economic theory of discrimination, pioneered by Becker, develops some theoretical insights, which explain how market equilibrium can occur with a racial wage gap at a given point in time, and which cast some light on other aspects of racial economics—including the segregation of occupations or enterprises by race, the differential return to education or training for the two races, and the stability of the wage-differentiated equilibrium over time.[6] This theory is reviewed in detail in Chapter 9. Insofar as it is based on generally valid economic motivations on the part of decisionmaking units, it should be as applicable to Malaysia as to the United States—at least for the private sector.

5. See, for example, Lester C. Thurlow, *Poverty and Discrimination* (Washington, D.C.: Brookings Institution, 1970).

6. Gary S. Becker, *The Economics of Discrimination* (Chicago: University of Chicago Press, 1957).

Table 6-1. Racial Distribution of Employees by Employer Type
(percentages of total for each employer type)

| | Race of employees | | | | | | Total employees | |
| | Kuala Lumpur | | | East Coast | | | | |
| Employer | Malay | Chinese | Indian and other | Malay | Chinese | Indian and other | Kuala Lumpur | East Coast |
|---|---|---|---|---|---|---|---|---|
| Malay private | 87 | 9 | 4 | 99 | 1 | ... | 6.9 | 30.1 |
| Chinese private | 6 | 92 | 2 | 34 | 65 | 1 | 45.2 | 35.6 |
| Foreign | 44 | 45 | 10 | 45 | 55 | ... | 13.6 | 2.5 |
| Government and public | 64 | 17 | 19 | 80 | 9 | 11 | 29.1 | 28.4 |
| Total | 34 | 55 | 11 | 67 | 28 | 5 | 100.0[a] | 100.0[a] |

... Zero or negligible.
a. Other employee types are not shown; hence, total of percentages do not add to 100.
Source: MES, 1975.

The overall effect of racially differentiated earnings levels is, how-ever, significantly affected in the Malaysian case by the substantial role of the public sector, which uses its employment and wage policies to redress the economic conditions of the disadvantaged race. Table 6-1 gives the percentage distribution of the population covered in MES by race and employer category. The Kuala Lumpur figures show nearly complete racial segregation of employment in the private sector, with Chinese employers (and consequently Chinese employees) dominating the sector as a whole. The public sector, however, which accounts for nearly 30 percent of total employment, provides a disproportionately high level of jobs for Malays. The situation is less extreme in the East Coast because Chinese employers provide jobs for a significant propor-tion of Malays, and Malay enterprises are important in the private sec-tor. Both groups of employers, however, still employ disproportionate percentages of workers of their own race. The public sector plays as important a role in the employment of Malays in the East Coast towns as it does in Kuala Lumpur.

## Migration and Income Distribution

Hypotheses about the differential effects of labor market segmenta-tion on earnings are often linked to the consequences of migration pat-terns for levels of earnings. Migration is generally thought to widen earnings differentials: two major variants of this hypothesis can be dis-tinguished.

The first, which has a long history in the literature, stresses the im-portance of long-term, established streams of migration. Migrants need peer group support while they are settling into their new environment. Without the promise of such support, the perceived risks associated with migration will outweigh the expected benefits in the minds of many potential migrants. For example, migrants to urban areas do not neces-sarily come from the poorest rural regions in the country, but often from those districts immediately surrounding the area of urban growth. Even when some migrants are attracted from more distant areas—notably to urban areas with a high rate of growth—lines of migration tend to get established, so that over time migrants come from the same hinterland even though it may itself develop into a relatively rich area. This phe-nomenon has an important consequence for income distribution in the economy as a whole. Migration may tend to narrow the gap between in-come levels in the established hinterland and the receiving area, but it may not help the poorest rural areas of the country; in certain cases, it may actually increase regional inequalities of income. The consequences for income distribution within the urban economy are less obvious, but also important. If the urban labor market is fragmented, the majority of the migrants from specific rural areas, or even from specific classes of the population within a given rural area, may gravitate to the low-income sector of the urban economy. Given limited mobility between the low- and high-income urban sectors, migration patterns might merely transfer existing inequalities of income from a rural to an urban setting. Caste and class selectivity among migrants entering the formal and informal sectors of the urban labor market in India is often believed to contribute to urban inequality in this way. In Malaysia the racial patterns of rural-urban migration are particularly worthy of attention in this context. Might it be that rural-urban earnings differentials seem to be much less for the Chinese than for the Malays because of selective patterns of migration between the two races? This question will be addressed in Chapter 11.

A second hypothesis has emerged in the recent literature of urban labor markets belonging to the class of Harris-Todaro models.[7] This view of migration, which is in some ways the opposite of the one that stresses the importance of established streams, emphasizes the gamble for high stakes. It sees migrants as responding to the gains they expect to achieve from their eventual entry into the high-wage formal sector of the urban economy, rather than to the earnings levels they are likely to achieve when they first arrive in the urban market. If this hypothesis is correct, new migrants will be found disproportionately in the informal urban sector, and the equilibrium level of their earnings at that stage will be lower than their long-run supply price (which they will achieve only when they manage to break into the formal sector). In other words, migrants may actually be willing to take a cut in their present earnings by moving to the city, because they believe their presence in the urban market to be an investment which will yield returns in the future. If this process operates on a significant scale, it will tend to worsen income distribution in the urban economy. Again, Chapter 11 examines the evidence for this hypothesis in the Malaysian context.

A third and rather different hypothesis about migration and sectoral differences in earnings in the urban economy has been developed based

7. J. R. Harris and M. P. Todaro, "Migration, Unemployment, and Development: A Two-Sector Analysis," *American Economic Review*, vol. 60, no. 1 (March 1970), pp. 126–42.

on an analysis of another Asian labor market—that of Bombay.[8] The evidence from this analysis suggests that earnings for labor of "equivalent quality" are lower in the informal sector than in the formal sector, not because risk-taking migrants who cannot break into the formal sector spill over into the informal sector, but because different types of migrants with different supply prices are attracted to the two sectors. In particular, temporary migrants with relatively low supply prices are found in disproportionate quantity in the informal sector, which has less demand for a stable work force and therefore for permanent migrants. The higher wage in the formal sector reflects the higher supply price of permanent family migration. Employers are willing to pay this higher wage, rather than to use cheaper but more temporary and unstable labor, because the correlation between the stability of labor and its productivity is strong in the formal sector. Chapter 11 will discuss the evidence for the coexistence of the different categories of migrants in Malaysia and will try to establish whether unmarried temporary migrants form as large a group in Malaysia as they do in Bombay and other Indian and African cities.

## Lifetime Earnings and Job Mobility

Dual labor market theories, while often formulated in terms of differences in initial wages, generally also include hypotheses about the lifetime earnings profiles of workers in the two sectors. The Doeringer-Piore formulation of the theory for the U.S. labor market stresses the lack of opportunity for developing skills among workers in the lower tier of the labor market.[9] This leads to a much flatter earnings profile for these workers by age level. The age-earning profile for a given group of workers is of course affected by two factors: the shape of the profile in any given sector or occupation, and the ability of workers to move from one sector to another during their career. Informal sector workers are believed to be at a disadvantage on both counts.

8. Dipak Mazumdar, "Labor Supply in Early Industrialization," *Economic History Review*, vol. 26, no. 3 (August 1973), pp. 477–96; and "Paradigms in the Analysis of Urban Labor Markets in LDCs: A Reassessment in the Light of an Empirical Survey in Bombay City," World Bank Staff Working Paper no. 366 (Washington, D. C., December 1979).

9. Peter B. Doeringer and Michael J. Piore, *Internal Labor Markets and Manpower Analysis* (Lexington, Mass.: D. C. Heath, 1971).

This hypothesis has much more serious implications for the prevalence of inequality of earnings in the urban economy than any theory about differences in entry wages. Cross-section data that pool information on individuals of different age cohorts at a given point in time can give some idea of age-earning profiles in different parts of the urban labor market. This material is covered in Chapter 8. Additional information on workers' lifetime performance is needed, however, to show the nature and extent of intersectoral mobility over time and to provide longitudinal data on changes in earnings. Information on job histories from the 1975 MES, discussed in Chapter 12, is based on respondents' recollections and is therefore probably more accurate for job mobility than for lifetime changes in earnings.

## The Regulated Sector in Urban Malaysia

The urban sector in Malaysia might be expected to offer relatively higher wages as a consequence of overt institutional influences of one kind or another. It can be broadly assumed that earnings are more likely to be regulated in the wage employment sector than among the self-employed. This is, of course, only partially the case in practice, because some of the self-employed—in the professional classes, for example—might be working in sectors of the market in which wages are regulated. For the purposes of this discussion, however, the wage employment sector will be considered to be regulated, and those in self-employment will be eliminated.

According to the population census of 1970, members of the labor force who were enumerated as "own account workers" or "family workers" accounted for 18 percent of the total in towns with populations of 75,000 or more, and 29 percent in towns with populations of 10,000 to 75,000. The difference between males and females was small; the higher proportion of self-employed males was offset by the higher proportion of family workers among the females. The self-employed, excluding family workers, accounted for 13 percent of the labor force in the large towns, and 20 percent in the small towns.

In regard to overt institutional influences in the wage employment sector, it is significant that trade unions cover only a small proportion of the work force in Peninsular Malaysia. The 1970 population census reported 1.38 million employees in the country as a whole, excluding own account and family workers, and total trade union membership was officially reported to be only 275,000 in 1970.[10] The 1973 Annual Report of the Trade Unions Registry stated: "1973 was a year during which the whole nation was faced with inflation. The yet unorganized wage earner was quick to recognize this fact and evidently felt the need to participate in the trade union movement in the quest for higher wages." Nevertheless, total membership of trade unions was reported to be only about 319,000 on December 31, 1973. Moreover, one large union—the National Union of Plantation Workers—accounted for 84,000 workers, most of whom were outside the urban economy under consideration here.[11] Membership figures for the other unions showed that only one—the National Union of Traders—had a membership of more than 10,000. Eight unions with memberships of between 5,000 and 10,000 accounted for another 18 percent of the total. The ten largest unions together covered about 70 percent of all unionized workers; working conditions for the rest of the work force, to the extent that they were covered by trade unions at all, were probably affected only slightly by organized collective bargaining.

A few workers in Malaysia are also affected by government wage regulations administered by Wages Councils. Four Wages Councils— covering dock workers in Penang, the catering and hotel industry, cinema workers, and shop assistants—fix minimum wages for employees in these trades. Shop assistants probably represent the largest of the four groups. The Wages Council for this category of labor fixed wages for 47,000 workers at three different levels, depending on the size of the town in which they worked. It is doubtful whether these levels were rigidly enforced, and in any case the minimum level seems to have been fairly low—between M$85 and M$100 a month for shop assistants above the age of twenty-one in 1974.

Sustained and pervasive institutional influences on wages in Malaysia are basically confined to the public sector. Wages in this sector have been regulated for a long time. Salary scales for persons with various qualifications have been the subject of periodic review by a variety of commissions, starting with the Benham Commission of 1947. Salary scales for the Civil Service were reviewed by the Suffian Commission in 1967, and the Harun Commission fixed scales for statutory authorities in 1972. A cabinet committee recently reported on the 1976 salary

10. Annual Report of the Ministry of Labor, 1971, p. 48.
11. Annual Report of Trade Unions Registry, 1973, p. 27.

scales for the entire public sector. All the discussions and recommendations of the various commissions were based on the principle of relating salary scales to formal educational qualifications. Even the recent
cabinet committee report, which rejected the recommendation of the
so-called Ibrahim Commission on the ground that "its wage structure is
solely determined on the principle of qualification and training," went
on to say that "qualifications can be accepted as a means of determining the various salaries and for the sake of convenience in classifying
the various schemes of service and categories of employees in a particular scheme of service."[12] In adopting this practice, of course, the
Malaysians are only following other countries' conventions. To provide
uniform guidelines for wages in different areas of its activities, the
public sector has to use formal schooling as a major determinant of
pay scales. It is, of course, possible for individuals to be paid differently
within established scales, but even this degree of flexibility is sometimes
limited by generally accepted seniority rules. There is also some evidence that the recommended scale of pay in the Malaysian public
services has been used to establish minimum wages above the levels pre-
vailing in the private sector. One of the objectives of the most recent
set of recommendations by the cabinet committee was to reduce the
differential between lower and higher categories of employees.[13]

The Manpower Survey of 1973 conducted by the Malaysian government has produced data on employment in the public sector. The table
below shows public sector employment by occupation as a percentage
of total employment in each group. The figures in parentheses show
the percentage of total national employment represented by each occupational group, as estimated by the Manpower Survey.

| Professional, technical, and related workers | Administrative and managerial | Clerical | Sales | Services | Agriculture | Production workers and laborers |
|---|---|---|---|---|---|---|
| 90.0 | 42.0 | 50.9 | 0.0 | 71.4 | 0.1 | 40.2 |
| (5.0) | (1.0) | (5.2) | (10.1) | (8.0) | (45.4) | (25.3) |

The weighted average for total public sector employment, using the
above figures in parentheses for weighting purposes, is 23.5 percent.
This average appears to be low because there are virtually no public

---

12. Report of the Cabinet Committee to Examine the Revised Report of the
Royal Salaries Commission, 1975, pp. 28–29.
13. Ibid., passim.

sector employees in sales or agriculture. In most other occupations, the public sector accounts for about half or more of total employment. Therefore, although separate figures for urban areas are not available, it can reasonably be inferred that public sector employment constitutes about 40 percent of total urban employment. For industrial rather than occupational groups, the Manpower Survey showed that two categories —"Transport, storage, and communication" and "Public administration and defense, education, health, and utilities"—accounted for 90 percent of all public sector employment; the latter alone contributed 76 percent of the total. Public sector employment in manufacturing was negligible. Thus, the large number of public sector employees shown as "production workers or laborers" in the occupational grouping were mostly unskilled workers in public administration and utilities.

Table 6-2. Educational Attainment of Public Sector Employees

| Category | Primary or less | Lower second-ary | Upper second-ary | Post second-ary | Diploma | Degree |
|---|---|---|---|---|---|---|
| Percentage in public sector of total employed at each educational level | 18.3 | 46.1 | 66.9 | 66.6 | 55.6 | 68.4 |
| Percentage distribution of total employed in each sector | | | | | | |
| Public | 28.4 | 21.8 | 40.1 | 2.2 | 2.2 | 5.5 |
| Private | 72.0 | 14.5 | 10.5 | 0.7 | 1.0 | 1.3 |

Source: Economic Planning Unit, Manpower Survey, 1973.

As might be expected, the better educated among the population are disproportionately highly represented in public sector employment. Less predictably, however, Table 6-2 shows the preponderance in the sector of all groups with educational attainment above the primary level.

# CHAPTER 7

# The Structure of Employment
# and Earnings

THIS CHAPTER PRESENTS A BROAD, DESCRIPTIVE PICTURE of the pattern
of employment in Malaysia's urban labor market and of the distribution of earnings for different groups of workers; the findings are primarily based on data from the 1975 World Bank Migration and
Employment Survey (MES), but also draw on Post-Enumeration Survey (PES) data. The first section discusses the differences between the
earnings of the self-employed and those of employees. Occupational
and intersectoral differences in earnings are discussed in the following
two sections.

## The Self-employed and Employee Groups

The MES questionnaire asked all earners about the type of enterprise
for which they worked, defining those who worked in their own or
family business as "self-employed" and those who worked for wages
in enterprises owned by others as "employees." The determinants of
the earnings of the employees will be analyzed in detail in Chapter 8;
this section outlines the different earnings patterns of the two employment groups.

As might be expected, a much greater proportion of the male labor
force is self-employed in the East Coast towns (34.7 percent) than in
Kuala Lumpur (16.4 percent). The contrast is even greater for the
female labor force in the two areas, where 32.2 and 9.6 percent, respectively, are self-employed. This finding is all the more striking since
females form a much smaller proportion of the labor force in the East
Coast towns than in Kuala Lumpur (15.5 percent against 23.2 percent); wage employment opportunities for females would appear to be
extremely restricted in the nonmetropolitan urban areas.

The activities of the self-employed are strongly concentrated in two occupational groups in both regions—especially in the case of Kuala Lumpur, where 35 percent of the self-employed are working proprietors or salesmen and 15 percent are hawkers and street vendors, the rest being distributed more or less evenly in other occupations. In the East Coast, 37 percent of the total are working proprietors or salesmen, 10 percent are street vendors, and 5 percent are farmers; the remainder is again fairly evenly distributed. Since the characteristics of the two major groups—working proprietors and street vendors—could be expected to differ, data for these two groups are shown separately wherever possible in the tabulations reported below.

It is frequently suggested that the self-employed group makes up the bulk of informal sector employment, which is characterized by ease of entry—and that the group therefore contains a disproportionate number of transient workers trying to improve their position on the employment ladder and workers who have slipped downward from more attractive jobs in the formal sector. If this is the case, the self-employed could be expected to be strongly biased as a group toward extremes of youth and age and to contain disproportionate numbers of the less educated. At the same time, the earnings of the self-employed could be expected to be distributed around a substantially lower mean level than those of the employees.

Data covering these variables are presented separately for the two regions. Table 7-1 gives the mean levels and Tables 7-2, 7-3, and 7-4 show the frequency distributions of different levels of education, age, and income, respectively, for employees and the self-employed and for individual categories within the latter group.

### Education

The educational difference between the two basic employment categories is as expected for both regions. Table 7-1 shows that both male and female employees have a higher mean educational level than the corresponding categories of the self-employed. The female employees are better educated than the males, but the opposite is true for the self-employed.

The frequency distribution by educational level in Table 7-2 shows that very few of the self-employed have passed the school certificate, whereas about 20 percent of the employees in each region have done so. Furthermore, a substantial proportion of the self-employed—particularly in the East Coast—have no formal schooling, whereas only a small per-

Table 7-1. Age, Education, and Income of the Self-employed and Employees

| Category of workers | Kuala Lumpur | | | Kuantan and Kota Bharu | | |
|---|---|---|---|---|---|---|
| | Mean age (years) | Mean education (years) | Mean income (Malaysian dollars a month) | Mean age (years) | Mean education (years) | Mean income (Malaysian dollars a month) |
| All self-employed | 35.19 | 2.39 | 346.20 | 36.65 | 2.22 | 245.60 |
| Male self-employed | 35.95 | 2.40 | 368.51 | 37.13 | 2.23 | 267.52 |
| Female self-employed | 30.74 | 2.37 | 199.08 | 33.75 | 2.13 | 114.09 |
| Working proprietors | 37.14 | 2.49 | 440.00 | 40.85 | 2.32 | 395.10 |
| Street vendors | 34.88 | 2.09 | 218.19 | 36.98 | 1.80 | 161.64 |
| Rest of self-employed (excluding working proprietors and street vendors) | 34.50 | 2.44 | 343.37 | 35.21 | 2.25 | 210.05 |
| All employees | 29.04 | 2.96 | 322.91 | 30.43 | 2.69 | 257.37 |
| Male employees | 30.18 | 2.95 | 350.65 | 31.16 | 2.65 | 265.35 |
| Female employees | 25.68 | 2.98 | 240.78 | 26.62 | 2.90 | 215.55 |
| Total labor force | 30.08 | 2.62 | 299.50 | 32.59 | 2.31 | 226.74 |

Note: In Kuala Lumpur 16.35 percent of the total labor force is self-employed; in Kuantan and Kota Bharu it is 34.71 percent.
Source: MES, 1975.

Table 7-2. Percentage Distribution by Educational Level
for Employees and Some Self-employed Groups

| Educational level | Employees | All self-employed | Shop owners | Vendors | Self-employed women |
|---|---|---|---|---|---|
| | | Kuala Lumpur | | | |
| No formal education | 4 | 8 | 4 | 17 | 16 |
| Primary | 39 | 54 | 51 | 72 | 41 |
| Some secondary | 30 | 31 | 34 | 10 | 32 |
| School certificate | 20 | 5 | 7 | . . . | 9 |
| Higher school certificate | 2 | 1 | . . . | . . . | 2 |
| Technical college diploma | 2 | . . . | . . . | . . . | . . . |
| University degree | 4 | 1 | 1 | . . . | . . . |
| | | Kuantan and Kota Bharu | | | |
| No formal education | 9 | 21 | 14 | 36 | 29 |
| Primary | 47 | 46 | 51 | 47 | 33 |
| Some secondary | 21 | 25 | 25 | 16 | 33 |
| School certificate | 19 | 7 | 9 | . . . | 5 |
| Higher school certificate | 2 | . . . | 1 | . . . | . . . |
| Technical college diploma | 1 | . . . | . . . | . . . | . . . |
| University degree | 1 | 1 | . . . | . . . | . . . |

. . . Zero or negligible.
Source: MES, 1975.

centage of the employees are in this category. As might be expected, street vendors and self-employed women have less education than those in other self-employed categories.

## Age

Unlike educational levels, the age variations between the self-employed and employees do not conform to the expected pattern. Both the summary figures in Table 7-1 and the detailed age distributions in Table 7-3 clearly show that the self-employed as a whole, as well as particular categories within the group, are older than the employees. The female self-employed category shown in Table 7-3 contains a larger proportion of the youngest age groups than the category for employees as a whole, but Table 7-1 shows that the average age of self-employed females in both regions is higher than that of the female

Table 7-3. Percentage Distribution by Age Group for Employees and Some Self-employed Groups

| Age group | Employees | All self-employed | Shop owners | Vendors | Self-employed women |
|---|---|---|---|---|---|
| | | Kuala Lumpur | | | |
| Under 20 | 16.3 | 9.5 | 5.3 | 9.7 | 20.3 |
| 21–25 | 27.9 | 16.7 | 9.5 | 17.7 | 28.8 |
| 26–30 | 22.1 | 14.9 | 18.9 | 11.3 | 11.9 |
| 31–35 | 11.6 | 14.4 | 15.8 | 14.5 | 10.2 |
| 36–40 | 8.7 | 12.9 | 14.7 | 17.7 | 10.2 |
| 41–45 | 5.9 | 10.0 | 15.8 | 9.7 | 8.5 |
| 46–50 | 5.1 | 10.0 | 10.5 | 8.1 | 1.7 |
| 51–60 | 1.8 | 7.2 | 6.3 | 8.1 | 5.1 |
| 61 and over | 0.5 | 3.6 | 3.2 | 3.2 | 3.4 |
| | | Kuantan and Kota Bharu | | | |
| Under 20 | 12.0 | 5.0 | . . . | 2.0 | 15.2 |
| 21–25 | 25.8 | 13.9 | 5.9 | 16.3 | 16.7 |
| 26–30 | 21.5 | 15.4 | 17.8 | 6.1 | 12.1 |
| 31–35 | 13.2 | 18.0 | 14.9 | 22.4 | 19.7 |
| 36–40 | 11.4 | 14.3 | 14.9 | 20.4 | 12.1 |
| 41–45 | 7.4 | 9.7 | 11.9 | 10.2 | 4.5 |
| 46–50 | 5.8 | 13.4 | 16.8 | 16.3 | 13.6 |
| 51–60 | 2.5 | 6.7 | 11.9 | 4.1 | 4.5 |
| 61 and over | 0.3 | 3.7 | 5.9 | 2.0 | 1.5 |

. . . Zero or negligible.
Source: MES, 1975.

employees. A point of particular interest is that the street-vendor category, which is supposed to attract young workers seeking their first jobs in the urban labor market, has an age distribution very similar to that of the self-employed group as a whole. In fact, a larger proportion of the under-25 age group is found among employees than among vendors—partly because young female workers are more commonly found in the former group.

At the upper end of the age distribution, it is clear that the self-employed form the bulk of the over-50 age groups in both regions; in fact, very few of the wage employees seem to stay on in the work force beyond the age of 50. A possible explanation for this phenomenon might be that employees leave the wage-earning labor force at this point and find work in the self-employed sector for the last portion of their careers. The quantitative significance of such a process, if it in fact exists, is small, however; the proportions of each group aged between 20 and 50 are more or less the same for the two groups of workers, and the remainder of each group is accounted for by the similar proportions of employees under 20 and self-employed over 50.

## Incomes

The first and most notable point to emerge from Table 7-1 is that self-employed males in both regions, and all self-employed taken together in Kuala Lumpur, have higher mean incomes than the corresponding categories of employees. Given the lower mean levels of education of the self-employed in these categories, the fact that they earn more than their counterparts in the employee sector becomes all the more striking.

The incomes of the self-employed are by no means homogeneous, however; in fact, they display a striking disparity compared with those of the employee group. Survey data not presented here show that in Kuala Lumpur the bottom 10 percent of the self-employed earn less than M$90 a month and the top 10 percent between M$600 and M$4,000 a month. The corresponding figures for the East Coast are less than M$60 a month and between M$600 and M$3,000 a month. Given the remarkably small variation in educational level among the self-employed (93 percent in Kuala Lumpur and 92 percent in the coastal towns have some secondary education or less), and given that experience seems to have little correlation with earnings (see below), it is necessary to look for some other explanation for the diversity of earnings of the self-employed.

Breaking down the earnings of the self-employed by sex provides the first element of the explanation. Women in both employment groups earn less than men, but the difference in earnings by sex is much greater for the self-employed. The percentage difference by sex for the self-employed is much greater in the East Coast, where, as noted earlier, wage-earning opportunities for women are very restricted and much the larger part of the female work force is self-employed.

Dividing the self-employed into different occupational groups throws a little more light on the causes of the wide disparity of earnings levels in the group. In principle, the working proprietors or shopkeepers might be expected to form a relatively well-off, even a "protected" subcategory of the self-employed group, and this is borne out by the facts. Data not reproduced here show that the working proprietors form by far the largest proportion of the self-employed in the top 10 percent of the earnings distribution (33 percent in Kuala Lumpur and 45 percent in the East Coast); moreover, their mean income is considerably higher than that of the rest of the self-employed, although they are not significantly more educated (they are somewhat older, however).

By contrast, Table 7-1 shows that the average earnings of the second largest group of the self-employed—the street vendors—are well below the average for the self-employed as a whole and less than 50 percent of what the shopkeepers earn. Despite this clear difference between the two main groups of the self-employed, the dispersion of earnings within each group persists. For example, it is apparent from Table 7-4 that a substantial proportion of the vendors earns more than

Table 7-4. Percentage Distribution by Income Level
for Employees and Some Self-employed Groups

| Income group (Malaysian dollars per month) | Employees | All self-employed | Shop owners | Vendors | Self-employed women |
|---|---|---|---|---|---|
| | | | Kuala Lumpur | | |
| Under 75 | 5.3 | 11.6 | 10.5 | 8.1 | 35.6 |
| 76–100 | 6.3 | 10.5 | 2.1 | 12.9 | 20.3 |
| 101–125 | 4.7 | 1.3 | 1.1 | . . . | 3.4 |
| 126–150 | 11.0 | 6.4 | 4.2 | 9.7 | 6.8 |
| 151–200 | 19.3 | 16.2 | 14.7 | 25.8 | 20.3 |
| 201–300 | 16.3 | 9.8 | 10.5 | 14.5 | 3.4 |
| 301–450 | 21.4 | 28.3 | 31.6 | 25.8 | 5.1 |
| 451–650 | 6.5 | 8.5 | 14.7 | 3.2 | 3.4 |
| 651–1,000 | 5.0 | 4.3 | 4.0 | . . . | 1.7 |
| 1,000 and over | 4.2 | 3.2 | 6.6 | . . . | . . . |
| | | | Kuantan and Kota Bharu | | |
| Under 75 | 8.4 | 13.4 | 4.0 | 16.3 | 31.8 |
| 76–100 | 9.0 | 19.0 | 5.9 | 22.4 | 27.3 |
| 101–125 | 6.8 | 7.8 | 3.0 | 12.2 | 9.1 |
| 126–150 | 12.1 | 10.6 | 9.9 | 14.3 | 10.6 |
| 151–200 | 22.4 | 18.4 | 23.8 | 16.3 | 15.2 |
| 201–300 | 13.6 | 4.1 | 2.0 | 4.1 | 1.5 |
| 301–450 | 16.5 | 13.6 | 20.8 | 10.2 | 3.0 |
| 451–650 | 6.7 | 6.7 | 17.8 | 2.0 | 1.5 |
| 651–1,000 | 3.7 | 4.8 | 9.0 | 2.0 | . . . |
| 1,000 and over | 0.9 | 1.5 | 3.9 | . . . | . . . |

. . . Zero or negligible.
Source: MES, 1975.

M$300 a month (roughly 30 percent in Kuala Lumpur and 15 percent in the East Coast), and a substantial proportion of the working pro-prietors earns less than M$150 a month (around 20 percent for both regions).

At this point it is worth examining the earnings structure of employ-ees and the self-employed as it emerges from the data set of the 1970 PES. Since the PES sample covers the whole urban sector in Malaysia, its large size makes it possible to compare the earnings distribution by occupational groups separately for males and females. Table 7-5 gives the earnings distributions for the employees and the self-employed as a whole, and also for two important occupational groups, broken down by sex. The data for all occupations reveal no real difference in the dis-tributions for the male self-employed and employee groups. The earn-ings distribution for self-employed females is definitely biased toward the lower end of the scale in comparison with that of the female employees, however, because of the high proportion of self-employed females in the bottom-income group.

A separate examination of earnings levels in the two largest occupa-tional groups in which the self-employed are found (other sales and production workers)[1] indicates that for males the distribution of self-employed earnings seems to be biased upward. A larger proportion of self-employed males than male employees has earnings above the middle-income range, notably in income groups 5-7 for sales, and groups 6-7 for production workers. By contrast, a much larger propor-tion of self-employed females is shown to be in the bottom income group. At the same time, however, Table 7-5 illustrates an interesting fact that did not show up in the aggregate distribution in Table 7-4: significantly larger percentages of self-employed females than of female employees are in the higher income groups (4-5 for sales and 5-6 for production workers). In spite of the small sample of females, the evi-dence is strong that a larger proportion of the self-employed among both sexes is in the above average earnings groups compared with the employ-ees. For the females only, this phenomenon goes hand in hand with a relative preponderance of the self-employed in the bottom income group.

In light of pronounced disparities in earnings within the self-employed group, it may be asked whether any simple relation exists

1. Each represents about 30 percent of total self-employed employment for both males and females. Since "other sales" have been distinguished from "higher sales" at the two-digit occupational classification, this group includes mostly the vendors and hawkers.

Table 7-5. Percentage Distribution of Earnings by Sex
and Occupation for Employees and the Self-employed
in All Urban Areas

| Income group (Malaysian dollars per month) | Male | | Female | |
|---|---|---|---|---|
| | Employed | Self-employed | Employed | Self-employed |
| *All occupations* | | | | |
| (1) 1–39 | 4.6 | 2.9 | 13.2 | 28.1 |
| (2) 40–79 | 9.6 | 11.0 | 27.4 | 28.3 |
| (3) 80–129 | 19.1 | 19.4 | 24.5 | 18.7 |
| (4) 130–179 | 17.4 | 16.0 | 9.8 | 8.6 |
| (5) 180–279 | 22.0 | 22.7 | 10.1 | 7.8 |
| (6) 280–479 | 15.4 | 17.5 | 10.2 | 5.6 |
| (7) 480–679 | 5.0 | 5.5 | 2.5 | 1.6 |
| (8) 680–979 | 3.1 | 2.3 | 0.8 | 0.6 |
| (9) 980 and over | 3.1 | 2.3 | 0.4 | 0.4 |
| Total | 100.0 | 100.0 | 100.0 | 100.0 |
| Total number | 5931 | 1539 | 2471 | 498 |
| *Other sales* | | | | |
| (1) 1–39 | 10.0 | 2.3 | 7.1 | 20.9 |
| (2) 40–79 | 20.1 | 11.7 | 40.9 | 33.5 |
| (3) 80–129 | 27.9 | 24.4 | 40.9 | 22.2 |
| (4) 130–179 | 19.0 | 21.4 | 3.9 | 13.9 |
| (5) 180–279 | 14.4 | 24.2 | 3.1 | 7.0 |
| (6) 280–479 | 6.3 | 12.0 | 2.4 | 1.9 |
| (7) 480–679 | 0.9 | 2.8 | . . . | . . . |
| (8) 680–979 | 1.0 | 0.7 | . . . | . . . |
| (9) 980 and over | . . . | . . . | . . . | . . . |
| Total | 100.0 | 100.0 | 100.0 | 100.0 |
| Total number | 672 | 426 | 127 | 158 |
| *Production workers* | | | | |
| (1) 1–39 | 4.7 | 2.6 | 19.9 | 41.4 |
| (2) 40–79 | 11.6 | 9.6 | 49.1 | 31.2 |
| (3) 80–129 | 22.8 | 21.9 | 22.9 | 14.9 |
| (4) 130–179 | 20.2 | 19.8 | 4.1 | 3.5 |
| (5) 180–279 | 27.9 | 23.7 | 2.8 | 5.7 |
| (6) 280–479 | 10.4 | 15.9 | 0.4 | 2.8 |
| (7) 480–679 | 1.2 | 3.4 | 0.2 | . . . |
| (8) 680–979 | 0.4 | 1.3 | 0.2 | 0.7 |
| (9) 980 and over | 0.3 | 1.0 | . . . | . . . |
| Total | 100.0 | 100.0 | 100.0 | 100.0 |
| Total number | 2283 | 384 | 532 | 141 |

. . . Zero or negligible.
Source: PES, 1970.

which might provide a starting point for the exploration of earnings in this category. Educational variations are small among the self-employed and therefore cannot explain the wide disparities in earnings. Since the majority of the self-employed spent only a few years in school, age could be a good proxy for experience and might be worth testing to see if it is systematically related to earnings. Accordingly, the following regression model was tested for the self-employed in each of the important subgroups in the MES sample:

$$\text{Log of earnings} = \alpha + \beta_1 \text{ (age)} + \beta_2 \text{ (age)}.$$

The results are shown in Table 7-6.

Except for male street vendors in Kuala Lumpur, age is not a significant explanatory variable for earnings in any of the groups studied. For the vendors of Kuala Lumpur, age, apart from being significant, explains a surprisingly large part of the variation in earnings. This result is, in fact, consistent with the traditional view of the self-employed sector. Street vending could be expected to provide an excellent opportunity for new job seekers to enter the labor market. This hypothesis suggests a positive relation between age and earnings; the young who get their first footing in the market as vendors will probably have to settle for low earnings while they are shopping around for better jobs, and those who continue to work as vendors as they grow older will tend to be the minority who manage to make good. The fact that no relation between age and earnings is observed for vendors in the East Coast suggests that the mechanism of entry and departure for this occupation is probably different in the coastal towns. Some support for this supposition is provided by the different age distributions that appear to exist among vendors in the two areas. Table 7-3 shows that nearly 40 percent of the vendors in Kuala Lumpur are under 30, but that vendors in the East Coast are much more evenly distributed among the different age groups. In the latter area, the sector probably offers long-term employment for the majority of those who enter it.

The results of the regression analysis are also consistent with the popular view that the self-employed groups in both areas have little opportunity to raise their earnings by increasing their skills through on-the-job training. This state of affairs contrasts sharply with that in the wage-earning sector, in which (as Chapter 8 will demonstrate in detail) experience accounts for a substantial proportion of the variation in earnings.

Contrary to general belief, the self-employed are not concentrated in a narrow range of occupations with low earnings, but this section has

Table 7-6. Significance of Age as an Explanatory Variable for Earnings among the Self-employed

| Group | Constant | F significance | $\beta_1$ | F significance | $\beta_2$ | F significance | $R^2$ |
|---|---|---|---|---|---|---|---|
| *Kuala Lumpur* | | | | | | | |
| Male shopowners | 4.44 | 12.74 | 0.071 | 1.34 | −0.009 | 1.62 | 0.02 |
| Male street vendors | 1.24 | 11.04 | 0.213 | 104.05 | −0.003 | 79.68 | 0.70 |
| Female self-employed | 3.03 | 3.03 | 0.119 | 1.39 | −0.199 | 2.28 | 0.09 |
| *Kuantan and Kota Bharu* | | | | | | | |
| Male shopowners | 4.95 | 23.08 | 0.031 | 0.391 | −0.003 | 0.285 | 0.007 |
| Male street vendors | 3.18 | 6.99 | 0.093 | 1.70 | −0.001 | 1.02 | 0.173 |
| Female self-employed | 2.29 | 2.51 | 0.093 | 1.23 | −0.009 | 0.674 | 0.056 |

*Source:* Data derived from MES, 1975.

not been able to explain—within the limits of its material—why some of the self-employed earn so much more than others. Some further explorations of possible causes of the widely observed income variations among the group will be made in Chapter 10, which deals with migration and mobility factors.

## Occupational Differences

The occupational classification of the sample in both the PES and the MES is based on the codes used in the *Dictionary of Occupational Classification* (Malaysia, 1968), prepared by the Ministry of Labor (which itself follows the ILO's International Standard Classification of Occupations). For the purposes of the present analysis, these codes have been aggregated into three groups: blue collar unskilled; blue collar semi-skilled and skilled; and white collar. Each group includes both manufacturing and service, sales, and agricultural workers:

*Blue collar unskilled*
—Sales workers: sales assistants, street vendors, canvassers, news vendors
—Service workers: waiters, bartenders, maids and related house-keeping workers, building caretakers, domestic servants, cleaners and related workers
—Agricultural workers: general farm workers
—Manufacturing: general laborers

*Blue collar semiskilled and skilled*
—Service workers: transport conductors, mail distribution clerks, telephone and telegraph operators, cooks, launderers, hairdressers, protective service workers (such as firemen and police)
—Agricultural workers: farm machinery operators, loggers, fishermen
—Production workers: all semiskilled and skilled production workers

*White collar*
—All professional and technical employees, administrative and managerial employees, senior clerical employees, and supervisory employees in the sales, service, and agricultural sectors.

This classification thus provides a rough framework for grouping workers by skill levels, irrespective of the particular occupational sector in which they work.

The earnings distributions for the three occupational categories are presented in Table 7-7, which shows the data separately for male and

Table 7-7. Percentage Distribution of Employees by Monthly Earnings

| | Income group (Malaysian dollars per month) | | | | | | | | Total number in group |
|---|---|---|---|---|---|---|---|---|---|
| Category | Less than 100 (1) | 100–150 (2) | 151–200 (3) | 201–250 (4) | 251–300 (5) | 301–400 (6) | 401–600 (7) | More than 600 (8) | |
| *Kuala Lumpur* | | | | | | | | | |
| Males | | | | | | | | | |
| Unskilled | 11.9 | 15.1 | 33.3 | 10.7 | 13.6 | 6.2 | 3.5 | 1.5 | 403 |
| Semiskilled | 7.4 | 15.7 | 20.5 | 15.7 | 17.9 | 14.1 | 5.1 | 2.3 | 689 |
| White collar | 2.1 | 7.1 | 12.5 | 10.9 | 17.3 | 12.1 | 13.6 | 24.6 | 667 |
| Females | | | | | | | | | |
| Unskilled | 43.4 | 33.1 | 13.1 | 1.7 | 1.7 | 0.6 | ... | 0.6 | 173 |
| Semiskilled | 56.5 | 19.6 | 14.1 | 3.3 | 1.1 | 1.1 | ... | ... | 98 |
| White collar | 7.4 | 13.3 | 14.8 | 11.8 | 13.0 | 12.2 | 16.3 | 10.4 | 270 |
| *East Coast Towns* | | | | | | | | | |
| Males | | | | | | | | | |
| Unskilled | 30.3 | 29.7 | 23.5 | 7.4 | 4.5 | 1.9 | 1.6 | 1.0 | 310 |
| Semiskilled | 17.0 | 20.7 | 25.9 | 11.5 | 14.2 | 5.5 | 4.2 | 1.0 | 401 |
| White collar | 12.8 | 9.9 | 17.1 | 7.7 | 9.9 | 11.8 | 15.7 | 15.0 | |
| Females | | | | | | | | | |
| Unskilled | 64.3 | 19.6 | 10.7 | 3.6 | 1.8 | ... | ... | ... | 56 |
| Semiskilled | 57.9 | 26.3 | 12.3 | ... | 1.8 | ... | ... | ... | 57 |
| White collar | 13.8 | 8.0 | 20.7 | 10.3 | 13.8 | 14.9 | 12.6 | 5.7 | 87 |

... Zero or negligible.
*Note:* The percentages are with respect to the total number of the subsample corresponding to each row. The percentage for each subsample whose income was not available has been left out of the table.

Source: MFLS 1975.

female employees. The figures relate to employees only; the self-employed are excluded from the distributions. Although the distribution data for male employees in Kuala Lumpur show a predictable shift toward higher income levels with successively more skilled occupational groups, there is considerable overlap between the three categories. For example, while the unskilled are heavily concentrated in the M$151–M$200 earnings group, a substantial portion of the other two occupational categories are to be found in this group as well. A fair number of all three categories are spread in the earnings groups up to group 5 (M$251–M$300). It is only above this level that representation begins to differ sharply among occupations. The unskilled category are a very small percentage, and white-collar employees form the bulk of those who earn more than M$400 a month.

In the East Coast, however, there seems to be a greater difference between the unskilled and the other two occupational categories in the two bottom earnings groups. More than 30 percent of unskilled male employees in Kuantan and Kota Bharu earn less than M$100 a month, and 60 percent of them earn less than M$150 a month. By contrast, the largest concentration of male employees in the other skill groups combined is in the M$150–M$200 income group. The break between skilled blue-collar and white-collar workers in the upper part of the distribution also comes at a lower level of earnings in the East Coast than in Kuala Lumpur. In the coastal towns, those earning more than M$300 are mostly white-collar workers; in Kuala Lumpur, the comparable figure was M$400.

The earnings distribution for female employees is illustrated in Figures 7-1 and 7-2. The figures show that the distributions for the unskilled and the blue-collar skilled are practically identical—and that they are virtually the same in both regions, with only a slight shift to higher earnings in the case of Kuala Lumpur. Most blue-collar female employees, whether unskilled or semiskilled, earn less than M$100 a month in both regions. The earnings of white-collar females vary more widely and are considerably higher than those of other groups. The figure for each region shows two peaks for the white-collar group: the first occurs in the M$151–M$200 earnings range for both regions; the second, in the M$301–M$400 earnings range in the case of the East Coast and in the M$401–M$600 earnings range in the case of Kuala Lumpur.

The earnings distribution data thus show a significant difference between the unskilled and the semiskilled only in the case of males in the East Coast towns, where median earnings of the semiskilled are

Figure 7–1. Distribution of Female Earnings by
Occupational Group: East Coast

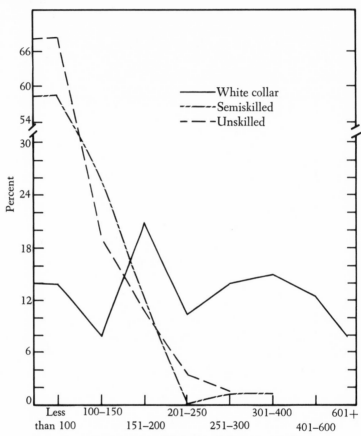

Income group (Malaysian dollars per month)

*Source:* MES, 1975.

about 52 percent higher than those of the unskilled. (The corresponding difference for Kuala Lumpur is only 12 percent.) White-collar
workers of both sexes have a widely dispersed pattern of earnings and
predictably make up the overwhelming majority of earners at the upper
end of the scale. Among the male workers, only the white-collar group
has a significant proportion of earners with monthly wages in excess
of M$300 in the East Coast and M$400 in Kuala Lumpur. Among the
females, white-collar workers begin to predominate at the M$150 level

Figure 7–2.  Distribution of Female Earnings by
Occupational Group: Kuala Lumpur

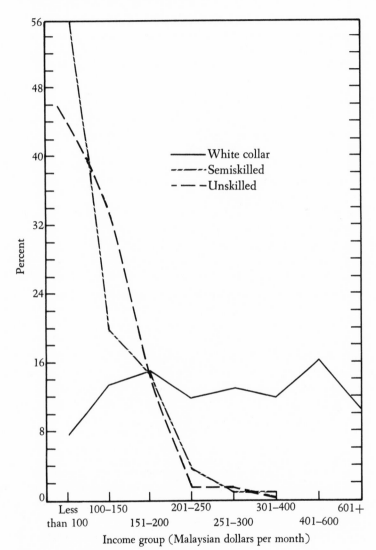

Income group (Malaysian dollars per month)

*Source:* MES, 1975.

in the East Coast and the M$200 level in Kuala Lumpur. The difference in median earnings for males between white-collar workers and unskilled is 67 percent for Kuala Lumpur and 77 percent for the East Coast.

One possible distinguishing characteristic of white-collar workers is their level of education, and differences in workers' earnings levels according to the number of years of their schooling might reasonably be expected to be one of the main explanatory factors underlying the broad pattern of the distribution of labor earnings. Education, however, may simply represent a ticket of entry into particular occupational groups with certain scales of earnings. It is a moot point whether differences in occupational earnings are determined by a real level of market demand for educated labor or by employment status factors. Some comparative studies of occupational differentials in other countries have found that the difference between the earnings of highly educated labor and those of unskilled labor is much more substantial in developing countries than in developed countries. This phenomenon is at least partly a result of the relative oversupply of uneducated labor that fills the jobs at the bottom of the occupational hierarchy.

In an interesting study of occupational differences, V. N. Kothari concluded: "On the whole, for Bombay and Ceylon it would be true to say that what are generally described as higher professions and superior managerial, executive and administrative posts attracted incomes 8 to 10 times as large as those obtained in unskilled manual labor occupations as against 2 to 2.5 times in the United States, and 3 to 3.5 times in Canada."[2] Whatever the difficulties of selecting comparable occupations in different countries, the difference in the earnings ratios is too large to be ignored as an indicator of the structure of earnings in South Asia on the one hand and North America on the other.

From the data collected and analyzed by Kothari, several other points of interest stand out. First, the mean earnings of clerical personnel in India and Ceylon were substantially higher than those of even skilled manual workers, whereas in the United States and Canada the earnings of clerks and traders were below the mean earnings of some of the skilled occupations such as electricians and masons. In South Asia low-level clerical workers earned roughly 25–30 percent more than skilled manual workers, whereas in North America the two groups earned roughly the same amounts.

2. V. N. Kothari, "Discipline in Relative Earnings among Different Countries," *Economic Journal*, September 1970, pp. 605–16.

Second, the difference in the number of years of schooling between clerical and manual workers was much greater in Bombay than it was for comparable groups in the United States. Hence, the difference in the earnings ratio could be ascribed to differences in numbers of years of schooling. But the real puzzle was that higher professionals in Bombay, with only a few more years of schooling than the clerical workers, enjoyed a much more substantial earnings premium over local clerical workers than existed for similar groups in the United States. Kothari's calculations on the internal rates of return to education in Bombay suggested that education can at best explain rather less than half the observed absolute earnings differential in the city's labor market.[3]

How do differences in mean earnings in urban Malaysia look compared with these results? Malaysia has a much more widespread system of primary education than either India or Ceylon had in the years covered by Kothari's study (1955 for Bombay and 1946 for Ceylon). By the early 1970s almost 95 percent of the relevant age group in Peninsular Malaysia had been exposed to primary education.[4] Data on differences in earnings in Malaysia for selected occupations (derived from a World Bank survey, which includes a cross-section of the urban population of Malaysia) are set out in Table 7-8. The data are intended to cover the same range of occupations as the information on occupational earnings in the United States (derived from the 1971 U.S. census) which is also given in the table.

It is clear from the figures that Malaysia differs from the United States in its pattern of occupational differences in much the same way as do Bombay and Ceylon. The index for superior white-collar earnings is a substantially greater multiple of that for the unskilled in Malaysia than it is in the United States. The same point holds true (although to a predictably lesser extent) for the relation between clerical and skilled manual earnings in the two countries. These differences do not appear to be as great as those observed by Kothari; the professional-unskilled earnings ratio, for example, is 7:1, not 10:1 or more. This may be due to the larger supply of workers with some formal education in Malaysia. But in spite of the relatively rapid spread of education in Malaysia (and especially the high rate of growth of secondary schooling), the earnings of clerical workers continue to be about 85 percent higher than those of the unskilled—a significantly

3. Ibid., p. 614.
4. See the appendix to Chapter 8 for a description of the educational system in Malaysia.

Table 7-8. Differences in Earnings by Occupation in Malaysia (1974) and the United States (1971)

| Malaysia | | United States | |
|---|---|---|---|
| Category | Index of monthly earnings | Category | Index of annual earnings |
| Higher professions | 718 | Professional and | |
| Administrators and | | technical | 182 |
| managers | 426 | Self-employed | 289 |
| Assistants to professionals | | Salaried | 160 |
| and technicians | 180 | Managers, proprietors, | |
| Clerical | 184 | and officials | 185 |
| Skilled engineering and | | Self-employed | 135 |
| metal workers | 122 | Salaried | 194 |
| Skilled transport | | Clerical | 133 |
| workers | 120 | Craftsmen | 140 |
| General laborers | 100 | Operations | 115 |
| | | Laborers, except farm | 100 |

*Sources:* Malaysia: Data processed from a World Bank survey (1974) for male employees only. United States: Data from the Bureau of Census, Current Population Reports, series P-60, no. 60, 1972, quoted by Lloyd G. Reynolds, *Labor Economics and Labor Relations,* 6th ed. (Englewood Cliffs, N.J.: Prentice-Hall, 1974).

larger difference than that shown for the United States, although perhaps somewhat less than that in Bombay or Ceylon at earlier dates.

## Differences in Earnings between the Goods-producing and the Service Sectors

Much of the popular literature on economic development makes the assumption that the urban tertiary sector, including commerce and services, has become an increasingly important source of jobs for the underemployed in the rural areas. The tertiary sector is broadly identified with both the informal sector and the self-employed segment of the urban labor market. There appear to be two main reasons for this widespread view of the role of the tertiary sector, one of them empirical and the other theoretical.

The empirical evidence pertains to the relatively rapid rate of growth of employment in the tertiary sector in developing countries, particularly in relation to the rate of growth in manufacturing.[5] In this respect, the experience of developing countries is at variance with the Clark-Fisher model, which maintained on the basis of the history of development of Western countries that the relative importance of tertiary sector employment should increase only at a relatively advanced stage of economic growth.[6] On the theoretical side, the phenomenon of rapid tertiary sector growth has suggested to many observers that tertiary sector employment in developing countries has typically been growing without a commensurate growth in production or income in this sector. Such a situation is theoretically possible if it is assumed that the model of monopolistic competition with easy entry is generally applicable in tertiary activity. The market structure associated with this model enables additional productive units to enter an industry even though its total output is not growing significantly; the total income generated is redistributed among a larger number of workers, however, leading to a fall in workers' average income. What is the evidence on the comparative level and distribution of earnings in the tertiary sector and in the goods-producing sector in Malaysia?

On the basis of the occupational classification of the Malaysian labor force,[7] it appears that a comparison needs to be made between the pattern of earnings in the clerical, sales, and service workers categories on the one hand and that of production workers on the other. Using the large data base provided by the PES for each of the first three groups, the earnings of managerial and supervisory workers and those of commercial travelers, insurance salesmen, and similar groups were removed by using the two-digit occupational codes to provide a set of service industry occupations that could validly be compared with the production worker group. The service industry data given in Tables 7-9 and 7-10 thus refer to the lower levels of clerical, sales, and service workers. The percentage distribution of workers is given separately for the sexes,

---

5. The Latin American evidence is summarized in Joseph Ramos, *Labor and Economic Development in Latin America* (New York: Columbia University Press, 1970). Similar trends are observed elsewhere.

6. A. G. B. Fisher, "Capital and the Growth of Knowledge," *Economic Journal*, vol. 18 (September 1933); and Colin Clark, *The Conditions of Economic Progress* (New York: Macmillan, 1957).

7. *The Dictionary of Occupational Classification* (Malaysia: Ministry of Labor, 1968), based on the International Standard Classification of Occupations issued by ILO in 1968.

Table 7-9. Earnings Distribution for Urban Males
(percent)

| Income group (Malaysian dollars per month) | Lower clerical workers | Lower sales workers | Lower service workers | Production workers |
|---|---|---|---|---|
| Urban areas[a] | | | | |
| 1–39 | 3.5 | 7.0 | 4.2 | 4.4 |
| 40–79 | 2.4 | 16.7 | 10.8 | 11.3 |
| 80–129 | 12.9 | 26.5 | 22.5 | 22.7 |
| 130–179 | 14.6 | 20.0 | 21.5 | 20.2 |
| 180–279 | 25.1 | 18.3 | 24.3 | 27.3 |
| 280–479 | 25.6 | 8.4 | 12.9 | 11.1 |
| 480–679 | 10.3 | 1.6 | 1.1 | 1.5 |
| 680–979 | 3.7 | 0.9 | 1.4 | 0.6 |
| 980 and over | 1.5 | . . . | 0.9 | 0.4 |
| Unknown | 0.3 | 0.5 | 0.5 | 0.4 |
| Total | 100.0 | 100.0 | 100.0 | 100.0 |
| Total number | 910 | 1,095 | 881 | 2,655 |
| Metropolitan towns[a] | | | | |
| 1–39 | 2.6 | 4.5 | 3.1 | 3.9 |
| 40–79 | 2.1 | 16.8 | 9.6 | 10.3 |
| 80–129 | 13.8 | 25.8 | 22.9 | 22.2 |
| 130–179 | 13.3 | 21.6 | 20.3 | 20.4 |
| 180–279 | 23.9 | 19.5 | 24.2 | 28.5 |
| 280–479 | 26.1 | 8.4 | 15.2 | 11.3 |
| 480–679 | 11.5 | 1.5 | 1.2 | 1.7 |
| 680–979 | 4.6 | 1.3 | 1.8 | 0.6 |
| 980 and over | 1.6 | . . . | 1.4 | 0.6 |
| Unknown | 0.5 | 0.6 | 0.4 | 0.4 |
| Total | 100.0 | 100.0 | 100.0 | 100.0 |
| Total number | 624 | 620 | 512 | 1,570 |

. . . Zero or negligible.

Note: Columns may not add to 100 because of rounding.

a. According to the PES, metropolitan towns were Johore Bahru, Malacca, Kuala Lumpur, Klang, Ipoh, and Georgetown. Urban areas are towns of more than 10,000 people.

Source: PES, 1970.

and for male workers it is separated for metropolitan towns and other urban areas. The following conclusions emerge:

—The distribution of earnings of clerical workers shows a bias toward the higher end of the income scale when compared with the other groups. This is to be expected in view of their greater number of years of schooling and the social stratification of jobs in most countries.

—For females, there are surprisingly larger percentages of production workers than clerical, sales, or service workers in the two bottom income groups.

—For males, the pattern of distribution of earnings is overall almost identical in the service and production sectors, but in the bottom-income groups the percentages are higher for sales workers than for service or production workers. These patterns hold for urban areas as a whole and for the metropolitan towns.

It will be shown in Chapter 8 that there is a significant correlation between the age and earnings of employees, especially among males. In particular, the earnings of workers up to about age 25 and over 50 are significantly lower than those of prime-age workers. Allowances must be made for this factor in drawing conclusions from the data in Tables 7-9 and 7-10 about the incidence of low earnings in different sectors of the urban economy. Table 7-11 shows the percentages of male workers in broad age groups whose earnings were below M$130 a month— roughly the average level of earnings of an unskilled male worker in

Table 7-10. Earnings Distribution for Urban Females
(percent)

| Income group (Malaysian dollars per month) | Lower clerical workers | Lower sales workers | Lower service workers | Production workers |
|---|---|---|---|---|
| 1–39 | 5.7 | 14.7 | 18.5 | 24.4 |
| 40–79 | 4.3 | 36.8 | 31.3 | 45.3 |
| 80–129 | 20.7 | 30.5 | 29.3 | 21.2 |
| 130–179 | 16.1 | 9.5 | 13.7 | 4.0 |
| 180–279 | 23.9 | 5.3 | 4.2 | 3.4 |
| 280–479 | 23.6 | 2.1 | 1.4 | 0.9 |
| 480–679 | 3.4 | . . . | 0.4 | 0.1 |
| 680–979 | 1.4 | . . . | . . . | 0.3 |
| 980 and over | 0.6 | . . . | . . . | . . . |
| Unknown | . . . | 1.1 | 1.3 | 0.3 |
| Total | 100.0 | 100.0 | 100.0 | 100.0 |
| Total number | 348 | 285 | 854 | 673 |

. . . Zero or negligible.
Note: Columns may not add to 100 because of rounding.
Source: PES, 1970.

Table 7-11. Male Workers Earning Less than M$130 per Month
by Age Group, Urban Malaysia, 1970
(percentage of total in each occupational group)

| Age group | Lower clerical | Lower sales | Lower services | Production workers | Agricultural workers |
|---|---|---|---|---|---|
| Under 25 | 14.2 | 28.4 | 18.0 | 22.2 | 14.4 |
| 25–50 | 3.3 | 14.5 | 11.9 | 11.5 | 25.2 |
| Over 50 | 11.3 | 7.3 | 7.6 | 4.7 | 18.1 |
| Total | 18.8 | 50.2 | 37.5 | 38.4 | 57.7 |

Source: PES, 1970.

organized industry in Malaysia in 1970.[8] This breakdown suggests that
the higher incidence of low earnings among male workers in the sales
sector, shown in Table 7-9, may be the result of the relative preponderance of young workers in this occupational category. The table shows
that the poorly paid sales workers were disproportionately concentrated
in the under 25 age group; in the prime age group, the percentages of
low-paid workers were almost identical for the production and lower
services sectors, and only slightly higher for the lower sales group.

Overall, in answer to the question posed earlier, available evidence
does not suggest that the tertiary wage-earning sector in Malaysia
represents a discrete pool of low-wage employees. This chapter has outlined the overall pattern of employment and earnings in urban
Malaysia. Chapter 8 will present a more analytical study of earnings,
and of the factors affecting differences in earnings among male
employees.

8. Ministry of Labor, *Handbook of Labor Statistics, West Malaysia* (Kuala
Lumpur, 1970).

# Education and Earnings

THIS CHAPTER ANALYZES DATA on individual earnings taken from both the Post-Enumeration Survey (PES) of 1970 and the Migration and Employment Survey (MES) of 1975, using the human capital model. The analysis is not intended to compare earnings levels at the two points in time represented by the survey dates. The time interval is too short for this purpose, and in any case the coverage is different; the PES is a large sample for all Malaysian urban areas, while the MES is confined to three towns. The latter, however, contains some additional information—on background variables, the type of employer, and other relevant variables—which will be useful in the course of the analysis.

## Analysis of the PES Data

Sudhir Anand has already undertaken some analysis of the PES data in respect to human capital.[1] He fitted the following equation to the data:

$$\log Y = \beta_0 + \beta_1 S + \beta_2 T - \beta_3 T^2$$

where $Y$ = earnings

$S$ = schooling (measured in years)

$T$ = experience, defined as age minus years spent in school.

### Anand's Results

The interpretation of the coefficient $\beta_1$ for the schooling variable $S$ is straightforward. Differentiating the equation partially produces:

$$\beta_1 = \frac{\triangle Y \ / \ Y}{\triangle S}.$$

1. Sudhir Anand, *Inequality and Poverty in Malaysia: Measurement and Decomposition* (New York: Oxford University Press, forthcoming), chap. 7.

If $\triangle S$ equals unity, then $\beta_1$ measures the percentage increase in earnings resulting from an additional year of schooling. No adjustment is made for unemployment or for varying participation rates. Fitting the equation to male urban employees, Anand found that an additional year of schooling increased the income of a Malay by 14.24 percent, of a Chinese by 13.87 percent, and of an Indian by 13.50 percent.

A comparative picture of the explanatory power of the simple model in Malaysia and in advanced countries can be obtained from Table 8-1. The inequality in the distribution of annual earnings, as measured by its log variance, is substantially higher in Malaysia than in the United States and even more so than in Britain—but so is the variance in schooling. Thus, the simple human capital model appears to be of considerably greater significance in the explanation of earnings in Malaysia.[2]

It has been noticed in both the United States and Britain that the share of schooling in the explanation of earnings inequality is substantially smaller than the share of experience. This follows directly from the fact that the variance in workers' years of schooling is so much less than that in their years of experience, and the difference in the coefficients of the two variables is not so great.[3] If only schooling (in years), and not experience, is used to explain earnings in the above

2. It is well known that the explanatory power of the model increases substantially in Britain and the United States when the number of weeks worked is included as one of the independent variables in the model. In Britain the $R^2$ goes up from 0.316 to 0.665 and in the United States from 0.285 to 0.525 (George Psacharapoulos and Richard Layard, "Analysis of the 1972 General Household Survey Data," *Review of Economic Studies* [July 1979]; and Jacob Mincer, "Progress in Human Capital Analysis," in Anthony B. Atkinson, ed., *The Personal Distribution of Incomes* [Boulder, Colo.: Westview, 1976]). But this is because of the endogeneity of weeks worked in the expanded model; that is, higher weekly earnings cause more weeks to be worked. A proper simultaneous equations approach does not give the human capital model a substantially higher explanatory power for either annual or weekly earnings than that noted in the text. (See Psacharapoulos and Layard, p. 12.) Information on weeks worked is not available from the PES data set for Malaysia. An informed guess would be that the low rate of unemployment among prime-age males and the low turnover rate in many urban sectors suggest that the variance in weeks worked during the year in urban labor markets in developing countries is probably much less than in advanced countries.

3. In the simple model estimated by Psacharapoulos and Layard, the contribution of schooling in Britain, holding experience constant, is equal to (coefficient of $S)^2$ Var $(S)$, which works out at 4.5 percent (as against the overall $R^2$ of 32 percent).

model, its explanatory power for U.S. and British differences in earnings is very low (5–6 percent). This fact has been taken by human capital theorists (Mincer, for example) as support for the thesis that investment in post-school learning such as on-the-job training, which is captured by the "labor market experience" variable, is of great importance in the explanation of earnings. It may or may not be legitimate to define "experience" in terms of postschool investment; other factors explaining the relation between rising earnings and experience include the ability of employers to discriminate between more and less productive workers over the long term, or the various factors which lead employers to relate wages to levels of seniority. For the present purpose, however, it is sufficient to note that formal schooling itself contributes substantially to the explanation of earnings in Malaysia, both because the coefficient of schooling shown in Table 8-1 is relatively high and because the variance in years of schooling is relatively great. In fact, it can be calculated from the values given in Table 8-1 that the schooling factor alone explains as much as 38 percent of the log variance of earnings (as against 49 percent of total variance explained by the model as a whole). This point will also arise later in this chapter when analysis of the data set from the MES using a rather different regression model shows that formal school qualifications alone account for a major share of the explained variance.

The differences illustrated above between Malaysia on the one hand, and the United States and Britain on the other, in the working of the standard human capital model are important for an understand-

Table 8-1. Comparative Performance of the Simple Human Capital Model

| Item | Malaysia (1970) | Britain (1972) | United States (1960) |
|---|---|---|---|
| Variance of log of annual earnings | 0.755 | 0.436 | 0.668 |
| Variance of years of schooling | 19.437 | 4.805 | 12.250 |
| Variance of years of experience | 197 | 207 | n.a. |
| $R^2$ | 0.492 | 0.316 | 0.285 |
| Coefficient of $S$ | 0.140 | 0.097 | 0.107 |
| Coefficient of $T$ | 0.098 | 0.091 | 0.081 |

n.a. Not available.

Sources: Malaysia: Anand, *Inequality and Poverty in Malaysia*, table 7.1. Britain: Psacharapoulos and Layard, "Analysis of the 1972 General Household Survey Data," p. 491. United States: Mincer, "Progress in Human Capital Analysis."

ing of Malaysia's labor market. Moreover, it is arguable that the observed differential importance of education as a determinant of earnings is probably a general phenomenon in developing countries.

### Further Analysis

Anand's regression equations had very good fits and explained about half the variance in earnings derived from survey data. But the return to education includes a number of components which are obscured by the type of model used. The following are some areas for further investigation: (1) The use of a continuous schooling variable is of only limited value because it measures the average effect of an additional year of schooling over the entire spectrum of education. It would be more useful to establish the varying amounts of additional income which result from schooling of *different levels*. (2) In considering different levels of schooling, therefore, a distinction needs to be made between those who have successfully completed a particular stage of schooling and obtained the relevant certificate, and those who have failed to do so (the dropouts). The earnings of workers with the same number of years of schooling will vary according to whether they have managed to obtain a particular certificate. This differential effect will be particularly strong if education does not affect an individual's productive capacity but serves more as a screening device used by employers to discriminate among the job seekers.[4] (3) In the analysis of the effect of education on earnings levels, an attempt could usefully be made to take account of explanatory variables that might influence the relation between the two. These include the location of employment (specifically, the type of urban area in which employees work), the nature of their educational experience (that is, level of schooling and language of instruction), and demographic factors (such as race and age).

The econometric model best suited to the task of analyzing earnings using a number of categories or classes of variables is that of multiple regression with sets of dummy variables. The dependent variable is the log of median earnings of the group selected.[5] The explanatory vari-

4. See, on this point, Richard Layard and George Psacharapoulos, "The Screening Hypothesis and the Returns to Education," *Journal of Political Economy*, September–October 1974.

5. The median income for the open-ended classes at the two extremes was calculated as the basis for an estimated distribution function, using Anand's function.

ables are age, educational level, race plus language used in school, type of town plus region, and name of the metropolitan town. The variables and the classes within each group are shown in Table 8-2, which also gives the detailed results. The regression covers all male workers (employees and self-employed) in urban areas, taking all occupations together.

The regression coefficients of the $E$ variables provide estimates of the percentage change in earnings for workers with different levels of education, controlling for other factors such as age, language, race and language of instruction, and location. Table 8-3 sets out the matrix of percentage increases in earnings by educational category. The figures along the left-hand diagonal of the matrix show the percentage increase in earnings resulting from each single increment in educational level ($E_1$ to $E_2$, $E_2$ to $E_3$, $E_3$ to $E_4$, and so on). The boldfaced figures along the diagonal mark these increments for the levels that represent completed educational phases. For example, $E_2$ is completed primary, and $E_4$ is completed lower certificate of education (LCE), but $E_3$ represents some education beyond primary without receipt of the certificate for the next grade.

Two findings about percentage increases in earnings are evident from the table. First, there is evidence of particularly high returns to education from completed educational phases after the primary level. $E_1$ is an amorphous category spanning a range of one to five years of primary schooling, and the coding of the data does not make it possible to subdivide this composite level. But completed primary ($E_2$) gives an earnings premium of 68 percent over those with no schooling ($E_0$). After that, completed LCE ($E_4$), completed school certificate, or Malaysian certificate of education (MCE) ($E_6$), and higher school certificate (HSC) ($E_8$) bring premiums of 27 percent, 59 percent, and 86 percent respectively over the previous completed stage ($E_2$ to $E_4$, $E_4$ to $E_6$, and so on). Increasing returns to education from secondary schooling have been found in other developing countries such as Kenya and Mexico.[6] The wage structure which produces this result and its persistence over time require careful examination. If it is persistent (and is determined by institutional rather than competitive factors), this phenomenon must powerfully increase the demand for secondary education on the

6. George Johnson, "An Empirical Model of the Structure and Wages in Urban Kenya," University of Michigan, draft, June 1972; and Martin Carnoy, "Earnings and Schooling in Mexico," *Economic Development and Cultural Change*, July 1967.

Table 8-2. Regression Analysis of Household Earnings: Male Employees and Self-employed

| Variables | Explanation of symbols | Years of schooling | β | Standard error | Proportion in category |
|---|---|---|---|---|---|
| Age (Base: 15–19) | | | | | |
| $A_1$ | 20–24 | | 0.635 | 0.032 | 0.157 |
| $A_2$ | 25–29 | | 1.078 | 0.033 | 0.141 |
| $A_3$ | 30–39 | | 1.394 | 0.030 | 0.243 |
| $A_4$ | 40–49 | | 1.577 | 0.032 | 0.174 |
| $A_5$ | 50 and over | | 1.406 | 0.033 | 0.166 |
| Education (Base: No schooling) | | | | | |
| $E_1$ | Some primary school, or now attending | 1–5 | 0.333 | 0.037 | 0.284 |
| $E_2$ | Completed primary school | 6 | 0.517 | 0.039 | 0.222 |
| $E_3$ | Forms I to III, no certificate | 7–9 | 0.593 | 0.038 | 0.147 |
| $E_4$ | Lower certificate of education or equivalent (completed lower secondary) | 9 | 0.758 | 0.052 | 0.041 |
| $E_5$ | Forms IV and V, no certificate | 10–11 | 0.897 | 0.042 | 0.077 |
| $E_6$ | School certificate or equivalent (completed upper secondary) | 11 | 1.225 | 0.041 | 0.092 |
| $E_7$ | Form VI, no certificate | 12 | 1.406 | 0.089 | 0.010 |
| $E_8$ | Higher school certificate | 13 | 1.845 | 0.065 | 0.021 |
| Race and language of instruction (Base: Chinese and English) | | | | | |
| $M_1$ | Malay and Malay | | −0.178 | 0.035 | 0.143 |

| | | | | |
|---|---|---|---|---|
| M$_2$ | Malay and English | 0.043[a] | 0.037 | 0.075 |
| M$_3$ | Chinese and Chinese | −0.064 | 0.029 | 0.365 |
| M$_4$ | Others and English | −0.019[a] | 0.035 | 0.083 |
| M$_5$ | Others and others | 0.070[a] | 0.146 | 0.003 |
| M$_6$ | Remainder | −0.360 | 0.034 | 0.097 |
| Strata (Base: Penang) | | | | |
| S$_1$ | Metropolitan towns | −0.032[a] | 0.032 | 0.577 |
| S$_2$ | All towns in Johore | 0.032[a] | 0.035 | 0.077 |
| S$_3$ | All towns in Kedah | −0.047[a] | 0.040 | 0.054 |
| S$_4$ | All towns in Kelantan | −0.206 | 0.046 | 0.038 |
| S$_5$ | All towns in Negri Sembilan | 0.076[a] | 0.056 | 0.024 |
| S$_6$ | All towns in Pahang | 0.226 | 0.044 | 0.042 |
| Metropolitan towns (Base: Georgetown) | | | | |
| T$_1$ | Johore Bahru | 0.191 | 0.045 | 0.053 |
| T$_2$ | Malacca | 0.042[a] | 0.052 | 0.033 |
| T$_3$ | Kuala Lumpur | 0.290 | 0.030 | 0.255 |
| T$_4$ | Klang | 0.176 | 0.047 | 0.043 |
| T$_5$ | Ipoh | 0.116 | 0.037 | 0.091 |
| Constant | | 3.477 | 0.039 | |
| $R^2 = 0.419$ | | | | |
| $F = 193.57$ | | | | |
| $N = 8,095$ | | | | |
| Mean $= 5.142$ | | | | |

a. Not statistically significant.
Source: Data derived from PES, 1970.

one hand, and severely limit the expansion of employment opportunities for school leavers on the other. Both effects would tend to increase unemployment among secondary school graduates.

Another striking feature of Table 8-3 is that the percentage increase in earnings does not increase uniformly for each year of schooling after the completed primary stage. In the case of each of the three post-primary levels considered, the percentage increase for those who drop out between completion of one phase and the next is relatively small (see the figures not in boldface along the diagonal of the matrix). This piece of evidence tends to support the "screening" hypothesis for the Malaysian education-earnings profile. It implies that more importance is attached by employers to workers' possession of a certificate of completion of a given phase of education than to the number of years of schooling. This in turn suggests the possibility of rigidities in the wage structure that are worth investigating.

## The Role of the Public Sector

Analysis of the PES data set has shown the very strong influence of formal education on earnings in urban Malaysia. This influence shows up both in the significant extent to which the education variable explains differences in earnings and in the large coefficients for the successive education levels used in the regression model. The point is emphasized further by the data in Table 8-3, which show, for example, that those with the highest qualification (HSC and higher) earn more than five times as much as those without any formal schooling. By way of comparison, a British earnings function study found that, other things being equal, people with degrees can earn twice as much as people with no qualifications. The much larger differential accruing to the better educated in Malaysia is in line with the substantially larger occupational differences in earnings found in Malaysia, and for that matter in India, which were discussed in Chapter 7. The importance of the public sector in the urban economy of Malaysia and its reliance on educational qualifications as a basis for its salary scales have already been discussed. This section examines the hypothesis that the role of the public sector may be linked with the large differences observed in the structure of employee earnings.

The data set from the MES (1975) provided information about respondents' employers. It is possible, therefore, to study the earnings function separately for the public and private sectors from this data

Table 8-3. Estimated Percentage Increases in Monthly Earnings
with Higher Levels of Education among Male Employees
and Self-employed

| From[a] | $To$[a] | | | | | | | |
|---|---|---|---|---|---|---|---|---|
| | $E_1$ | $E_2$ | $E_3$ | $E_4$ | $E_5$ | $E_6$ | $E_7$ | $E_8$ |
| $E_0$ | 39 | 68 | 81 | 113 | 145 | 241 | 308 | 533 |
| $E_1$ | | 20 | 30 | 53 | 76 | 144 | 193 | 354 |
| $E_2$ | | | 8 | 27 | 46 | 103 | 143 | 277 |
| $E_3$ | | | | 18 | 36 | 88 | 126 | 250 |
| $E_4$ | | | | | 15 | 59 | 91 | 203 |
| $E_5$ | | | | | | 39 | 66 | 158 |
| $E_6$ | | | | | | | 20 | 86 |
| $E_7$ | | | | | | | | 55 |

Note: Estimated percentage increases between any two educational levels are
calculated by finding the antilog of the difference in earnings coefficient between
the two educational levels, subtracting one, and multiplying by 100. For example,
moving from $E_0$ to $E_1$ means taking antilog $(E_1 - E_0)$ which is antilog $(0.333) =$
1.39. 100 $(1.39 - 1) = 39$ percent.
a. The educational levels to which the abbreviations in the table refer are explained in Table 8-2.
Source: Data derived from PES, 1970.

set. The analysis should also provide an additional check on the influence of formal education on earnings.

Before undertaking this analysis, it is necessary to clarify a point
about the data on labor market experience. It has been recognized in
the human capital literature that both age and experience, together with
education, affect earnings, but that it is better to use experience in the
earnings function. To quote Mincer:

> More educated workers of the same age have less experience since
> they enter the labor market later. Since growth rates of earnings
> reflect investment rates, and since these are a (negative) function of
> experience, growth rates of earnings are stronger for more than for
> less educated workers at given ages. This is the essence of the uni-
> versally observed and econometrically bothersome age-schooling inter-
> action effect. With experience as an explicit variable, the interaction
> effect on earnings vanishes.[7]

7. Mincer, "Progress in Human Capital Analysis," p. 148.

Experience is defined as age minus the years of schooling. The more intensive questionnaire administered to the respondents in the MES sought to obtain information on the age at which they left school. In the analysis of the earnings function based on this sample, therefore, it would be possible in principle to take the number of years of schooling and of experience, defined in the way just described, as variables. There is, however, a problem about the respondents' reports of the ages at which they left school, which is specific to the urban economy of Malaysia. The aggregate data show that the ages at which a significant proportion of the sample said they had left school were much higher than might normally be expected for given levels of schooling. The relevant data are given in Table 8-4.

The age at which a student could be expected to complete primary education would be twelve or thirteen at the outside. Yet over half the Malays in Kuala Lumpur with primary education or less, and a larger proportion in the East Coast towns, said they had left school after the age of thirteen. A similar pattern holds for Chinese primary school leavers, and for both races with respect to the other educational levels given in Table 8-4. Such a proportion of abnormally high school-leaving ages could be only partially caused by errors in recollection. The uniformity of the "bias" for the different regions and levels of schooling suggests that there must be a substantive reason for the phenomenon. In connection with the analysis of the problem of unemployment in Part III, it will be argued that the widely reported high school-leaving ages actually represent "passive unemployment" connected with the difficulty of obtaining employment at the relatively young ages which would be considered to be normal in many other societies. A detailed discussion of this argument is given in Chapter 17. For the moment, however, it is only necessary to recognize that experience, as calculated by the difference between present age and the reported age of leaving school, will not have the same significance in Malaysia as it did in Mincer's work in the United States. Consequently, the further analysis of the earnings function in Malaysia undertaken here continues to use present age, not experience, as an explanatory variable along with education.[8]

The simple human capital model was fitted to the data from the MES separately for the public and the private sector employees, and the

8. Anand, in *Inequality and Poverty in Malaysia*, did use experience as an explanatory variable, but his variable was calculated theoretically from the usual (normal) age of leaving school for each educational level.

Table 8-4. Percentage of Male Employees Who Left School at Different Ages by Level of Schooling, Region, and Race

| Age left school | Kuala Lumpur | | | | | | East Coast towns | | | | | |
|---|---|---|---|---|---|---|---|---|---|---|---|---|
| | Malay | | | Chinese | | | Malay | | | Chinese | | |
| | A | B | C | A | B | C | A | B | C | A | B | C |
| Less than 12 | 10.0 | 9.4 | | 9.5 | 5.0 | | 6.5 | 7.8 | | 9.6 | 3.4 | |
| 12 | 19.9 | | | 14.4 | | | 24.3 | | | 15.7 | | |
| 13 | 16.2 | 6.8 | 18.2 | 24.8 | 8.3 | 7.0 | 12.3 | 5.2 | 16.3 | 13.2 | 3.4 | 12.2 |
| 14 | 7.9 | 7.4 | | 14.4 | 11.2 | | 13.0 | 3.9 | | 12.0 | 18.6 | |
| 15 | 16.6 | 20.3 | | 11.6 | 14.0 | | 15.2 | 26.0 | | 16.9 | 13.6 | |
| 16 | 12.9 | 13.5 | | 7.0 | 13.2 | | 12.3 | 18.2 | | 10.8 | 16.9 | |
| 17 | 5.0 | 11.5 | 13.6 | 6.7 | 13.2 | 5.6 | 4.3 | 15.6 | 13.0 | 6.0 | 20.3 | 8.2 |
| 18 | 17.5 | 15.5 | 20.1 | 7.7 | 16.1 | 23.9 | 8.7 | 11.7 | 29.3 | 6.0 | 8.5 | 18.4 |
| 19 | | | 20.8 | | | 14.8 | | | 4.3 | | | 14.3 |
| 20 and over | 4.2 | 15.6 | 27.3 | 3.7 | 19.0 | 48.6 | 3.3 | 11.7 | 37.0 | 9.6 | 15.2 | 46.9 |
| All ages | 100.0 | 100.0 | 100.0 | 100.0 | 100.0 | 100.0 | 100.0 | 100.0 | 100.0 | 100.0 | 100.0 | 100.0 |
| Number | 241 | 148 | 154 | 326 | 242 | 142 | 276 | 77 | 92 | 83 | 59 | 49 |

*Note:* A = No formal schooling and primary school; B = Some secondary school; C = Passed school certificate and some additional education.
*Source:* MES, 1975.

results are presented in Table 8-5. The subsample used for this analysis consisted of male principal household earners who were also employees (secondary earners as well as the self-employed were excluded). Two striking results emerge from the table: the proportion of variance explained is twice as high for the public employees as it is for the private sector workers, and it reaches an astonishingly high value of 67 percent for the former group. This underlines the importance of education and age variables in a public sector wage determination system that emphasizes formal schooling and seniority.

The frequency distribution of actual earnings is compared with that predicted by the simple human capital model in Figure 8-1. In the private sector the model predicts a much stronger mode than is actually observed, and seriously underestimates the proportion of employees earning more than M\$300 a month. The much better fit of the model for the public sector produces substantial agreement between predicted and actual percentages of employees. In the case of those earning M\$200–M\$299, who make up the modal earnings group for both public

Table 8-5. Earnings Functions for Principal Male Earners

| Variables | Coefficients for public employees | Coefficients for private employees |
|---|---|---|
| Primary | 0.18094 | 0.46488 |
|  | (0.11274) | (0.07466) |
| Some secondary | 0.61736 | 0.73803 |
|  | (0.11861) | (0.08331) |
| Passed school certificate | 1.06092 | 1.20577 |
|  | (0.11797) | (0.09459) |
| Higher school certificate | 1.29040 | 1.10177 |
|  | (0.14665) | (0.25834) |
| Technical diploma | 1.69851 | 1.38405 |
|  | (0.14242) | (0.21617) |
| University degree | 2.02645 | 1.80108 |
|  | (0.12814) | (0.15612) |
| Age | 0.05095 | 0.03470 |
|  | (0.01096) | (0.01227) |
| Age$^2$ | −0.00033 | −0.00022 |
|  | (0.00016) | (0.00017) |
| Constant | 3.781 | 4.02135 |
| $R^2$ | 0.67 | 0.31 |
| F | 137.3 | 40.5 |

Note: Standard errors are in parentheses.
Source: Data derived from MES, 1975.

Figure 8–1. Percentage Distribution of Public and
Private Employees by Monthly Earnings Group

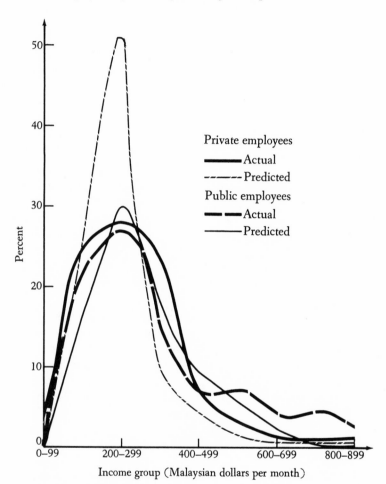

Source: MES, 1975.

and private sector employees, the model is a strikingly better predictor
for the former worker sample than for the latter. The model for the
private sector generally underestimates the proportion of high earners
much more seriously than does the one for the public sector. It follows
that factors other than formal education and age contribute to the
ability of employees in the private sector to attain high earnings.

Table 8-6. Differences in the Values of Coefficients of Successive
Educational Categories in the Human Capital Model

| Educational level | Public | Private |
|---|---|---|
| No schooling | Base | Base |
| Primary | 0.18 | 0.47 |
| Some secondary | 0.44 | 0.27 |
| Passed school certificate | 0.44 | 0.47 |
| Higher school certificate | 0.23 | −0.11 |
| Technical diploma | 0.41 | 0.28 |
| University degree | 0.33 | 0.42 |

Source: Table 8-5.

The incremental effects of successive levels of education in the two
sectors can be judged by looking at differences in the values of the
regression coefficients of the education dummies.[9] Table 8-6 shows that
the incremental coefficients are generally higher for the public than for
the private sector, with the exception of primary education. Primary
education seems to have a stronger positive influence on earnings in the
private sector than in the public sector, but the returns to higher levels
of education are, by and large, more substantial in the latter.

Finally, to reiterate a point already mentioned in connection with the
model used by Anand, education plays a relatively large part in the
explanation of earnings. For public sector employees, the education
dummies alone explained 57 percent of the variance; the addition of the
age and age$^2$ variables added another 10 percent to the $R^2$. For the
private sector, the corresponding percentages were 24 and 8. The contrast with the results of the earnings function analysis in both Britain
and the United States is quite striking: as noted, education by itself
explains no more than 5 to 6 percent of the variance in those countries.

## The Influence of Background Variables

In some studies an individual's earnings have been shown to be
affected by his or her father's occupation or education. A recent British
study of hourly earnings of full-time males, for instance, found that the
earnings of a worker were 10 percent higher if the earner's father were

9. The actual values of the coefficients are to be found in Table 8–5.

a professional or other white-collar worker than if the father were unskilled (holding other factors constant).[10] Admittedly, the effect of this particular influence on earnings was small compared with that of the educational attainment of the respondent, for example. In less developed countries observers have often been impressed by the importance of familial ties and social connections in determining a person's status in the job market, and therefore his earnings. In the Malaysian case, however, the inclusion of the father's occupation or education as an explanatory variable in the earnings function did not prove to be significant in any of the many experiments that were tried. This negative finding should not come as a surprise. In a study of the returns to education in Mexico, Martin Carnoy concluded:

> The rates to finishing primary school and other levels, except for completion of university, are somewhat lowered by holding the distribution of father's occupations constant at the mean of the total sample. Since this distribution varies greatly among schooling categories, the small effect of holding it constant implies that the change in the composition of skills of fathers of students completing any level of schooling will only slightly affect the rate of return to the investment in that level.[11]

Carnoy was quick to point out that this does not mean that parental background was wholly irrelevant to the determination of earnings. The point is that parental status influenced earnings indirectly through its effect on the number of years of schooling; in fact, the mean years of schooling went up consistently with higher parental status. There is evidence that this same tendency exists in Malaysia, but it is important to emphasize that the father's occupation or education is no substitute for the earner's schooling. Moreover, as Table 8-7 shows, education levels can vary widely for a given category of paternal occupation.

## The Rate of Return to Education

The returns to successive levels of education discussed in previous sections do not take into account the private costs of education. These

10. Royal Commission on the Distribution of Income and Wealth, Background Paper no. 5 (London, 1978), p. 42.
11. Carnoy, "Earnings and Schooling in Mexico," p. 336.

Table 8-7. Percentage Distribution of Educational Levels of Respondents by Father's Occupation

| Father's occupation | Educational level of respondent | | | | | | | Total | Column percentage |
|---|---|---|---|---|---|---|---|---|---|
| | No formal schooling | Primary | Secondary | Passed school certificate | Higher school certificate | Technical diploma | University degree | | |
| Professional, managerial, and administrative | 2.8 | 29.0 | 23.3 | 25.6 | 4.0 | 4.0 | 11.4 | 100.0 | 9.8 |
| Clerical | 3.6 | 27.7 | 25.9 | 28.3 | 3.6 | 2.4 | 7.8 | 100.0 | 9.2 |
| Skilled blue collar | 6.7 | 52.6 | 26.6 | 10.2 | 1.0 | 1.2 | 1.6 | 100.0 | 27.1 |
| Unskilled blue collar | 8.7 | 63.9 | 17.5 | 7.8 | 0.3 | 1.2 | 0.6 | 100.0 | 18.4 |
| Farmer | 10.6 | 55.0 | 16.4 | 10.8 | 1.9 | 0.8 | 4.5 | 100.0 | 20.9 |
| Trade proprietors | 3.8 | 41.6 | 25.4 | 18.4 | 2.7 | 2.7 | 5.4 | 100.0 | 10.2 |
| Unspecified | 15.2 | 49.4 | 20.3 | 11.4 | 1.3 | 1.3 | 1.3 | 100.0 | 4.4 |
| Total | 7.3 | 49.3 | 22.0 | 14.0 | 1.8 | 1.7 | 3.9 | 100.0 | 100.0 |

Source: MES, 1975.

private costs have two major components: (1) the out-of-pocket educational costs, which include expenditure on books, uniforms, transport, and additional food costs (for example, lunches in addition to school fees); and (2) the earnings forgone by the student while he or she is at school.

A World Bank research project has tried to quantify the value of out-of-pocket costs for different levels of education.[12] The method was that of a sample survey of households which obtained information on the costs and benefits of various types of services, including education. In addition, the Malaysian Ministry of Education collected information on these costs in 1973. The following are the figures of out-of-pocket costs per student in Malaysian dollars a year for different levels of education obtained from the ministry:

|  | | | | *Secondary form* | | | | |
|---|---|---|---|---|---|---|---|---|
| | *Remove* | | | | | | *Lower* | *Upper* |
| *Primary* | *form* | *I* | *II* | *III* | *IV* | *V* | *VI* | *VI* |
| 114 | 253 | 260 | 259 | 283 | 341 | 424 | 509 | 619 |

Private costs increase quite sharply through the various grades of secondary level education. Meerman found that his figures for private costs obtained from the household survey agreed remarkably closely with the Ministry of Education figures.[13] His study also contained data on out-of-pocket costs by household income levels. His finding on this point is best expressed in his own words:

Households in the lowest income quintile have a mean yearly household income of M$1,152. . . . the mean out-of-pocket cost for a secondary student in the lowest income quintile was M$208 a year. This by itself implies an educational burden of 13 percent of income. Even if all payments to school were eliminated, the burden would still be 11 percent. Clearly, those in the "poorest forty" [percent] of the income distribution can ill afford the out-of-pocket costs of maintaining even two students in school, particularly if one is at the secondary level. This factor is doubtless a principal reason for the rapid decrease in enrollment rates irrespective of level, as incomes fall.[14]

12. Jacob P. Meerman, *Public Expenditure in Malaysia: Who Benefits and Why* (New York: Oxford University Press, 1979).

13. Ibid., pp. 113–14 and table C–4.

14. Ibid., p. 115.

Supporting children in secondary school can impose a significant financial burden on families; nevertheless, some simple calculations show that the quantitative importance of this factor is small in relation to the private return to education over the lifetime of a school leaver. The earnings functions discussed in this chapter suggest that obtaining a lower secondary certificate of education (LCE) would increase a school leaver's earnings by 27 percent above those of another who has only completed primary schooling. The former's additional out-of-pocket costs would probably amount to about eight or nine months of average earnings (assuming a primary school graduate earns about M$100 a month). Inasmuch as the increased level of earnings is likely to persist for the greater part of twenty years, the private out-of-pocket expenses seems to be of minor significance. Even for those who do not obtain their LCE but merely stay in school, the additional years raise their earnings by about 8 percent above the level of those with completed primary only, and thus the increased out-of-pocket costs can be paid off relatively quickly. These calculations, moreover, do not take into account the more favorable age-earnings profiles associated with increases in educational levels.

The speed with which the costs of schooling can be recovered from earnings, even by those with relatively low educational attainments, suggests that a student's forgone earnings during the period of his or her additional schooling might represent a much more sizable item than out-of-pocket costs on the cost side of the private rate of return calculation. In his study of the rate of return to schooling in Latin America, Martin Carnoy observed:

> One of the most important findings of the study is that earnings forgone by students while attending school, as calculated from the earnings of young people of equal age and education not attending school, exceed annual per student *institutional* costs as early as the fourth year of primary school, and represent about 60 percent of total expenditures on schooling from the fifth or sixth grade of primary school through university.[15]

This estimate of the importance of forgone earnings assumes even greater weight when it is remembered that Carnoy included public expenditures as well as private out-of-pocket educational costs in institu-

15. Martin Carnoy, "Rates of Return to Schooling in Latin America," *Journal of Human Resources*, vol. 2, no. 3 (1966), p. 362.

tional costs. In the Malaysian case, Meerman estimated that at the primary level out-of-pocket costs accounted for about half the public cost of a student, while at the secondary level out-of-pocket costs very nearly equalled the public current costs.[16] In estimating the net private return to education, the cost of forgone earnings—where it exists—must account for the lion's share of the private costs of education.

In any realistic calculation, however, it is important to be sure that the student who elects to stay on in school is in fact likely to forgo employment before including forgone employment as a cost of education. Carnoy in his Latin American work did not allow for unemployment or low participation rates among school leavers in the early years of education. His conclusion about the importance of forgone earnings is, therefore, an overestimate in practical terms. In the Malaysian case the element of forgone earnings in the costs of education would be grossly overestimated if the earnings of those of school age who do work were counted as forgone by all those of the same age who were still in school. This is because a very long waiting period before starting work is typical for Malaysian school leavers. A detailed analysis of the school leaver's waiting period before finding employment, based on material obtained from the World Bank's 1973 School Leavers Survey (SLS), is presented in Chapter 14. The hypothesis is developed there that probably a socially imposed "minimum age" of employment is consciously or unconsciously accepted by employers, and that this minimum age is considerably higher than the normal school-leaving age for much of the population of urban Malaysia. School leavers with an LCE, who would normally leave school at the age of fourteen or fifteen, tend to wait for about two or three years before becoming absorbed into the labor force. The SLS, which specifically asked respondents about the nature of their unemployment, identified a long period of active unemployment for a large number of school leavers. In a household survey—in which respondents are not asked about their unemployment in detail—the difficulty of breaking into the labor market before a certain age would be expressed in terms of data showing a good deal of passive unemployment, taking the form of a low participation rate for the relevant age group (including reports of abnormally late school-leaving ages). Evidence on this point is presented below in Chapters 14 and 17. For the moment, it is simply worth noting that, in the MES, respondents reported not only late school-leaving ages, but also even later mean ages for starting work (see Table 8-8).

16. Meerman, *Public Expenditure in Malaysia*, p. 115.

Table 8-8. Mean Number of Years Elapsed between Leaving School and Starting Work: Male Employees at Three Levels of Education

| Age left school | Kuala Lumpur Malay A | B | C | Kuala Lumpur Chinese A | B | C | East Coast towns Malay A | B | C | East Coast towns Chinese A | B | C |
|---|---|---|---|---|---|---|---|---|---|---|---|---|
| Less than 12 | 4.6 | | | 4.6 | | | 6.8 | | | 4.0* | | |
| 12 | 6.2 | 5.1 | | 3.2 | 1.8 | | 4.1 | 5.3 | | 3.8 | * | |
| 13 | 6.2 | 6.3 | 5.3 | 2.4 | 3.0 | 2.0 | 3.1 | 3.0* | 2.3 | 1.5 | * | 1.2* |
| 14 | 5.0 | 1.5 | | 2.1 | 3.4 | | 3.8 | 6.7* | | 1.1 | * | |
| 15 | 4.3 | 3.6 | | 2.0 | 3.2 | | 3.0 | 2.5 | | 0.6 | 0.5 | |
| 16 | 3.6 | 4.4 | | 1.3 | 1.3 | | 2.5 | 1.6 | | 1.1* | 1.4 | |
| 17 | 2.7 | 2.5 | 2.2 | 1.9 | 1.4 | 0.8 | 0.7 | 1.8 | 0.5 | 1.4* | 3.3 | 0.5* |
| 18 | 2.2 | 1.4 | 1.4 | 1.5 | 1.2 | 1.4 | 1.0 | 2.4 | 1.1 | 0.2* | 0.6 | 0.4* |
| 19 | | | 1.3 | | | 0.7 | | | 1.0* | 0.2* | | 0.9* |
| 20 and over | 1.2 | 1.8 | 1.0 | 0.8 | 1.1 | 0.6 | 1.1 | 0.9 | 0.4 | 0.2* | 0.4 | 0.0 |
| All ages | 4.6 | 3.1 | 2.1 | 2.4 | 1.9 | 0.9 | 3.2 | 2.4 | 1.0 | 1.6 | 1.2 | 0.3 |

* Base has too few cases.

Note: A = No formal schooling and primary school; B = Some secondary school; C = Passed school certificate and some additional education.

Source: MES, 1975.

The conclusion to be drawn from this body of information is that school leavers in the 13–17 age group would be very unlikely to be able to obtain a steady income from employment, given the structure of the labor market in the urban economy of Malaysia. Thus, it is not unreasonable to exclude forgone earnings from the calculation of the costs and benefits of additional education.

## Age-Earnings Profiles

Thus far, this chapter has examined the rates of return to various levels of education without reference to the ways in which they vary over time with the age of the earner. In effect, the different rates of return to various levels of education have been calculated on the assumption that the age of the sample is held constant. For some purposes, however, it is useful to know how the different returns vary at different points of earners' working lives. There is, of course, no guarantee that the age-earnings profiles for different educational levels derived from cross-section data will remain unchanged for the present generation. In the absence of better information, however, the different shapes of the expected age-earnings profiles will have some effect on people's perception of the private rate of return to education. It is well known that in advanced countries the experience profiles for different groups are roughly parallel (with earnings measured in logs); in other words, the percentage differences in earnings for different levels of schooling remain roughly constant over the entire period of a working life.[17] The profiles derived for Malaysia from the earnings function of the MES are graphed in Figure 8-2.

An inspection of the profiles shows that they do not form a system of parallel curves. The profiles for those with no formal schooling and for those with primary education are more near parallel to each other than to the other profiles, but even in this case there is a perceptible narrowing of the earnings gap with increasing age. For other levels of education, the relation of the earnings difference to age is in the opposite direction. For the successive grades the profiles diverge with age, at least up to the points of peak earnings on the profiles.

---

17. See Layard and Psacharapoulos, "Analysis of the 1972 General Household Survey Data."

Figure 8–2. Mean Earnings of Males by Age and Educational Level

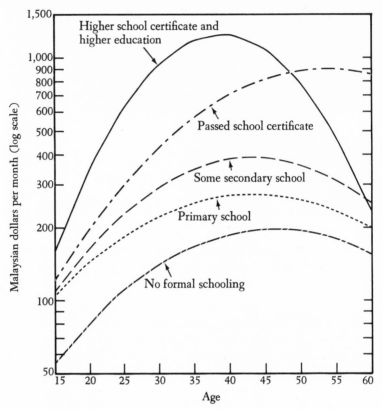

Source: MES, 1975.

This pattern of age-earnings profiles poses a problem of interpretation. If it is believed that the earnings of the young with different educational levels will have the same patterns in the future as those of the older wage groups today, it might be concluded that the labor market in Malaysia functions in such a way that the relation between education and earnings becomes much more strongly established at later ages. But the cross-section picture need not reflect lifetime profiles. In particular, returns to education (at least for the postprimary levels) may have fallen for recent years.

Appendix: The Education System of Peninsular Malaysia

The federal government of Malaysia has primary responsibility for the education system in the Peninsula. Most schools are "assisted," that is, they are financed by the government either entirely or in part, with additional support from nonprofit organizations. Private schools, although of some importance for the Chinese at the middle level, do not account for many students. A survey undertaken by Meerman in connection with a World Bank research project found that 97, 94, and 81 percent of all primary, secondary, and postsecondary students, respectively, were enrolled in assisted schools.[18]

The basic system of education in Peninsular Malaysia is represented schematically in Figure 8-3. Six years of primary education are followed by three of lower secondary. Promotion is automatic through the third form of the secondary, but there are major examination hurdles afterward. One important component of the Malaysian government's education policy is the process of phasing out the use of the English language. In 1974 the timetable for this process was as follows: primary schools, 1970–75; secondary schools, 1976–80; higher schools (sixth form), 1981–82. Vocational and technical schools were started with the idea of providing an alternative to the academic curriculum of the traditional upper secondary schools. But they have not accounted for a large proportion of the students enrolled in this grade.

Enrollment is voluntary throughout the various stages of the school system, but attendance at primary school had reached more than 90 percent of the population of the relevant age group some time ago. Figure 8-4 graphs the enrolled as a percentage of the population of different ages for two dates, 1965 and 1972. It shows that primary education has probably reached its saturation point. It also illustrates that, in spite of serious government efforts, there was no dramatic increase in enrollment ratios during the period. The ratio of enrollment to the total of the relevant age group increased by a few percentage points at the lower secondary level and rose much more sharply at the upper secondary stage—by 50 percent to be precise—but even in 1972 the overall enrollment ratio at this level was very low. The school age popula-

18. Meerman, *Public Expenditure in Malaysia*, chap. 4, p. 100.

Figure 8–3. Structure of the Formal System of Education in Peninsular Malaysia, 1974

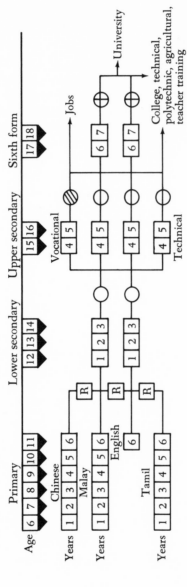

○ Lower certificate of education

⊕ Malaysian certificate of education or school certificate (SPM, MCE, or SC)

⊕ Higher school certificate (STP or HSC)

◍ Malaysian vocational certificate (SVM or MVC) or city, guild, and state trade examinations

R = Remove class

*Note:* For postprimary education, an extra year must be added for those proceeding through the remove class. Private schools exist, but they are not shown in the chart. The numbers in the boxes in the first row of the chart give the approximate age of a typical student in each grade. The numbers in the other boxes refer to years of schooling.

*Source:* Ministry of Education.

Figure 8–4. Enrollments in Assisted Schools, 1965 and 1972

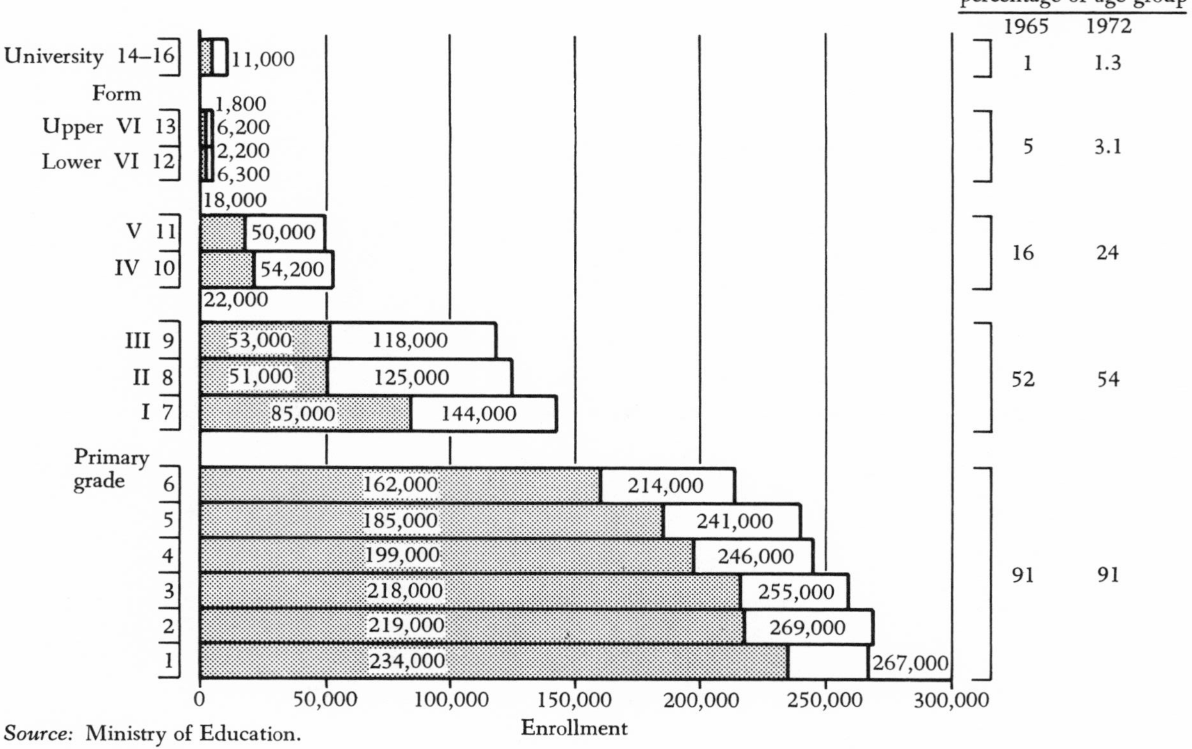

| | Enrollment as a percentage of age group | |
|---|---|---|
| | 1965 | 1972 |
| University 14–16 | 1 | 1.3 |
| Form Upper VI 13 | 5 | 3.1 |
| Lower VI 12 | | |
| V 11 | 16 | 24 |
| IV 10 | | |
| III 9 | 52 | 54 |
| II 8 | | |
| I 7 | | |
| Primary grade 6 | 91 | 91 |
| 5 | | |
| 4 | | |
| 3 | | |
| 2 | | |
| 1 | | |

University 14–16: 11,000

Form
Upper VI 13: 1,800 / 6,200
Lower VI 12: 2,200 / 6,300

V 11: 18,000 / 50,000
IV 10: 54,200

III 9: 22,000 / 53,000 / 118,000
II 8: 51,000 / 125,000
I 7: 85,000 / 144,000

Primary grade 6: 162,000 / 214,000
5: 185,000 / 241,000
4: 199,000 / 246,000
3: 218,000 / 255,000
2: 219,000 / 269,000
1: 234,000 / 267,000

Enrollment

Source: Ministry of Education.

147

Figure 8–5. Retention Rates and Dropout Rates in the Education System

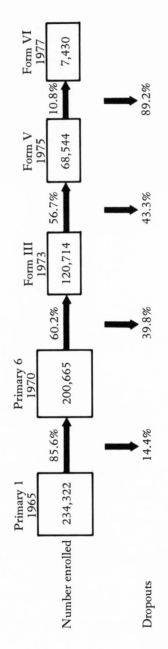

Source: Ministry of Education.

Table 8-9. Enrollment in Assisted Academic Schools
(thousands)

| Year | Primary | Lower secondary | Upper secondary |
|------|---------|-----------------|-----------------|
| 1965 | 1,217   | 189             | 63              |
| 1972 | 1,493   | 386             | 104             |
| 1974 | 1,547   | 457             | 132             |
| 1980 | 1,779   | 593             | 241             |
| 1985 | 2,132   | 711             | 291             |

Note: The figures are the totals for all forms in the particular class of schooling. Totals for 1965–74 are actual; for 1980 and 1985 they are projected.
Source: Ministry of Education.

tion was growing quite rapidly during the period, and therefore data for changes in enrollment ratios may provide a less useful impression of the explanation of the education system than the absolute numbers of those enrolled (see Table 8-9). The rate of growth of the numbers enrolled in secondary grades has been quite remarkable—more than doubling in the seven years between 1965 and 1972. The Malaysian government projected that the growth rate would slow somewhat but remain high at around 5 percent a year through the early 1980s.

The Ministry of Education provides annual statistics of enrollment for each form in assisted schools, which can be used to build up a picture of the pattern of survival and dropping-out through the various stages of schooling. Figure 8-5 gives the overall picture.

CHAPTER 9

# Segmentation of the Labor Market and Differences in Earnings: Evidence from Three Towns

THIS CHAPTER DISCUSSES THE IMPORTANCE of a group of factors, which can be subsumed under the general term "labor market segmentation," for the determination of earnings in Peninsular Malaysia. The analysis uses the material collected by the 1975 World Bank Migration and Employment Survey (MES) in Kuala Lumpur and the two East Coast towns of Kuantan and Kota Bharu and is confined to the earnings of male employees only.

The human capital framework has been used widely—and up to a point successfully—to explain earnings as a function of education and experience. But occupational location can also play an important part in the distribution of personal earnings in the urban economy; as noted in Chapter 6, the introduction to Part II, workers of the same quality may earn different amounts depending on their location in the market (defined as the type of enterprise in which they work). One rather stringent definition of labor market segmentation is that a difference in earnings can be attributed to institutional factors over and above what is accounted for by labor quality variables such as education and experience. This definition is a stringent one because differences in the quality of labor are only partially captured by measurable variables. Moreover, the magnitude of the rate of return to education and to experience may itself reflect some institutional influences rather than being fully accounted for by productivity differences.[1] The first objective of this chapter is to assess the evidence for the existence of labor

---

1. This proposition assumes either a large nonprofit maximizing sector of employers such as the government, or high costs of gathering information about employees, which induce employers to value credentials as such. Unionism may also contribute.

market segmentation in urban Malaysia in this narrow sense, and to form some judgment about its quantitative importance compared with the influence of the standard human capital factors.

Even if education and experience turn out to be the major determinants of earnings, the returns to these factors may be different in different segments of the labor market. This is a second interpretation of labor market segmentation. A specific location in the labor market does not so much shift the earnings function for a typical worker as alter its slope with respect to the human capital variables used in the function. This possibility is here examined separately for three skill categories and also for workers in three different categories of size of enterprise. The use of unskilled, skilled blue-collar, and white-collar groups to represent different grades of labor is an obvious choice. Enterprise size was chosen as an alternative way of dividing the labor market because it turned out to be the institutional variable which helped significantly to explain levels of earnings after allowing for the human capital attributes of the employees.

Several hypotheses can be suggested about the relative returns to education and experience on different rungs of the labor market ladder. It might be useful to set out a few of these hypotheses at the outset to clarify results discussed later in the chapter.

*Hypothesis 1.* On-the-job training or assessment may be used as an alternative to formal educational qualification in evaluating the productivity of a worker. Thus, if returns to education in a given segment of the market were high, the returns to experience would be low, and vice versa.

*Hypothesis 2.* At the higher levels of the labor market, returns to education may be greater either because of the effect of "credentialism" or because employers are able to use educated labor more productively.

*Hypothesis 3.* Opportunities for skill formation during the worker's career may be small at the lower end of the labor market. Thus, the experience-earnings profile in these sectors would be relatively flat.

It should be noted that the hypotheses are not complementary. For example, if both hypotheses 2 and 3 are true, hypothesis 1 will be contradicted.

## The Sample

It is appropriate to begin the discussion with a descriptive summary of the most important segments of the labor markets in the two regions

—Kuala Lumpur and the East Coast towns. Three sets of characteristics provide a basis for segmentation: (1) the type of employer—which in the Malaysian context can be classified as government (including public corporations), Malay private, Chinese private, and foreign; (2) the nature of the employee's job—in particular the broad skills classification of his occupation, here divided into unskilled, semiskilled and skilled manual, and white collar; and (3) the type of enterprise in which the employee works. The sample survey distinguished four basic types: small (employing 10–99 workers), large (employing 100 or more workers), and own or family businesses (which covers the self-employed).

The MES was based on a household sample and relied on the workers themselves for information about the enterprises in which they worked. It was not possible to mount a follow-up survey of the enterprises. Thus, several major factors about the character of any enterprise (for example, the type or value of capital employed) could not be covered. Efforts were made, however, to collect information which workers could reasonably be expected to know and which would have a bearing on the determination of wage levels in the enterprises.

One important aspect about which respondents were asked was the size of the enterprise. As discussed in the introduction to Part II, any wage difference between the formal and informal sectors of the urban labor market can be ascribed to one of two influences: overt institutional factors, such as unions or public sector employment, or management's recognition of the strong relation between wage levels and efficiency (in other words, higher wages produce more than proportionate increases in worker efficiency). If the latter is the case, it becomes necessary to explain why the relation between wages and efficiency is stronger in some enterprises than in others. The answer might involve differences between enterprises in technology or in the structure of the work force. These differences can in turn be equated with differences in the size of enterprises. It is plausible to maintain that the larger the number of workers employed, the more formally structured the work force will tend to be; to a lesser but still realistic extent, the size of the enterprise is also likely to be positively correlated with the greater use of modern technology.

Apart from being asked the number of employees, respondents in the MES were questioned about several variables that might be associated with formal work arrangements or modern technology. These included the proportion of white-collar workers in the enterprise, the presence of staff with university qualifications, the existence of written or orally agreed terms of employment, the use of fixed or variable hours of work, and the period of advance notice of departure required. These variables will be tested, together with number of employees, as possible explanatory factors of levels of earnings.

The major characteristics of the employees in the sample, by type of employer and of enterprise, are described below. The description will illustrate some of the more interesting interrelations between the different characteristics.

## Type of Employer

This subsection analyzes the sample's employment by employer type— Malay and Chinese private sector employers, foreign employers, and government and public sector employers. A large proportion of the employees in the sample works in the government or public sector—29 percent in Kuala Lumpur and 27 percent in the East Coast. The foreign sector is also important in Kuala Lumpur (13 percent) but not in the East Coast towns. One major difference between the two regions is that private sector enterprises owned by Malays are quite prominent in the East Coast towns (30 percent) but make up a very small part of the labor market scene in Kuala Lumpur.

Large enterprises are disproportionately represented in the public sector. Table 9-1 shows that 41.9 percent of the sample who were in the public sector in the East Coast towns were working in enterprises with 100 or more employees; the proportion was even larger in Kuala Lumpur where 61.3 percent worked in large enterprises.

Unionization is also relatively important in the public sector. As Table 9-2 shows, unionization is generally of minor importance in the Malaysian economy. The Chinese private sector, at one extreme, is barely unionized at all; Malay-owned private sector enterprises, especially in the East Coast towns, were also not significantly unionized. There is some unionization in the Malay private sector in Kuala Lumpur, but the proportion of employment in this sector in Kuala Lumpur is itself quite small. By contrast, roughly half the sample who said they worked in the public sector in both regions were employed by enterprises in which 75 percent or more of the employees belonged to a union.

What are these public sector enterprises with more than 100 workers and a substantially unionized labor force? Are they large offices employing predominantly white-collar workers? Table 9-3 gives the percentages of the sample working in enterprises with varying proportions of white-collar workers. The government sector clearly has a larger proportion than the others of enterprises made up of white-collar employees —more so in the East Coast than in Kuala Lumpur. Public sector enterprises are by no means exclusively white-collar, however. Even if white-collar enterprises are defined as having three-quarters of their employees from the white-collar occupational group, the proportion of the sample working in such enterprises represents just over one-quarter of the public sector total in Kuala Lumpur, and about 40 percent of the total in the East Coast.

## Type of Enterprise

This subsection analyzes the sample of the type of enterprise in which respondents worked—small, medium, large, and family businesses. Since enterprises employing mainly white-collar workers are strongly represented in the public sector (which also contains a significant proportion of large enterprises), is it also the case that large enterprises as a whole are heavy employers of white-collar workers? Data dealing with this question (see Table 9-4) clearly show that the answer is negative. Among the small and family-owned enterprises in both areas substantial

Table 9-1. Percentage of Total Workers for Each Employer Type by Size of Enterprise

| Employer type | Less than 10 employees | 10–99 employees | More than 100 employees | Own or family business |
|---|---|---|---|---|
| *Kuala Lumpur* | | | | |
| Malay private | 16.7 | 30.8 | 41.0 | 11.5 |
| Chinese private | 34.4 | 34.4 | 16.2 | 14.9 |
| Foreign | 14.3 | 38.3 | 42.2 | 5.2 |
| Government and public sector | 10.6 | 25.2 | 61.3 | 3.0 |
| Total | 22.7 | 32.4 | 34.7 | 10.1 |
| *East Coast towns* | | | | |
| Malay private | 25.1 | 21.4 | 10.3 | 43.2 |
| Chinese private | 38.7 | 20.6 | 9.8 | 31.0 |
| Foreign | 40.0 | 30.0 | 20.0 | 10.0 |
| Government and public sector | 17.1 | 27.9 | 41.9 | 13.1 |
| Total | 28.7 | 23.0 | 19.2 | 29.2 |

Source: MES, 1975.

Table 9-2. Percentage of Total Workers for Each Employer Type
by Degree of Unionization

| Employer type | Less than three-fourths unionized | Between three-fourths and all unionized | All unionized | No unions | Percentage in sample[a] |
|---|---|---|---|---|---|
| *Kuala Lumpur* | | | | | |
| Malay private | 5.1 | 10.3 | 20.5 | 62.8 | 6.9 |
| Chinese private | 5.5 | 5.1 | 3.7 | 84.3 | 45.2 |
| Foreign | 7.7 | 40.9 | 15.6 | 33.8 | 13.6 |
| Government and public sector | 21.9 | 27.8 | 24.5 | 25.8 | 29.1 |
| Total | 10.3 | 17.7 | 12.6 | 57.9 | 100.0 |
| *East Coast towns* | | | | | |
| Malay private | 2.8 | 2.9 | 5.3 | 88.9 | 30.1 |
| Chinese private | 3.8 | 0.3 | 1.4 | 94.1 | 35.6 |
| Government and public sector | 14.9 | 26.6 | 23.0 | 34.7 | 27.5 |
| Total | 6.8 | 9.3 | 9.4 | 74.1 | 100.0 |

*Note:* The percentage of foreign employers in the East Coast is so small (2.5 percent) that they have been omitted from this table.
a. The sample for Kuala Lumpur numbered 1,131 and for the East Coast, 806.
*Source:* MES, 1975.

proportions employ no white-collar workers at all, but the large units do not have a particularly white-collar character. The proportion of the sample working in large enterprises, which employ almost entirely white-collar workers (or even those which have more than half their work force in the white-collar category), is only a little higher than the comparable proportion for the sample as a whole. Enterprises with 25 to 50 percent white-collar employment are, however, more common in the large enterprise subgroup than in the sample as a whole.

Table 9-5 looks at all three occupational groupings[2] of the sample by the size of the enterprise in which members of each grouping work. As might be expected, the proportion of white-collar workers employed in the large firms is larger than the average for the sample, but the differences are not very striking. The relative unimportance of white-collar workers in small enterprises is again confirmed in this table. The fact

2. The occupational grouping is the same as that used in Chapter 7.

that there is not a very strong correlation between enterprise size and the occupational category of workers is of some importance for the subsequent analysis in this chapter. It makes it possible to study the different categories of enterprises separately but still to obtain a reasonable spread of education and occupational groupings for the purposes of the regression analysis of earnings.

Other institutional variables included in the sample survey might be expected to be well correlated with enterprise size. A few examples will indicate the general results of the labor market studies. Unionization (taken to mean that three-quarters or more workers belong to unions in the enterprises covered) accounts for about 30 percent of the total sample in Kuala Lumpur and 18 percent in the East Coast; in the large enterprises the corresponding percentages are 45 and 33, respectively. Written contracts of employment do not seem to be the rule in the Malaysian economy. In Kuala Lumpur 40 percent of the sample said they had such contracts, but in the East Coast towns the proportion was only half as high. Even in the large firms, only 60 percent of

Table 9-3. Percentage of Total Workers for Each Employer Type by Level of White-Collar Employment in the Enterprise

| Employer type | Almost all | 51–90 percent | 26–50 percent | 25 percent and under | None | Not known |
|---|---|---|---|---|---|---|
| Kuala Lumpur | | | | | | |
| Malay private | 8.6 | 4.3 | 7.2 | 32.9 | 32.9 | 14.3 |
| Chinese private | 7.4 | 3.4 | 6.7 | 31.4 | 41.6 | 9.6 |
| Foreign | 5.8 | 11.6 | 20.1 | 29.9 | 17.5 | 14.9 |
| Government and public sector | 16.2 | 21.0 | 13.3 | 23.3 | 12.4 | 13.8 |
| Total | 10.2 | 10.2 | 11.0 | 28.5 | 27.3 | 12.8 |
| East Coast towns | | | | | | |
| Malay private | 14.6 | 1.3 | 1.9 | 26.5 | 46.2 | 9.5 |
| Chinese private | 3.8 | 3.3 | 5.7 | 45.5 | 30.3 | 12.5 |
| Government and public sector | 33.8 | 13.2 | 9.0 | 21.2 | 1.4 | 21.6 |
| Total | 17.4 | 5.9 | 6.4 | 31.9 | 23.7 | 14.8 |

Note: The percentage of foreign employers in the East Coast is so small that they have been omitted from this table.
Source: MES, 1975.

Table 9-4. Percentage of Total Workers in Each Enterprise Type by Level of White-Collar Employment in the Enterprise

| Type of enterprise | Almost all | 51–90 percent | 26–50 percent | 25 percent and under | None | Not known |
|---|---|---|---|---|---|---|
| Kuala Lumpur | | | | | | |
| 1–9 employees | 4.9 | 7.4 | 7.3 | 30.8 | 25.1 | 14.6 |
| 10–99 employees | 13.4 | 10.0 | 8.4 | 32.6 | 27.3 | 8.4 |
| 100 and more employees | 10.8 | 13.5 | 15.8 | 26.3 | 16.4 | 17.2 |
| Own or family business | 8.0 | 4.5 | 9.1 | 17.0 | 55.7 | 5.7 |
| Total | 10.2 | 10.2 | 11.0 | 28.5 | 27.3 | 12.8 |
| East Coast towns | | | | | | |
| 1–9 employees | 14.4 | 3.5 | 8.0 | 31.4 | 32.3 | 10.4 |
| 10–99 employees | 24.0 | 11.1 | 2.9 | 32.8 | 15.8 | 13.5 |
| 100 and more employees | 16.3 | 6.8 | 9.5 | 34.7 | 10.2 | 22.4 |
| Own or family business | 15.2 | 2.8 | 5.6 | 29.2 | 32.6 | 14.6 |
| Total | 17.4 | 5.9 | 6.4 | 31.9 | 23.7 | 14.8 |

Source: MES, 1975.

respondents in Kuala Lumpur and 40 percent in the East Coast towns had written contracts. In contrast, rather more than half the workers in both regions said they worked fixed rather than variable hours even in the small firms and family businesses. In the medium and large firms the proportion with fixed hours was 70 percent or more. A majority of the workers in all the enterprise groups, except the largest firms, said that they were required to give either no notice or less than a month's notice of departure. About half the enterprises employing respondents in Kuala Lumpur had some staff with university qualifications; in the East Coast towns the comparable proportion was one-third. Although the proportion of enterprises having staff with university qualifications rose with enterprise size, even among family businesses and small firms in the East Coast such enterprises constituted 20 to 25 percent of the total. This finding may be linked with the above-average levels of white-collar employment in family businesses in both regions (shown in Table 9-5).

Table 9-5. Occupational Distribution of Male Employees
by Size of Enterprise

| Occupational category | Less than 10 employees | 10–99 employees | More than 100 employees | Own or family business | Total |
|---|---|---|---|---|---|
| Kuala Lumpur | | | | | |
| Unskilled | 3.7 | −2.0 | −1.4 | 2.7 | 22.6 |
| Skilled blue collar | 14.0 | 8.2 | −5.2 | −9.7 | 38.6 |
| White collar | −17.8 | −6.3 | 6.5 | 6.9 | 38.9 |
| Total | 13.0 | 27.2 | 39.4 | 19.9 | 100.0 |
| Number | 232 | 485 | 703 | 356 | 1,786 |
| East Coast towns | | | | | |
| Unskilled | 0.6 | −1.9 | −11.1 | 7.0 | 28.0 |
| Skilled blue collar | 19.0 | 4.4 | 7.8 | −17.0 | 35.2 |
| White collar | −19.6 | −2.4 | 3.3 | 10.0 | 36.8 |
| Total | 18.4 | 28.5 | 18.1 | 35.6 | 100.0 |
| Number | 203 | 326 | 207 | 406 | 1,142 |

Note: Figures in each cell (except for totals and number) represent differences in the percentages of each enterprise category from the corresponding total percentage given in the last column.
Source: MES, 1975.

## The Methodology

The purpose of the remainder of this chapter is to identify and, where possible, quantify the extent to which institutional factors of the kind discussed in the previous section cause differences in earnings between male employees in the two urban regions of the Malaysian economy covered by the MES. It is generally accepted that earnings are determined by the personal characteristics of workers, and particularly by the amount of human capital invested in them, measured principally by education and experience. Earnings may also, however, be influenced by institutional factors which create segmentation in the labor market; a worker's location in a particular segment of the market, as well as his personal attributes, could influence the level of his earnings.

One way of disentangling the effects of personal and institutional factors on earnings would be to start with an empirical model that tries to explain earnings solely on the basis of human capital variables. The next stage would be to add institutional variables to the estimated model to see which of them might have a significant effect on earnings and what additional variation in earnings they might explain. A model of this kind can be represented symbolically as:

(Model 1)

$$\ln Y = f\,(H)$$
$$\ln Y = g\,(H, S)$$

where ln $Y$ is the log of monthly earnings, $H$ is a vector of human capital factors, $S$ is a vector of institutional factors which are expected to contribute to a labor market segmentation, and $f$ and $g$ are functional forms in the successive regression equations.

The trouble with this model is that $H$ and $S$ will be very likely to be correlated if $S$ is in fact important in influencing earnings, because the quality of labor tends to adjust to the level of earnings. If, in fact, institutional factors succeed in raising the earnings of a particular type of labor to a level higher than its opportunity cost, then the natural reaction of employers would be to offer the high-wage job to workers who (from the employers' point of view) have superior personal attributes. Human capital variables such as education and experience are precisely the kind of attributes which, in the minds of employers, are proxies for the quality of labor. If this mechanism were operating in any significant way, Model 1 would not identify the influence of $S$ in any meaningful way.

The alternative is to start with an attempt at identification of the institutional factors causing differences in earnings, and then to add human capital variables to the model:

(Model 2)

$$\ln Y = f'\,(S)$$
$$\ln Y = g'\,(S, H).$$

Of course, if the quality of labor is adjusted to earnings in the way discussed in the last paragraph, collinearity problems would still occur in the second stage of Model 2, and human capital variables would most likely dominate. At least in the first stage, however, it might be possible to identify the type of institutional influences that tend to create differences in earnings in the first place. Moreover, as in Model 1, some institutional factors may continue to be significant, in addition to the human capital variables, in the second stage of the regression Model 2.

Needless to say, an approach like that of Model 2 is only possible in a study of the earnings of workers within a fairly narrow range of occupations. The logic of the model is that workers of different education (or experience) levels are substitutable for each other in the jobs in question. The type of worker who gets a particular job is determined by the wage level established for that job by institutional factors.

The sample was broken down for analytical purposes into three occupational groups: unskilled workers, other semiskilled and skilled blue-collar workers, and white-collar workers.[3] The institutional variables used in addition to the human capital ones were:

| | |
|---|---|
| NE 1, NE 2, and NE 3: | Enterprises with 1–9, 10–99, and 100 or more employees, respectively. |
| Union 1, Union 2, and Union 3: | Enterprises with 1–75 percent of employees unionized, with 75 percent or more unionized, and with no union, respectively. |
| WCOL 1, WCOL 2, and WCOL 3: | Enterprises with none, less than 25 percent, and more than 25 percent white-collar employees, respectively. |
| Government, Foreign, and Private: | Types of employer. |

In the first set of runs, in which the log of earnings was regressed on the above set of institutional variables only, the proportion of variance explained was quite small. The value of $R^2$ ranged from 5 percent for the unskilled and 7 percent for the blue-collar skilled to 10 percent for the white-collar group. The only set of variables which consistently turned out to be significant in all three regressions for the occupational groups separately was that for the size of enterprise. WCOL was significant for the unskilled and the white-collar occupations. The unionization variables generally turned out to be of little importance. The type of employer seemed to be significant only for the earnings of white-collar employees, which were higher in government and higher still in foreign firms than in privately owned enterprises. As might be expected from the group's higher $R^2$ value, the regression model for white-collar employees had the largest number of significant explanatory variables.

When human capital variables were added at the second stage of the regression exercise, all the institutional variables except for enterprise size turned out to be insignificant. This result lends support to the hypothesis that institutionally determined levels of earnings cause appropriate adjustments in the quality of labor employed (in human capital terms). But even after allowing for such adjustments, enterprise size

---

3. Definitions of the categories are as given in Chapter 7.

exercises a separate and independent influence on earnings. It is, in fact, the only institutional variable that identifies a group of sectors of the labor market in which labor with the same human capital attributes seems to earn varying amounts by sector. The next section presents a multiple classification analysis (MCA) of earnings which quantifies these differences. The relative importance of the variables of human capital and enterprise size for differences in earnings can be readily assessed from this analysis.

## Analysis by Occupational Groups

The results of the MCA are presented in Tables 9-6, 9-7, and 9-8 for the three occupational groups separately.[4] The unadjusted deviations are the gross differences of the log of earnings of the sample in each category from the overall grand mean given at the top of the tables. The adjusted deviations are the net differences after controlling for the influence of the other explanatory variables used in the analysis. The ($\beta$) values give an idea of the importance of the particular variable in the explanation of the log of earnings, if the other variables are held constant.

The tables do not show the degree of significance of the variables included in the analysis. Some idea of the role of the individual variables, and of the two-way interactions among them, is shown below:

| Occupational group | Variables significant at 99 percent probability | Significance of F for other variables | Interaction which was significant at up to 95 percent probability |
|---|---|---|---|
| Unskilled | All except region | Region (0.077) | Race and age |
| Skilled blue-collar | All except size | Size (0.002) | None |
| White-collar | Education and age only | Size (0.002)<br>Others not significant | None |

4. In all the earnings functions reported in this section and the next, the question has to be asked: Are the coefficients of the independent variables for each occupation (or sector) significantly different from those of the others? The appropriate analysis of variance test for this purpose is the so-called Chow test (see John Johnston, *Econometric Methods* [New York: McGraw-Hill, 1963], pp. 136–37). All the results discussed in the text passed the standard Chow test, and the differences in the coefficients of the separate equations were highly significant.

Table 9-6. Log of Earnings of Unskilled Male Employees:
Multiple Classification Analysis

| Variable and category | Number in sample | Unadjusted deviation | Eta value | Adjusted for independents' deviation | Beta value |
|---|---|---|---|---|---|
| *Region* | | | | | |
| Kuala Lumpur | 558 | 0.04 | | −0.00 | |
| Kuantan | 154 | −0.02 | | 0.10 | |
| Kota Bharu | 137 | −0.15 | | −0.10 | |
| | | | 0.08 | | 0.07 |
| *Race* | | | | | |
| Malay | 430 | −0.19 | | −0.15 | |
| Chinese | 344 | 0.22 | | 0.21 | |
| Indians and others | 75 | 0.05 | | −0.11 | |
| | | | 0.23 | | 0.21 |
| *Education* | | | | | |
| No schooling | 53 | −0.33 | | −0.46 | |
| Primary | 372 | −0.16 | | −0.16 | |
| Some secondary | 246 | −0.00 | | 0.03 | |
| School certificate | 178 | 0.44 | | 0.44 | |
| | | | 0.28 | | 0.30 |
| *Age* | | | | | |
| Less than 20 | 70 | −0.50 | | −0.49 | |
| 20–24 | 227 | −0.16 | | −0.22 | |
| 25–29 | 190 | 0.11 | | 0.02 | |
| 30–34 | 119 | 0.17 | | 0.18 | |
| 35–39 | 86 | 0.14 | | 0.17 | |
| 40–44 | 67 | 0.12 | | 0.22 | |
| 45–49 | 53 | 0.15 | | 0.33 | |
| 50 and over | 37 | 0.07 | | 0.27 | |
| | | | 0.23 | | 0.27 |
| *Size* | | | | | |
| 1–9 employees | 159 | −0.18 | | −0.16 | |
| 10–99 employees | 308 | −0.03 | | −0.06 | |
| 100 or more employees | 350 | 0.06 | | 0.07 | |
| Don't know | 32 | 0.60 | | 0.54 | |
| | | | 0.17 | | 0.16 |
| Multiple $R^2$ | | | | | 0.220 |
| Multiple R | | | | | 0.469 |

*Note:* Grand mean = 5.38.
*Source:* Data derived from MES, 1975.

Table 9-7. Log of Earnings of Skilled Blue-Collar Male Employees: Multiple Classification Analysis

| Variable and category | Number in sample | Unadjusted deviation | Eta value | Adjusted for independents' deviation | Beta value |
|---|---|---|---|---|---|
| *Region* | | | | | |
| Kuala Lumpur | 561 | 0.08 | | 0.05 | |
| Kuantan | 165 | 0.06 | | 0.09 | |
| Kota Bharu | 156 | −0.36 | | −0.27 | |
| | | | 0.27 | | 0.21 |
| *Race* | | | | | |
| Malay | 410 | −0.12 | | −0.09 | |
| Chinese | 411 | 0.11 | | 0.09 | |
| Indians and others | 61 | 0.08 | | −0.05 | |
| | | | 0.18 | | 0.14 |
| *Education* | | | | | |
| No schooling | 47 | −0.41 | | −0.51 | |
| Primary | 497 | 0.03 | | −0.03 | |
| Some secondary | 274 | −0.04 | | 0.06 | |
| School certificate | 64 | 0.25 | | 0.36 | |
| | | | 0.19 | | 0.25 |
| *Age* | | | | | |
| Less than 20 | 91 | −0.67 | | −0.69 | |
| 20–24 | 200 | −0.20 | | −0.27 | |
| 25–29 | 188 | 0.13 | | 0.09 | |
| 30–34 | 129 | 0.23 | | 0.25 | |
| 35–39 | 104 | 0.04 | | 0.08 | |
| 40–44 | 64 | 0.30 | | 0.36 | |
| 45–49 | 58 | 0.27 | | 0.32 | |
| 50 and over | 48 | 0.17 | | 0.35 | |
| | | | 0.46 | | 0.51 |
| *Size* | | | | | |
| 1–9 employees | 226 | −0.18 | | −0.11 | |
| 10–99 employees | 347 | −0.01 | | 0.01 | |
| 100 or more employees | 291 | 0.14 | | 0.06 | |
| Don't know | 18 | 0.18 | | 0.16 | |
| | | | 0.20 | | 0.11 |
| Multiple $R^2$ | | | | | 0.372 |
| Multiple $R$ | | | | | 0.610 |

Note: Grand mean = 5.32.
Source: Data derived from MES, 1975.

Table 9-8. Log of Earnings of White-Collar Male Employees: Multiple Classification Analysis

| Variable and category | Number in sample | Unadjusted deviation | Eta value | Adjusted for independents' deviation | Beta value |
|---|---|---|---|---|---|
| *Region* | | | | | |
| Kuala Lumpur | 293 | 0.04 | | 0.03 | |
| Kuantan | 47 | −0.07 | | 0.01 | |
| Kota Bharu | 67 | −0.11 | | −0.16 | |
| | | | 0.06 | | 0.07 |
| *Race* | | | | | |
| Malay | 193 | −0.10 | | −0.03 | |
| Chinese | 159 | 0.04 | | 0.06 | |
| Indians and others | 55 | 0.24 | | −0.05 | |
| | | | 0.12 | | 0.05 |
| *Education* | | | | | |
| Primary | 76 | −0.68 | | −0.74 | |
| Some secondary | 80 | −0.50 | | −0.37 | |
| School certificate | 142 | 0.12 | | 0.13 | |
| Higher school certificate | 22 | 0.42 | | 0.54 | |
| Technical college | 25 | 0.59 | | 0.53 | |
| University | 62 | 0.81 | | 0.68 | |
| | | | 0.54 | | 0.51 |
| *Age* | | | | | |
| Less than 20 | 16 | −1.17 | | −0.94 | |
| 20–24 | 87 | −0.59 | | −0.61 | |
| 25–29 | 104 | 0.04 | | −0.10 | |
| 30–34 | 65 | 0.35 | | 0.27 | |
| 35–39 | 62 | 0.21 | | 0.32 | |
| 40–44 | 34 | 0.46 | | 0.52 | |
| 45–49 | 22 | 0.39 | | 0.55 | |
| 50 and over | 17 | 0.35 | | 0.68 | |
| | | | 0.45 | | 0.47 |
| *Size* | | | | | |
| 1–9 employees | 48 | −0.75 | | −0.39 | |
| 10–99 employees | 152 | 0.02 | | 0.01 | |
| 100 or more employees | 204 | 0.16 | | 0.08 | |
| Don't know | 3 | −0.14 | | 0.16 | |
| | | | 0.30 | | 0.15 |
| Multiple $R^2$ | | | | | 0.529 |
| Multiple $R$ | | | | | 0.728 |

Note: Grand mean = 6.07.
Source: Data derived from MES, 1975.

Generally, the analysis was successful because practically no interaction terms were significant enough to detract from the influence of the individual variables. The tables show that education and age dominate the explanatory power of the model. The importance of education, as judged by the beta values, is more or less the same for the unskilled and blue-collar skilled—0.25 and 0.30, respectively—but increases sharply to 0.51 for the white-collar. This is clearly due to the presence of employees with postsecondary qualifications in the sample. The education coefficients for the unskilled category bring out the point that primary education increases earnings sharply (by about 30 percent) even for this group by comparison with those without any formal schooling.

The coefficients of age are interesting because it has sometimes been hypothesized that low-grade labor would have a relatively flat age-earnings profile in less-developed countries, owing to the presence of surplus labor. The results for the unskilled group refute this hypothesis. It is true that the beta values for the skilled blue-collar and white-collar employees are higher, reflecting the fact that the deviations from the grand mean are higher for the younger and older workers in these groups. Looked at diagramatically, the age-earnings profile for the unskilled will certainly be relatively flat compared with those for the other groups. The actual magnitudes of the deviation—varying from about 50 percent below for those under twenty to 33 percent above for the 45–49 age group in which earnings peak—are substantial, however, and do not give a flat profile by any absolute standard. The earnings of the unskilled fall for those over fifty and taper off for skilled blue-collar workers after the age of forty-five, but white-collar earnings continue to increase even for those aged fifty and over. The effect of seniority rules on payments is obviously significant for the latter group.

The quantitative significance of the enterprise size variable—the only institutional variable found to be significant after preliminary analysis —can be assessed from the results of the MCA. Although the tables show that the variable is significant for all three occupational groups, its actual effect on earnings is small (the beta values are quite low). When age, education, and other factors are controlled, employees in the smallest enterprises earn 16 percent less than the grand mean in the unskilled occupations, 11 percent less in the skilled blue-collar occupations, and 39 percent less in white-collar jobs. The earnings of those in the very large enterprises employing 100 or more workers are 7 percent, 16 percent, and 16 percent more than the grand mean in the unskilled, skilled, and white-collar occupations, respectively. As a rule of thumb, the spread in earnings (net of other effects) is about 30 percent of the mean earnings in each occupation. The spread seems to be higher in the white-collar occupations because of the particularly low earnings of these workers in the smallest enterprises, but the number in this subsample is small. Thus, the quantitative effect of enterprise size on earnings differences is not spectacular. The point can be appreciated better by contrasting this picture with the results of the analysis of another labor market undertaken by the author—that of Bombay.[5] In that instance, similar calculations provided a spread of earnings between the lowest paid casual workers and those in the largest factories of as much as 106 percent of the grand mean after controlling for other factors. The employment size of the enterprise was the single most important variable with a beta value of 0.68, substantially higher than the values for the education and age variables.

## Analysis by Size of Enterprise

The previous section showed that earnings increase with enterprise size, even after human capital variables are controlled, in each of the three occupational groups considered. But the multivariate analysis undertaken takes account of only horizontal shifts in the function for each category of enterprise size, and the coefficients of the age and education variables must be averages of those for the various enterprise size groups. These coefficients may differ significantly from each other for different size groups. Separate regressions need to be run to identify these differences for the sample of employees working in each of the three types of enterprise.

It has been noted that white-collar employees are disproportionately represented in large enterprises. Since it is possible that employees with a particular level of education (or experience) would be earning more in white-collar occupations than in blue-collar jobs, to lump all occupational groups together in the estimation of earnings functions by enterprise size might exaggerate the differences in coefficients of, say, education by enterprise size. That is to say, differences attributable to occupational classes might be added to differences owing to the size

5. See Dipak Mazumdar, "Paradigms in the Study of Urban Labor Markets in LDCs: A Reassessment in the Light of an Empirical Survey in Bombay City," World Bank Staff Working Paper no. 366 (Washington, D.C., December 1979), p. 47.

of the enterprise. Thus, it is important to control for differences in the occupational mix as much as possible when comparing returns to education and experience in different size categories of enterprise.

In order to develop separate coefficients as described above, the sample was divided into two broad occupational categories—the blue-collar and the white-collar—and earnings functions were calculated separately for each of the three enterprise size groups. Since there were only a very few white-collar employees in the smallest enterprise size group (those with less than ten employees), the functions for this occupational group were estimated only for the medium and large enterprises. The results of the regression model explaining the log of earnings are reported in Tables 9-9 and 9-10.

The differences in the coefficients of age for different size groups can be used to test the hypothesis that opportunities for skill formation are limited in small firms, producing a markedly flatter age-earnings profile for these firms than that for larger, more complex enterprises. This is a version of the dual labor market theory, which suggests that the disadvantage of belonging to the informal sector may be attributed not so much to a low entry wage as to a slow growth in lifetime earnings. Table 9-11 reproduces the coefficients of age and the square of age from the estimated regression equations. The values given negate the hypothesis of a flatter age-earnings profile for the smaller enterprises. Blue-collar workers in the smallest enterprises have a much higher growth rate of earnings, and the differences in the ages of peak earnings are not very large; it can easily be calculated that the age of peak earnings is forty-six, forty-four, and fifty for the small, medium, and large enterprises, respectively. In the smaller enterprise, the white-collar employees have a very sharp rise in earnings, which peak at age forty-five. By contrast, there is a slow, almost linear growth in earnings right through the worker's life in the large firms. This suggests that the results are the exact opposite of the surmise of the dual labor market hypothesis. Smaller firms seem to attach value to seniority or experience more than large firms for both types of workers.

The returns to education for the different sizes of enterprises can be judged from Table 9-12, which presents the differences in the coefficients of successive educational grade dummies derived from Tables 9-9 and 9-10. That is, the values in the table give the increase in the log of earnings produced by each increment in educational level. The general pattern is quite clearly one of returns to education, which increase with plant size in both categories of occupations. For the blue-collar workers the point can be seen most clearly by comparing the coefficients for the

Table 9-9. Regression Model Explaining Log of Earnings
of Blue-Collar Male Employees by Enterprise Size

| | 1–9 employees | | | 10–99 employees | | | 100 or more employees | | |
| Variable | Beta value | Standard error | Proportion/ mean | Beta value | Standard error | Proportion/ mean | Beta value | Standard error | Proportion/ mean |
|---|---|---|---|---|---|---|---|---|---|
| Education | | | | | | | | | |
| No schooling (base) | — | — | 0.11 | — | — | 0.06 | — | — | 0.06 |
| Primary | 0.52 | 0.12 | 0.56 | 0.18 | 0.08 | 0.54 | 0.51 | 0.13 | 0.41 |
| Some secondary | 0.63 | 0.13 | 0.28 | 0.29 | 0.09 | 0.27 | 0.74 | 0.14 | 0.34 |
| School certificate | 0.81 | 0.17 | 0.05 | 0.74 | 0.09 | 0.11 | 1.08 | 0.14 | 0.18 |
| Higher school certificate | —ª | —ª | —ª | 0.93 | 0.15 | 0.02 | 1.49 | 0.21 | 0.02 |
| Diploma | —ª | —ª | —ª | 1.15 | 0.32 | 0.003 | 1.79 | 0.28 | 0.01 |
| Age | 0.12 | 0.02 | 30.07 | 0.08 | 0.01 | 29.81 | 0.07 | 0.02 | 30.65 |
| Age² | −0.0014 | −0.0002 | — | −0.0009 | 0.0002 | — | −0.0007 | 0.0002 | — |
| Race | | | | | | | | | |
| Malay | −0.17 | 0.09 | 0.34 | −0.20 | 0.08 | 0.44 | 0.04 | 0.07 | 0.66 |
| Chinese | −0.05 | 0.15 | 0.61 | 0.09 | 0.08 | 0.52 | 0.20 | 0.08 | 0.21 |
| Other (base) | — | — | 0.05 | — | — | 0.04 | — | — | 0.13 |
| Region | | | | | | | | | |
| Kuala Lumpur | 0.21 | 0.10 | 0.52 | 0.29 | 0.05 | 0.61 | 0.10 | 0.08 | 0.75 |
| Kota Bharu | 0.31 | 0.10 | 0.21 | 0.27 | 0.06 | 0.21 | 0.10 | 0.09 | 0.15 |
| Trengganu (base) | — | — | 0.27 | — | — | 0.18 | — | — | 0.10 |
| | Constant = 2.21 | | | Constant = 3.22 | | | Constant = 3.02 | | |
| | $R^2$ = 0.30 | | | $R^2$ = 0.40 | | | $R^2$ = 0.27 | | |
| | N = 381 | | | N = 657 | | | N = 648 | | |

Not applicable.    a. Only one case.    Source: MFLS 1975.

Table 7.10 Regression Model Explaining Log of Earnings of White-Collar Male Employees by Enterprise Size

| Variable | 10–99 employees | | | 100 or more employees | | |
|---|---|---|---|---|---|---|
| | Beta value | Standard error | Proportion/ mean | Beta value | Standard error | Proportion/ mean |
| Education | | | | | | |
| Primary (base) | — | — | 0.15 | — | — | 0.13 |
| Some secondary | 0.26 | 0.13 | 0.23 | 0.24 | 0.18 | 0.16 |
| School certificate | 0.83 | 0.12 | 0.36 | 0.65 | 0.16 | 0.39 |
| Higher school certificate | 0.93 | 0.19 | 0.06 | 1.25 | 0.25 | 0.05 |
| Technical diploma | 1.06 | 0.18 | 0.07 | 1.32 | 0.22 | 0.07 |
| University diploma | 1.16 | 0.15 | 0.13 | 1.45 | 0.18 | 0.20 |
| Age | 0.18 | 0.03 | 31.85 | 0.05 | 0.03 | 30.31 |
| Age$^2$ | −0.0019 | 0.0004 | — | −0.00006 | 0.0005 | — |
| Race | | | | | | |
| Malay | 0.03 | 0.15 | 0.44 | −0.07 | 0.14 | 0.57 |
| Chinese | 0.24 | 0.15 | 0.48 | 0.02 | 0.15 | 0.27 |
| Other (base) | — | — | 0.08 | — | — | 0.16 |
| Region | | | | | | |
| Kuala Lumpur | 0.23 | 0.10 | 0.50 | 0.05 | 0.16 | 0.82 |
| Kota Bharu | 0.20 | 0.13 | 0.18 | −0.20 | 0.23 | 0.06 |
| Trengganu (base) | — | — | 0.24 | — | — | 0.12 |
| | Constant = 1.60 | | | Constant = 4.08 | | |
| | R$^2$ = 0.64 | | | R$^2$ = 0.48 | | |
| | N = 151 | | | N = 206 | | |

— Not applicable.
Source: MES, 1975.

Table 9-11. Coefficients of Age and Age² by Enterprise Size

| Occupation | 1–9 employees | 10–99 employees | 100 or more employees |
|---|---|---|---|
| Blue collar | | | |
| Age | 0.12 | 0.08 | 0.07 |
| Age² | −0.0014 | −0.0009 | −0.0007 |
| White collar | | | |
| Age | — | 0.18 | 0.05 |
| Age² | — | −0.0002 | −0.00006 |

— Not applicable.
Source: Tables 9-9 and 9-10.

largest enterprises with those for the medium size. In the large enterprises, workers with school certificates earn 108 percent more than those with no schooling, and those with a higher school certificate earn 149 percent more; the corresponding percentages for workers in medium-size firms are 74 and 93, respectively. It is difficult to compare the smallest enterprises with the largest because of the limited range of educational levels over which the comparison can be made. There are no observations for workers with more qualification than a school certificate in the small-size group. As Table 9-12 shows, the percentage increase in earnings of those with primary education over those with no formal schooling is largest for the smallest enterprises, so that the large earnings differential discriminating against the blue-collar workers in small plants is substantially reduced for those with primary education. Nevertheless, the earnings of blue-collar workers in large enterprises increase more rapidly with the addition of the next educational grade than do the earnings of those in small plants.

A similar result is obtained by comparing the white-collar workers in large enterprises with those in the medium-size group, although the substantially higher returns in the former seem to come only at the higher school certificate level. Employees in large enterprises with higher school certificate qualifications earn 125 percent more than primary school leavers, as against an increment of 93 percent for higher school certificate over primary education in medium firms. Those with university education obtain relative increments of 145 percent and 116 percent.

Taken together, these divergent patterns of returns to education and experience by size of enterprise suggest a plausible mechanism for the determination of earnings in the Malaysian labor market. In the larger enterprise, because of its larger number of employees, it is relatively difficult to establish a personal relation with individual workers and judge them on their intrinsic merits. Employers therefore look for a more formal selection and grading system, which is most readily provided by the educational qualifications of the employees. Formal education, in other words, represents a signaling device that takes precedence over on-the-job training (years of work experience) as a determinant of higher earnings. Another influence working in the same direction is that the larger enterprises are more likely to be sufficiently organized to implement "conventional" differences in earnings for different educational groups.

In smaller enterprises, however, a more personal evaluation of employees leads to a pattern of earnings more closely related to the individual worker's ability to benefit from less formal opportunities for skill formation in the labor market—hence the stronger correlation in this size group between experience and earnings.

The earnings functions shed considerable light on the possibility raised in the literature that earnings in the formal sector of the labor market may be significantly higher than those in the informal sector. If the informal sector is equated with the enterprises employing less

Table 9-12. Differences in the Coefficients of Education Dummies for Blue-Collar and White-Collar Workers

| Education | 1–9 employees | 10–99 employees | 100 or more employees |
|---|---|---|---|
| Blue collar workers | | | |
| No schooling (base) | — | — | — |
| Primary | 0.52 | 0.18 | 0.51 |
| Some secondary | 0.11 | 0.11 | 0.23 |
| School certificate | 0.18 | 0.45 | 0.34 |
| Higher school certificate | —[a] | 0.19 | 0.41 |
| Diploma | —[a] | 0.22 | 0.30 |
| White collar workers | | | |
| Primary (base) | | — | — |
| Some secondary | | 0.26 | . . . |
| School certificate | | 0.53 | 0.65 |
| Higher school certificate | | 0.10 | 0.60 |
| Diploma | | 0.13 | 0.07 |
| University degree | | 0.10 | 0.13 |

. . . Not significant.
a. No observation.
Source: Tables 9-9 and 9-10.

than ten workers, the constant terms of the regressions show that the earnings of employees with no education and little labor market experience (as measured by age) are, indeed, lowest in this size group. The magnitude of the difference is not very great, however; the gap between small enterprises on the one hand and medium and large ones on the other is one of perhaps 25 to 30 percent. It is not even clear that workers with some formal education would earn more in larger enterprises over their lifetime, since the higher returns to education in these enterprises are balanced by the higher returns to experience in the small ones. Education selectivity by enterprise size operates in the sense that no workers with more than a school certificate are to be found in the small enterprises, but the earnings of those with either some secondary school or a school certificate and sixteen to twenty years of experience are—according to the regression models—practically the same in all three groups. Workers with education beyond the level of school certificate, however, do better in large enterprises than in medium-size ones: in this case, the higher return to education is not offset by a lower return to experience.

## The Utility of Sectoral Earnings Functions

There is likely to be substantial intersectoral mobility over the lifetime of the workers in the sample. Thus the coefficients of the education (and experience) variables in an earnings functions calculated for the sector out of which workers tend to move to better jobs will underestimate the returns to human capital. For example, there is likely to be a net movement over the lifetime of workers from the small-scale to the large-scale sectors. Both higher education and longer experience in the labor market are likely to favor such a movement, and those who move successfully will have higher earnings than others. A discussion which is limited to workers in the small-scale sector excludes these observations of higher earnings associated with higher education and experience. It follows that the coefficients of sectoral earnings functions cannot be interpreted as the returns to human capital of those who started their life in a particular sector. They do, however, represent the average experience of those who did not make a transition to the better-paid sectors, and their usefulness derives entirely from the empirical observation of the proportion of workers who did not make such a transition.

Chapter 12 studies the material on intersectoral mobility for the MES sample. It appears from the data presented there that the small-scale sector (employing less than ten workers) had between 15 and 20 percent more workers in first jobs than it had in current jobs. By contrast, the large-scale sector (with more than 100 workers) had between 5 and 10 percent more workers in current jobs than in first jobs. Thus, the sample shows the expected net upward movement, but the magnitude of the movement is not large enough to invalidate the study of sectoral earnings.

# CHAPTER 10

# Racial Differences in Earnings

THE PROBLEM OF LABOR MARKET DISCRIMINATION is logically distinct from the wider issue of observed differences in incomes between groups of workers. Labor market discrimination can contribute to differences in earnings, but is not a necessary condition for the existence of such differences. Conceptually, discrimination causes workers belonging to a particular (perhaps racial) group to be paid less than another group of workers with similar skills, for reasons which cannot be ascribed to supply and demand factors. The first step in any analysis of the extent of discrimination, therefore, is to discover whether there is an unexplained gap in earnings between, say, two different racial groups after controlling for the groups' different levels of skill.

## Theories of the Earnings Gap

Defining equivalent skill levels for different workers is a major problem in applied economics. Unless worker skills can be defined in observable and measurable terms, the question of equivalence becomes unanswerable. Reliance on measurements of earnings gaps corrected for skill differences is consequently limited because few of the factors underlying a worker's skill level (with regard to his potential productivity) will be measured by generally available statistics.

Faced with this limitation, empirical economists have generally relied on a simple human capital framework for establishing skill equivalences. A worker's skills are defined rather narrowly by his years (or levels) of formal education and by the length of his experience in the labor market. In fact, as earlier chapters have shown, education and experience do account for a substantial part of the variance in earnings in Malaysia, as elsewhere. It is not unreasonable, therefore, to begin the analysis by examining differences in earnings for groups with equivalent education and experience.

An important general point, which first arose in studies of the racial earnings gap in the United States, is that the black-white income ratio declines with the level of education; in other words, the extent of discrimination increases progressively with higher levels of education.[1] At the same time, within particular education categories the age-earnings profiles of blacks are considerably flatter than those of whites. If the age-earnings profiles are considered as representing returns to on-the-job training, the two sets of findings can be interpreted as evidence of either greater discrimination against the more skilled blacks, or less acquisition of human capital by the blacks per year of schooling and experience. In fact, these two explanations are opposite sides of the same coin. If market returns to an additional year of schooling or experience are lower for blacks, their rational response as investors is to make less of an effort than whites to acquire extra skills: students in school will opt for more leisure, and workers will be less likely to demand training from foremen. The idea that groups which are discriminated against experience a lower rate of return to investment in human capital is plausible, but it was soon realized that the hypothesis was based on incomplete evidence, insofar as it assumed the availability of the same quantity of resources per year of schooling for the two races. Welch first tackled this question empirically in connection with the analysis of the racial earnings gap for rural males in the southern United States.[2] Of the many factors affecting school quality, he was able to analyze only two for which data were available: teacher quality (approximated by salary paid to the teachers) and secondary school size. (The latter was important because of the "apparent scale economies in school size which are probably related to the lack of teacher specialization implicit in small rural schools.") Welch's statistical work showed that even these two variables accounted for 37 percent of the differential return accruing to a white male for a year's schooling. Nevertheless, the racial gap was still very large after controlling for school quality.[3]

1. See the analysis of the 1960 census mentioned by Gary Hancock, "An Economic Analysis of Earnings and Schooling," *Journal of Human Resources,* vol. 2 (Summer 1967), pp. 310–29; and by R. D. Weiss, "The Effect of Education on the Earnings of Blacks and Whites," *Review of Economics and Statistics,* vol. 52 (May 1970), pp. 150–59.

2. Finis Welch, "Labor Market Discrimination: An Interpretation of Income Differences in the Rural South," *Journal of Political Economy,* vol. 75 (June 1967), pp. 225–41.

3. Ibid., Task 2, pp. 235 and 237. The estimated value of one unit of schooling (eight years) to whites was US$1,160 and to blacks, US$320. Of the huge gap of US$840, US$537 was left after adjusting for school quality.

Differences in the quality of schooling, however, have consequences of much greater importance than the explanation they provide for a portion of the estimated gap in the returns to schooling. In most societies the differences in the quality of schooling for different races can generally be expected to fall over the years. In the United States the quality of education of the disadvantaged race has improved noticeably in the past few decades. Such a secular reduction in different quality of schooling affects the estimation of the return to human capital in a systematic way. The point can be clarified with reference to Figure 10-1, which shows the hypothetical returns to experience curves for two generations of blacks separated in time (with the educational distribution held constant). Curve A for the later generation lies above curve B of the older generation at all points because of the overall improvement in the quality of schooling. An econometric study of the relation between earnings and experience based on cross-section data, however, would reflect neither of the curves. The point of observation in a study made, say, in the 1960s would lie along the dotted line of Figure 10-1 and would lump together the returns to experience of both the new labor market entrants with a 1960s education and the surviving older workers with a 1920s schooling level. The result is an apparent experience and earnings profile which is flatter than either of the real profiles.

Figure 10–1. Hypothetical Returns to Experience for Two Generations of Blacks

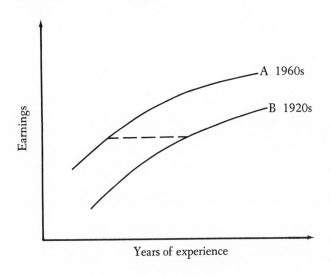

The returns to education calculated on the basis of cross-section data will be misleading in a similar way, because the results for younger blacks with more recent schooling (and a relatively high rate of return to education) will be mixed up with those for older, more experienced blacks from an earlier educational vintage (who will have relatively low returns to schooling). Since the majority of the adult population is likely to come from these earlier vintages, the weighted average return to schooling will be biased toward the low levels of past periods when the quality of education for blacks was very poor. A more recent study undertaken by Welch in 1973 used data from the 1966 Survey of Economic Opportunity as well as 1960 census data. In both samples the return to schooling was found to be higher for blacks at low levels of experience (of up to seven years), was more or less equal for both races with intermediate levels of experience (from seven to twelve years), and was distinctly lower for blacks in cohorts with more than twelve years of experience.[4]

Thus, it is hard to establish racially determined differences in earnings with any accuracy on the basis of comparative analyses of current levels of education. The future earnings levels of the present generation are not known, and analyses using cross-section data include observations for individuals belonging to different educational generations. The quality of education has been singled out for discussion as being particularly relevant to the problem of defining labor of equivalent skills, but any substantial secular change in labor market conditions— such as major reductions in discrimination practices or new government hiring programs and policies—will create similar problems of analysis and interpretation of data.

### The "Crowding" Theory

Even if it is possible to resolve the difficulties mentioned so far and to establish on a valid basis a racial difference in earnings for labor of similar skills, the task of explanation will have only begun. The question then to be asked is: Why should it pay an employer to offer higher pay to some workers, when others with the same level of skills but belonging to a particular racial group are available at a lower wage?

One of the earliest theories on this question, which still looms large in the discussion of the economic disadvantages faced by particular

4. Finis Welch, "Black-White Differences in Returns to Schooling," *American Economic Review*, vol. 63 (December 1973), pp. 897–98.

groups, was suggested by Edgeworth in connection with the problem of the relatively low earnings of females.[5] On this hypothesis, only a narrow band of occupations is generally open to women workers, and this crowding of women in a few job categories reduces their supply price, not only in these occupations (because of the relative abundance of supply), but also throughout the economy. Hence, even when a woman worker manages to be accepted in an occupation other than the traditionally female ones, she will be forced to accept a wage which reflects her relatively low supply price in the crowded categories.

The crowding hypothesis still does not explain why employers do not hire more females in the occupations where they are underrepresented, when it would be profitable for them to do so. It also does not indicate what factors determine the particular occupations in which the disadvantaged group is crowded and how the boundaries of the crowded sectors change over time. Nevertheless, the theory is important because it draws attention to an empirical fact that needs to be studied. Crowding of women in particular occupations does occur in most societies, and the crowded occupations are often remarkably similar for different countries. In the case of the United States, occupational crowding by race is an important feature of the economic scene. A recent writer has the following comment on the racial division of labor in the United States:

> It is very easy to document. . . . I have included in the list [from the 1960 census] only those occupations in which the majority of those employed had not achieved a complete high school education. For each of these occupations, an "expected" number of non-white employees [males only] was computed by assuming that non-whites would share in employment in each occupation to the degree that they shared in the educational achievement shown by all persons in that occupation. On this basis, of the twenty-nine occupations, eighteen had significant deficits of non-whites and eight had surpluses. Of the eighteen deficit occupations, fifteen had deficits of non-whites of more than 50 percent. The surpluses of non-whites were heavily concentrated. Two occupations, service workers and non-farm laborers, accounted for 82 percent of the surpluses.[6]

5. F. Y. Edgeworth, "Equal Pay to Men and Women," *Economic Journal*, vol. 32 (December 1922), pp. 431–57.

6. Barbara R. Bergmann, "The Effect on White Incomes of Discrimination in Employment," *Journal of Political Economy* (March/April 1971), p. 297.

In the analysis of racial differences in earnings in Peninsular Malaysia, it will be important to see whether there is any evidence of the existence of similar occupational divisions between the two major races.

## The Becker Hypothesis

EMPLOYEE DISCRIMINATION. The current economic theory of discriminatory behavior stems from the analysis set out by Becker in his *Economics of Discrimination*.[7] The theory suggests that there is some disutility cost to the use of a unit of labor belonging to the group discriminated against (call it $B$) which is added to the cost of the wage paid to that unit. According to one hypothesis, this disutility might be perceived by employees belonging to the group which is not discriminated against (call it $W$). In formal terms, the discrimination practiced by employees in group $W$ (who attach a negative value to working with those in group $B$) leads to the proposition that $W$ workers need to be compensated by the amount $(B/W) D_w$ for the disutility of working with $B$ workers, where $D_w$ (as a function of the ratio of $B$ to $W$ workers) is a term giving the equivalent (in wage units) of the intensity of discriminatory feelings. As Becker pointed out, if $B$ and $W$ workers are perfect substitutes, employee discrimination will lead to segregated work forces, not to wage differences in a state of equilibrium. The wage cost of a $W$ worker in segregated establishments will be less than in enterprises using both types of workers. There will be a positive incentive for employers to use one or the other type of worker as long as they are perfect substitutes.

If their skill compositions are different, however, $W$ and $B$ workers are likely to be complementary in production. For instance, if there are large numbers of unskilled $B$ workers in the economy, some $W$ workers will have to work with them in integrated establishments. In this case, profit-maximizing employers will not hire workers of the two groups at the same wage. An increase in the number of $B$ workers tends to increase the wage cost of $W$ workers, while an increase in the number of $W$ workers tends to lower the cost of other (complementary) $W$ workers. The marginal cost of each type of worker is different from his wage rate. In equilibrium, $B$ workers will have a wage of less than their marginal product (which equates with their higher marginal

7. Gary S. Becker, *The Economics of Discrimination* (Chicago: University of Chicago Press, 1957).

cost), while $W$ workers will have a wage of more than their marginal product (which equates with their lower marginal cost).

Apart from its implication of an equilibrium wage difference, this theory has two other features relevant to the topics discussed above:

1. The segregationist implications of the hypothesis lend some support to the idea of occupational crowding. Although the complementarity between $W$ and $B$ workers requires integrated establishments, the disutility cost of association can be minimized by segregated occupations within establishments. At the same time, the employment of small numbers of $B$ workers in occupations new to them may produce substantial marginal costs—a consideration which might prevent the easy erosion of segregationist boundaries around specific occupations once they had been built up. Occupational segregation, however, does not necessarily imply a wage difference. The $B$ workers will have lower wages only because of specific supply-demand situations in the occupations in which they have been crowded at a specific point in time. The theory has nothing to say about the possibility of such a situation emerging.

2. The theory predicts different returns to schooling for $B$ and $W$ workers, which are the opposite of what has been observed in the U.S. labor market. Since black skilled workers are in relatively short supply, discrimination by whites, in a situation where skilled and unskilled workers are complementary in production, will produce wage differences only against the unskilled categories of blacks. Skilled blacks can escape the costs of white employee discrimination by associating only with unskilled blacks in segregated establishments. Some unskilled blacks, however, must work with skilled whites, whose discriminatory feelings will produce a wage gap in the way described above. This prediction, of course, goes against the apparent results in the U.S. studies which found the black-white earnings ratio to be negatively related to education. It is important, however, to reiterate the measurement problems associated with a sample spanning several generations, especially when there have been substantial changes in the quality of schooling.

EMPLOYER DISCRIMINATION. Becker has developed an alternative hypothesis relating to discrimination by employers. The concept of an employer's perception of the disutility cost of employing $B$ workers produces a relatively straightforward explanation for the wage gap against such workers. In equilibrium the marginal product of a $B$ worker is equated not to his actual wage, but his wage plus $d_B$, where $d_B$ measures the cut the employer is willing to take in profit for reducing his $B$ labor by one unit. Since there is no such additional cost of employing $W$

labor, and the marginal products of the two types of labor are equated in equilibrium, the wage paid to $W$ labor exceeds the wage paid to $B$ labor.

The employer's discrimination coefficient $d_B$ will vary with the ratio of $B$ to $W$ workers. All employ some $B$ workers at first. As more $B$ workers are employed in relation to $W$ workers their marginal cost increases. They are employed up to the point that their marginal cost is equated to the wage of the $W$ worker. In the case in which all firms have the same utility function (in particular an identical function relating $d_B$ to the ratio of $B$ and $W$ workers), Arrow has shown that employers neither gain nor lose by their discriminatory behavior. The entire effect is that of a transfer from $B$ to $W$ workers. In the more general case, with different utility functions for different employers, a higher proportion of $W$ workers will be found in firms with a higher $d_B$. Thus, there is a partial degree of segregation, with a tendency for $B$ workers to be in the less discriminatory firms and for $W$ workers to be in the more discriminatory ones.[8] Furthermore, since the marginal product of labor is no longer the same in different firms, production is less efficient and profits may be lower than otherwise.

In this model there is no prediction of occupational segregation, unless it is assumed that particularly discriminatory employers are to be found in enterprises that make use of certain types of occupations rather than others. It is difficult to think of reasons why the tendency toward discrimination should be linked with given types of occupation in this way.

In regard to the other important empirical observation noted earlier —the differential return to investment in human capital—it is necessary to make special assumptions to get a specific prediction. Suppose employers are divided into two categories—the public sector employers who do not behave in a discriminatory manner, and owners of capital who employ workers in the private sector and tend to have a significant discrimination coefficient. If, as seems likely in the United States at the present moment, capital is more complementary to educated than to uneducated labor, the $B$ workers will experience a lower return to education than $W$ workers—provided the public sector does not play a significant offsetting role.

The hypothesis of employer discrimination does provide a straightforward explanation of how different rewards for labor of the same skill

8. Kenneth J. Arrow, in *Discrimination in Labor Markets*, Orley Ashenfelter and Albert Rees, eds. (Princeton, N.J.: Princeton University Press, 1973).

can arise, but it does not offer a satisfactory rationale for the persistence of these different rewards. Since the basic assumption is that employers with a taste for discrimination sacrifice profits to satisfy their prejudice, less discriminatory firms should be able, in the long run, to undercut the more discriminatory firms. Market forces would thus wipe out discrimination over time. It becomes necessary then to take refuge in arguments involving nonconvexities to escape from the long-run instability of the model.[9]

In the long run, the hypothesis of employee discrimination runs into rather similar difficulties. As already noted, this theory has strong segregationist implications, but as long as there are many more unskilled than skilled blacks, some unskilled blacks and some skilled whites will work in integrated firms, provided the gains from complementarities exceed the diseconomies of association. Wage differences appear against unskilled blacks and in favor of skilled blacks. In time, this should lead to increases in the proportion of skilled blacks in the black labor force. The hypothesis thus leads to the prediction that the two racial groups will become increasingly segregated in employment, and that wage differences will tend to disappear.[10]

To sum up, then, it appears that the current economic theory of discrimination offers some explanation of the existence of the racial wage gap at a point in time, but cannot be considered to have satisfactory explanatory power because its dynamic implications do not fit the facts over a long period of U.S. history. The predictions of the model on points other than the wage gap—principally occupational crowding and different returns to schooling and experience—are hazy and sensitive to the sources of discrimination.

This brief discussion has, however, suggested some areas which are worth following up in the Malaysian context. The next section of this chapter examines the occupational distribution of Malays and Chinese, to test, among other things, whether crowding exists in Malaysia's urban economy. The following section undertakes a decomposition of the Malay-Chinese earnings difference from the data set generated by the World Bank's Household Survey in Kuala Lumpur and the two East Coast towns. Its purpose is to assess the relative importance in the differ-

9. Ibid., pp. 13–20.

10. This point has been noted by Finis Welch, "Human Capital Theory: Education, Discrimination, and Life Cycles," *American Economic Review*, vol. 65, no. 2 (May 1975), pp. 63–73.

ences in earnings of educational attainment, occupational distribution, and the level of earnings within an occupational group. The final section pursues differences in returns to human capital for the two races.

## Racial Differences in Occupational Patterns in Urban Malaysia

Any discussion of occupational patterns in the urban economy of Malaysia needs to take account of the argument that it is not legitimate to draw conclusions about either the existence or the effects of crowding from only one part of the economy—the urban sector. It is well known that there is marked occupational crowding in the economy of Peninsular Malaysia as a whole and that Malays are disproportionately represented in agriculture. Insofar as earnings in agriculture are at a lower level than in nonagricultural activities, this phenomenon in itself depresses the relative earnings of Malays in the economy as a whole. Moreover, the relative income of Malays within the agricultural sector is very low. Anand, using the PES data, found that racial differences in earnings were not large for the economy as a whole, except in farming and the sales sector:

> The racial disparity ratios among farmers are greatest, with Chinese farmers earning more than two-and-a-half times as much as Malay farmers, and Indian farmers (constituting only 1 percent of the category) earning almost twice as much as Malay farmers. These differentials strongly suggest that average Chinese landholdings are much larger than average Malay landholdings . . . but there are no independent data to check on the distribution of land in Malaysia.[11]

The existence of this disparity suggests that the supply price of Malay migrants to the towns might be relatively low; this should in turn cause Malay earnings to be lower than the earnings of non-Malays in the urban economy. In principle, unless barriers to entry exist in particular urban occupations, employers would tend to hire Malays (who have a lower supply price) more frequently than non-Malays. It therefore becomes necessary to ask why non-Malays get employed at all in urban

11. Sudhir Anand, *Inequality and Poverty in Malaysia: Measurement and Decomposition* (New York: Oxford University Press, forthcoming), chap. 6.

jobs requiring skills which can be supplied more cheaply by Malays. In other words, to explain the persistence of a racial earnings difference for labor with similar skills in the urban sector, it is necessary to identify barriers to employment for Malays within the urban economy.

In the family-owned business sector, the relatively high income of the non-Malays might be explained partly by a distribution of assets or by cooperant factors more favorable to the non-Malays, similar to the pattern observed in the agricultural economy. For this reason, this section is limited to a discussion of whether there is any significant racial segregation of *employees* by occupation in the urban economy, as suggested by the hypothesis of occupational crowding (which was significant in the United States). Before the occupational distribution by race of the employee group is discussed, however, the overall employment patterns of both employees and the self-employed by racial group will be reviewed.

### Employment Status

Table 10-1 gives the 1970 census distribution for males broken down by race, employment status, and other categories. The major point of interest is that racial differences in the type of employment are generally minor except in the metropolitan areas, in which the figures for self-employed Chinese and Malay employees are disproportionately high. Differences in participation rates are not as large between the two races, but the market entry rate of unemployment (the percentage represented by those looking for their first job) is considerably higher among the Malays than the Chinese (see Part III).

The distribution for females given in Table 10-1 suggests some important points. The proportion of females who work for themselves or as family workers is astonishingly low in the metropolitan regions (although it is higher for the Chinese); it is much more substantial in the nonmetropolitan urban economy, where the racial difference is reversed, with a larger proportion of self-employed Malay women.

The data also illustrate a major difference between the races in the availability of employment for women in all three types of urban areas. The female market entry unemployment rates for both races are more than twice as high as those for males and, as with males, are substantially higher for Malays than for Chinese. In addition, however, the participation rate is significantly lower for Malay females. This phenomenon seems likely to be at least partially due to limited job oppor-

Table 10-1. Percentage Distribution of Males and Females
by Work Status, Race, and Size of City, Together
with Participation Rates

| | Metropolitan | | Large urban | | Small urban | |
| Status | Malay | Chinese | Malay | Chinese | Malay | Chinese |
|---|---|---|---|---|---|---|
| **Males** | | | | | | |
| Employer | 3.0 | 5.9 | 4.0 | 6.9 | 4.1 | 5.8 |
| Self-employed | 5.8 | 18.8 | 25.8 | 22.1 | 28.1 | 30.2 |
| Employee | 83.2 | 66.3 | 59.7 | 59.5 | 58.3 | 46.3 |
| Family worker | 1.3 | 5.1 | 3.9 | 7.6 | 4.9 | 14.7 |
| Looking for first job | 6.7 | 3.9 | 6.6 | 3.8 | 4.6 | 3.0 |
| Work force | 100.0 | 100.0 | 100.0 | 100.0 | 100.0 | 100.0 |
| Participation rate[a] | 61.4 | 63.1 | 54.9 | 60.4 | 60.8 | 61.5 |
| Participation rate[b] | 65.8 | 65.6 | 58.8 | 62.8 | 63.6 | 63.5 |
| **Females** | | | | | | |
| Employer | 3.1 | 2.7 | 3.2 | 3.4 | 3.3 | 2.6 |
| Self-employed | 4.4 | 9.0 | 25.0 | 10.9 | 26.4 | 16.4 |
| Employee | 73.0 | 69.9 | 42.4 | 62.2 | 36.6 | 49.2 |
| Family worker | 4.4 | 9.2 | 17.9 | 14.7 | 24.2 | 27.3 |
| Looking for first job | 15.0 | 9.1 | 11.5 | 8.8 | 9.6 | 4.5 |
| Work force | 100.0 | 100.0 | 100.0 | 100.0 | 100.0 | 100.0 |
| Participation rate[a] | 17.6 | 26.3 | 17.6 | 22.9 | 18.2 | 30.5 |
| Participation rate[b] | 20.7 | 29.0 | 19.9 | 25.2 | 10.1 | 31.9 |

Note: "Not stated" is not included in the total in the computation of participation rates.
a. Excludes from the work force those looking for first job.
b. Includes in the work force those looking for first job.
Source: Malaysian Census, 1970.

tunities for Malay women, some of whom would appear to have been discouraged from entering the labor force.[12]

*Occupational Distribution*

Table 10-2 presents the distribution of male and female employees in the labor force by one-digit occupational groups. The data are

12. The statement in the text is a strong surmise, not a certainty. It might be useful to recall, as a point of comparison, that nonwhite women in the United States have a *higher* participation rate—a phenomenon frequently attributed to economic necessity.

Table 10-2. Index of Malay Crowding and Occupational Distribution

| Occupation | Index of crowding[a] | | | Percent of labor force in occupational group (all races) | | |
|---|---|---|---|---|---|---|
| | Metro-politan | Large urban | Small urban | Metro-politan | Large urban | Small urban |
| *Males* | | | | | | |
| Professional, technical | 1.17 | 1.59 | 2.72 | 7.0 | 7.6 | 5.3 |
| Administrative, managerial | 0.50 | 0.50 | 0.78 | 2.5 | 1.6 | 1.0 |
| Clerical and related | 1.48 | 1.60 | 2.26 | 12.8 | 8.3 | 4.3 |
| Sales, high | 0.24 | 0.48 | 0.39 | 6.4 | 7.6 | 6.8 |
| Sales, other | 0.19 | 0.26 | 0.27 | 11.5 | 10.6 | 7.4 |
| Service, high | 0.29 | 0.50 | 0.61 | 1.5 | 1.6 | 1.7 |
| Protective services | 18.22 | 13.82 | 19.69 | 6.4 | 4.6 | 3.9 |
| Other services | 0.94 | 1.04 | 1.02 | 5.7 | 5.0 | 4.1 |
| Agriculture workers | 1.52 | 2.19 | 0.96 | 2.7 | 10.9 | 33.5 |
| Production workers | 0.61 | 0.59 | 0.60 | 30.3 | 28.6 | 19.8 |
| Laborers (n.e.c.)[b] | 2.61 | 1.35 | 1.68 | 5.6 | 6.6 | 5.7 |
| Not adequately described | 1.40 | 1.00 | 1.29 | 1.1 | 1.1 | 0.9 |
| Not stated | 1.48 | 1.47 | 1.24 | 6.5 | 6.8 | 5.6 |
| Total | | | | 100.0 | 100.0 | 100.0 |
| *Females* | | | | | | |
| Professional, technical | 1.55 | 1.59 | 3.42 | 12.2 | 11.8 | 5.9 |
| Administrative, managerial | 0.72 | 0.65 | 0.69 | 0.3 | 0.7 | 0.1 |
| Clerical and related | 1.25 | 0.90 | 1.90 | 15.0 | 6.4 | 2.1 |
| Sales, high | 0.53 | 2.63 | 2.46 | 1.5 | 2.9 | 2.3 |
| Sales, other | 0.30 | 0.59 | 0.82 | 6.6 | 6.2 | 4.8 |
| Service, high | 0.69 | 2.42 | 2.56 | 0.9 | 1.3 | 0.9 |
| Protective services | 6.64 | 4.15 | 4.37 | 0.2 | 0.2 | 0.1 |
| Other services | 1.09 | 0.91 | 1.30 | 24.2 | 16.0 | 7.6 |
| Agriculture workers | 0.26 | 1.05 | 0.63 | 2.3 | 20.0 | 50.5 |
| Production workers | 0.46 | 0.70 | 1.06 | 18.4 | 16.3 | 10.2 |
| Laborers (n.e.c.)[b] | 1.69 | 0.28 | 0.48 | 2.6 | 2.5 | 2.4 |
| Not adequately described | 1.42 | 0.68 | 1.34 | 12.4 | 7.9 | 7.9 |
| Not stated | 1.85 | 1.72 | 1.84 | 3.4 | 8.5 | 5.3 |
| Total | | | | 100.0 | 100.0 | 100.0 |

a. Index of crowding is:

$$\left( \frac{\text{Percentage of Malay in occupation } i}{\text{Percentage of Chinese in occupation } i} \right) \div \left( \frac{\text{Percentage of Malay in work force}}{\text{Percentage of Chinese in work force}} \right)$$

b. Not elsewhere classified.
*Source:* Malaysian Census, 1970.

broken down by the size of the urban area. The first three columns give the index of crowding of Malays in the particular urban group and occupational category. A value of unity means that the representation of the Malays and the Chinese is in proportion to their shares of the work force in the urban area concerned, while a value exceeding unity indicates overrepresentation of Malays. Overrepresentation of a particular racial group may, of course, occur in an occupation in which there are relatively few workers. To check on this, the last three columns of each table give the share of each occupational group in the total work force of the particular urban area.

Production work (that is, manufacturing activity as distinct from agriculture) forms only a minor part of the economic activity of towns. In the metropolitan areas it accounts for only one-third of the male and one-fifth of the female labor force. A feature of the classification of rural and urban areas in Malaysia is the importance of agriculture in nonmetropolitan towns, particularly the small towns. In spite of the fact that all areas with less than 10,000 inhabitants are classified as rural, the table shows fully one-third of the male and one-half of the female labor force in the small towns as being in agriculture.

There does seem to be a perceptible occupational separation by race in the broad classification presented in Table 10-2, but it is not obvious that there is a concentration of Malays in the low-grade categories. Of the sixty-six indexes of crowding presented in the table (eleven occupational groups for the two sexes in the three urban sectors), less than ten have a value reasonably close to unity. All the other values are substantially below or above unity, indicating overrepresentation of one or the other of the two races. But if occupational crowding systematically discriminated against the Malays, there should be a value well above unity in the three categories most likely to contain the low earners—laborers, other services, and other sales. In fact, a significant overrepresentation of Malays is observed only for laborers for both sexes in the metropolitan areas, and for males only in the other urban areas. The "other sales" group contains a disproportionate number of non-Malays. Contrary to some popular myths, the "other services" category provides employment to Malays and non-Malays roughly in proportion to the representation of the two racial groups in the total work force. The data illustrate the special importance of the "other services" category for female employment; fully a quarter of female employees in the metropolitan towns are found in this group. But for the females, as with the males, Malays are not generally crowded into this occupation. This finding is in sharp contrast to the situation observed in the United

States, where the overcrowding of black females in personal and related services is one of the main causes of the low earning capacity of this racial group.

The data in Table 10-2 bear out the widely held view that Malays are significantly underrepresented in manufacturing and related activities. It is not possible to differentiate on the basis of census data between employees with different levels of skill in the nonagricultural production sector. For all production workers together, however, the crowding index for Malays is very much below unity in this single most important category for employment in the urban economy of Malaysia. If this sector were thought to provide employment at relatively high levels of income, there might be some support for the hypothesis of occupational crowding into other sectors as a factor in the lower economic performance of Malays. But the hypothesis that earnings in nonagricultural production in the urban economy are high is doubtful in the Malaysian context. The analysis of PES income data in Chapter 7 showed that the distribution of earnings in services was almost identical to that in the production sector for males. It is, of course, arguable that production activities can offer more opportunities for skill formation and a better lifetime earnings profile than the other sectors. The factors affecting the rate of growth of lifetime earnings are many, and a detailed multivariate analysis would be needed to isolate the influence on it of the employee's sector of activity. Issues of this kind are discussed in Chapter 11.

The underrepresentation of Malays in semiskilled and skilled blue-collar jobs in urban Malaysia is balanced by their overrepresentation in the public sector (as noted earlier) and in a range of white-collar jobs. (For example, Table 10-2 indicates that protective services constitute a significant part of total urban male employment, particularly in metropolitan areas, and that this occupation is almost entirely dominated by Malays.) Public sector wages are maintained by the government at somewhat higher levels than those in comparable private activities. Malays are also disproportionately represented in the large clerical sector and—contrary to popular belief—in professional and technical occupations. Malays are significantly underrepresented in administrative and managerial jobs, but this sector employs relatively few workers.

### Segregation by Race of Employer

Although the evidence on overcrowding in the traditional sense of an overrepresentation of the disadvantaged groups in low-paid occupations is thus not strong, the degree of racial segregation of employees in the public and private sectors is quite striking in the Malaysian economy. Private enterprises owned by Malays in both Kuala Lumpur and the East Coast towns and those owned by the Chinese in the capital employed their own race almost exclusively. Only Chinese-owned enterprises in the East Coast towns made use of a substantial number of Malays, who made up about a third of the employees in these enterprises. The public sector is dominated by Malays, but more so in the East Coast—the percentage of Malay employees being 80 percent in this area as against 64 percent in Kuala Lumpur (see Table 6-1).

The percentage distribution of employees of the two races by type of employer is shown in Table 10-3. At first sight the segregation of employees in the private sector by the race of the owner might be thought to contribute to a difference in earnings against the Malays— particularly in Kuala Lumpur where the importance of Malay-owned firms seems to be rather low. (Only 7 percent of all employees were in private Malay firms in Kuala Lumpur as against 30 percent in the East Coast towns.) On reflection, however, the point does not appear to be well taken. As stated earlier, if *employees* of one race dislike working with colleagues belonging to another race, the model predicts the segregation of employees by race in separate establishments rather than an interracial wage difference, because the former would be the best way for profit-maximizing employers to minimize their costs. If discrimination originates with *employers,* however, racial segregation by establishments can occur only if the discrimination coefficient (measured by the monetary loss the employer is willing to incur to satisfy his desire to discriminate) of the least discriminatory employer exceeds the racial wage difference. In other words, with employer discrimination, segre-

Table 10-3. Percentage Distribution of Employees by Race and Type of Employer

| Employer | Kuala Lumpur | | East Coast | |
|---|---|---|---|---|
| | Malay | Chinese | Malay | Chinese |
| Malay private | 18 | 1 | 44 | 1 |
| Chinese private | 6 | 75 | 18 | 81 |
| Foreign | 18 | 11 | 2 | 5 |
| Government or public sector | 54 | 9 | 34 | 10 |
| Other | 4 | 4 | 2 | 3 |
| Total | 100 | 100 | 100 | 100 |

Source: MES, 1975.

gation would be a reflection of a relatively small racial wage gap rather than the cause of a large one.

If this reasoning is correct, the observed pattern of racial segregation by establishments predicts that the wage level of Malays will be significantly below that of equivalent Chinese labor in the East Coast, but not in Kuala Lumpur. The next section confirms this.

## Decomposition of Racial Differences in Earnings

The previous section argued that a version of the crowding hypothesis does not provide a strong explanation of important racial differences in earnings in urban Malaysia. It is now necessary to widen the discussion to include an assessment of the influence of racial differences in education on disparities in earnings.

The distribution by educational attainment of the subsample of employees from the MES in Table 10-4 shows some interesting differences

Table 10-4. Education Distribution of Employees
by Race, Sex, and Region
(percent)

| | Kuala Lumpur | | East Coast towns | |
| Education | Malay | Chinese | Malay | Chinese |
|---|---|---|---|---|
| *Males* | | | | |
| No formal school | 2.0 | 3.5 | 9.4 | 4.1 |
| Primary school | 42.7 | 43.5 | 55.2 | 40.0 |
| Some secondary | 27.2 | 33.7 | 16.1 | 30.3 |
| Passed secondary | 19.7 | 12.4 | 15.3 | 20.0 |
| Passed higher school | 1.8 | 1.8 | 2.0 | 2.1 |
| Technical college diploma | 2.6 | 1.2 | 0.8 | 1.5 |
| University | 4.0 | 4.0 | 1.2 | 2.3 |
| Total | 100.0 | 100.0 | 100.0 | 100.0 |
| *Females* | | | | |
| No formal school | 1.5 | 7.1 | 14.8 | 7.7 |
| Primary school | 25.7 | 39.0 | 10.9 | 30.9 |
| Some secondary | 26.5 | 26.3 | 14.8 | 40.4 |
| Passed secondary | 36.0 | 24.0 | 32.1 | 17.3 |
| Passed higher school | 3.7 | 1.3 | 3.7 | —ᵃ |
| Technical college diploma | 2.9 | 1.3 | 1.2 | 1.9 |
| University | 3.7 | 1.0 | 2.5 | —ᵃ |
| Total | 100.0 | 100.0 | 100.0 | 100.0 |

a. Too few in subgroup.
Source: MES, 1975.

between the two racial groups. In the East Coast towns Chinese males
are clearly better educated than Malays; there are larger percentages of
Chinese at all levels of attainment above the primary. The racial earnings difference in the coastal towns may be partly attributable to this
factor. The situation seems to be reversed for male workers in Kuala
Lumpur and for females in both regions.

To show relative earnings by levels of education, the educational
groups have been combined into three larger categories with income
ratios (Malay: Chinese) as follows:

| Education | Male employees | | Female employees | |
|---|---|---|---|---|
| | Kuala Lumpur | East Coast | Kuala Lumpur | East Coast |
| No formal schooling and primary school | 0.80 | 0.79 | 1.24 | 0.77 |
| Some secondary school and passed school certificate | 0.84 | 0.64 | 0.73 | 1.10 |
| Higher school certificate and some additional education | 0.97 | 0.74 | 0.94 | (Too few in sub-group) |

There is clearly a bias in earnings against male Malay employees by
broad educational groups, particularly in the East Coast. The difference
is much smaller in Kuala Lumpur, particularly for the higher educational groups. It has already been noted that the educational level of the
Chinese is higher in the East Coast, which accentuates the income disparity between the races in this region. (Female earnings ratios are
erratic; given the smallness of the sample, nothing very meaningful can
be said about them.)

Schooling affects earnings through its influence on both the occupation a person is able to enter and the income level the person attains
within the occupational group. The average earnings level of any
group ($E_i$) will be the product of three terms:

$$E_i = S_i \times O_i \times Y_i$$

where $S_i$, the schooling vector, gives the distribution of the population
among the various educational categories; $O_i$, the education-occupation
matrix, shows how each educational group is distributed among different occupations; and $Y_i$ is the vector of mean earnings for each occupation covered.

In itself this equation does not say much, but it can be used to compare the different average earnings of two groups—in this case the
Malays and the Chinese—in a way that may shed light on the causes

of the differences in earnings. The differences in observed earnings between the two racial groups can be decomposed into three components by starting with the values of the three terms on the right-hand side of the identity for one race, and then substituting each of the values for the other race for each of the three terms in the equation. For example, if $S_C$—the schooling vector for the Chinese—is substituted into the equation for the Malays' earnings—a product of $S_M$, $O_M$, and $Y_M$—the product will be the hypothetical earnings of the Malays if their schooling vector were like that of the Chinese, but with no other difference either in the education-occupation matrix or in the occupation-earnings vector. The difference between this hypothetical figure for earnings and the actual earnings of the Malays represents the part of the racial gap in earnings which could be ascribed to a difference in educational attainment. (For the purposes of this calculation it is assumed that the three terms of the identity expressed are independent of each other.) The decomposition of the racial earnings gap into the three components caused by differences in $S_i$, $O_i$, and $Y_i$ is a useful first step. The orders of magnitude involved will suggest the nature of the problem and may provide helpful indications of regional variations in the relative importance of the different components.

To simplify the calculations for the numerical exercise, both the educational and the occupational categories have been grouped into three classes. The educational classes are the same as those just discussed—no formal schooling and primary school; some secondary school and passed school certificate; and higher school certificate and some additional education. The occupational categories are white collar, semiskilled, and unskilled. The calculations are made only for male employees in both regions, and the results are in Malaysian dollars per month (differences refer to Chinese earnings *minus* Malay earnings):

|  | Kuala Lumpur | East Coast |
|---|---|---|
| Average earnings |  |  |
| Malay | 328 | 232 |
| Chinese | 361 | 309 |
| Actual differences in earnings | 33 | 77 |
| Difference due to schooling vector $(S_i)$ | —3 | 18 |
| Difference due to education-occupation matrix $(O_i)$ | —30 | —19 |
| Difference due to occupation-income vector $(Y_i)$ | 65 | 80 |

The education-occupation matrix is less favorable for the Chinese. If the Malays had the $O_i$ value given for the Chinese and the other two terms of the equation were unchanged, their earnings would be reduced by nearly 10 percent in both regions. This is consistent with the finding in the previous section that there is no evidence of crowding of Malays in low-grade occupations.

Much the most important source of the racial gap in earnings is the difference in mean earnings between the two races within each occupational group. The occupation-income vectors for the races (in Malaysian dollars per month) are:

| | Kuala Lumpur | | East Coast | |
|---|---|---|---|---|
| Occupation | Malay | Chinese | Malay | Chinese |
| White collar | 440 | 560 | 360 | 456 |
| Skilled | 280 | 279 | 187 | 245 |
| Unskilled | 227 | 266 | 169 | 251 |

Although the relative importance of the intraoccupational racial difference in earnings has been noticed before, the current exercise reveals its magnitude. Malays would be better off by 20 percent in Kuala Lumpur and by a third in the East Coast, if they had the Chinese earnings vector $(Y_C)$.

The schooling vector produces only a negligible difference in Kuala Lumpur. In the East Coast it favors the Chinese; if the Malays shared the higher educational attainments of the Chinese, their earnings could be increased by about 8 or 9 percent.

The relative importance of the occupation-income vector in accounting for the racial earnings gap would at first tend to suggest that the returns to education would be higher for the Chinese in this economy. This is not necessarily so, however. The decomposition has not related education directly to earnings, but has instead worked through an intermediate stage of occupational distribution. The earnings difference in favor of the Chinese does not necessarily increase with the skill level of the occupational grouping. In Kuala Lumpur white-collar Chinese have a relatively high earnings differential (27 percent as against 19 percent for unskilled occupations), but the situation is the other way around in the East Coast. Moreover, the decomposition procedure does not establish probable relationships; it is merely an accounting breakdown of the sources of the racial earnings gap. To establish a statistically significant relation between education and earnings which would be more generally valid, it is necessary to compute earnings functions separately for the two races.

Table 10-5. Earnings Functions for Male Employees by Race (Whole Sample)

| Variable | Malay employees | | | | | Chinese employees | | | | |
|---|---|---|---|---|---|---|---|---|---|---|
| | Coefficient | F ratio | Beta value | $R^2$ | Proportion/mean | Coefficient | F ratio | Beta value | $R^2$ | Proportion/mean |
| Age | 0.112 | 141.06 | 1.58 | 0.11 | 30.0 | 0.133 | 79.29 | 1.44 | 0.10 | 30.5 |
| $Age^2$ | −0.0012 | 81.96 | −1.20 | 0.13 | 985.1 | −0.0016 | 54.06 | −1.19 | 0.15 | 1031.4 |
| $E_2$ | 0.38 | 37.54 | 0.29 | 0.26 | 0.49 | 0.16 | 1.26 | 0.09 | 0.17 | 0.43 |
| $E_3$ | 0.66 | 90.95 | 0.42 | 0.30 | 0.22 | 0.20 | 1.89 | 0.10 | 0.22 | 0.33 |
| $E_4$ | 0.99 | 187.34 | 0.58 | 0.30 | 0.18 | 0.58 | 12.52 | 0.22 | 0.22 | 0.14 |
| $E_5$ | 1.33 | 134.09 | 0.28 | 0.32 | 0.02 | 0.92 | 14.13 | 0.14 | 0.22 | 0.02 |
| $E_6$ | 1.51 | 154.06 | 0.29 | 0.35 | 0.02 | 1.16 | 18.78 | 0.14 | 0.23 | 0.01 |
| $E_7$ | 1.93 | 338.12 | 0.48 | 0.55 | 0.03 | 1.33 | 41.02 | 0.27 | 0.28 | 0.04 |
| Kuala Lumpur | 0.02 | 0.39 | 0.02 | 0.57 | 0.28 | −0.10 | 1.96 | −0.05 | 0.28 | 0.79 |
| Kota Bharu | −0.20 | 26.72 | −0.14 | 0.58 | 0.52 | −0.34 | 7.50 | −0.09 | 0.29 | 0.07 |
| Plant size | | | | | | | | | | |
| 10–99 | 0.11 | 6.79 | 0.08 | 0.58 | 0.34 | 0.05 | 0.60 | 0.03 | 0.29 | 0.44 |
| 100 and over | 0.16 | 13.88 | 0.12 | 0.59 | 0.52 | 0.21 | 7.45 | 0.10 | 0.39 | 0.22 |
| Occupation | | | | | | | | | | |
| Manual | 0.08 | 6.63 | 0.07 | 0.60 | 0.43 | −0.11 | 3.01 | 0.06 | 0.29 | 0.43 |
| White collar | 0.27 | 43.33 | 0.19 | 0.60 | 0.36 | 0.09 | 1.31 | −0.05 | 0.30 | 0.32 |

Constant: Malay employees, 2.409; Chinese employees, 2.967.
Note: The education categories are as described in Table 8-2.
Source: MES, 1975.

## Racial Earnings Functions

The racial earnings functions have been obtained from the combined samples for the three towns in the World Bank Household Survey, using dummies to control for any difference in earnings attributable to location (see Table 10-5). The analysis, which is confined to male employees, suggests two general propositions.

*Proposition 1.* Education plays a much more important role in augmenting the earnings of Malays than those of Chinese.

For the Malays, the coefficients of the education dummies used in the model are significant for every level of education. For the Chinese, however, primary education does not seem to increase earnings significantly above the level of those without formal education, and secondary education (without upper secondary school certificate) is barely significant at the 85 percent level.

The log variance of earnings explained by education alone is as much as 42 percent for the Malays and only 13 percent for the Chinese. It should be noted, however, that the dispersion of earnings is substantially larger for the Chinese. The standard deviation of the log of earnings is 0.66 for the Malays and 0.92 for the Chinese—nearly 50 percent higher for the latter. The regression model accordingly performs much less well for the Chinese than for the Malays. But even when the substantially lower $R^2$ in the case of the Chinese is taken into account, the role of education can be seen to be less important. Less than half the overall $R^2$ of 0.28 is accounted for by education for the Chinese. In the case of the Malays it is 42 percent of the overall 60 percent of the variance explained.

Changes in the values of the coefficients for successive levels of education, calculated from the full regression model, are presented in Table 10-6. These incremental values give the successive increases in the log of earnings with each step upward in the educational hierarchy. The incremental changes in $R^2$ are also included in this table. Increments at the middle levels of education (passed school certificate or higher school certificate) raise the earnings of Malays and Chinese by about the same percentages. At either end of the educational spectrum, however, there are major differences; the incremental values of the coefficients as well as the changes in $R^2$ are much larger for the Malays for primary and some secondary education on the one hand, and for university education on the other.

Table 10-6. Effect on the Log of Earnings of Successive Levels of Education

| | Malay | | Chinese | |
|---|---|---|---|---|
| Education | Increase in values of education coefficient | Increase in R² | Increase in values of education coefficient | Increase in R² |
| Primary | 0.38 | 0.13 | 0.16 | 0.02 |
| Some secondary | 0.28 | 0.13 | 0.04 | 0.05 |
| Passed school certificate | 0.33 | 0.00 | 0.38 | 0.00 |
| Higher school certificate | 0.34 | 0.02 | 0.34 | 0.00 |
| Diploma | 0.18 | 0.03 | 0.24 | 0.01 |
| University degree | 0.42 | 0.20 | 0.17 | 0.05 |

*Source:* Table 10-5.

The regression model presented in Table 10-5 can also be used to compute the predicted earnings of the two races for the different educational levels. The predicted earnings are calculated by adding the coefficients of the education dummies to the earnings of the base group with no formal education; the latter is calculated by using the mean values of the noneducation variables in the model. The results of the calculation are given in Table 10-7, where the right-hand column shows that the earnings differential in favor of the Chinese is at its greatest for those without any formal education. With primary and some secondary education the Malays succeed in reducing their disadvantage to some extent. For middle levels of education the relative difference

Table 10-7. Predicted Log of Earnings of the Chinese

| Education | Log of earnings | Excess of earnings over those of Malays |
|---|---|---|
| No formal schooling | 4.73 | 0.56 |
| Primary | 5.11 | 0.34 |
| Some secondary | 5.39 | 0.10 |
| Passed school certificate | 5.72 | 0.15 |
| Higher school certificate | 6.06 | 0.15 |
| Diploma | 6.24 | 0.21 |
| University degree | 6.66 | −0.04 |

*Source:* Table 10-5.

in earnings remains more or less unchanged. Malays have higher earnings at the level of university education.

*Proposition 2.* Occupation makes a greater difference to the earnings
of the Malays.

The value of the coefficient of white-collar occupations is substantial
for the Malays. Their earnings, if they are in white-collar jobs, are 27
percent higher than those of the unskilled, after allowance is made for
the effects of age, education, and other variables in the model. The
corresponding coefficient for the Chinese is insignificant. In blue-collar,
semiskilled occupations, Malays have higher earnings than in the unskilled group (by about 8 percent); for the Chinese, earnings in this category are significantly *lower* (around 11 percent). This last point might
seem surprising, except that the division of the occupations into three
groups left some of the sales workers in the unskilled category. The
Chinese are heavily represented in the sales sector, and their earnings in
this sector tend to be relatively high.

Education augments earnings in two ways: by providing opportunities
for entry into higher skilled occupations and by permitting a relatively
well-educated worker to increase his earning strength within a particular occupational group. Insofar as there is a correlation between levels
of education and the earners' occupations, there may be some bias in
the estimates as a consequence of including both variables in the same
regression model. The same point will hold to a lesser degree for the
enterprise size variables. The empirical content of this possible bias can
be judged by comparing the education coefficients of the model when
the log of earnings is regressed solely on age and education (the simple
human capital model) with those given in Table 10-5. Column (1)
below for each race gives the coefficients of the simple human capital
model; column (2) gives the coefficients from Table 10-5:

|  | Malay | | Chinese | |
|---|---|---|---|---|
|  | *(1)* | *(2)* | *(1)* | *(2)* |
| $E_2$ | 0.48 | 0.38 | 0.16 | 0.16 |
| $E_3$ | 0.85 | 0.66 | 0.25 | 0.20 |
| $E_4$ | 1.26 | 0.99 | 0.70 | 0.58 |
| $E_5$ | 1.59 | 1.33 | 1.15 | 0.92 |
| $E_6$ | 1.85 | 1.51 | 1.33 | 1.16 |
| $E_7$ | 2.26 | 1.93 | 1.57 | 1.33 |

As might be expected, the education coefficients for both races are
higher for the simple model. The values of the *differences* in coefficients for successive levels of education are not altered, however. Thus
the conclusions reached in the discussion of Proposition 1 stand. In

particular, examination of the coefficients of the simple model confirms the fact that the differential advantage to the Malays from increased education is strongest at either end of the educational spectrum.

### Race, Education, and Poverty

The findings on the racial earnings functions should help to illuminate two different questions pertaining to race, educational attainment, and low earnings. First, does formal education help reduce the racial earnings gap among low earners? Second, are low earnings accounted for partly by the race of the earner, over and above what is accounted for by human capital factors?

The discussion above has shown that little of the average earnings disparity between the races is accounted for by differences in schooling—and whatever can be ascribed to this factor is significant only for the East Coast towns. Focusing on differences in average earnings could, however, obscure factors which lead to differences in the *shapes* of the racial earnings distributions. The conclusion from the racial earnings function amplifies one such point. Table 10-7 shows that both primary and secondary schooling substantially reduces the disparity in earnings between Malays and Chinese. In this sense, the government policy to encourage secondary education, together with the effect of public sector hiring of more educated Malays, has affected the racial gap at the lower end of the distribution. A similar effect can be seen at the upper end of the distribution, where university-educated Malays are shown to earn somewhat more than the Chinese.

The second question posed above can be partly answered by a comparison of the predicted distributions of earnings by earnings functions for the two races with the actual distributions. The distributions are plotted for the two races separately in Figure 10-2. In both cases there are larger percentages of earners than predicted at the lower and the upper ends of the distribution. At the lower end of the earnings distribution, the crossover point for the predicted and actual curves occurs at a higher income level for the Malays—M$101 to M$150—than for the Chinese. In addition, the percentage of male employees with lower actual monthly earnings than those predicted by their human capital attributes is rather large for the Malays:

|  | Less than M$100 | | Less than M$150 | | More than M$450 | |
|---|---|---|---|---|---|---|
|  | Actual | Predicted | Actual | Predicted | Actual | Predicted |
| Malay | 9.7 | 2.4 | 31.1 | 22.0 | 9.3 | 5.8 |
| Chinese | 9.5 | 2.0 | 18.8 | 13.9 | 12.0 | 9.6 |

Figure 10–2. Distribution of Actual and Predicted Earnings
among Malays and Chinese

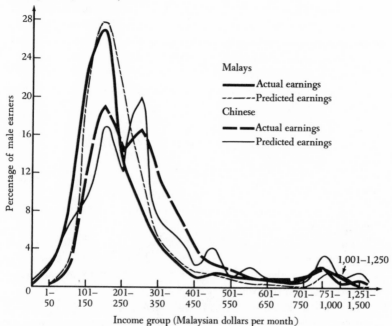

Income group (Malaysian dollars per month)

*Source:* MES, 1975, and derived data.

Thus, there appears to be some truth to the hypothesis that levels of earnings cannot be wholly accounted for by human capital factors; the extent to which actual values fall short of predicted ones at the lower end of the scale and exceed them at the upper end is substantially stronger for the Malays than for the Chinese. The above figures suggest, however, that the overall quantitative importance of this phenomenon is not very large.

## Age-Earnings Profiles

It has already been noted that studies of racial earnings differentiation in the United States have drawn attention to the disadvantage for blacks represented by the flatness of their age-earnings profile compared with that of whites. Such a difference between the profiles by race suggests that returns to experience as well as to education are significantly lower for the disadvantaged group. This is a consequence of the more limited opportunities for skill formation available to blacks. It will need to be established whether there is any hint of a similar disadvantage for the Malays in the sample analyzed here.

The coefficients of age and age² in the earnings functions reported in Table 10-5 are:

|         | Age   | Age²    |
|---------|-------|---------|
| Malay   | 0.112 | −0.0012 |
| Chinese | 0.133 | −0.0016 |

The higher coefficient for the Chinese suggests that their earnings do in fact grow at a higher rate than those of the Malays. But the age-earnings profile for the Malays cannot in any way be called flat; their earnings grow with age at a high absolute rate of 11 percent a year. The profiles are the normal U-shape for both races, although the curve is more pronounced (with a steeper rise and fall) for the Chinese. The coefficients show that the Chinese reach their maximum earnings at age forty-one, and the Malays at age forty-six.

This picture contrasts sharply with that observed for black-white income differences in the United States. Given that the relative economic position of the younger generation of Malays has improved in recent years (as it has for younger blacks in the United States), their age-earnings profile on the basis of cross-section data might be expected to be relatively flat. The fact that the coefficient of age has a high positive value in the Malays' earning function, despite this statistical effect, clearly shows that Malays do not suffer from a low return to experience.

## Conclusions

Chinese employees have an earnings advantage over Malays in the urban economy of Malaysia. The Malaysian experience does not, however, follow the general pattern observed in the classic case of the black-white differences in the United States, on which much of the economic literature about racial differences in earnings is based. In particular, the relative disadvantage of the Malays cannot be ascribed to their crowding into badly paid occupations. There is a perceptible racial segregation of the two major communities into broadly defined occupational groups, but the underrepresentation of Malays in semiskilled and skilled blue-collar jobs is balanced by their overrepresentation in the public sector and in a range of white-collar jobs.

The decomposition of the sources of racial difference in earnings identified the difference in average earnings within each occupational group (rather than differences in educational attainment or in the occupation-education matrix) as the principal factor. In fact, although the distribution of education is less favorable to the Malays in the East Coast (but not in Kuala Lumpur), the education-occupation matrix is *more* favorable to them in both regions. It was noted that the racial earnings gap, which can be ascribed to a difference in average earnings in the same occupational group, was larger in the East Coast towns. The discussion of the racial segregation of employees by establishments in the two sample regions suggested that the observed pattern was consistent with the predictions of the Becker hypothesis of employer discrimination.

This last point suggests that the economic return to education may be higher for the Malays than for the Chinese, a hypothesis in fact borne out by the study of racial earnings functions. Returns to education are substantially higher for the Malays at either end of the educational spectrum, although there does not seem to be a significant racial difference at the middle levels. The analysis revealed that the predicted earnings for the Malays were lowest for those without formal education, improved substantially with primary and lower secondary education, and actually were higher than those for the Chinese in the case of university-educated employees. Returns to experience are substantial for both racial groups and are not very different in magnitude.

The evidence presented in this chapter of a higher return to human capital for the relatively disadvantaged racial group is of major importance for the urban labor market of Malaysia and is in sharp contrast to the situation in the United States. It offers the possibility that in Malaysia the group with lower earnings can catch up with the favored group, given increased investment in human capital resources. Clearly the role of public sector employment and wage policy is crucial in achieving this state of affairs for the disadvantaged group. The "vintage effect" noticed at the beginning of this chapter (which tends to reduce the returns to education and experience in a cross-section analysis for blacks in the United States) will also be statistically significant for the Malays in Malaysia; thus the evidence of higher returns to the human capital factors in their case, in spite of the statistical bias, is particularly encouraging.

# CHAPTER 11

# Migration

THIS CHAPTER PRESENTS A SHORT ACCOUNT of the process of migration in Malaysian urban labor markets, based on data from the 1975 World Bank Migration and Employment Survey (MES). The survey questionnaire began by identifying migrants as those born outside the towns of enumeration, and then established some details about the characteristics of migration. Some basic facts about the scale of migration in Malaysia are given below, followed by comparative data on the economic characteristics of migrant and native urban residents. The influence of the size and nature of the migrants' community of origin on their economic characteristics is assessed, as well as the extent to which the flows of migrants represent only temporary moves, as opposed to long-term resettlement.

Questioning migrants in the towns to which they have migrated, as was done in the MES, yields only partial data. Important information about economic conditions in the migrants' areas of origin which may have influenced their decision to migrate can best be derived from a survey directed at would-be migrants or members of migrants' families who have stayed behind. Moreover, the migrant population identified by the MES (residents of Kuala Lumpur, Kuantan, and Kota Bharu who were born elsewhere) is likely to include mainly migrants who have succeeded in the town of enumeration; it does not provide any information about return flows of migrants back to their place of origin. Despite these limitations, some points of interest about migration emerge from the data.

The extent of migration in Malaysia (including both rural-urban movement and migration from one town to another) is illustrated by the fact that nearly 60 percent of the sample in Kuala Lumpur and 55 percent in the two coastal towns were not born in the cities where they now live and work. There is an important racial difference in the capital, but not in the coastal towns; a quite extraordinary proportion of the Malay population in Kuala Lumpur (83 percent) was born outside the city.

Table 11-1. Percentage of Migrants in the Total Urban Sample
and in Each Race for Each Age Group

| Age group | Total urban sample | Malay | Chinese | Indian |
|---|---|---|---|---|
| 15–19 | 100.0 | 100.0 | . . . | . . . |
| 20–24 | 76.7 | 87.0 | 53.3 | 60.0 |
| 25–29 | 66.2 | 80.1 | 48.2 | 34.2 |
| 30–34 | 53.6 | 64.9 | 41.6 | 55.0 |
| 35–39 | 58.1 | 71.0 | 47.6 | 55.6 |
| 40–44 | 49.1 | 49.5 | 49.5 | 43.7 |
| 45–49 | 45.8 | 49.5 | 41.4 | 50.0 |
| 50 and over | 30.8 | 40.6 | 25.3 | . . . |
| Total | 55.1 | 66.4 | 43.6 | 49.2 |

. . . Zero or negligible.
Source: MES, 1975.

Table 11-1 gives the percentage of migrants in each age group of the sample—for the three cities pooled together—broken down by race. The proportion of migrants is highest among Malays for all age groups, and astonishingly high among those under the age of thirty.

The definition of migration by place of birth lumps several different types of geographical movement together. People born elsewhere could have moved as children to the town where they were surveyed. As adults they might have moved directly to the town, or they might have stopped at one or more intermediate points for varying lengths of time. The two types of adult migrants can be called "one-shot" and "stage" migrants respectively. Other types of movement are also possible. Those born in the town surveyed (and those who had arrived as migrants of one type or another) might have moved to another location for a period and returned to the town of the survey. Movement of this kind can be called "circulatory" migration.

Stage migration appears to be of unusual importance in Malaysia. It is even more common in Kuala Lumpur than in the East Coast towns, but it represents the dominant migratory pattern in both regions and accounts for between two-thirds and three-quarters of the adult migrants to the towns surveyed. Stopping temporarily at a place adjacent to the three towns of enumeration is a strong possibility in a country such as Malaysia, and all migrants doing this would be classed as stage migrants. The intermediate stops were made in different types of communities: 27.2 percent in rural areas, 37.7 percent in towns of 10,000–75,000 inhabitants, 27.8 percent in metropolitan areas,[1] and 7.4 percent in major towns, that is, all other large towns with populations of more than 75,000. The percentage recorded for those who had stopped in a metropolitan area would include those who had settled in the environs of Kuala Lumpur before coming to the city itself. Nevertheless, the phenomenon of the intermediate stop—particularly in small towns and other rural areas—is an unusual and interesting feature of migration in Malaysia, and more than half the stage migrants made more than one intermediate stop. The overall picture, therefore, becomes one of a very fluid, geographically mobile population.

## Migrants and Natives

The first point to establish in an assessment of migration is how well the migrants perform in their community of adoption. Whereas the rate of return to migration can be gauged only by comparison with the economic conditions of those who did not migrate, useful insights can be gained by comparing the performance of migrants with that of natives in the towns where the survey was conducted.

### Education

Since the expansion of the education system has been more rapid in urban areas, migrants from the hinterland will be less exposed to educational progress. If migrants have a higher level of education (controlling for age), it can be hypothesized either that better-educated adults have a disproportionate tendency to migrate or that child migrants have a high propensity for education.

Table 11-2 shows that in Kuala Lumpur the level of education is higher for migrants of all ages, except the oldest group (41–50), and for all races. The pattern is different in the East Coast. Generally, migrants under the age of thirty seem to be less educated than the natives, while those over thirty have somewhat more education. For the sample in the East Coast as a whole—without reference to age groups—an interesting racial difference is that Malay migrants are more educated than Chinese, a finding which may be based on a relation between the age and race of migrants.

---

1. Metropolitan areas are Georgetown, Johore Bahru, Kuala Lumpur, and Ipoh.

Table 11-2. Mean Values of Education for Migrants and Natives
by Age, Race, and Region

| | Kuala Lumpur | | East Coast | |
| Age and race | Migrants | Natives | Migrants | Natives |
|---|---|---|---|---|
| Age group | | | | |
| 15–20 | 3.31 | 2.94 | 2.85 | 3.43 |
| 21–25 | 3.14 | 3.04 | 2.90 | 2.92 |
| 26–30 | 3.51 | 3.12 | 2.69 | 2.79 |
| 31–35 | 2.91 | 2.65 | 2.83 | 2.49 |
| 36–40 | 3.06 | 2.48 | 2.44 | 2.49 |
| 41–50 | 2.37 | 2.61 | 2.00 | 1.85 |
| Race | | | | |
| Malay | 2.96 | 2.85 | 2.81 | 2.21 |
| Chinese | 3.07 | 2.68 | 2.68 | 3.02 |
| Indian and other | 3.50 | 3.48 | 3.48 | 2.56 |
| All | 3.05 | 2.81 | 2.59 | 2.46 |
| Entire population | 2.96 | | 2.53 | |

Note: The values are means of distribution by educational categories scaled from
0 to 7.
Source: MES, 1975.

More detailed analyses of the data by age and education groups (not
shown here) suggest a point that does not emerge in the summary figure: for both regions, migrants with primary education or with a
school certificate are heavily overrepresented in the youngest age group
(15–25). The large proportion of migrants with these qualifications by
comparison with natives is balanced by a comparatively low representation of migrants with some secondary education. It is plausible to
suppose that secondary education has spread more rapidly in the urban
areas in which the natives were brought up. At the same time, most of
those from areas of migration that offer secondary education do in fact
migrate if they have obtained a school certificate.

The differences between migrants and natives are less marked at
levels of education other than those just mentioned. The detailed data
confirm the fact noted above that, among the older age groups in Kuala
Lumpur, the migrants are better educated—the point of inflection coming at the level of "passed school certificate." There is a clear racial
difference between Kuala Lumpur and the East Coast towns in the
comparative educational patterns of migrants and natives; Chinese
migrants are less educated in the latter areas, the divergence again being
at the school certificate level.

*Earnings*

The differences in the mean earnings levels of migrants and natives are given in Table 11-3. Migrants as a whole appear to earn more than natives, but the age distribution of earnings is noticeably different. In both regions migrants in the youngest age group earn less than natives in the same age group, and it is only in the 26–30 age group that they draw level before pulling ahead later. The difference in earnings between the two major races is exactly the opposite in the two regions. In Kuala Lumpur, native Malays earn more than migrants of the same race, and Chinese migrants earn more than native Chinese; this pattern is reversed in the East Coast.

The gross income comparisons do not take account of the many factors affecting earnings and their varying importance for migrants and natives. For example, it has been shown that migrants and natives in both regions have differing educational levels; a valid comparison of the performance of migrants and natives in a particular urban labor market must therefore control for the effects of education on earnings. Thus, earnings functions have been computed for migrants and natives in the

Table 11-3. Mean Income for Migrants and Natives
by Age, Race, and Region
(Malaysian dollars per month)

| Age and race | Kuala Lumpur | | East Coast | |
|---|---|---|---|---|
| | Migrants | Natives | Migrants | Natives |
| *Age group* | | | | |
| 15–20 | 200 | 255 | 179 | 193 |
| 21–25 | 340 | 337 | 199 | 236 |
| 26–30 | 452 | 415 | 282 | 256[a] |
| 31–35 | 466 | 339 | 342 | 361 |
| 36–40 | 515 | 354 | 359 | 283[a] |
| 41–50 | 449 | 520 | 275 | 234 |
| *Race* | | | | |
| Malay | 342 | 371 | 219 | 190[a] |
| Chinese | 555 | 379 | 441 | 517 |
| Indian and other | 551 | 518 | 480 | 201[a] |
| All | 436 | 400 | 290 | 267[a] |
| Entire population | 423 | | 280 | |

a. Significantly different at 90 percent level of confidence.
*Source:* MES, 1975.

two regions separately, using education, experience,[2] race, and type of business as explanatory variables. The analysis is confined to male employees only because of the uncertainties associated with the calculation of earnings functions for the self-employed noted previously. The results are presented in Table 11-4.

The coefficients of the computed equations can be used to calculate migrants' and natives' experience-earnings profiles (see Figures 11-1 and 11-2). The intercepts of the profiles are calculated by adding to the constants of the respective regression equations the additional earnings of the sample attributable to variables other than experience (the contributions of the variables being determined by the proportion of each category in the sample). In the case of Kuala Lumpur, the experience coefficient for migrants is larger than that for natives. Hence, as the figure shows, the net difference in earnings in favor of the migrants is quite modest to begin with, but continues to increase until the peak of the experience-earnings profile is reached for the migrants at thirty-two years of experience. By contrast, the experience coefficient of the earnings function of migrants in the East Coast is smaller than that of natives. Figures 11-1 and 11-2 therefore show a narrowing of the earnings difference over the years and a crossover in the two groups' experience-earnings profiles. Since the initial difference in earnings (the intercept) in the East Coast is quite strongly favorable to the migrants, the earnings of the two groups are equalized only at thirty-six years of experience. Thus, migrants earn significantly more than natives over most of their working lives in both regions, after allowance is made for education and other factors that influence earnings.

It is also apparent from the figures that although the earnings difference in favor of migrants in the East Coast diminishes over their working lives, it is much larger in the East Coast than in Kuala Lumpur for the early years. In fact, it is not until the two racial groups have accumulated twenty years of experience that the relative difference is of the same magnitude in the two regions. A comparison of the values of the constant terms in the regression equations for the migrants and the natives in the two regions shows that the larger relative difference in the East Coast is attributable to the better overall performance of the migrants rather than to their having a markedly different mix of the variables included in the regression models. This evidence of a higher

---

2. Experience is defined as the actual age minus an estimated value of the "normal" age of a person having the particular level of education.

Table 11-4. Earnings Regression for Migrants and Natives, Both Regions, Male Employees Only

| | Natives | | | Migrants | | |
|---|---|---|---|---|---|---|
| Variable | Proportion in sample | Coefficient | t-ratio | Proportion in sample | Coefficient | t-ratio |
| | | | Kuala Lumpur | | | |
| Education | | | | | | |
| Primary | 0.42 | 0.48 | 3.67 | 0.39 | 0.34 | 1.78 |
| Some secondary | 0.36 | 0.69 | 5.07 | 0.28 | 0.68 | 3.44 |
| Passed school certificate | 0.11 | 1.26 | 8.46 | 0.20 | 1.24 | 6.21 |
| Passed higher school | 0.01 | 1.67 | 7.35 | 0.02 | 1.84 | 7.58 |
| Technical college diploma | 0.01 | 1.82 | 6.28 | 0.02 | 2.16 | 9.18 |
| University degree | 0.03 | 2.12 | 10.94 | 0.05 | 2.61 | 12.07 |
| Experience (years) | 17.49 | 0.080 | 9.39 | 15.24 | 0.092 | 10.00 |
| Experience$^2$ | 433.32 | −0.001 | −6.60 | 316.97 | −0.001 | −6.12 |
| Race | | | | | | |
| Chinese | 0.72 | 0.208 | 2.76 | 0.33 | 0.164 | 3.25 |
| Indian and other | 0.13 | 0.105 | 1.06 | 0.08 | 0.080 | 1.02 |

208

East Coast

| Education | | | | | | |
|---|---|---|---|---|---|---|
| Primary | 0.51 | 0.59 | 6.12 | 0.48 | 0.18 | 1.95 |
| Some secondary | 0.21 | 0.98 | 8.35 | 0.19 | 0.54 | 5.02 |
| Passed school certificate | 0.14 | 1.48 | 11.91 | 0.19 | 0.98 | 9.07 |
| Passed higher school | 0.02 | 1.98 | 9.46 | 0.03 | 1.27 | 7.71 |
| Technical college diploma | 0.01 | 2.20 | 6.22 | 0.02 | 1.64 | 8.24 |
| University degree | 0.01 | 2.53 | 7.13 | 0.02 | 1.70 | 9.89 |
| | | | | | | |
| Experience (years) | 19.09 | 0.098 | 10.257 | 16.85 | 0.073 | 9.01 |
| Experience$^2$ | 491.9 | -0.001 | -7.13 | 378.9 | -0.001 | -6.56 |
| | | | | | | |
| Race | | | | | | |
| Chinese | 0.29 | 0.334 | 5.25 | 0.23 | 0.286 | 5.16 |
| Indian and other | 0.04 | 0.039 | 0.28 | 0.07 | 0.330 | 3.95 |

*Note:* The dependent variable is the log of earnings. The category "no schooling" is the omitted variable for education, and Malays for race. The coefficients of the education and race dummies thus give the increment of the log of earnings over the omitted categories.
*Source:* MES, 1975.

Figure 11–1. Experience-Earnings Profiles for Migrants and Natives, Male Only: Kuala Lumpur

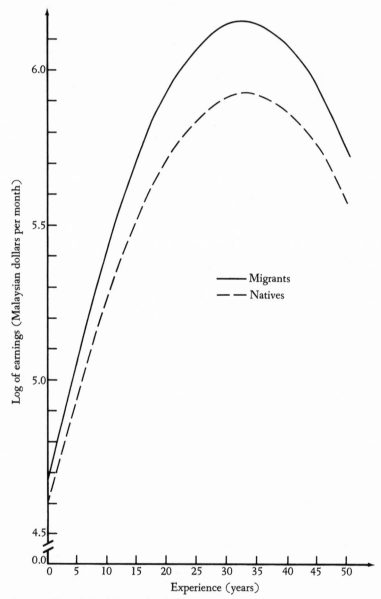

*Source:* Data derived from MES, 1975.

Figure 11–2. Experience-Earnings Profiles for Migrants
and Natives, Male Only: East Coast

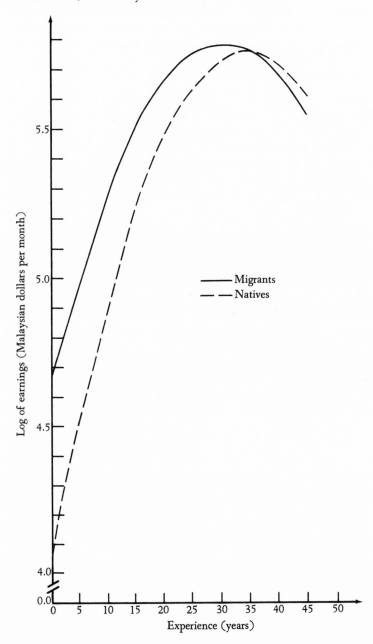

return to migration in the growing labor markets of the East Coast, as against the established market of the capital, is of considerable general interest.

## Background of Migrants

This section discusses the effect of the size and nature of the migrants' community of origin on their economic characteristics, and whether this effect is significantly different for different racial or age groups. Table 11-5 gives the percentages of migrants to Kuala Lumpur and the East Coast towns from communities of different sizes. In grouping the communities of origin, four large metropolitan areas (Kuala Lumpur, Georgetown, Ipoh, and Johore Bahru and their suburbs) were taken together because the total number of migrants from these areas was relatively small, and they could be expected to behave in a similar manner and to have similar characteristics.

The most striking point is the extent to which migrants to both the capital and the two coastal towns come from relatively urbanized areas.

Table 11-5. Percentage Distribution of Migrants to Kuala Lumpur and the East Coast by Size of Community of Origin and by Race

| Community of origin | Malay | Chinese | Indian and other | Total |
|---|---|---|---|---|
| | | *To Kuala Lumpur* | | |
| Towns of 75,000 or more | 9.8 | 15.9 | 17.9 | 12.9 |
| Metropolitan areas[a] | 5.6 | 17.9 | 21.3 | 12.0 |
| Towns with 10,000–75,000 | 36.0 | 31.4 | 30.4 | 33.7 |
| Towns with less than 10,000 and rural areas | 48.6 | 34.7 | 30.4 | 41.4 |
| Total | 100.0 | 100.0 | 100.0 | 100.0 |
| | | *To East Coast towns* | | |
| Towns of 75,000 or more | 3.9 | 12.9 | 7.4 | 6.6 |
| Metropolitan areas[a] | 1.5 | 24.1 | 18.5 | 8.7 |
| Towns with 10,000–75,000 | 45.2 | 30.2 | 37.0 | 40.7 |
| Towns with less than 10,000 and rural areas | 49.5 | 32.8 | 37.0 | 44.0 |
| Total | 100.0 | 100.0 | 100.0 | 100.0 |

Note: Columns may not add to 100 because of rounding.
a. The four metropolitan regions centered in the cities of Kuala Lumpur, Georgetown, Ipoh, and Johore Bahru.
Source: MES, 1975.

The supposition that domestic flows of migrants to large towns in Asia are principally rural-urban in character appears to be false for Malaysia; in both regions about half the Malay migrants and more than two-thirds of the Chinese migrants follow an urban-to-urban pattern. In conjunction with the predominance of stage migration noted earlier, the Malaysian picture is more akin to that described by Bruce Herrick for Chile than it is to that for Asia or Africa.[3] Admittedly, the bulk of the urban-to-urban migrants come from the smaller towns, but in Malaysia all communities with less than 10,000 people are defined as rural. The difference in size of community of origin by migrants' racial group is interesting; very few Malay migrants (especially to the East Coast towns) come from the larger towns or cities, but the Chinese from these areas make up about a third of the total migrants in both regions.

To retain an impression of the changing importance of various sources of migration over time, the migrants were broken down into three broad age groups for Malays and Chinese separately; Indians and others were too few to permit a division of this nature and were ignored. The data are not shown here, but the principal findings are: (1) For migrants to Kuala Lumpur, the type of community of origin did not vary by age for the Malays, but there was a distinct shift to urban origin for the younger Chinese. While migrants from rural areas made up a roughly constant 48 percent of all age groups among the Malays, the corresponding percentages among the Chinese fell markedly from 41.5 percent for the older age group to 24.3 percent for the young—who had significantly higher levels of migration from the smaller towns as well as from the four metropolitan areas. (2) In the East Coast towns, rural areas were again the principal source of Malay migrants, but more younger migrants came from the smaller towns than from the larger urban areas. Among the Chinese, far more young migrants came from outlying large towns and far fewer from the metropolitan areas. There thus seems to have been some diffusion over time of the sources of Chinese migration to the East Coast towns, with the less urbanized areas a more important source for the younger age groups. This is the reverse of the pattern for Kuala Lumpur.

3. Bruce H. Herrick, *Urban Migration and Economic Development in Chile* (Cambridge, Mass.: MIT Press, 1966). In a recent study of the Bombay labor market it was found that most migrants to the city came from rural areas (Dipak Mazumdar, "Paradigms in the Analysis of Urban Labor Markets in LDCs: A Reassessment in the Light of an Empirical Survey in Bombay City," World Bank Staff Working Paper no. 366 [Washington, D.C., December 1979]).

Tables 11-6 and 11-7 present data for the sample of migrants in the two regions by education and race. The very small proportion of the group with higher school certificate or above makes it necessary to concentrate the analysis on those with primary education and less and those with secondary schooling. The tables show that the rural areas and the small towns supply broadly similar proportions of migrants at both levels of education. In Kuala Lumpur, as one would expect, a larger proportion of those with secondary schooling come from small towns than from a rural background, but as many as 39 percent of the Malays and 28 percent of the Chinese with this level of education are of rural origin. Conversely, rather less than half the Chinese and just a little more than half the Malays with primary education or less came from rural areas. In the East Coast towns the proportion of Malay migrants from rural areas with secondary education (57 percent) is 10 percentage points higher than that for those with primary education (47 percent), while the share of Chinese migrants from rural areas is practically the same

Table 11-6. Percentage Distribution of Migrants to Kuala Lumpur by Size of Community of Origin and by Educational Level

| Community of origin | Educational group | | |
|---|---|---|---|
| | Primary or less | Secondary | Higher school certificate |
| *Malay* | | | |
| Towns of 75,000 or more | 9.6 | 11.4 | 5.6 |
| Metropolitan areas | 3.6 | 7.1 | 11.1 |
| Towns with 10,000–75,000 | 31.7 | 43.0 | 33.3 |
| Towns with less than 10,000 and rural areas | 55.1 | 38.6 | 50.0 |
| Total | 100.0 | 100.0 | 100.0 |
| Proportion in sample | 52.7 | 36.0 | 11.4 |
| *Chinese* | | | |
| Towns of 75,000 or more | 15.3 | 14.2 | 25.0 |
| Metropolitan areas | 10.8 | 24.5 | 21.4 |
| Towns with 10,000–75,000 | 30.6 | 33.0 | 28.6 |
| Towns with less than 10,000 and rural areas | 43.2 | 28.3 | 25.0 |
| Total | 100.0 | 100.0 | 100.0 |
| Proportion in sample | 45.3 | 43.3 | 11.4 |

Source: MES, 1975.

Table 11-7. Percentage Distribution of Migrants to the East Coast by Size of Community of Origin and by Educational Level

| Community of origin | Educational group | | |
| | Primary or less | Secondary | Higher school certificate |
| --- | --- | --- | --- |
| *Malay* | | | |
| Towns of 75,000 or more | 3.6 | 5.6 | 0.0 |
| Metropolitan areas | 2.0 | 0.0 | 0.0 |
| Towns with 10,000–75,000 | 47.7 | 37.5 | 50.0 |
| Towns with less than 10,000 and rural areas | 46.7 | 56.9 | 50.0 |
| Total | 100.0 | 100.0 | 100.0 |
| Proportion in sample | 69.4 | 25.6 | 5.0 |
| *Chinese* | | | |
| Towns of 75,000 or more | 9.4 | 15.3 | 25.0 |
| Metropolitan areas | 27.4 | 23.8 | 0.0 |
| Towns with 10,000–75,000 | 30.2 | 28.8 | 50.0 |
| Towns with less than 10,000 and rural areas | 34.0 | 32.2 | 25.0 |
| Total | 100.0 | 100.0 | 100.0 |
| Proportion in sample | 45.7 | 50.9 | 3.4 |

*Source:* MES, 1975.

for the two education groups. Another interesting feature of the migration pattern is that while Chinese migrants with primary education, as well as those at the secondary level, come in sizable proportions from the large towns with populations of 75,000 or more, this is not the case for Malays.

Table 11-8 gives data on the geographical origins of migrants, showing that Malay migrants seem generally to move shorter distances than do the Chinese. This pattern is plainly apparent for migrants to Kuala Lumpur. Almost all the Malays come from the West Coast states and more than 50 percent come from the southwest and south. The Chinese come from more varied geographical backgrounds. Pahang contributes 10 percent and Perak the highest proportion of 33 percent. The share of migration from the south is smaller, but it still constitutes a significant percentage of the total.

The pattern for the coastal towns is less clear, because the two towns from which the sample was collected are fairly far apart and in different

Table 11-8. State of Origin of Migrants to Kuala Lumpur
and the East Coast by Race
(percent)

| | Kuala Lumpur | | | East Coast | | |
|---|---|---|---|---|---|---|
| State of origin | Malay | Chinese | Indian and other | Malay | Chinese | Indian and other |
| Selangor | 20.5 | 22.0 | 26.8 | 1.8 | 17.2 | 25.9 |
| Negri Sembilan | 12.3 | 6.5 | 8.9 | 1.8 | 7.8 | 3.7 |
| Malacca | 15.1 | 8.2 | 5.4 | 3.2 | 2.6 | 7.4 |
| Johore | 13.2 | 8.6 | 8.9 | 2.8 | 10.3 | 11.1 |
| Pahang | 0.9 | 10.2 | 3.6 | 14.6 | 14.7 | 14.8 |
| Trengganu | 1.6 | 0.4 | 0.0 | 23.8 | 10.3 | 0.0 |
| Kelantan | 3.2 | 0.0 | 1.8 | 45.6 | 12.9 | 11.1 |
| Perak | 18.9 | 32.7 | 32.1 | 3.6 | 18.1 | 22.2 |
| Penang | 5.7 | 9.4 | 10.7 | 1.1 | 5.2 | 3.7 |
| Kedah | 8.5 | 2.0 | 1.8 | 1.8 | 0.9 | 0.0 |
| Total | 100.0 | 100.0 | 100.0 | 100.0 | 100.0 | 100.0 |

Source: MES, 1975.

states. The difference between the mobility of the races, in terms of distance moved, nevertheless persists. Trengganu and Kelantan (the two home states) contribute 70 percent of the Malay migrant sample but only 23 percent of the Chinese. Perak is still an important source of Chinese migrants, and Selangor and Johore also contribute proportionately more Chinese migrants than Malays. Thus, it appears that Malays tend to move to a city from neighboring areas, but that the Chinese tend to come from certain areas that are general sources of migration to different cities, and to have better defined migration streams than the Malays.

Table 11-9 presents migrants' estimates of their families' economic status at the time of their departure from their place of birth, subdivided by the migrants' races and educational levels. Although these estimates are subjective and subject to all the biases inherent in self-assessment, the data by race show a fairly consistent pattern. Three of the four groups in the table are divided about two to one between average and below average status; the Malay migrants to Kuala Lumpur give a different estimate, with only 20 percent reporting a below average background. Very few migrants said that they came from an above average background. The breakdown of the migrants' perceptions of their families' economic status by their own educational attainments confirms the expected linkage between perceived economic status and educational level. Migrants to the East Coast towns with primary education or less tend to have come from humbler family economic backgrounds than those at the same educational level who migrated to Kuala Lumpur; at higher levels of education, however, migrants to the East Coast have a somewhat higher family status than those to Kuala Lumpur. This probably reflects the relatively slow spread of postprimary education into the more depressed areas which supply migrants to the East Coast towns.

A more objective picture of migrants' socioeconomic backgrounds can be obtained by looking at the occupational group to which their families belonged and, for those with a farming background, examining the amounts of land owned and the use made of it. The importance of urban-to-urban and stage migration in Malaysia is linked to the fact that although farming is the single most important occupation of the typical migrant's family, it is not nearly so overwhelmingly important as in

Table 11-9. Migrants' Family Economic Status by Destination, Educational Level, and Race of Migrants

| Destination, education, and race | Family economic status | | | |
|---|---|---|---|---|
| | Above average | About average | Below average | Don't know |
| Kuala Lumpur | | | | |
| Education | | | | |
| Primary | 1.8 | 63.6 | 32.5 | 2.1 |
| Secondary | 6.3 | 70.1 | 22.5 | 1.1 |
| Higher school certificate or above | 12.2 | 67.1 | 19.5 | 1.2 |
| Race | | | | |
| Malay | 5.8 | 71.8 | 21.8 | 0.6 |
| Chinese | 3.0 | 62.9 | 31.8 | 2.3 |
| East Coast | | | | |
| Education | | | | |
| Primary | 0.6 | 55.0 | 41.9 | 2.4 |
| Secondary | 5.6 | 71.3 | 19.7 | 3.4 |
| Higher school certificate or above | 20.7 | 69.0 | 10.3 | 0.0 |
| Race | | | | |
| Malay | 3.3 | 61.3 | 32.9 | 2.5 |
| Chinese | 3.5 | 59.6 | 34.8 | 2.1 |

Source: MES, 1975.

many other developing countries. Farming accounted for 29 percent of migrants' families' occupations in the Kuala Lumpur sample and for 48 percent in the East Coast towns, but there are important racial differences in the composition of these percentages. In both regions Chinese migrants with agricultural backgrounds made up approximately the same proportion of the total—around 20 percent. But the proportions of Malay migrants to the two urban areas from farming families was sharply different—62 percent in the coastal towns as against only 37 percent in Kuala Lumpur. The other major racial difference in family occupational backgrounds is the substantially higher proportion of Chinese migrants who came from sales and blue-collar (production work) backgrounds. Proportionately more Malays than Chinese in both regions came from service occupations.

Tables 11-10 and 11-11 give data on migrants' families' landholdings by race and destination of migrants. The tables show the proportions of families by use and ownership of land, the distribution of landholdings by size, and the breakdown of those who used land for growing com-

Table 11-10. Migrants' Families' Land Use and Size of Landholding by Race and Destination of Migrants
(percent)

| Families' land use and size of holding | Kuala Lumpur | | | East Coast | | |
|---|---|---|---|---|---|---|
| | Malay | Chinese | Total | Malay | Chinese | Total |
| Land use | | | | | | |
| Growing food | 44.8 | 15.1 | 30.1 | 45.9 | 8.6 | 33.5 |
| Commercial crops | 40.4 | 14.3 | 26.7 | 25.6 | 10.3 | 20.0 |
| Both purposes | 64.4 | 21.2 | 42.9 | 53.7 | 18.1 | 41.3 |
| Some family business | 13.2 | 21.2 | 16.5 | 9.6 | 18.1 | 12.5 |
| Owned all the land used | 89.2 | 61.5 | 82.3 | 82.1 | 33.3 | 76.6 |
| Landholding (acres) | | | | | | |
| 0–1 | 9.8 | 15.7 | 12.5 | 7.3 | 28.6 | 10.3 |
| 1–2 | 15.1 | 7.8 | 13.2 | 15.2 | 14.3 | 14.9 |
| 2–3 | 15.1 | 15.7 | 14.7 | 21.9 | 4.8 | 19.4 |
| 3–4 | 11.7 | 5.9 | 10.2 | 15.2 | 14.3 | 14.9 |
| 4–5 | 8.3 | 2.0 | 6.8 | 11.9 | 0.0 | 10.9 |
| 5–6 | 10.2 | 5.9 | 9.1 | 6.6 | 9.5 | 6.9 |
| 6–10 | 13.2 | 5.9 | 11.3 | 10.6 | 4.8 | 9.7 |
| 10–15 | 7.8 | 13.7 | 9.4 | 7.3 | 9.5 | 8.0 |
| 15 and more | 8.8 | 27.5 | 12.8 | 4.0 | 14.3 | 5.1 |

Source: MES, 1975.

Table 11-11. Commercial Use of Land by Migrants' Families
by Race and Destination of Migrants
(percent)

| Amount of landholding used for commercial crops | Kuala Lumpur | | | East Coast | | |
|---|---|---|---|---|---|---|
| | Malay | Chinese | Total | Malay | Chinese | Total |
| At least three-quarters | 40.5 | 31.4 | 38.1 | 21.2 | 52.4 | 25.1 |
| At least half | 50.7 | 31.4 | 46.0 | 30.5 | 57.2 | 33.7 |
| At least one-quarter | 60.9 | 60.8 | 59.6 | 43.7 | 57.2 | 45.1 |
| At least some | 62.4 | 66.7 | 61.9 | 47.7 | 57.2 | 48.5 |
| None | 37.6 | 33.3 | 38.1 | 52.3 | 42.9 | 51.5 |

Source: MES, 1975.

mercial crops. The information helps to define the migrant group's overall economic status and highlights some important interracial and geographic differences within it.

It has already been noted that many more Malay than Chinese migrants come from farming backgrounds, notably in the East Coast; and Table 11-10 shows that a correspondingly higher proportion of Malay families used land for growing either food or commercial crops in both regions. In fact, the proportion of Malay migrants to Kuala Lumpur who say that their families use land for growing food (45 percent) is considerably higher than the proportion who gave farming as their families' principal occupation (37 percent). This suggests that many families had small holdings for growing food crops as a subsidiary occupation. No such phenomenon is observed in the East Coast towns, which is consistent with the fact that a larger proportion of migrants to these urban areas said that they had come from families of below average economic status. A much larger proportion of the East Coast migrants' families apparently used their land for subsistence agriculture only.

The Chinese migrants to the two regions appear to have similar patterns of family land use; about 20 percent of their families made use of land for growing both food and commercial crops (Table 11-10). In contrast to the Malays, however, the proportion of Chinese migrants' families using most of their land for commercial crops is *higher* in the East Coast than in Kuala Lumpur (Table 11-11).

Table 11-11 shows that, in spite of some interracial and interregional difference, the bulk of the migrants did *not* come from subsistence farming households, that is, those that used none of their land for commercial crops. Even the group with the highest proportion of subsistence farmers—the Malays of the East Coast—recorded just over half their families as using their land for subsistence only.

Although a significant proportion of migrants' families owned the land they used, the extent of ownership was lower for the Chinese, especially for families of Chinese migrants to the East Coast towns. The distribution of total landholdings also varies substantially by race, with more extreme variations in the size of holding for the Chinese migrants' families than for the Malays. While some of the former appear to have been large landholders, a relatively large proportion (16 percent for the Chinese in Kuala Lumpur and 29 percent in the East Coast) had very small holdings of an acre or less; the corresponding figures for the Malays' families are 10 percent and 7 percent, respectively. In contrast, 41 percent of the Chinese in Kuala Lumpur and 24 percent in the coastal towns recorded more than ten acres of family land; the corresponding figures for the Malays were 17 percent and 11 percent in the two regions, respectively.

The survey also provided data about migrants' links with their places of birth. Overall, these links appear to be weak, suggesting that migration into the towns surveyed was not temporary, with the migrants returning to their native towns after a limited time. According to data not reproduced here, only one-sixth of the migrants in Kuala Lumpur said that they had a place to which they could return if they were out of a job. Of these, 55 percent said they were able to return to a family business, and 35 percent, to a family smallholding. This figure is of special interest when it is recalled that the overall sample proportions for those with a family business were much lower than those coming from families with landholdings. It appears, then, that those with some form of family business maintain stronger connections with their place of origin than the sample as a whole. Further, when the migrants were grouped by size of community of origin, it was found that those who came from rural areas or small towns had even weaker links with their place of origin than the sample as a whole. Of those who had links with their birthplace, 28 percent and 30 percent came from small towns and rural areas, respectively, whereas the proportions coming from these areas for the sample as a whole are 34 percent and 41 percent. It also appears that very few of the small proportion who did visit their family landholdings outside Kuala Lumpur actually work on them. About 90 percent classified their last visit to the place where they had their family holding as purely social, and most of these visits were of short duration (less than two weeks). Nearly 60 percent of this group of migrants had visited their family holding in the three months before the date of interview, suggesting that they had only a short distance to travel for these visits.

The pattern for the East Coast is similar but, surprisingly, the proportion of migrants with a place to fall back on was even lower than in Kuala Lumpur (about one-eighth), and nearly all of them came from families with some form of business, rather than a smallholding. Again, half of those who had visited their place of family business had done so within the previous three months, but the length of visits was less than two weeks for almost all of them (98 percent).

## Degree of Permanence

This section briefly discusses the relation between sectoral differences in wages and the degree of permanence of migration, examining the hypothesis that the level of earnings in the informal sector might be relatively low because of the large number of temporary migrants in this sector. In Chapter 6 this conclusion was suggested by alternative theories of urban wage determination. In the Harris-Todaro model wages in the formal sector are maintained at a high level by institutional factors, but because migrants use the informal sector to enter the urban labor market in the expectation of eventually getting a well-paid job in the formal sector, wages in the informal sector are depressed. In the Mazumdar hypothesis, wages in the informal sector are geared to the supply price of individual short-term migrants; this is lower than the supply price of more permanent family migrants in the formal sector because of the greater efficiency of the more stable labor supply. Chapter 9 showed that differences in earnings do exist by enterprise size, after allowance is made for human capital factors for each occupational group,[4] so that it is worth investigating the hypotheses about migration and wages for the employees in the different categories of firms. It would also be useful to look at the self-employed separately, on the assumption that a large proportion of them would be in the informal sector.

Temporary migration can mean two different things. It can refer to seasonal migrants who work in the city for part of the year, but who also

4. The differences in earnings are, however, not nearly so great as in some other urban labor markets, for example, in Bombay.

take part in economic activity in their rural areas of origin. The Malaysian labor markets covered by the MES do not appear to contain any significant number of migrants who are temporary in this sense. As noted above, half the migrants had visited their place of origin during the three months before their interviews, but most of their visits were of less than two weeks. About 90 percent classified their last visit as purely social.

A second interpretation of temporary migration takes account of the prevalence of migrants who return to their place of origin after a few years, when the balance of economic advantage (and social pressure) shifts against the urban area. Unfortunately, no accurate quantitative measure of return migration can be obtained from a single survey in an urban area. Generally, a labor market with substantial proportions of recent migrants, single migrants, or household heads without their families will be likely to have a high incidence of return migration; in the Malaysian case, however, only a qualitative judgment can be made.

Despite the high levels of migration to the three cities surveyed, the number of single persons or even small families among the migrants is very small. Only about 5 percent of the migrant households in the sample consisted of one person; another 10 percent were two-member families. Even among very recent migrants—those who had lived for one year or less in the cities—the proportion of single-member households was only 10 percent, and that of two-member families another 20 percent. These percentage levels are in sharp contrast to the figures for the Bombay labor market in which return migration is a significant phenomenon. In the Bombay study single-member families accounted for 45 percent of all migrant households in the casual sector, 49 percent of the total in the small-scale sector, and 28 percent in the factory sector of the labor market.[5]

The distribution of migrants by duration (the number of years at their destination) is largely as might be expected in labor markets that are growing rapidly as a consequence of migration. The percentage distribution of the sample by duration (years since migration) is:

| 1 or less | 6–10 | 11–15 | 16–20 | 21–25 | 26–30 | 31 or more | Natives |
|---|---|---|---|---|---|---|---|
| 18.7 | 12.6 | 10.7 | 6.2 | 3.8 | 2.8 | 0.5 | 44.8 |

If either the Harris-Todaro or the Mazumdar hypothesis were valid for the Malaysian labor markets surveyed, the data would show different

5. See Mazumdar, "Paradigms in the Analysis of Urban Labor Markets."

distributions of migrants by duration in the formal and informal sectors of the market. A relatively much larger proportion of recent migrants in the informal than the formal sector is a necessary condition for the hypothesis of a greater incidence of return migration in this sector; this condition alone is not a determinant, however, since many of the new migrants move to other sectors of the urban market.

The distribution of migrants by duration for the different sectors of the labor market (Table 11-12) shows just the reverse of the Harris-Todaro or Mazumdar hypotheses. Easily the largest percentage of very recent migrants (those with a duration of a year or less) is found in the most "formal" grouping, that is, in firms employing more than 100 workers. Apparently quite a high proportion of new migrants to the urban labor markets in Malaysia move straight into large enterprises— perhaps into public sector jobs. Equally interesting is the substantially less than average percentage of recent migrants in the self-employed category. Neither this nor the small-scale sector seems to be providing a first footing for migrants coming into the cities. Again, the contrast with the Bombay labor market on this point is remarkable.[6]

## Conclusions

The three cities covered in the MES depend heavily on in-migration for their growth, so much so that at the time of the survey those born outside the cities constituted a majority of their populations. Migration is especially important among Malays in Kuala Lumpur. The pattern of migration into the cities studied differs in many respects from the stereotypes in the literature of internal migration in developing countries. A large proportion of adult migrants comes from other urban areas, and a surprisingly large fraction had made one or more inter-mediate stops before arriving in the town of enumeration. The migration was, for the most part, permanent, and migrants maintained relatively weak links with their places of origin.

Migrants generally performed better economically than the natives in the towns surveyed. They also seemed generally better educated than the natives, suggesting that the tendency to migrate is probably selective in favor of the more educated. Nearly 30 percent of the migrants came from families whose economic position in their place of origin was below

6. Ibid., pp. 27–32 in particular.

Table 11-12. Percentage Distribution of Sample by Duration of Migration in Different Sectors

| Sector | Years since migration | | | | | | | |
|---|---|---|---|---|---|---|---|---|
| | 1 or less | 6–10 | 11–15 | 16–20 | 21–25 | 26–30 | 30 or more | Natives |
| Plant size | | | | | | | | |
| 1–9 employees | 15.5 | 11.3 | 10.8 | 7.5 | 3.8 | 3.8 | 1.4 | 46.0 |
| 10–99 employees | 19.1 | 13.3 | 13.1 | 5.1 | 2.7 | 2.2 | 0.4 | 44.0 |
| 100 or more employees | 27.5 | 16.8 | 11.7 | 7.3 | 4.0 | 2.0 | 0.0 | 30.6 |
| Self-employed | 9.8 | 8.8 | 7.7 | 6.2 | 4.9 | 3.6 | 0.9 | 58.1 |

Source: MES, 1975.

average, but more than twice this percentage reported coming from families of average economic status. A minority of migrants came from farming families, particularly among the Chinese—another striking difference from other Asian countries. Even among those coming from a farming background, an overall minority came from purely subsistence farming households.

The patterns of migration outlined in this chapter provide some explanation for the failure of internal migration to do more to equalize rural-urban differences in income levels in Peninsular Malaysia, which are much more pronounced for the Malays than for the Chinese. While Malay migrants tended to come from communities relatively close to the cities studied, the Chinese have a more extensive network of streams of migration, in spite of (or perhaps because of) their better economic position in the rural areas. Moreover, migration into the cities was not predominantly rurally based for either race. For these reasons, the number of low-income Malay families in depressed pockets of the agricultural and rural economy tends not to be reduced by migration to the bigger cities.

The only point emerging from this chapter about the relation between migration and variations in sectoral earnings is that migrants in the towns studied are definitely *not* concentrated in small enterprises or in self-employment. In fact, contrary to the prediction of both the Harris-Todaro and the Mazumdar hypotheses, new migrants seem to be disproportionately represented in the large and medium-size enterprises.

CHAPTER 12

# Job Mobility

THE QUESTIONNAIRE USED in the World Bank Migration and Employment Survey (MES) obtained data on the job histories of interviewees, which are used to throw some light on the patterns of employment mobility and the economic implications for the labor market. This chapter provides an overview of job mobility by examining total number of jobs held by those in the survey sample during their careers. It then focuses on labor market entry and first jobs and describes the main types of worker movement across sectors and industries. The last section tackles the influence of job mobility on the economic performance of the sample throughout their working lives.

The analysis of the earnings data in Chapter 10 suggested that experience is important in determining male employees' earnings. In particular, it was found that unskilled workers and those employed in small enterprises seemed to have a steep age-earnings profile. The analysis depended necessarily on cross-section data, which presented the predictable problems associated with pooling information on workers from different generations in order to compute hypothetical lifetime profiles. In this chapter the earlier findings are supplemented by an examination of the earnings data given by individuals as they recalled them (the best approach available in the absence of genuine longitudinal data).

## Total Jobs Held

Table 12-1 indicates the extent of job mobility by cross-tabulating the number of jobs held against various levels of age and education. These two variables have separate and significant effects on job mobility. As might be expected, the number of jobs held increases with age; less predictably, the number decreases within each age group as the educational level of the respondent increases. Data of this kind, however, can provide only a basic summary of the position at a given point in time. The influence of other variables—such as race, place of birth, the size

Table 12-1. Number of Jobs Held by Age and Education Group
(percentage of total workers in each group)

| | Number of jobs | | | | | |
|---|---|---|---|---|---|---|
| | 1 | 2 | 3 | 4 | 5 | 6 or more |
| *Kuala Lumpur* | | | | | | |
| Age 15–25 | | | | | | |
| Primary education or less | 30.4 | 35.4 | 13.9 | 8.9 | 8.9 | 2.5 |
| Secondary education | 46.8 | 32.3 | 10.1 | 7.6 | 1.9 | 1.3 |
| Higher school certificate and above | 60.9 | 26.1 | 8.7 | 0.0 | 4.3 | 0.0 |
| Age 26–35 | | | | | | |
| Primary education or less | 18.1 | 22.7 | 22.2 | 17.6 | 10.6 | 8.8 |
| Secondary education | 38.0 | 24.4 | 16.1 | 9.8 | 7.8 | 3.9 |
| Higher school certificate and above | 30.2 | 41.3 | 15.9 | 11.1 | 1.6 | 0.0 |
| Age 36–50 | | | | | | |
| Primary education or less | 18.0 | 20.4 | 17.6 | 18.8 | 12.5 | 12.6 |
| Secondary education | 29.6 | 20.4 | 15.7 | 15.7 | 9.3 | 9.3 |
| Higher school certificate and above | 17.4 | 26.1 | 30.4 | 17.4 | 8.7 | 0.0 |
| *East Coast* | | | | | | |
| Age 15–25 | | | | | | |
| Primary education or less | 18.0 | 26.2 | 31.1 | 13.1 | 8.2 | 3.2 |
| Secondary education | 47.8 | 26.1 | 13.0 | 8.7 | 3.3 | 1.1 |
| Higher school certificate and above | 66.7 | 33.3 | 0.0 | 0.0 | 0.0 | 0.0 |
| Age 26–35 | | | | | | |
| Primary education or less | 13.4 | 19.3 | 16.6 | 25.1 | 15.0 | 10.6 |
| Secondary education | 37.7 | 23.8 | 27.9 | 6.6 | 3.3 | 0.8 |
| Higher school certificate and above | 64.7 | 23.5 | 11.8 | 0.0 | 0.0 | 0.0 |
| Age 36–50 | | | | | | |
| Primary education or less | 14.6 | 19.3 | 17.3 | 12.2 | 18.1 | 18.5 |
| Secondary education | 47.3 | 23.6 | 12.7 | 7.3 | 7.3 | 1.8 |
| Higher school certificate and above | 55.6 | 22.2 | 22.2 | 0.0 | 0.0 | 0.0 |

*Source:* MES, 1975.

of the enterprise in which the respondent first secured employment, and the number of location changes in his working life—cannot be ignored. To find out whether these factors play significant roles in mobility, the number of jobs held was regressed against a number of independent variables.

Table 12-2. Multiple Regression on the Number of Full-Time Jobs Held

| | Kuala Lumpur | | | | East Coast | | | |
|---|---|---|---|---|---|---|---|---|
| Independent variable | β | t-ratio | Introduced in step no. | Sample proportion | β | t-ratio | Introduced in step no. | Sample proportion |
| Age (Base: 15–25) | | | | | | | | |
| 26–35 | 0.448 | 2.95 | 6 | 0.45 | 0.396 | 2.08 | 6 | 0.429 |
| 36–50 | 0.749 | 4.46 | 2 | 0.34 | 0.612 | 3.03 | 5 | 0.378 |
| Education (Base: Primary or less) | | | | | | | | |
| Some secondary | −0.695 | −5.46 | 4 | 0.41 | −1.49 | −9.38 | 1 | 0.333 |
| Higher school certificate and above | −1.03 | −5.40 | 5 | 0.12 | −2.24 | −7.29 | 2 | 0.054 |
| Race (Base: Malay) | | | | | | | | |
| Chinese | 0.921 | 7.54 | 1 | 0.43 | 0.367 | 2.25 | 4 | 0.264 |
| Indian and other | 0.463 | 2.27 | 7 | 0.10 | −0.548 | −1.83 | 7 | 0.058 |
| Number of place changes | 0.195 | 5.22 | 3 | 2.15 | 0.218 | 5.05 | 3 | 2.43 |
| Constant | 1.88 | 11.59 | — | — | 2.72 | 14.08 | — | — |
| $R^2$ | 0.213 | | | | 0.265 | | | |
| F | 26.64 | | | | 27.02 | | | |
| N | 698 | | | | 534 | | | |
| Mean value of dependent variable | 2.79 | | | | 3.10 | | | |

Source: MES, 1975.

In the case of the Kuala Lumpur sample, neither the size of the respondents' birthplace population nor that of the first enterprise in which they had found employment helped to explain the variation in the number of jobs held. None of the dummy variables for the size of the birthplace community was significant; they were therefore not included in the regression. Only those who started work as employees in very small firms had any tendency to change more jobs than everyone else in the sample, and the tendency was not very significant. Since information on the sector of the first job was not given for all respondents, the final equation was estimated without this variable in order to provide a larger sample size. The results are presented in Table 12-2 and support the general picture obtained from the cross-tabulations of Table 12-1. Education reduces the number of jobs respondents are likely to have held after standardizing for age, and Malays are likely to change jobs less frequently than Chinese or Indian workers. The number of location changes plays a very significant role. The effect is not to reduce the explanatory powers of the other variables but to add nearly 0.04 to the $R^2$. When the regression was run without this variable, it was found that only the coefficients of age were altered slightly; the other coefficients were virtually unaffected, although the constant term was significantly higher. While it is to be expected that the number of location changes will strongly affect the number of jobs held, even after the introduction of location changes as an independent variable, other factors in the equation were still important. Thus, these factors have a direct effect on job changes and are not acting as a proxy for geographical mobility in any way.

The results are similar for the sample in the East Coast towns. Again, the size of the respondent's birthplace makes no difference to the number of jobs he has held, and the size of the first firm he worked for is only slightly significant if he started work for a very large firm (in which case it reduces the likelihood of his moving jobs). As for Kuala Lumpur, the equations exclude the "sector of first job" variable because of the need to obtain as large a sample as possible. Again there is a close relation between job mobility and location changes. After the regression was run both with and without this variable, it was found that its addition did not detract from the explanatory powers of the other variables. The only coefficients to be significantly altered were the constant term and (to a lesser degree) the coefficients of age (which were reduced). As in the case of the Kuala Lumpur data, the addition of this variable increased the $R^2$ by 0.04 and reduced the constant term by nearly 0.5.

Table 12-2 yields some important interregional differences, however. First, the mean value of the dependent variable is higher in the East Coast, as is the overall explanatory power of the regression itself. The second difference lies in the relative magnitudes of the various coefficients and in the order in which the explanatory variables are introduced in the step-wise regressions. Age seems to have a smaller quantitative effect on job movement in the East Coast than in Kuala Lumpur; the coefficients of both the age groups are smaller in the former than in the latter. This is more than made up for the much greater effect of education on the number of jobs that the East Coast subject is likely to hold in his working life. Not only are the education variables the first to be introduced in the step-wise regression on the East Coast, but they are more than twice the size of their corresponding coefficients in Kuala Lumpur. The effect of race is also different. The Chinese are again more likely to change jobs, but the quantitative difference is much smaller in the East Coast; for Indians and other racial groups the sign of the coefficient itself changes. In the East Coast they are less likely to change jobs than the Malays, although this difference is only significant on a 90 percent confidence level.

It can also be helpful to look at the mean number of jobs held per year of working life:

|  | Kuala Lumpur | East Coast |
|---|---|---|
| Entire population | 0.25 | 0.23 |
| Age 15–25 | 0.32 | 0.25 |
| Age 26–35 | 0.24 | 0.25 |
| Age 36–50 | 0.13 | 0.13 |

Overall, each person in the sample changes jobs every four years of his working life in both regions. (The fact that the constant terms in the estimated regression equations of Table 12-2 showed a higher value for the East Coast suggests that the mobility of the base group, made up of those with primary education or less, is relatively high in this region.) The interesting point, however, is the relatively high degree of mobility among the 15–25 age group in Kuala Lumpur. Those over thirty-five years old in both regions change jobs, on the average, only every eight years.

## The First Job

Since the MES could collect only a limited amount of information about each job held by respondents, it was decided to confine the questions about types of job to two items. The first asked about the sector of employment, defined by the size (number of employees) of the enterprise together with the self-employed category. The second asked about the industry group to which the employer enterprise belonged. An important issue in the literature on job mobility in the labor markets of developing countries is the role of the informal sector as a stepping-stone to certain types of job. Two hypotheses mentioned in the literature are examined here:

*Hypothesis 1*: Low grade labor has to enter the labor market through the informal sector and moves only later into the formal sector.

*Hypothesis 2*: Migrants entering the urban labor market do so through the informal sector.

For present purposes, the informal sector can be defined either by the sector of employment or by the industry. The MES distinguished four employment sectors: (1) enterprises with 1 to 9 workers; (2) enterprises with 10 to 99 workers; (3) enterprises with 100 or more workers; and (4) the self-employed. The informal sector could be defined to include both the small-scale sector, made up of the smallest enterprise size group (those with 1 to 9 employees) and the self-employed sector, which is believed to provide relatively free entry for new workers. It was decided to group the industrial categories into four broad groups: (1) agriculture; (2) manufacturing, gas, water and electricity, and construction; (3) transport, finance, public administration, sanitary services, social and community services, and international services; and (4) trade, recreational services, personal and household services.[1] The distinction between (4) and (3) is intended to bring out the difference between the informal tertiary or service sector and its more formal component; group (4) is expected to include many of the activities into which entry is apparently easy and in which operations are carried out in small units with relatively little use of capital. Thus, for both the sector and industry grouping categories (1) and (4) represent the informal sector and categories (2) and (3) the more formal part of the labor market.

To test the validity of the hypotheses stated above, in particular hypothesis 2 about migrant entry into urban labor markets, the sample was subdivided into natives and migrants, so that the categories into

---

1. These distinctions are based on the Malaysian Industrial Classification.

which the first jobs of migrants and natives fell could be examined separately. The percentage distribution by first jobs for the sample of natives among the four industry and sector groups is:

|          | (1)  | (2)  | (3)  | (4)  | Total |
|----------|------|------|------|------|-------|
| Sector   | 37.7 | 31.1 | 16.2 | 15.0 | 100.0 |
| Industry | 11.7 | 28.4 | 22.6 | 37.4 | 100.0 |

The informal type of job is of major importance to the native subgroup in both the sectoral and the industrial categories, accounting for fully half the first jobs reported by the natives. It is possible to test whether the experience of low-grade labor differs from this pattern by looking specifically at the subsample of the natives who have primary education or less. Data not reproduced here show that the distribution of first jobs does *not* differ much for this group from that for the natives as a whole. Those with primary education or less had about 10 percent more first jobs in the small-scale sector than those with higher education. There is practically no difference in the distribution among the industrial categories for the poorly educated and the subgroup as a whole; the larger share of agriculture in the first jobs of the less educated is almost exactly offset by the smaller share of the informal tertiary category. There was also very little difference between the distributions for the Kuala Lumpur labor market and the East Coast towns. Thus, hypothesis 1 appears not to be confirmed for the subgroup of natives of the urban areas surveyed.

Hypothesis 2 refers not to the first jobs of all migrants (defined as all those born elsewhere, including those who may have come to the city as children) but only to the first jobs of those migrants who came to the town of enumeration as adults. The percentage distribution of the first jobs of this group among the sectors and industries defined above is:

|          | (1)  | (2)  | (3)  | (4)  | Total |
|----------|------|------|------|------|-------|
| Sector   | 26.5 | 36.5 | 25.0 | 12.0 | 100.0 |
| Industry | 11.5 | 41.0 | 20.0 | 27.5 | 100.0 |

The figures refute hypothesis 2. In the towns surveyed, a substantially smaller proportion of adult migrants than natives worked in the informal sector. This finding is consistent with the importance of stage migration in Peninsular Malaysia in that migrants who have stopped at intermediate points might be expected to find it relatively easy to find a foothold in the more formal sector of the labor market by the time they move into the larger towns.

# Movement between Sectors and Industries

Some idea of the pattern of movement of workers between jobs in the four employment sectors can be developed by comparing the sector of respondents' first jobs with the sector in which they currently work. This approach gives only a limited indication of mobility patterns, because it does not take into account any jobs held between the first and present ones, and because younger respondents in particular may not have had more than one job. To reduce the latter problem, the analysis which follows will include an older group in the sample as well as all those who had held more than one job.

## Movement between Sectors

About two-thirds of the sample of about 1,200 respondents in Kuala Lumpur reported having held both a first and a current job. A rather larger proportion of the East Coast sample—about three-quarters—is currently employed in a job other than the first. The basic matrixes for the two regions are given in Table 12-3. In both regions the propensity to move out of the sector of first employment is highest for those whose first jobs were in the small-scale wage sector. The retention rate of this sector—the proportion of those with a first job in this sector whose current job is also in the sector—is 18 percent in Kuala Lumpur and 22 percent in the East Coast towns. For the oldest age group in the sample (those aged between thirty-six and fifty), the retention rates are even lower—17 and 14 percent for the two regions, respectively.

The variations in retention rates by employment sector are broadly similar for Kuala Lumpur and the East Coast towns, with the important exception of the rates for the large enterprises, which employ an abnormally large proportion of workers in the labor market in the capital. This sector has the highest retention rate for the sample as a whole in Kuala Lumpur, and the rate is more or less the same for the subsample of those aged thirty-six or older. Large firms account for a much smaller proportion of employment in the East Coast, however, and the retention rate among those who started their career in large firms is substantially lower in this labor market than in Kuala Lumpur (32 percent against 62 percent).

Table 12-3. Transition Matrix of Change in Job Sector

| | Sector of current job | | | | | |
| | Size of enterprise | | | | | |
| Sector of first job | 1–9 | 10–99 | 100 or more | Self-employed | Total | Num |
|---|---|---|---|---|---|---|
| Kuala Lumpur | | | | | | |
| Size of enterprise | | | | | | |
| 1–9 employees | 17.9 | 21.3 | 25.5 | 33.2 | 100.0 | 23! |
| 10–99 employees | 7.7 | 39.3 | 32.0 | 19.1 | 100.0 | 27: |
| 100 or more employees | 4.3 | 19.7 | 62.4 | 12.4 | 100.0 | 23. |
| Self-employed | 11.7 | 20.0 | 30.0 | 38.3 | 100.0 | 6( |
| Number | 80 | 215 | 311 | 182 | | 80. |
| East Coast | | | | | | |
| Size of enterprise | | | | | | |
| 1–9 employees | 22.4 | 25.6 | 11.4 | 39.7 | 100.0 | 21! |
| 10–99 employees | 9.1 | 39.4 | 20.5 | 28.8 | 100.0 | 13: |
| 100 or more employees | 12.2 | 29.3 | 31.7 | 23.2 | 100.0 | 8 |
| Self-employed | 15.4 | 24.1 | 16.0 | 42.6 | 100.0 | 16. |
| Number | 96 | 171 | 104 | 213 | | 59! |

Note: The raw percentages do not add exactly to 100.0 because of a few misfuncti
ing cases.
Source: MES, 1975.

Another way of assessing the extent of mobility by sector is to compare the net difference for each sector between its percentage shares of first and current jobs. The figures are:

| | Size of enterprise | | | |
| Region | 1–9 | 10–99 | 100 or more | Family-owned |
|---|---|---|---|---|
| Kuala Lumpur | −13.3 | −7.2 | 9.6 | 15.2 |
| East Coast | −20.7 | 6.5 | 3.7 | 8.6 |

It is perhaps unexpected that the self-employed show by far the largest increases in their shares of total employment in both regions. Far from offering an easy initial entry into the labor market for newcomers, the family-owned business seems to be an employment source to which a significant proportion of workers gravitate in their later career. This point is reinforced by data for those aged over thirty-six, for whom the increase in the self-employed's percentage share of total employment is substantially larger than that for each of the regional samples as a whole

(20 and 13 percent respectively for Kuala Lumpur and the East Coast). Of course, the information given so far does not show whether this pattern is associated with increases in real incomes for those making the move.

The finding that there is a net lifetime movement out of wage employment into self-employment runs contrary to a number of myths in the literature.[2] At least one study, however—perhaps the best known one of lifetime mobility in a developing country—did put forward the view that it is more useful to view self-employment as a sector of advancement than as a reservoir of workers seeking more lucrative wage employment. Reporting on male workers in Monterrey, Mexico, the study found that self-employment was a very heterogeneous category, but that there was a large intermediate group in the "middle levels of the stratification hierarchy" of self-employment which provided an opportunity for workers to enter without much capital (material or human) and offered the prospect of a decent income. "It is such positions to which manual workers can and do aspire to move."[3] The authors noted that "Self-employment is an important goal for many men both in industrial and industrializing societies, for it signifies independence which is highly valued. Self-employed men are often evaluated as holding better positions than employees, even when there is little difference in income and level of living."[4] In Monterrey more than half the moves to self-employment (57 percent) among the men aged forty-five and over involved an upward move in the study's classification of occupational grades. "In the majority of cases it was an unskilled manual worker becoming either a grocery store owner, an independent craftsman, or a driver-owner of a vehicle. . . . On the other hand, fifty-four percent of the men who left self-employed positions entered an occupation at a lower level."[5]

Because of the importance of the view expressed (and substantiated) in the Monterrey study that self-employment can represent a source of upward mobility in the labor market, it is worth briefly setting out some causal factors which tend to confirm its validity in labor markets in developing countries.

2. Michael P. Todaro, "A Model of Urban Unemployment in LDC's," *American Economic Review*, vol. 59, no. 1 (1970), pp. 138–48.

3. Jorge Balán, Harley L. Browning, and Elizabeth Jelin, *Men in a Developing Society* (Austin and London: University of Texas Press, 1973), p. 216.

4. Ibid., p. 215.

5. Ibid., pp. 221–22.

First, the move to self-employment in a developing country depends more on human than financial resources. The self-employed may require some capital, but the cash outlay is often quite minimal. With sufficient energy and imagination, the entrepreneur can go a long way by using his own labor to build up the required capital (including the physical building he may need). In other words, capital formation in the self-employed sector need not require substantial initial funds and often the assets created are a classical example of "congealed labor." Since wage labor does not provide an opportunity for capital formation in this way, self-employment represents an appealing opportunity for those who have been able to identify a promising area of the market to exploit.

Second, opportunities for skill formation may not be available for workers at the bottom of the skills hierarchy, especially in economies in which a labor aristocracy has developed. In such an environment, advancement for the lower-paid workers is limited by formal craft unions or informal pressure groups among the more skilled workers, which tend to adopt a closed shop policy toward the less skilled. The problem can be accentuated in some countries by discrimination against ethnic or linguistic groups with or without the support of the state. Under these conditions, a move to self-employment becomes not merely an attractive possibility but a logical necessity for the ambitious worker with a low position in the formal hierarchy.

Third, macroeconomic policies in many developing countries can adversely affect the growth rate of the sectors of the urban economy which provide wage employment. Although this is probably not an important problem in Malaysia, extreme cases exist in which government fiscal and monetary policies create conditions of inflation and falling real wages in the wage-earning sector. The only way for workers to protect their living standards may be to seek a niche in the self-employed sector—even on a part-time basis. It is common to refer to the riskiness of self-employment, but this risk may be no greater than that of wage employment in a situation of inflation accompanied by controls on wages and salaries. If wages are held steady, the consequence can often be the stagnation of living standards.

## Movement between Industries

Labor mobility can also take the form of movement by workers out of one type of productive activity and into another. The examination which follows of the extent of this kind of mobility in Malaysia's urban labor markets is based on an analysis of first and current jobs held by the sample in the four broad industrial categories defined above. Table 12-4 is based on information available for the 1,358 individuals who reported their first and current jobs. It shows that the agricultural category has suffered a very large percentage loss of workers who had started their careers in it. This is, of course, to be expected in an economy in which the urban sector has been developing with substantial migration from rural areas and small towns. The overall importance of agriculture as the source of initial employment is surprisingly small, however; consequently the net loss imposed on the industry by the overall mobility of the sample is much smaller in absolute terms than its very low percentage retention rate might suggest. About half of those employed in the other industrial groups changed their jobs but did not change industries in the process. The retention rate was similar for all three nonagricultural industrial groups.

Because the pattern of mobility of low-grade labor is of particular interest, information on interindustry mobility provided by respondents with primary education or less is shown separately in the table. This group differs from the sample as a whole in that a significantly larger percentage of the less educated started their career in agriculture. Since the agricutural retention rate for the group is barely greater than that

Table 12-4. Changes in Industrial Category
during the Workers' Careers

| Item | Agri-culture | Manu-facturing | Informal services | Formal services |
|---|---|---|---|---|
| Percentage with the first job in the industry | | | | |
| Total sample | 18.3 | 24.6 | 33.2 | 23.9 |
| Primary education or less | 25.6 | 25.8 | 32.7 | 15.9 |
| Retention rate[a] | | | | |
| Total sample | 10.8 | 48.5 | 55.0 | 56.5 |
| Primary education or less | 11.6 | 52.1 | 57.1 | 50.7 |
| Net gain or loss of industry[b] | | | | |
| Total sample | −14.2 | 6.6 | −0.4 | 8.0 |
| Primary education or less | −20.2 | 8.3 | 1.1 | 9.9 |

a. Percentage of those currently employed in each industry whose first job was in the same industry.
b. Present percentage share of jobs minus percentage share of first jobs.
Source: MES, 1975.

for the full sample, it follows that a substantially larger proportion of the less educated than of the better qualified moved to other sectors in their subsequent careers.

The figures for net gain by industry group show that the manufacturing and the formal service sectors were proportionately the most attractive alternative sources of employment for those with little education who left agriculture (as for the sample as a whole). If the informal service sector is identified with relatively low or stagnant earnings, the pattern of interindustry mobility suggested by these data is one of upward movement through the workers' career. There is, however, no evidence in Table 12-4 that the informal service sector is a dead end, with an unusually high retention rate for the less educated, or that it typically provides low-grade workers with their first jobs before they manage to move on to better work in manufacturing or the formal service sector. In fact, the proportions of those with first and current jobs in the informal service sector are similar for the less educated group and for the sample as a whole.

To summarize the mobility patterns analyzed here, those who reported having had more than one job appear to have changed employment sectors more than they changed industry categories. The net losers from job mobility are the small-scale employment sector and the agricultural category. Although there may be some overlap between these two groupings, the former is much the larger source of first jobs for the sample. The retention rates for the informal service sector turned out to be only marginally different from those for formal services or manufacturing. In addition, data presented above for movement between industry categories suggest that the experience of the poorly educated portion of the sample was not significantly different from that of the whole sample; data not shown here confirm this conclusion for intersectoral job changes as well.

## Mobility between Sectors and Change in Income

This section discusses the extent to which job mobility helps to increase workers' earnings; it concentrates on mobility between sectors, which is more extensive than mobility between industries. It was shown above that movement out of the small-scale sector was a major element in overall sectoral mobility, as was the net gain in employment of the self-employed sector. This section will assess the extent of changes in earnings associated with these movements.

Table 12-5. Current Monthly Income by Sectoral Change
between First and Current Job
(Malaysian dollars per month)

| | Sector of current job | | | | | |
| | Size of enterprise | | | | | |
| Sector of first job | 1–9 | 10–99 | 100 or more | Self-employed | Mean | t-ratio |
|---|---|---|---|---|---|---|
| Size of enterprise | | | | | | |
| 1–9 employees | 252 | 274 | 287 | 326 | 291 | 2.92 |
| 10–99 employees | 243 | 409 | 491 | 491 | 435 | 2.81 |
| 100 or more | | | | | | |
| employees | 225 | 360 | 465 | 439 | 421 | 2.35 |

Source: MES, 1975.

Table 12-5 shows the current mean income of male workers by sector of first and current jobs. There are clear and significant variations in the mean incomes of those who started in a given sector but ended up in a different one. For those who started their careers in the small-scale wage sector and moved, job earnings rise with each level of enterprise size in the wage sector; the highest earnings are attained in the self-employed sector. A similar pattern exists for those who started work in medium-size enterprises (with 10 to 99 employees) and moved to large ones (100 or more employees). The move to self-employment produces no incremental gain for this group, however—and actually leads to a loss for those who started work in the large enterprises. For those who started in the large and medium enterprises and moved to a job in a smaller one, current monthly earnings fall substantially.

Earnings levels are, of course, influenced by age, education, and other factors, as noted earlier. An assessment of the impact on earnings of sectoral mobility will require a multivariate analysis which includes mobility as one of its explanatory variables. For the purpose of this discussion, however, the effect of mobility on *levels* of earnings, though interesting, is of less significance than its effect on the *difference* between earnings before and after a move. Therefore, the regression analysis which follows takes the current income of the worker in relation to his initial income. The problem here is, of course, that respondents may have inadequate recollections of their initial incomes. In addition, price changes over time will exaggerate (or understate, depending on whether the price level rises or falls) the real value of any nominal differences in the initial incomes of different age cohorts. To some extent, this problem is taken care of by including the age of the respondent as one of the explanatory variables. The coefficient of the age variable is thus an amalgam of the effect of the length of experience and of the price change relevant to the cohort in question.

To make the calculations manageable, the sector mobility variable has been reduced to a few categories, as shown in the following matrix:

|  | Sector of current job | | | |
|---|---|---|---|---|
|  | Size of enterprise | | | |
| Sector of first job | 1–9 | 10–99 | 100 or more | Self-employed |
| Size of enterprise |  |  |  |  |
| 1–9 employees | A | B | B | C |
| 10–99 employees | R | A | B | C |
| 100 or more employees | R | R | A | C |
| Self-employed | Missing data | Missing data | Missing data | A |

The survey data provided no information on the initial income of those who had started work in their own businesses and had then moved on to the wage sector (although the reported changes in income of those who had continued to work in the self-employed sector were available). Therefore, the cells marked "missing data" are omitted from the analysis. The other cells were divided into four categories as shown in the matrix; these were used as dummy variables in the regression models to explain earnings differences between first and current jobs. The category R was used as the reference group (or base) and was omitted from the set of dummies. Thus the other dummies account for the marginal effect on the earnings difference of the other types of mobility in relation to the type represented by category R. The definitions of the four types are:

R = A downward movement with respect to the size of the enterprise
A = No change of sector
B = An upward movement with respect to the size of the enterprise
C = Movement into self-employment.

Various forms of the dependent variable were tried, including the ratio of current income to starting pay, the logarithm of this ratio, and log (current income — starting pay). The regression model which used the last of these three as its dependent variable was by far the most efficient in terms of the proportion of variance explained. The results are set out in Table 12-6.

Table 12-6. Regression Model Explaining Log of Current Income Minus Starting Pay

| Variable | B | Beta | F-ratio | $R^2$ | Proportion |
|---|---|---|---|---|---|
| *Step 1 Age* | | | | | |
| 15–25 (base) | — | — | — | — | 0.14 |
| 26–30 | 0.43 | 0.18 | 27.6 | 0.000 | 0.26 |
| 31–35 | 0.66 | 0.25 | 55.8 | 0.005 | 0.19 |
| 36–40 | 0.66 | 0.23 | 49.6 | 0.009 | 0.16 |
| 41–50 | 0.91 | 0.37 | 104.8 | 0.056 | 0.23 |
| *Step 2 Education* | | | | | |
| No school (base) | — | — | — | — | 0.05 |
| Primary | 0.50 | 0.24 | 18.5 | 0.134 | 0.54 |
| Some secondary | 0.82 | 0.33 | 41.2 | 0.142 | 0.22 |
| School certificate | 1.40 | 0.43 | 105.2 | 0.148 | 0.12 |
| Higher school certificate and above | 2.02 | 0.50 | 176.4 | 0.294 | 0.07 |
| *Step 3[a] Move* | | | | | |
| R (base) | — | — | — | — | 0.11 |
| A | 0.16 | 0.07 | 3.2 | 0.301 | 0.37 |
| B | 0.35 | 0.15 | 14.5 | 0.301 | 0.27 |
| C | 0.43 | 0.18 | 20.8 | 0.312 | 0.25 |
| *Step 4 Region* | | | | | |
| Trengganu (base) | — | — | — | — | 0.11 |
| Kota Bharu | −0.29 | −0.11 | 20.8 | 0.369 | 0.18 |
| Kuala Lumpur | 0.15 | 0.07 | 10.8 | 0.377 | 0.63 |
| *Step 5 Race* | | | | | |
| Other (base) | — | — | — | — | 0.08 |
| Malay | −0.18 | −0.08 | 3.3 | 0.428 | 0.44 |
| Chinese | 0.38 | 0.18 | 16.3 | 0.430 | 0.48 |

Constant = 3.447
$R^2 = 0.43$
$F = 48.6$
$N = 984$
Mean = 5.153

a. R = a downward movement with respect to the size of the enterprise; A = no change of sector; B = an upward movement with respect to the size of the enterprise; and C = movement into self-employment.
*Source:* MES, 1975.

The results show that all the mobility dummies have a significant effect on the change in earnings, and the effects are in the expected direction. No change of sector has a positive effect on the earnings difference, other things remaining equal, compared with the base group with downward mobility. Category B, representing a move to an enterprise with a larger labor force, adds a percentage improvement in earnings between first and current jobs which is more than twice as high as the advantage experienced by the nonmovers over the base group. It is of special interest to note that movement into self-employment leads to the greatest increase in lifetime earnings.

Mobility factors do not, however, account for a great deal of the variance explained. The lion's share of the total $R^2$ is accounted for by education. In particular, primary and postsecondary education add 8 and 15 percent respectively to the $R^2$. This is an important result and is consistent with the conclusions reached in Chapter 7 (on the basis of cross-section material) that the effect of education on earnings is strong at the upper levels of the labor market (that is, in the white-collar occupations). The coefficients of the education variables are very high— even higher than the coefficients for age, which should provide the most direct explanation of the difference between current and starting incomes. The net effects of region and race on the earnings difference— after controlling for other variables—are also worthy of note.

Generally, the multivariate analysis shown in Table 12-6 gives surprisingly good results, with no variable having a coefficient with a contraintuitive sign or magnitude; this suggests that the data obtained on the past and present earnings of the sample can be treated with confidence. Nevertheless, the reliability of past earnings data obtained by the recall method is always open to question. Partly for this reason, and partly because it is an interesting (and different) question in itself, the effect of job mobility on the level of current earnings is examined separately below.

In the earnings function obtained by a step-wise multiple regression program (not reproduced here), the job mobility variables were entered

Table 12-7. Coefficients of Mobility Variables in Earnings Function Explaining Log of Current Earnings

| Variable | B | Beta | F-ratio | Proportion |
|---|---|---|---|---|
| Constant | 4.63 | — | — | — |
| To self-employment | 0.18 | 0.11 | 11.2 | 0.21 |
| Always self-employed | 0.15 | 0.05 | 4.6 | 0.07 |
| To larger enterprise | 0.09 | 0.05 | 3.0 | 0.22 |
| No sector change | 0.06 | 0.04 | 1.6 | 0.31 |
| From self-employment | 0.04 | 0.02 | 0.5 | 0.10 |
| To smaller enterprise (base) | — | — | — | 0.09 |

Source: MES, 1975.

at the very end—after the education, age, race, and region variables. Consequently, the incremental $R^2$ attributable to the mobility variables was quite small (around 1 percent of the total of 57 percent of the variance explained). Nevertheless, several of the categories of mobility turned out to have significant net effects on current earnings. The coefficients of the mobility variables used in the final regression (not shown) are given in Table 12-7.

Of the six categories of mobility identified in this model, the first three, and possibly the fourth, add significantly to current earnings. The results are broadly in line with the model used to explain changes between initial and current earnings. The movement from wage employment to self-employment adds most to current earnings, just as it did in the earlier model. An additional result shown in Table 12-7 is that those who have always been self-employed also have higher earnings—other things remaining the same (data on initial earnings are not available for this category). Movement to a larger enterprise in the wage-employment category also has a significant positive effect on the level of current earnings.

# Part III

# *Unemployment*

# CHAPTER 13

# Introduction to Part III

PART III ADDRESSES THE PROBLEM of unemployment in Peninsular Malaysia, with particular reference to the urban areas. The dimensions of the problem are identified in Chapter 14. Given the high growth rate of Malaysia compared with many other developing countries (including several in Asia), the rate of open unemployment is high and has been even higher in the recent past. The high incidence of unemployment appears to be caused by the unusual difficulties which new entrants—particularly young school leavers—face when trying to break into the labor market. Young people's long wait for employment is in turn reflected in the high rate of joblessness. The succeeding chapters of Part III attempt to shed light on the various factors which contribute to this problem, and to offer an internally consistent explanation of it.

The long period of waiting between leaving school and starting work can be explained by either the job search hypothesis or the rationing hypothesis. The distinction between the two corresponds roughly to the difference between voluntary and involuntary unemployment. According to the job search hypothesis, job seekers attach a high value to shopping around for the best job. The duration of the search—and hence the length of the waiting period—will increase with the extent to which the perceived or expected benefits to be derived from the search outweigh the perceived or expected costs of unemployment. On this hypothesis, unemployment is voluntary; it is assumed that job seekers would be able to get a job more quickly if they were willing to settle for a lower starting salary.

The hypothesis makes the implicit assumption that job seekers' benefits in the form of returns to job searches would fall significantly if they were to accept low-paid employment even temporarily. This may be due to one or a combination of the following reasons: (1) mobility between jobs may be low because of institutional bottlenecks which discourage frequent changes of employer; (2) a low-paid starting job may "spoil" the worker's job record, by making it difficult to obtain subsequent employment at a substantially higher wage; and (3) the job search process may require the searcher's active presence in the labor market (at employment exchanges or in pursuit of personal contacts), which precludes temporary employment. The job search hypothesis thus proposes an "equilibrium waiting period" in the labor market, which the typical job seeker reaches by equating benefits (the expected return to search) with costs (earnings forgone during the period of search). Consequently, on this hypothesis, there will be an equilibrium rate of unemployment associated with the equilibrium period of waiting.[1]

In contrast, the rationing hypothesis starts with the assumption of a rigid structure of wages which, for institutional reasons, is insensitive to the excess supply of labor produced by the educational system. School leavers thus have to queue up for the limited number of opportunities for paid employment which become available in a particular period. Although they are all eventually absorbed into employment, most of them have to endure a period of involuntary unemployment while waiting for their turn to come.

In theory these alternative hypotheses of unemployment are clearly distinguishable from each other. Involuntary unemployment requires a labor market with rigid institutionally determined wages; voluntary unemployment requires only a wide dispersion of wages. In principle, the latter can exist without the former, but it is difficult to imagine that this will be the case in the real world. If the same type of labor faces a wide variety of wages, the dispersion will almost certainly be caused, at least in part, by institutionally maintained wages in some segments of the market.

It was shown in Chapter 9 that institutional factors were of minor significance in the determination of earnings compared with standard human capital factors. The size of the enterprise had a significant influence on employees' wage levels, but several other factors which might have been expected to have affected earnings independently—most notably public sector employment—were surprisingly unimportant. For the purposes of the present discussion, however, this conclusion needs to be qualified.

First, the analysis in Chapter 9 was designed to test for the net effect of institutional factors on earnings through channels other than education-experience variables. Even if such independent effects are weak, institutional factors can still significantly influence the ways in

1. The waiting period will be approximately equal to $U/E$, where $U$ is the number of unemployed school leavers, and $E$ is the annual output of school leavers.

which, and the extent to which, educational qualifications determine earnings. In other words, the association of higher earnings with higher educational levels may reflect not only strictly economic factors such as the greater productivity of better-educated workers, but also (perhaps even predominantly) the institutionally-determined weight attached to the acquisition of credentials. Insofar as this is the case, wage rigidities may be important in the economy even though institutional factors appear to have a low degree of significance as independent variables in the determination of earnings.

Second, the analyses in Part II were based on cross-section data for the current earnings of several generations of workers. A more relevant starting point for the study of the problem of unemployment of new entrants to the labor market would be the pattern of earnings in the market when they enter it. This body of data, which is available from the World Bank's School Leavers Survey (SLS), may reveal the importance of factors other than human capital variables more clearly than pooled cross-section data which span several generations. In any event, the pattern of earnings which will be influential for school leavers will be that of their own generation, however it is determined; an analysis of the causes of youth unemployment, therefore, needs to be based on this pattern.

The evidence presented in Chapter 8 showed that earnings were linked with educational attainment in urban Malaysia in a way that strongly suggests the predominance of "credentialism." The material on entry wages from the SLS also points to the existence of wage premiums in particular sectors of the economy (notably the public sector) and to wide variations in earnings for a given level of education. These characteristics suggest that the Malaysian labor market would be likely to foster both a desire to acquire educational credentials and extensive job searches and consequential unemployment as market entrants shop around for the more lucrative jobs.

Nevertheless, it would be a gross oversimplification to ascribe urban unemployment among Malaysian school leavers entirely to the search for jobs. Only a small proportion of the unemployed identified at the time of the SLS had had previous job experience. Questions about any job offers rejected by school leavers failed to elicit much substantive information. There was little evidence of active job search, in the sense of job seekers looking at and consciously rejecting various alternatives before eventually accepting a job. In any event, the average period of waiting was found to be much too long to be explained by any plausible theory of job search.

If some element of rationing of jobs and involuntary unemployment does enter into the explanation of extensive unemployment among school leavers, it becomes necessary to establish the nature of the rigidities in the labor market. It should be clear that wage rigidities in particular occupations or particular types of employment, such as government jobs, cannot alone constitute a sufficient explanation. The market mechanism can operate quite effectively within a rigid system of occupational wages through a process of upgrading the educational qualifications associated with successively lower strata of jobs. As the supply of educated labor runs ahead of the demand for it in the face of wage rigidities based on credentials, more educated persons get selected for jobs previously filled by less educated applicants. Less educated persons, in their turn, now accept lower-paid jobs in occupations they previously would have considered below their standards. The market, in other words, works round any system of occupation-specific wage rigidities, through the revision of expectations and consequential changes in the education-occupation matrix.

Chapter 16 looks at the available material on the education-occupation matrix in Malaysia in recent years. The survey data indicate that the educational attributes of broad occupational groups have changed substantially in recent years. The direction of the change—as might be expected in an economy with a surplus of educated labor—is toward a general upward revision of the educational level of workers in most occupational categories. The School Leavers Survey asked about job seekers' earnings expectations when they left school, and the great majority of respondents accepted jobs at wages substantially below their expectations.

These pressures in the labor market and the responses to them are in line with the expectations of economic theorists. In principle, the pattern of responses can be expected gradually to eliminate the problem of unemployment among school leavers—both by increasing demand for them as their relative wages fall, and by reducing their supply as private demand for education contracts in response to the fall in the rate of return to education. Is the problem of the high rate of open unemployment in Malaysia therefore only a transitional one? Chapter 14 shows that over the 1967–74 period both the rate of unemployment and the period of waiting as measured by national sample survey data have fallen significantly. The improvement is only relative, however. The absolute incidence of unemployment remains high, and the peculiar nature of the problem in Malaysia, exemplified by the inordinately long wait before the typical school leaver finds his first job, needs to be explained.

The SLS study of lower secondary and upper secondary school leavers (LCE and MCE/MCVE certificate holders) which the World Bank undertook in 1973, and which is discussed in detail in the chapters which follow, showed that large numbers of school leavers were still looking for jobs four or five years after their LCE examinations. Of course, a survey which depends on mailed questionnaires is inherently biased toward locating the unemployed more easily than the employed. Hence the information derived from the survey is less useful for measuring the absolute dimensions of the unemployment problem than for analyzing the characteristics of different groups of school leavers in the labor market (including both those with jobs and the unemployed). Nevertheless, it is significant that even the employed reported that the median length of time it took them to get their first job was about one and one half years for those who left school after getting their LCE, and nine months for those with the MCE/MCVE; moreover, as will become clear from Chapter 17, the time taken to get a first job reported by the employed sample in the SLS generally underestimates the average period of waiting in the labor market.

One index of the efficiency with which pressures in the labor market work in reducing the imbalance between supply and demand is the private rate of return to education. The discussion in Chapter 8 made use of three sets of data on earnings related to education—the Post-Enumeration Survey of 1970 (which covers the population of all ages in urban Malaysia), the World Bank's School Leavers Survey of 1973 (which is confined to recent LCE and MCE/MCVE graduates throughout urban Malaysia), and the World Bank's Migration and Employment Survey of 1975 (which again covers the population of all ages but is confined to a sample in three large towns). The three surveys were administered over too short a time, and the material is too diverse, to permit any firm conclusions about the trends in the private rate of return to education. The problem is complicated because, as was shown in Chapter 8, the age-earnings profiles for workers with different educational attainments are not parallel in Malaysia as they are in many industrial economies. Analysis of both the 1970 and 1974 cross-section samples showed that successive levels of education tend to yield progressively larger returns from the age of twenty-five until the age of maximum earnings. This pattern immediately suggests a question which is unanswerable by the present data: Is a major change taking place in the rate of return to higher education, with a reduction in the return for the more recent age cohorts? Will the observed return to education for the older cohorts no longer be valid for today's younger generation as they in turn become older?

The 1975 cross-section data show that for the younger age groups (those between fifteen and twenty-five), the return to education is highest for those with primary education, followed by that for middle over lower secondary education, and least for lower secondary over primary education. Nevertheless, the return to lower secondary education, although small, is positive and significant in the early years. Further, the earnings data from the 1973 SLS show a wide dispersion of earnings in the first job for the lower secondary certificate holders (LCES). It would be surprising if this pattern did not lead to more substantial subsequent returns to lower secondary education for those who had "made good." The general inference to be drawn from this body of data is that there is likely to be a substantial positive return to job searches at the start of a school leaver's career.

Overall, therefore, available evidence suggests that the pressures in the Malaysian labor market over the last decade or so have been in the right direction, toward reducing the surplus supply of educated labor, but that the process has not been moving nearly rapidly enough. The initial period of waiting and the rate of unemployment on the one hand, and the return to further schooling on the other, all remain at levels which would be considered inconsistently high in an industrial economy. What special factors exist in the Malaysian labor market (and in other developing countries) which so perversely slow down the process of adjustment over time?

One element in the dynamic process of labor market adjustment, which has been singled out for discussion in some analyses as a possible causal factor, is the way in which an increasing supply of educated labor tends to induce larger demand for such labor in the market.[2] As a surplus of labor of a particular educational level builds up in the market, employers have a tendency to upgrade the educational requirement of jobs previously filled by less educated people. At the most elementary level, such a tendency might be traced to employers' intrinsic respect for formal education and their uncertainty about the ideal educational re-

2. See Mark Blaug, Richard Layard, and Maureen Woodhall, *The Causes of Graduate Unemployment in India* (London: Allen Lane, 1969), especially pp. 36–39.

quirement of any particular job. This tendency would be encouraged if, as seems likely in most markets other than that of temporary unskilled labor, it costs less to raise employees' entry qualifications than to raise wages.

The process of upgrading the educational requirements of jobs would be further fueled if the expansion in the quantity of education leads to a decline in its quality.[3] As rapid expansion in the education system breeds congestion (through shortages of teaching material and amenities as well as reductions in the quality of teaching), employers find that the new middle secondary graduates perform at the level achieved by lower secondary school leavers a few years ago. Thus the upgrading process, which might have started as a supply-induced phenomenon, soon tends to justify itself and leads to further demand-induced upgrading. The rate of return to education falls at all levels of education, but falls most at the lower levels. Thus the *differential* rate of return to successive levels of schooling may not fall very much, if at all. Similarly, the incidence of unemployment is shifted downward, with the highest rates observed at the lower educational levels. The net effect of the whole process is to encourage school leavers at successive levels to stay on longer in the school system rather than to enter the labor market. This leads to further dilution of school quality and to the development of a truly vicious circle.

Thus the strong economic forces which cause rightward shifts in the supply curve of school leavers may in fact generate pressures which shift demand curves in the same direction. This process naturally slows down the market clearing mechanism. A subsidiary but quantitatively important point is that a clearing mechanism which works through the upgrading of job qualifications reduces unemployment less successfully than one which works through changes in wage rates. The process of upgrading itself increases the dispersion in wage rates facing a school leaver. The net effect is to increase the value of job searches in school leavers' calculations, both by raising the prospective gains from searches and by lowering the alternative earnings forgone in the "free entry" sector.

It has been assumed in the preceding paragraphs that adjustments in the quality of labor are made by employers with reference to the formal educational qualifications of job seekers. It has only rarely been noted in the literature that employers might be equally interested in the age

3. Ibid.

of new entrants when fixing their hiring policies. In certain sectors of the economy, particularly the public and formal private sector, the long-term commitment of the new recruit to the job might be of real interest to employers. In interviews I conducted, employers stressed the importance of judging the maturity of teenagers who applied for jobs; many of them strongly preferred applicants at least seventeen or eighteen years old so that they could form such judgments with a reasonable hope of accuracy. Insofar as a large proportion of secondary school leavers might be interested in working in these sectors, their mean waiting time after leaving school would tend to be long.

As the stock of job seekers with education beyond the primary level increases and jobs are upgraded, it is probable that formal educational attainment and age would become joint criteria for hiring new employees. This development is also likely to occur as employers redefine an increasing proportion of jobs in terms of a more formally structured work force.

Why do secondary school leavers not enter areas of the labor market where the age barrier does not exist? The answer probably lies partly in job seekers' evaluations of the gains from job searches while they are wholly unemployed and partly in the occupational preferences of school leavers. The sales and services sector is likely to be the major source of the least formally structured employment opportunities, and it will be shown that this is the sector which secondary school leavers typically tend to avoid.

A detailed analysis of the determinants of unemployment and of the waiting period is undertaken in Chapter 17. It is preceded by a description of the sample of the School Leavers Survey in Chapter 15. In addition to their emphasis on the causes of unemployment, these chapters discuss other points of interest, including the parental background of different types of school leavers, their pattern of geographical mobility, differences in the period of waiting by racial group, and differences in the employment experience of academic and vocational school leavers.

CHAPTER 14

# The Problem of Unemployment
# in Peninsular Malaysia

THIS CHAPTER BEGINS WITH A BRIEF DISCUSSION of the different types of unemployment which need to be distinguished in any analysis of the problem. The second and third sections analyze unemployment patterns in Malaysia and the ways in which they have changed over time and offer some comparisons with other Asian countries which put the Malaysian situation in perspective.

## Types of Unemployment

Unemployment is generally measured by a rate at a point in time. It relates the number of those counted as unemployed during a reference period (say, a week) to the total labor force during the same period. This provides an overall unemployment rate in the reference week; separate rates can be calculated in the same way for individual groups defined by age, sex, race, or other common characteristics. Conceptually these rates imply the measurement of a static amount, the stock of the unemployed in the week in question. But the stock of unemployment measured by the percentage rate at a given point in time includes in one figure two dynamic dimensions of the unemployment problem: the number of people who become unemployed a week (or the rate of flow into unemployment) and the duration of unemployment which a person suffers before finding a job (which is a way of expressing the rate of flow out of unemployment). If, in fact, the stock rate of unemployment is steady, there is a simple relation between these three concepts:

Number of unemployed at a point in time = Number becoming unemployed a week *times* average completed duration in weeks

or,

Percentage unemployed at a point in time (stock rate) = Percentage
becoming unemployed a week (flow rate) *times*
average completed duration (in weeks).

The concept of duration in the above identity refers to completed duration; in other words, it covers only those who have moved out of their
state of unemployment and have found a job. A sample survey of the
unemployed at a given point in time will, of course, yield data only
on the uncompleted spell of unemployment.

It is clear that various combinations of flow rates and average dura-
tions will yield the same stock rate of unemployment, although they
will have widely different implications for economic welfare. Differences
in observed stock rates of unemployment between demographic groups
may also obscure the fact that the flow rate or the average duration of
unemployment may be increasing for one group and decreasing for
another. For example, teenagers in all economies have a higher stock
rate of unemployment than people in the prime age groups. This is
generally because of the much larger flow rate of unemployment among
the young—reflecting the fact that new members of the labor force are
regularly coming into the market and looking for their first job, or the
tendency for a significant proportion of the new workers to try out several jobs before settling into a satisfactory one. In some economies these
high flow rates are at least partly offset by a relatively short average
duration of completed unemployment for the younger workers.

### Frictional and Hard-Core Unemployment

Economists have often made a distinction between frictional unemployment—which a relatively large number of workers could be expected to suffer (or even choose to incur) for short spells, because the
labor market is not able to match demanders and suppliers of labor
perfectly without any time lag—and the more serious phenomenon of
structural or hard-core unemployment, which keeps a smaller proportion of the work force idle for long spells. A substantial proportion of
youth unemployment in an economy is likely to be frictional, while a
larger proportion of the unemployed among older age groups tends to
fall into the hard-core category; this group continues to be a problem
even when conditions in the labor market as a whole are generally good.

Recent studies of the U.S. labor market have, however, called into
question the usefulness of distinguishing between the frictional and

hard-core categories entirely by the duration of the unemployment. In particular, available data do not indicate the existence of a group suffering lengthy and continuous unemployment. The following data on the duration of unemployment in the United States are given for a relatively "good" year (1968) and a relatively "bad" year (1971); they show the percentage of the total unemployed workers by the number of weeks of their unemployment:[1]

| Year | Less than 5 weeks | 5–14 weeks | 15–26 weeks | 27 weeks and over |
|------|------|------|------|------|
| 1968 | 56.6 | 23.3 | 14.6 | 5.5 |
| 1971 | 44.7 | 21.2 | 23.7 | 10.4 |

Even in an exceptionally difficult year such as 1971 only about 10 percent of the unemployed were out of work for more than six months. Generally, rather more than half of those unemployed had been out of work for less than five weeks.

New workers trying to break into the labor market did not typically appear to face the problem of long spells of initial unemployment. Comparative figures for the duration of unemployment among the young generally confirm the point made above about the stock rate of unemployment for this group being a function of high flow rates. The U.S. data below are for April 1969 (a good month), and again show the percentage of the total in each unemployed group by the number of weeks of unemployment:[2]

| Sex and age | Less than 5 weeks | 5–14 weeks | 15–26 weeks | 27 weeks and over |
|------|------|------|------|------|
| Both sexes, 16–19 years | 60.1 | 25.6 | 7.3 | 7.0 |
| Male, 20 years and over | 47.9 | 26.2 | 18.4 | 7.4 |
| Female, 20 years and over | 55.1 | 25.6 | 14.5 | 4.9 |

The stock rate of unemployment for the 16 to 19 age group was significantly higher than that for the labor force as a whole, but it is clear from the table that unemployment in this age group was much more strongly concentrated in the short-term categories than it was for those

1. U.S. Department of Labor, *Handbook of Labor Statistics, 1972* (Washington, D.C., 1973).

2. U.S. Bureau of Labor Statistics, *Employment and Earnings*, vol. 15 (May 1969), quoted by Robert E. Hall, "Why Is the Unemployment Rate So High at Full Employment?" *Brookings Papers on Economic Activity*, vol. 3 (1970), p. 385.

aged 20 and over. By the same token, the proportion of those aged under 20 in the two longer-term categories was significantly lower than that for those over 20 taken together.

While the duration of unemployment for an individual may not be very long in any age group, there is a problem of abnormal unemployment related to the phenomenon of labor turnover. As Hall puts it, "The true problem of hard-core unemployment is that certain members of the labor force account for a disproportionate share of unemployment because they drift from one unsatisfactory job to another, spending time between jobs either unemployed or out of the labor force."[3]

For 1968 Hall calculated that the implied average time gap between spells of unemployment for a given individual was about twenty-seven months, so that the probability that a "normal" worker would suffer unemployment more than once during the same year would be very low indeed. Data on unemployment histories, however, showed that a third of those who had been unemployed at all in 1968 had had two or more spells of unemployment. This phenomenon had been noted twenty years earlier by Fichandler for 1943–50. He wrote, "In each year the percentage of workers who became unemployed at least twice during the year has been much greater than it would have been if a random distribution is assumed."[4] Some sections of the labor force in the United States have always shown a disproportionate tendency toward relatively frequent spells of unemployment. Work in progress by Holt and Smith shows that "the quitting rate for blacks is roughly double that for whites; the layoff rate of blacks is double that of whites. Together these account for most of the unemployment differential" between blacks and whites.[5]

Thus, proneness to frequent spells of unemployment need not be characteristic of a particular age group; it could, for example, be the typical cause of unemployment among blacks of all age groups in the United States. The large proportion of teenage workers with a short spell of unemployment is, however, compatible with an equal or larger incidence of the phenomenon of recurrent unemployment.

3. Hall, "Why Is the Unemployment Rate So High?" p. 389.

4. Thomas C. Fichandler in Waldimir S. Woytinsky and associates, *Employment and Wages in the United States* (New York: Twentieth Century Fund, 1953), p. 403.

5. Charles Holt, "Comment" on Hall, "Why Is the Unemployment Rate So High?" in *Brookings Papers on Economic Activity*, vol. 3 (1970), p. 406.

## Unemployment of Young Workers

The employment patterns of new entrants in the labor market are of considerable interest in any economy. Data on spells of unemployment may not be collected in the regular surveys, but if recurrent unemployment is in fact serious for this group, the existence of the problem will be signaled by the relatively small proportion of young job seekers reported as looking for a job for the first time.

The length of initial unemployment experienced by new entrants, expressed as the time it takes them to find their first job, will tend to vary from one economy to another—and this variation can affect levels of youth unemployment. Indeed, it might appear that an economy in which the average duration of unemployment among new job seekers is relatively long will also have a relatively high stock rate of unemployment compared with another economy in which the average duration is shorter (provided that the two have similar demographic and educational structures). This is not the case, however, because the flow rate of unemployment, the other component of the unemployment rate, is not determined only by the age structure of the population and its pattern of schooling. In an economy in which the school leaver finds it relatively difficult to get a first job, new job seekers will be typically sluggish in entering the labor market to make active job searches. This will reduce the flow rate of unemployment, and the lower flow rate will in turn partly or wholly offset the longer duration of active unemployment in the economy. It will be shown that this is in fact the situation in Malaysia, in contrast to, for example, the Philippines.

## The Basic Issues

The analysis in this section of unemployment in Malaysia depends heavily on a special survey undertaken for 1967–68 by the Malaysian Department of Statistics.[6] (A labor force sample survey exists for 1962

6. N. S. Chaudhry, *Socio-Economic Sample Survey of Households—Employment and Unemployment* (Kuala Lumpur: Department of Statistics, 1970), hereafter referred to as SES. In recent years the Department of Statistics has undertaken quarterly labor force surveys which provide summary statements of unemployment rates by certain categories. These will be referred to later. The household surveys

but is less detailed.) Unfortunately, no data were collected on the number of spells of unemployment suffered by the sample during the year; no direct evidence is available, therefore, as to whether any particular part of the labor force is disproportionately prone to relatively frequent periods of unemployment of the kind noted by Holt and Smith. Available evidence suggests, however, that this is by no means the central problem of unemployment in Malaysia. The major problem appears to be that of getting a start in the labor market, and Malaysia's high unemployment rate is largely owing to the long delay experienced by new workers before they can get their first jobs.

Unemployment in Malaysia is very heavily concentrated among the young (see Table 14-1). The rate of unemployment falls sharply with age; the 15–19 age group alone accounted for nearly half the total unemployed, and those aged 15–24 accounted for 75 percent of the total. As a point of comparison, teenagers in the United States (the 16–19 age group) accounted for about 25 percent of all the unemployed in the late 1960s. The evidence seems to be overwhelmingly against the hypothesis that the young move from job to job before settling down; in other words, it appears not to be the case that Malaysia's high rate of unemployment reflects high labor turnover in the younger age groups. First-time job seekers accounted for 60 percent of the male and 72 percent of the female stock of unemployed of all ages and for as much as 80 percent of the unemployed in the 15–24 age group.[7]

The difficulty of breaking into the labor market is revealed in the extraordinarily long average duration of unemployment for first job seekers (see Table 14-2).[8] Half the first-time unemployed of all ages had been unemployed for one year or more (the proportion is the same for the 15–24 age group). The difficulty of obtaining the first job is

---

undertaken by the Malaysian government and the World Bank have tried to find out about the state of unemployment in the sampled population, but for reasons to be discussed below a household questionnaire is not the appropriate instrument for obtaining information on unemployment. The major characteristics of the unemployment problem revealed by the 1967–68 survey, however, remain valid even now, as can be inferred from pieces of information available from the Malaysian quarterly surveys, the household surveys, and the School Leavers Survey—although the *quantitative* importance of the problem may have changed somewhat. For this reason, material from the 1967–68 survey is presented in some detail, and the present tense is used for ease of exposition.

7. SES, p. 120.

8. Unfortunately the data are not presented separately in the SES for the age groups 15–19 and 20–24.

Table 14-1. Unemployment as a Percentage of the Labor Force by Sex and Age Group, 1967

| Unemployed | Aged 15–19 | | | Aged 20–24 | | | Aged 25–34 | | |
|---|---|---|---|---|---|---|---|---|---|
| | Male | Female | Total | Male | Female | Total | Male | Female | Total |
| Actively | 20.8 | 20.1 | 20.5 | 10.9 | 12.7 | 11.5 | 2.7 | 5.0 | 3.5 |
| Passively | 3.8 | 8.6 | 5.8 | 0.8 | 5.2 | 2.4 | 0.4 | 3.9 | 1.5 |
| Total | 24.6 | 28.7 | 26.3 | 11.7 | 17.9 | 13.9 | 3.1 | 8.9 | 5.0 |

| | Aged 35–54 | | | Aged 55–64 | | | Aged 15–64 | | |
|---|---|---|---|---|---|---|---|---|---|
| | Male | Female | Total | Male | Female | Total | Male | Female | Total |
| Actively | 1.7 | 2.2 | 1.9 | 2.3 | 1.3 | 2.0 | 6.2 | 8.1 | 6.8 |
| Passively | 0.6 | 2.0 | 1.0 | 1.0 | 1.4 | 1.1 | 1.1 | 4.3 | 2.2 |
| Total | 2.3 | 4.2 | 2.9 | 3.3 | 2.7 | 3.1 | 7.3 | 12.4 | 9.0 |

*Source:* SES, Annex, p. 107.

Table 14-2. Percentage Distribution of First-Time Unemployed and Others by Waiting Period, Sex, and Age Group

| Sex and waiting period | First-time unemployed | | | | Others | | | |
|---|---|---|---|---|---|---|---|---|
| | Subtotal | Aged 15–24 | Aged 25–34 | Aged 35–64 | Subtotal | Aged 15–24 | Aged 25–34 | Aged 35–64 |
| Male | 100.00 | 100.00 | 100.00 | 100.00 | 100.00 | 100.00 | 100.00 | 100.00 |
| Less than 3 months | 13.76 | 13.71 | 11.78 | 36.04 | 35.07 | 32.94 | 45.49 | 32.21 |
| 3–6 months | 13.52 | 13.93 | 1.40 | 15.91 | 14.68 | 16.24 | 13.41 | 13.27 |
| 6–12 months | 23.59 | 23.71 | 20.43 | 20.70 | 16.99 | 20.49 | 13.97 | 14.41 |
| 1–3 years | 34.63 | 35.00 | 26.60 | 15.91 | 22.00 | 2.84 | 18.65 | 22.97 |
| 3–5 years | 10.44 | 10.07 | 22.53 | ... | 5.46 | 4.09 | 6.07 | 6.01 |
| 5 years and more | 4.05 | 3.54 | 17.25 | 11.36 | 5.07 | 2.37 | 2.38 | 11.12 |
| Female | 100.00 | 100.00 | 100.00 | 100.00 | 100.00 | 100.00 | 100.00 | 100.00 |
| Less than 3 months | 16.42 | 16.00 | 17.49 | 22.37 | 27.97 | 28.77 | 23.70 | 31.03 |
| 3–6 months | 14.27 | 14.86 | 9.03 | 14.31 | 16.12 | 16.95 | 15.16 | 15.66 |
| 6–12 months | 21.05 | 22.58 | 9.34 | 17.22 | 15.99 | 16.86 | 16.13 | 14.29 |
| 1–3 years | 34.99 | 36.93 | 25.45 | 19.77 | 25.99 | 28.42 | 27.00 | 20.57 |
| 3–5 years | 7.73 | 6.65 | 17.20 | 7.47 | 6.76 | 4.79 | 9.87 | 6.94 |
| 5 years and more | 5.54 | 3.06 | 21.41 | 18.86 | 7.19 | 4.20 | 8.11 | 11.50 |

.... Zero or negligible.
Source: SES, Annex, p. 137.

supported by evidence that the duration of unemployment appears to be significantly less for those who have had a job than for first-job seekers for each separate age and sex group. For example, the median duration of unemployment for males who have worked before is six months, while for first-job seekers it is one year (the mode of the distribution is less than three months for the former and one to three years for the latter). To put the issue in perspective, a young entrant into the market in the United States would typically be unemployed for about a month before obtaining his first job, whereas in Malaysia he would most likely wait at least a year.

Unemployment associated with initial entry into the labor market, especially among the young, is much more important in Malaysia than either the classical hard-core unemployment or the high turnover unemployment affecting some groups in the United States. With regard to the latter phenomenon, it has been shown that the majority of the unemployed were first-job seekers (and that this was overwhelmingly the case among the young who make up the bulk of total unemployment). With regard to the hard-core unemployed, this group can be defined, somewhat arbitrarily, as those aged over twenty-five who have been unemployed for more than one year. This is not an insignificant percentage of the total, but the absolute numbers are small—about 8,000 males and as many females (out of a total of 176,000 of both sexes).

### Unemployment by Educational Level

In 1967–68 about 9 percent of the unemployed had no formal education, 48.8 percent had primary education, 32.4 percent had lower or middle secondary education, and 8.1 percent had upper secondary education. These figures provide a basic educational profile of the unemployed; to relate unemployment and education levels in an analytically useful way, however, it is necessary to develop a profile of the unemployment levels of workforce groups with varying types of educational attainment. Figure 14-1 gives the unemployment rates (as percentages of the labor force) of groups with different levels of education. The curve follows an inverted U-shaped pattern—much more pronounced for females—which has become common in developing countries in recent years. The figure shows a strong mode of the distribution for those with upper secondary qualifications (ten to eleven years of education). Although the absolute number of persons with upper secondary education is considerably smaller than that with lower second-

Figure 14–1. Male, Female, and Total Unemployment as a
Percentage of the Labor Force by Years of Education, 1967

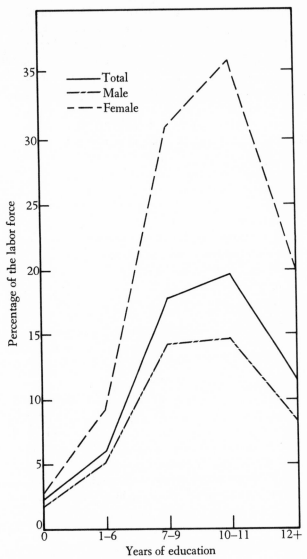

Source: SES, 1970, annex, pp. 32, 122.

ary education, the unemployment rate among the former is higher, presumably because there are more people at this educational level who are actively seeking employment.

The relatively high percentages of unemployment among those with lower and middle secondary school educations may reflect the fact that unemployment is concentrated in the younger age group, which is likely to make up a large proportion of the segment of the labor force with secondary education, because of the recent expansion of the education system. Thus it is necessary to control for the age factor in coming to conclusions about the incidence of unemployment at different levels of education.

Data can be extracted from SES on rates of unemployment for separate age and sex groups by levels of education (see Table 14-3). If those with higher education (whose absolute numbers are small) are omitted, the overwhelming impression from the table is the extremely high incidence of unemployment among secondary school leavers of

Table 14-3. Unemployment Rates as a Percentage of the Labor Force by Education, Sex, and Age Group, 1967

| Years of education and sex | Aged 15–65 | Aged 15–19 | Aged 20–24 | Aged 25–64 |
|---|---|---|---|---|
| 12 or more | | | | |
| Male | 8.5 | 46.4 | 17.2 | 1.4 |
| Female | 20.1 | 44.7 | 22.6 | 4.6 |
| Total | 11.9 | 45.5 | 19.4 | 2.0 |
| 10–11 (upper secondary; forms IV, V) | | | | |
| Male | 14.7 | 47.0 | 22.2 | 3.9 |
| Female | 35.9 | 71.9 | 40.0 | 10.5 |
| Total | 19.7 | 55.1 | 27.9 | 5.0 |
| 7–9 (lower secondary; forms I–III) | | | | |
| Male | 14.5 | 33.5 | 15.6 | 3.3 |
| Female | 30.8 | 44.8 | 28.1 | 11.8 |
| Total | 17.6 | 36.6 | 18.5 | 4.3 |
| 1–6 (primary) | | | | |
| Male | 5.1 | 16.0 | 7.8 | 2.2 |
| Female | 9.1 | 15.9 | 8.0 | 4.7 |
| Total | 6.0 | 16.0 | 7.8 | 2.6 |
| No formal education | | | | |
| Male | 1.8 | 7.6 | 4.5 | 1.5 |
| Female | 2.8 | 10.8 | 5.3 | 2.1 |
| Total | 2.4 | 9.9 | 5.1 | 1.9 |

Source: SES, Annex, pp. 33, 122.

the younger age groups—both male and female. It is substantially higher than for primary school leavers and reaches a peak level of 50 percent or more for upper secondary school leavers. The high overall rate of unemployment in Peninsular Malaysia is clearly due to the remarkably high rates among secondary school leavers, persisting even for the 20–24 age group.

*Unemployment of Males and Females*

As Table 14-4 shows, females represent about 40 percent of the unemployed who are actively seeking work in the Malaysian urban labor

Table 14-4. Active Unemployment by Educational Attainment for Urban and Rural Areas

| Educational attainment | Actively unemployed | | | | | |
| | Number (thousands) | | Percentage of total | | Percentage of labor force | |
| | Urban | Rural | Urban | Rural | Urban | Rural |
|---|---|---|---|---|---|---|
| No formal education | 6.4 | 9.3 | 7.9 | 9.7 | 5.6 | 1.7 |
| Male | 1.6 | 2.8 | 3.7 | 4.5 | 3.6 | 1.4 |
| Female | 4.8 | 6.6 | 13.2 | 18.9 | 6.9 | 1.9 |
| Primary | 30.8 | 55.4 | 38.2 | 57.7 | 7.4 | 5.3 |
| Male | 19.4 | 37.0 | 43.6 | 60.5 | 6.0 | 4.7 |
| Female | 11.4 | 18.3 | 31.6 | 52.7 | 12.1 | 7.2 |
| Lower/middle secondary | 33.0 | 24.2 | 41.0 | 25.2 | 17.6 | 18.7 |
| Male | 18.8 | 17.1 | 42.2 | 28.0 | 13.3 | 16.0 |
| Female | 14.2 | 7.1 | 39.2 | 20.3 | 31.0 | 31.3 |
| Upper secondary | 9.3 | 5.0 | 11.5 | 5.2 | 14.5 | 23.7 |
| Male | 4.0 | 3.1 | 9.1 | 5.1 | 8.9 | 19.2 |
| Female | 5.3 | 1.9 | 14.5 | 5.4 | 27.5 | 39.1 |
| Religious | 0.3 | 2.0 | 0.4 | 2.1 | 13.8 | 12.4 |
| Male | 0.2 | 1.1 | 0.4 | 1.8 | 12.7 | 9.7 |
| Female | 0.1 | 1.0 | 0.4 | 2.7 | 15.5 | 17.9 |
| Teachers, technical university, and other | 0.8 | 0.1 | 0.9 | 0.1 | 2.5 | 0.7 |
| Male | 0.4 | 0.1 | 0.8 | 0.2 | 1.7 | 9.5 |
| Female | 0.4 | . . . | 1.2 | . . . | 4.1 | . . . |
| Total | 80.7 | 96.0 | 100.0 | 100.0 | 9.9 | 5.4 |
| Male | 44.5 | 61.2 | 100.0 | 100.0 | 7.7 | 5.4 |
| Female | 36.2 | 34.8 | 100.0 | 100.0 | 15.2 | 5.5 |

. . . Zero or negligible.
*Source:* SES, p. 134.

market. The female unemployment rate is twice that for males in the urban market, but about the same as the male rate in the rural areas (where females represent just over one-third of the unemployed). The high overall urban rate of female unemployment is largely due to the very large proportions of the female labor force represented by jobless lower/middle and upper secondary school leavers. In absolute numbers nearly as many females as males in these two groups were unemployed, and the higher female percentages reflect their lower participation rate in the labor force.

The data in Table 14-4 refer to the actively unemployed, that is, those without jobs who are actively searching for them. It is sometimes observed that female members of the working age groups do not actively look for work in the labor market but would be willing to accept remunerative employment should the opportunity present itself. The SES tried to identify these "passively unemployed" potential workers as a group separate from those actively looking for work. As might be expected, three quarters of the passively unemployed are females; a substantial portion of them are concentrated in the rural areas and have no more than primary education. If the actively and passively unemployed groups are taken together, the distribution of the unemployed is as follows:[9]

|        | Urban  | Rural  |
|--------|--------|--------|
| Male   | 48,200 | 76,000 |
| Female | 47,600 | 60,700 |

Thus, females form about 50 percent of the total unemployed in the cities and nearly as large a proportion in rural areas. To the extent that the passively unemployed are defined as willing to enter employment if a suitable job opportunity becomes available, the figures above represent a more complete (and more negative) picture of the imbalance between labor supply and available jobs in the market than do the data for the active unemployed alone.

### Rural-Urban Differences

As might be expected, the rate of active unemployment (shown below as a percentage of the labor force) is higher for urban than for

9. SES, vol. 2, pp. 35–36.

rural areas. The differences are, however, much more striking for females than for males:[10]

|  | Male | Female | Total |
|---|---|---|---|
| Metropolitan | 7.8 | 16.1 | 10.1 |
| Other urban areas | 7.6 | 14.4 | 9.7 |
| Rural areas | 5.4 | 5.5 | 5.4 |

The age distribution of the unemployed is basically the same for
urban and rural areas, with persons under the age of twenty-five con-
stituting the bulk of the unemployed in both types of markets. Urban
and rural unemployment rates vary, however, with respect to the two
principal racial groups, Malays and Chinese. The incidence of active
unemployment (as a percentage of the labor force) is significantly
higher for the Malays in the urban areas for both sexes, but especially
among males; in the rural areas it is slightly higher for the Chinese,
notably among the females:[11]

|  | Urban | Rural |
|---|---|---|
| *Males* | | |
| Malay | 10.2 | 4.7 |
| Chinese | 6.0 | 4.9 |
| *Females* | | |
| Malay | 15.8 | 4.6 |
| Chinese | 13.9 | 5.8 |

## Differences by Race

In spite of the Malays' relatively high urban unemployment rate, the
nationwide incidence of unemployment is actually smaller for the
Malays than it is for the Chinese or the Indians. As the following
figures show, the Indians have a much higher unemployment rate
(as a percentage of the labor force) than the other two races:[12]

|  | Males | Females | Total |
|---|---|---|---|
| Malay | 5.7 | 6.0 | 5.8 |
| Chinese | 5.5 | 9.7 | 6.9 |
| Indian | 9.7 | 11.7 | 10.3 |

From a comparison of the rates of unemployment by educational
levels for the principal races (see Table 14-5), it is apparent that more

10. SES, p. 130. Metropolitan areas in the table are Johore Bahru, Malacca,
Kuala Lumpur, Klang, Ipoh, and Georgetown.
11. SES, p. 133.
12. SES, p. 110.

Table 14-5. Unemployment as a Percentage of the Labor Force
by Sex, Race, and Education

| Education | Male | | Female | | Total | |
|---|---|---|---|---|---|---|
| | Malay | Chinese | Malay | Chinese | Malay | Chinese |
| No formal | 2.3 | 4.3 | 4.6 | 5.3 | 3.7 | 5.0 |
| Primary | 6.2 | 4.7 | 17.3 | 10.7 | 8.6 | 6.4 |
| Lower secondary | 20.6 | 9.5 | 50.6 | 26.2 | 26.0 | 13.3 |
| Middle secondary | 25.9 | 9.7 | 41.5 | 34.5 | 29.6 | 16.4 |
| Upper secondary | 18.6 | 10.9 | 39.5 | 28.6 | 24.1 | 16.5 |

Source: SES, Annex, p. 120.

Malays than Chinese are unemployed at all levels of education except for the lowest (no formal education). The higher levels of Malay unemployment are particularly marked for the lower and middle secondary levels, as already noted. Since the number of Malays with more than primary education is substantially smaller than the number of the Chinese with such educational attainment, Malay unemployed secondary school leavers amount to about 27 percent of total Malay unemployment whereas the similar percentage for the Chinese is as high as 42 percent. But the *rates* of unemployment among those in urban areas and those with some secondary school qualification are significantly higher for the Malays than for the Chinese—two politically important aspects of the problem of unemployment in Malaysia.

There is some evidence to suggest that the duration of unemployment is also higher in general for Malays than for Chinese, and that it takes the first-time Malay job seekers longer to break into the market (see Table 14-6). Statistics on duration of unemployment are not, however, available separately from the SES data for urban job seekers or for groups with different educational qualifications. It is thus impossible to tell whether the relatively high rates of unemployment among the Malays in the urban areas or with secondary school qualification are specifically associated with longer periods of waiting for first jobs.[13]

13. This question is addressed in the material collected by the School Leavers Survey (SLS); see Chapter 17.

Table 14-6. Percentage Distribution of First-Time Unemployed by Age, Race, and Waiting Period

| Waiting period | Aged 15–24 | | Aged 25–34 | |
| --- | --- | --- | --- | --- |
| | Malay | Chinese | Malay | Chinese |
| Less than 3 months | 14.6 | 17.4 | 19.8 | 15.0 |
| 3–6 months | 12.6 | 17.0 | 4.8 | 5.9 |
| 7–12 months | 21.4 | 24.8 | 7.9 | 14.0 |
| 1–3 years | 37.0 | 33.7 | 24.7 | 24.7 |
| 3–5 years | 10.4 | 5.0 | 19.3 | 20.0 |
| 5 years and over | 4.0 | 2.5 | 23.4 | 20.5 |
| Total | 100.0 | 100.0 | 100.0 | 100.0 |

Source: SES, Annex, p. 140.

## Changes in Unemployment over Time

The first systematic survey of unemployment in Malaysia was made in 1962.[14] Although it is not possible to compare details from different sample surveys, a general comparison of some of the basic data from the 1962 survey with SES data for 1967 suggests that the problem of unemployment probably increased over the period. According to Table 14-7, unemployment rates increased for both sexes in urban areas and for males in rural areas; the increases by age group were especially marked among young males.

The increase in unemployment was relatively more pronounced for the groups with at least secondary school education. Table 14-8 sets out the nature of the growth of the labor force and the increase in unemployment for the decade 1957–67. The spread of education is revealed in the high rate of growth of the labor force with ten or more years of education. The most significant point, however, is that the rate of growth of unemployment was higher than the growth rate of the labor force for the two top educational groups. The unemployment rate for those with no education dropped markedly, although the labor force in this group continued to increase to some extent.

14. Federation of Malaysia, *Report on Employment, Unemployment, and Underemployment, 1962* (June 1963); hereafter referred to as 1962 Survey.

Table 14-7.  The Unemployed and Those Outside the Labor Force
by Urban or Rural Residence, Age Group, and Sex, 1962 and 1967

| Age group and sex | Unemployment rate (percentage of labor force) | | | | Outside labor force (percentage of population) | | | |
|---|---|---|---|---|---|---|---|---|
| | Urban | | Rural | | Urban | | Rural | |
| | 1962 | 1967 | 1962 | 1967 | 1962 | 1967 | 1962 | 1967 |
| 15–19 | | | | | | | | |
| Male | 24.0 | 29.2 | 14.1 | 17.7 | 55.4 | 51.2 | 36.1 | 33.6 |
| Female | 30.6 | 29.9 | 15.4 | 15.6 | 69.9 | 64.3 | 56.9 | 51.5 |
| Total | 26.4 | 28.0 | 14.6 | 16.8 | 62.2 | 57.3 | 46.3 | 45.7 |
| 20–24 | | | | | | | | |
| Male | 11.2 | 13.5 | 6.1 | 9.4 | 9.2 | 9.3 | 7.0 | 5.8 |
| Female | 18.3 | 19.9 | 8.5 | 8.5 | 55.8 | 50.9 | 53.5 | 51.5 |
| Total | 13.6 | 15.8 | 6.9 | 9.1 | 33.0 | 30.9 | 30.6 | n.a. |
| All ages[a] | | | | | | | | |
| Male | 7.0 | 7.7 | 4.4 | 5.4 | 16.0 | 15.7 | 13.0 | 11.7 |
| Female | 14.6 | 15.2 | 6.1 | 5.5 | 70.1 | 65.7 | 54.2 | 52.1 |
| Total | 8.9 | 9.9 | 5.0 | 5.4 | 42.5 | 40.9 | 33.0 | 32.2 |

a. All ages in 1962 refer to those aged 15–70 and in 1967 to those aged 15–64.
*Sources:* 1962 Survey, tables 1-7 (a) and (b); ses, p. 132.

The increase in the labor surplus in the decade up to 1967 is reflected in an increase in duration of unemployment. Figure 14-2 shows
the marked increase in the percentage of long-term unemployed among
the jobless aged 18–24 (who make up the bulk of total unemployment),

Table 14-8.  Percentage Distribution of the Labor Force
and of the Unemployed by Years of Education

| Years of education | 1957 | | 1967 | | Percentage change, 1957–67 | |
|---|---|---|---|---|---|---|
| | Labor force | Unemployed | Labor force | Unemployed | Labor force | Unemployed |
| 10 and more | 5.9 | 10.1 | 10.0 | 22.7 | 120.8 | 193.3 |
| 7–9 | 8.1 | 14.9 | 7.6 | 19.1 | 22.5 | 68.2 |
| 1–6 | 44.9 | 48.6 | 57.1 | 50.5 | 65.0 | 6.1 |
| 0 | 41.2 | 26.4 | 25.3 | 7.7 | 20.2 | 6.5 |
| Total | 100.0 | 100.0 | 100.0 | 100.0 | 30.0 | 31.1 |

*Source:* D. R. Snodgrass, "The Growth and Utilization of Labor Supply in
West Malaysia" (Kuala Lumpur, February 1972; processed), tables 3 and 13, pp.
12 and 41.

Figure 14–2. Percentage of the Unemployed Aged 15–24 by Waiting Period, 1962 and 1967

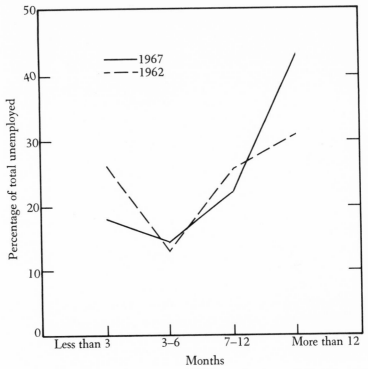

Sources: 1962 Survey, annex, tables 2.10(a) and (b); SES, 1970, annex, p. 137.

and the relative decline of the percentage who were unemployed for a short period.

No detailed survey of the unemployed has been undertaken in Malaysia since 1967, but the Malaysian Department of Statistics has administered a sample survey of labor force status roughly twice a year since 1971. Because of the experimental nature of these surveys, it is not possible to compile a reliable time series on unemployment rates. A special effort was made, however, in the April-May 1974 survey to obtain reliable data on unemployment and, in particular, to tackle carefully the question of passive unemployment. During this period a Socioeconomic Household Survey was also undertaken by the department, which included questions about the employment status of the sample.

In the Household Survey the passively unemployed included all those who were not seeking work but said without prompting that they would accept a job if it were offered. Since this highly subjective statistic was heavily dependent on the respondent, in the April-May Labor Force Survey it was decided to adopt more fully the U.N. recommendation for counting those who showed direct or indirect evidence of wanting work. This approach produced a substantially higher rate of passive unemployment as a percentage of the labor force:[15]

|                      | Active | Passive | Total |
|----------------------|--------|---------|-------|
| Household Survey     | 4.5    | 0.7     | 5.3   |
| Labor Force Survey   | 4.4    | 2.9     | 7.4   |

Because of the different ways used to establish the number of passively unemployed and the inevitable changes in definition, it is difficult to make a precise comparison of the incidence of unemployment in 1967 and 1974. According to Table 14-1 the rates for 1967 were 6.8 percent for active and 2.1 percent for passive unemployment, giving an overall total of 9.0 percent. It is clear that the active unemployment rate fell over the seven-year period by about a third, but no clear conclusion is possible about the passive unemployment rate. The alternative estimates provided by the two 1974 surveys show it either falling very sharply or rising slightly by comparison with 1967. This uncertainty in turn makes any judgment about changes in the total incidence of unemployment (active and passive) uncertain. While it is clear that the overall rate had fallen significantly by 1974 from its 1967 level, the 7.4 percent for 1974 shown by Labor Force Survey data is still high by Asian standards (see below).

One of the consequences of the approach to passive unemployment used in the 1974 Labor Force Survey is a reduction in the difference between the overall rates of unemployment in the rural and the urban areas—passive unemployment, of course, accounting for a much more substantial part of unemployment in rural areas:

|         | Urban | Rural |
|---------|-------|-------|
| Active  | 5.7   | 3.9   |
| Passive | 2.3   | 3.2   |
| Total   | 8.0   | 7.1   |

15. Department of Statistics, *Report of the Labor Force Survey, April/May 1974* (Kuala Lumpur, 1977), p. 144. The total labor force estimated by the Labor Force Survey was somewhat higher than that by the Household Survey.

The other major characteristic of unemployment in Malaysia mentioned earlier—the inverted U-shaped pattern of the unemployment rates with respect to educational attainment—was as striking in 1974 as in 1967. The highest unemployment rate was observed for those with lower secondary qualification (10 percent for males and 20 percent for females) with the upper secondary school leavers following closely behind.

It was shown earlier in this section that the increase in the overall rate of unemployment between 1962 and 1967 was accompanied by a lengthening of the duration of unemployment, and in particular by a substantial increase in the proportion of the unemployed who had been out of work for more than a year. It might be expected that the reduction in the unemployment rate between 1967 and 1974 would similarly lead to a shortening of the duration of unemployment. This is indeed the case, as can be seen from a comparison of material from two surveys (see Table 14-9). The long-term unemployed nevertheless remained a substantial proportion of the total, even in 1974.

Table 14-9. Distribution of the Unemployed
by Duration of Unemployment, 1967 and 1974

| Sex and year | Less than 3 months | 3–6 months | 7–12 months | More than 1 year | Total |
|---|---|---|---|---|---|
| Males | | | | | |
| 1967 | 22.6 | 14.0 | 21.0 | 42.5 | 100.0 |
| 1974 | 30.8 | 23.6 | 15.2 | 30.5 | 100.0 |
| Females | | | | | |
| 1967 | 19.6 | 14.8 | 19.7 | 46.0 | 100.0 |
| 1974 | 25.3 | 20.1 | 15.7 | 38.9 | 100.0 |

Sources: SES and Labor Force Survey, 1974.

The basic characteristics of unemployment illustrated by the 1974 survey data remain unchanged from their 1967 patterns. Youth unemployment is still predominant; the share of the 15–19 and 20–24 age groups in the total unemployed remain practically unchanged at 42 and 26 percent, respectively. The incidence of unemployment within these age groups is, however, reduced from the 1967 level in line with the general fall in unemployment rates. As figures in Table 14-10 show, the female unemployment rate was substantially higher than the male rate, and it can be inferred from the larger male-female differential after age

Table 14-10.  Active and Inactive Unemployment as a Percentage
of the Labor Force, April-May 1974

| Category | Aged 15–19 | Aged 20–24 | Aged 25–29 | All ages |
|---|---|---|---|---|
| Urban | 21.2 | 10.6 | 4.7 | 7.9 |
| Rural | 20.2 | 11.2 | 3.5 | 7.1 |
| Both | 20.4 | 11.0 | 3.9 | 7.4 |
| Male | 19.1 | 8.0 | 2.6 | 5.9 |
| Female | 21.9 | 15.3 | 6.7 | 10.0 |

Source: Labor Force Survey, 1974.

twenty that this is due to the longer waiting period of females in the
labor market. Data not shown here suggest that, compared with 1967,
the proportion of new entrants without previous job experience in the
total unemployed seems to have been reduced somewhat. About half
the total unemployed had worked before; this was true of the 20–24 age
group as well, but only 30 percent of the 15–19 age group had had
previous job experience.

## Comparison of Unemployment in Malaysia and in Other Asian Countries

Unemployment rates for rural and urban areas in selected countries
of South and Southeast Asia have been brought together in Table 14-11.
Because of the importance of youth unemployment in Malaysia, the
statistics are presented separately for the younger age groups. Unemployment statistics are often viewed with suspicion, and differences between
countries as wide as those in Table 14-11 can lead to the assumption
that the data are not really comparable. In the present case, however, at
least in the urban areas, the differences in measured open unemployment rates are real. The definitions used in the various surveys are
given in the appendix to this chapter and seem to be comparable between countries. Moreover, the different countries come up with much
the same rates of unemployment in successive surveys.

Table 14-11 shows that Malaysia's overall rate of unemployment is
exceeded only by that of Sri Lanka. The Philippines seems to have a
rate of unemployment close to that of Malaysia—but the latter's level
of urban unemployment among females is much higher. Furthermore,

Table 14-11. Unemployment Rates as a Percentage of the Labor Force by Country, Sex, Age Group, and Urban or Rural Residence

| Country and sex | Aged 15–19 | | | Aged 20–24 | | | Aged 15–24 | | | Total[a] | | |
|---|---|---|---|---|---|---|---|---|---|---|---|---|
| | Urban | Rural | Total | Urban | Rural | Total | Urban | Rural | Total | Urban | Rural | Total |
| India (1966–67) | | | | | | | | | | | | |
| Male | 5.6 | 3.7 | 4.7 | 4.1 | 2.5 | 3.3 | n.a. | n.a. | n.a. | 1.5 | 1.8 | 1.7 |
| Female | 5.7 | 6.9 | 6.3 | 4.4 | 4.7 | 4.7 | n.a. | n.a. | n.a. | 1.8 | 4.3 | 3.1 |
| Total | n.a. | n.a. | n.a. | n.a. | n.a. | n.a. | n.a. | n.a. | n.a. | n.a. | n.a. | n.a. |
| Indonesia (1971) | | | | | | | | | | | | |
| Male | 13.7 | 4.4 | 5.8 | 11.9 | 4.0 | 5.7 | 12.5 | 4.2 | 5.7 | 5.0 | 1.9 | 2.4 |
| Female | 11.1 | 2.4 | 3.5 | 9.6 | 1.8 | 3.0 | 10.4 | 2.1 | 3.3 | 4.5 | 1.4 | 1.3 |
| Total | 12.8 | 3.7 | 4.9 | 11.3 | 3.2 | 4.8 | 11.9 | 3.5 | 4.8 | 4.8 | 1.7 | 2.2 |
| Philippines (1968) | | | | | | | | | | | | |
| Male | 25.2 | 11.2 | 14.5 | 17.2 | 10.0 | 12.5 | 20.3 | 10.7 | 13.5 | 8.8 | 5.0 | 6.3 |
| Female | 11.1 | 19.9 | 16.5 | 15.1 | 17.9 | 16.3 | 13.7 | 19.1 | 16.7 | 9.5 | 12.6 | 11.7 |
| Total | 17.4 | 14.2 | 15.3 | 16.2 | 12.5 | 14.1 | 16.7 | 13.4 | 14.7 | 9.1 | 7.4 | 3.1 |

| Sri Lanka (1969–70) | | | | | | | | | | | |
|---|---|---|---|---|---|---|---|---|---|---|---|
| Male | n.a. | n.a. | 39.9 | n.a. | n.a. | 28.3 | 36.7 | 33.2 | 33.3 | 13.0 | 10.2 | 10.7 |
| Female | n.a. | n.a. | 40.6 | n.a. | n.a. | 40.1 | 55.5 | 51.2 | 40.3 | 31.1 | 27.1 | 20.5 |
| Total | n.a. | n.a. | 40.1 | n.a. | n.a. | 32.4 | 42.2 | 42.2 | 35.6 | 16.9 | 16.9 | 13.2 |
| **Thailand (1969)** | | | | | | | | | | | | |
| Male | 4.5 | 0.7 | 1.0 | 4.7 | 0.2 | 0.8 | 4.6 | 0.5 | 0.9 | 1.5 | 0.2 | 0.3 |
| Female | 1.6 | n.a. | 0.1 | 2.8 | n.a. | 0.4 | 2.2 | n.a. | 0.2 | 1.0 | n.a. | 0.1 |
| Total | 3.0 | 0.4 | 0.6 | 3.8 | 0.1 | 0.6 | 3.4 | 0.3 | 0.6 | 1.3 | 0.1 | 0.2 |
| **Peninsular Malaysia (1967–68)** | | | | | | | | | | | | |
| Male | 29.2 | 17.7 | 20.9 | 13.5 | 9.4 | 10.9 | 20.3 | 14.0 | 15.3 | 7.7 | 5.4 | 6.2 |
| Female | 29.9 | 15.6 | 20.1 | 19.9 | 8.5 | 12.7 | 26.7 | 13.6 | 16.7 | 15.2 | 5.5 | 8.1 |
| Total | 29.0 | 16.8 | 20.5 | 15.3 | 9.1 | 11.5 | 22.7 | 13.8 | 16.1 | 9.9 | 5.4 | 6.8 |

n.a. Not available.

a. India includes all ages; Philippines, 10 and over; Sri Lanka, 15–64; Thailand, 11 and over; Indonesia, 10 and over; and Peninsular Malaysia, 15–64.

Sources: Ronald S. Ridker and Harold Lubell, eds., Employment Problems of the Near East and South Asia, vol. 1 (Delhi: Vikas Publications, 1971), pp. 219–20; Indonesia Central Bureau of Statistics, 1971 Population Census, Advance Tables (Djakarta, 1973); Philippines Bureau of the Census and Statistics, BCS Survey of Households Bulletin (Manila, 1968), pp. 31, 32, 38; [Sri Lanka] Department of Census and Statistics, Preliminary Report on the Socio-Economic Survey of Ceylon, 1969–70 (Colombo, 1971), pp. 23, 24, 28, 47; Thailand National Statistical Office, Final Report of the Labor Survey, July–Sept., 1969 (Bangkok, 1970), pp. 22, 23, 29, 32, 103, 104, 107; SES, pp. 18, 130, 132.

the duration of unemployment in the Philippines is not so long as in Malaysia—a point which will be discussed later.

India and Thailand have strikingly low rates of unemployment. It might be plausible to argue that the Thai economy, particularly in the urban sector, is approaching a full employment level, but the Indian case is puzzling. One hypothesis is that the unorganized or informal sector may be more important in India than in Malaysia, and consequently that job seekers who cannot find employment in the formal sector manage to earn some kind of income in the informal sector. A related point is that because the general level of household income is higher in Malaysia, job seekers there can afford to be unemployed better than their counterparts in a poor country such as India.

It is possible to hypothesize that countries which show relatively high rates of urban unemployment might have a relatively large proportion of young people living in urban areas (the group which suffers from the highest rate of unemployment) and a higher participation rate among the population in this age group. Statistics on these points have been brought together in Table 14-12, but it does not appear that Peninsular Malaysia has a notably greater proportion of the urban population in the 15–24 age group than the other countries of the region. Of the six countries, Indonesia clearly has the highest concentration of urban youths. Only India has a lower percentage of its population in this age group than Malaysia.

Participation rates, probably the only meaningful rates for comparative purposes, are shown in Table 14-13 for urban areas. The female participation rate is considerably higher for the younger age groups in Malaysia than in India, Indonesia, and even Sri Lanka. These lower participation rates in India and Indonesia must partly account for the lower unemployment rates among their young female population. The male participation rates are significantly higher in Malaysia than in the Philippines and Indonesia, which may make those countries' unemployment rates for these groups lower than otherwise.

The rate of unemployment is not the only measure of the seriousness of the problem of open unemployment; the duration of unemployment among job seekers is equally important. The very long periods for which some job seekers are unemployed in Malaysia compared with other countries represent a critical feature of the labor market scene in Malaysia. The situation in the Philippines is of special interest. Actual rates of unemployment—particularly for males—were comparable to those in Malaysia, but only about 7 percent of the unemployed in the Philippines had been without jobs for more than twenty-nine weeks,

Table 14-12. Shares of Young Population in Urban Areas
by Country, Sex, and Age Group

| Country and sex | Aged 0–14 | Aged 15–24 | All ages |
|---|---|---|---|
| India (1961) | | | |
| Male | 37.3 | 19.0 | 100.0 |
| Female | 41.0 | 18.5 | 100.0 |
| Total | 39.0 | 18.8 | 100.0 |
| Indonesia (1971) | | | |
| Male | 17.8 | 28.6 | 100.0 |
| Female | 17.3 | 28.8 | 100.0 |
| Total | 17.6 | 28.7 | 100.0 |
| Philippines (1968) | | | |
| Male | n.a. | 49.9 | 100.0 |
| Female | n.a. | 50.3 | 100.0 |
| Total | n.a. | n.a. | n.a. |
| Sri Lanka (1968) | | | |
| Male | 38.2 | 22.3 | 100.0 |
| Female | 37.6 | 22.3 | 100.0 |
| Total | 37.9 | 22.6 | 100.0 |
| Thailand (1969) | | | |
| Male | 42.7 | 19.7 | 100.0 |
| Female | 37.8 | 21.6 | 100.0 |
| Total | 40.2 | 20.7 | 100.0 |
| Peninsular Malaysia (1967–68) | | | |
| Male | 43.9 | 19.3 | 100.0 |
| Female | 42.2 | 20.4 | 100.0 |
| Total | 43.0 | 19.9 | 100.0 |

n.a. Not available.
Sources: Institute of Applied Manpower Research, Fact Book on Manpower,
Pt. I (New Delhi, 1968), pp. 26–28; United Nations, Demographic Yearbook,
1970 (New York, 1971), pp. 274, 276, 292; Jacques Hallak, Financing and
Educational Policy in Sri Lanka (Ceylon) (Paris, 1972), p. 30; Thailand National
Statistical Office, Final Report of the Labor Survey, July–Sept., 1969 (Bangkok,
1970), p. 22; SES, table 1-0-0, p. 70 (Statement 18); International Labour Or-
ganisation, Yearbook of Labor Statistics, 1973 (Geneva, 1973), p. 26; [Sri Lanka]
Department of Census and Statistics, Preliminary Report on the Socio-Economic
Survey of Ceylon, 1969–70 (Colombo, October 1971), p. 1.

while as many as 43 percent in Malaysia were still unemployed after as
many as forty-eight weeks. Data on the duration of unemployment are
unfortunately not available in as detailed a form for Sri Lanka, where
the rates of measured unemployment are higher than anywhere else in
South Asia. According to one survey, however, 61 percent of those
unemployed had been without work for more than a year (48 weeks)

Table 14-13. Urban Labor Force Participation Rates
by Country, Sex, and Age Group

| Country and sex | Aged 15–19 | Aged 20–24 | Aged 15–24 | Total[a] |
|---|---|---|---|---|
| India (1961) | | | | |
| Male | 42.9 | 76.3 | 68.8 | 82.4 |
| Female | 14.6 | 37.8 | 16.0 | 39.6 |
| Total | 32.8 | 57.4 | 43.7 | 59.8 |
| Indonesia (1971) | | | | |
| Male | 32.9 | 67.0 | 47.0 | 61.2 |
| Female | 17.4 | 23.6 | 20.1 | 22.5 |
| Total | 25.2 | 44.4 | 33.4 | 41.7 |
| Philippines (1968) | | | | |
| Male | n.a. | n.a. | 45.1 | 59.8 |
| Female | n.a. | n.a. | 39.0 | 34.5 |
| Total | n.a. | n.a. | 41.8 | 46.5 |
| Sri Lanka (1969–70) | | | | |
| Male | n.a. | n.a. | 61.3 | 85.0 |
| Female | n.a. | n.a. | 24.7 | 23.0 |
| Total | n.a. | n.a. | 42.8 | 53.9 |
| Thailand (1969) | | | | |
| Male | 35.0 | 74.4 | 57.0 | 62.8 |
| Female | 38.0 | 54.9 | 46.5 | 40.3 |
| Total | 36.5 | 63.6 | 51.7 | 51.1 |
| Peninsular Malaysia (1967–68) | | | | |
| Male | 49.8 | 90.7 | 66.1 | 84.3 |
| Female | 35.7 | 49.1 | 41.2 | 34.3 |
| Total | 42.7 | 69.1 | 53.4 | 59.1 |

a. India includes all ages; Philippines, 10 and over; Sri Lanka, 15–64; Thailand, 11 and over; Indonesia, 10 and over; and Peninsular Malaysia, 15–64.

Sources: Institute of Applied Manpower Research, Fact Book on Manpower, Pt. I (New Delhi, 1968), p. 89; Philippines Bureau of the Census and Statistics, BCS Survey of Households Bulletin (Manila, 1968), no. 26, pp. xvii, 9, 22, 32, 38; [Sri Lanka] Department of Census and Statistics, Preliminary Report on the Socio-Economic Survey of Ceylon, 1969–70 (Colombo, 1971), pp. 1, 11, 23, 24; Final Report of Labor Force Survey, pp. 22, 28, 29, 32, 104, 107; SES, pp. 18, 19, 79, 119; Central Bureau of Statistics, 1971 Population Census: Advance Tables (Djakarta, 1973), table 6.

in Sri Lanka, which was significantly higher than the corresponding figure of 43 percent in Malaysia. Qualitatively, it would seem that Peninsular Malaysia and Sri Lanka face similar problems—a heavy open rate of unemployment (particularly among the young and those with some schooling), combined with a long waiting period before securing a job—but that quantitatively Sri Lanka's problem is significantly worse than Malaysia's (see Table 14-14). It cannot be overstressed that it is the long duration of unemployment—not just the rate at a given time—which makes the problem of unemployment in Malaysia so serious. Rates of unemployment as high or higher than that observed for urban Malaysia can be found in many African and Latin American countries. Unemployment rates are often not the most serious labor market problem in these countries, however, because individuals tend to leave the pool of the unemployed reasonably quickly.

Table 14-14. Rates of Long-term Unemployment
by Weeks of Duration

| Country and duration | Rate |
| --- | --- |
| India (1966–67)[a] | |
| 12 weeks | 67.7 |
| 24 weeks | 46.9 |
| 48 weeks | 21.3 |
| Philippines (1968)[b] | |
| 4 weeks | 68.4 |
| 9 weeks | 26.5 |
| 19 weeks | 12.1 |
| 29 weeks | 7.2 |
| Sri Lanka (1969) | |
| 24 weeks | 92.3 |
| 44 weeks | 73.9 |
| Thailand (1969) | |
| 5 weeks | 33.3 |
| 9 weeks | 22.3 |
| 14 weeks | 9.0 |
| Peninsular Malaysia (1967–68) | |
| 12 weeks | 78.6 |
| 24 weeks | 64.3 |
| 48 weeks | 43.9 |
| 144 weeks | 18.2 |

a. Urban areas only.
b. First-time unemployed males only. Females suffer a longer period of unemployment among both the first-time unemployed and the previously employed.
Sources: Ridker and Lubell, eds., Employment and Unemployment Problems of the Near East and South Asia, p. 238; Philippines Bureau of the Census and Statistics, BCS Survey of Households Bulletin (Manila, 1968), p. 32; Final Report of Labor Force Survey, p. 113; SES, table 61-0-0 (b); R. K. Srivastava, "The Unemployment Problem with Special Reference to the Rural Sector," MARGA Quarterly Journal, vol. 2, no. 2 (1973), p. 55.

Berry's study of unemployment in Colombia for 1967 provides a useful example of this point. In the urban areas of Colombia, which had an overall unemployment rate of 10 percent, the median length of unemployment for most categories of the previously employed was a little less than three months; for first-time job seekers, the comparable period was four to five months. Taking this fact into account, together with the observation that about a third of the job seekers were looking for relatively high-income jobs (professional, executive, and clerical), Berry concluded that "perhaps 3–5 percent of the labor force is unemployed and in bad straits."[16] By contrast, the very long waiting period without a job faced by the typical unemployed Malaysian makes the problem quantitatively more serious in Malaysia than it is in almost any of the other countries examined in this section.

## Appendix: Definitions of Unemployment

*India*: All persons who were reported as not working during the reference week and who were either seeking work or, if not seeking, were available for work.

*Indonesia*: Persons who have never worked before and are seeking work; persons who do not work at the time of enumeration but are looking for work; persons released from duty and seeking work.

*Peninsular Malaysia*: All persons who, having no job or enterprise of their own, did not work at any time during the reference week and were looking for a job or work.

*Philippines*: All persons who were reported as wanting and looking for full-time work. The desire to work must be sincere and the person must be serious about working. Also included are persons reported as wanting work but not looking for work because of temporary illness, bad weather, or some other valid reason.

*Sri Lanka*: All persons who did not fall into the employed category. The employed are: (1) all those in regular employment and in receipt of remuneration either as employers, employees (including apprentices), or own-account workers during the month preceding the survey, even though they may have been away from work temporarily because of illness or other reasons; (2) those such as farmers or fishermen who

16. Albert Berry, "Unemployment as a Social Problem in Urban Colombia," Yale Economic Growth Center Discussion Paper no. 145 (May 1972), p. 58.

were mainly engaged in seasonal occupations, even though they may not have been fully employed during the period of investigation; (3) those who had worked on a temporary or casual contract, if they had worked for at least ten days during the month preceding the survey; and (4) unpaid family workers assisting in a household enterprise if they had worked at least ten days during the month or the season preceding the survey.

*Thailand*: All persons who did not work at all during the survey week but wanted to work and were able to do so. Also included are those who, during the survey week, did not work at all but were looking for work or would have been looking for work had they not been ill.

CHAPTER 15

# Characteristics of Secondary School Leavers

DURING THE SECOND HALF OF 1973 the World Bank conducted a School Leavers Tracer Study (SLS) to obtain data on the incidence of unemployment and the factors affecting it among those of young working age (seventeen to twenty-six years).[1] This chapter describes some of the basic characteristics of the survey sample. Relevant data on sample selection, response rates, and demographic characteristics are given in the appendix.

The survey focused on graduates of the secondary school system at the lower (LCE) and upper secondary levels (MCE/MCVE). (The upper secondary school system has developed a small vocational program that awards graduates the MCVE certificate, as opposed to the MCE which the more numerous students in the academic and technical stream obtain.) One purpose of the survey was to see whether the two additional years of schooling in the middle secondary stage improved the employability of lower secondary school leavers, and whether graduates of the vocational stream performed differently from academic graduates. Survey questionnaires were therefore administered to a sample of lower and upper secondary school graduates selected from those who had obtained the LCE certificate in 1968 and 1969, and from those who had received the MCE or MCVE certificate two years later in 1970 and 1971.

The overall sample size was increased by including two subsamples, one of registrants at employment offices and the other of those enrolled in Industrial Training Institutes. These subsamples were also confined to those with either an LCE or an MCE/MCVE certificate, but the respondents had graduated over a wider range of years than those in the first

1. This survey was made possible by the generous and active cooperation of the Malaysian government, particularly the Manpower Department, Ministry of Labor, and the Economic Planning Unit. It was administered in Malaysia by Shigeko Asher from the Bank.

subsample. Taken together the three subsamples make it possible to analyze the labor market experience of lower and upper school certificate holders over the 1968–73 period. They do not cover the experience of school leavers who failed to complete the lower secondary course successfully, that is, those who went into secondary schools but did not obtain the LCE certificate.

The survey excluded Chinese private schools, so that very few respondents had had Chinese as their medium of instruction. (It appears that job seekers who used the employment exchanges were not generally graduates of Chinese schools.) Nearly all the Chinese and Indian school leavers in the sample had been taught English, but Malays from both Malay- and English-speaking school systems were adequately represented.

About a quarter of the total sample of about 6,500 were females. This suggests that females may have been underrepresented, since registration figures for public secondary schools in 1971 show females amounting to about 40 percent of the population. Sufficient numbers of respondents of both sexes are available, however, to allow a comparison of different groups' experiences, which is the primary purpose of the present analysis.

Thanks to the cooperation of the Ministry of Labor, which collected the returned questionnaires, the response rate was exceptionally high for this kind of survey—about 52 percent for the whole sample. As the details in the appendix show, however, the level of response was substantially higher for the upper secondary school leavers than for the lower ones. Many of the LCE holders had graduated several years before the survey was made, and it is possible that a number of them had moved away from their last known addresses. Nevertheless, the response rate for this group was about one-third—large enough for a comparison of its more important characteristics with those of the MCE/MCVE streams.

## Current Employment Status

Table 15-1 shows the employment status of school leavers at the time of the SLS. The respondents from the Industrial Training Institutes differ from those drawn from employment offices and the secondary schools in that nearly all of the former are classified as studying in some way at the time the survey was administered. A high proportion were both employed and studying, which reflects the fact that some students

Table 15-1. Present Employment Status of the Sample Groups
(percent)

| Sample group | Unemployed and looking | Unemployed and not looking | Studying and looking | Studying and not looking | Employed and studying | Employed and not studying | Total Percent | Total Number |
|---|---|---|---|---|---|---|---|---|
| Industrial Training Institutes | | | | | | | | |
| LCE | 3.3 | ... | 52.2 | 1.8 | 42.0 | 0.7 | 100.0 | 274 |
| MCE | 0.5 | ... | 37.0 | 1.6 | 60.3 | 0.5 | 100.0 | 184 |
| MCVE | ... | ... | 27.6 | ... | 65.5 | 6.9 | 100.0 | 29 |
| Employment offices | | | | | | | | |
| LCE | 54.5 | 0.1 | 7.2 | 0.4 | 11.4 | 26.5 | 100.0 | 740 |
| MCE | 44.1 | 0.2 | 15.4 | 1.0 | 18.6 | 20.6 | 100.0 | 1,464 |
| MCVE | 52.1 | 0.3 | 13.7 | 0.3 | 14.3 | 19.2 | 100.0 | 307 |
| Secondary schools | | | | | | | | |
| LCE | 53.0 | 2.4 | 7.1 | 0.7 | 6.1 | 30.7 | 100.0 | 841 |
| MCE | 36.9 | 0.8 | 21.0 | 5.0 | 19.7 | 16.7 | 100.0 | 1,674 |
| MCVE | 43.5 | 0.5 | 8.3 | 1.0 | 18.3 | 28.4 | 100.0 | 996 |
| Total | | | | | | | | |
| LCE | 46.3 | 1.1 | 13.8 | 0.8 | 13.5 | 24.6 | 100.0 | 1,855 |
| MCE | 38.1 | 0.5 | 19.4 | 3.1 | 21.5 | 17.5 | 100.0 | 3,322 |
| MCVE | 44.5 | 0.5 | 10.0 | 0.8 | 18.4 | 25.8 | 100.0 | 1,332 |

... Zero or negligible.
Source: SLS, 1973.

at the Industrial Training Institutes are sponsored by their employers. The employment status of the other two sample subgroups is broadly similar for each of the three types of qualification, as is the overall division between the employed and the unemployed—the unemployment percentage being in the 50–60 percent range. The only difference between the LCE and the MCE/MCVE samples is that a substantially larger proportion of the upper secondary group, particularly those from the academic and technical stream (MCE), said that they were continuing to study while being unemployed. This pattern was also apparent among those who had found employment.

The inordinately high rate of unemployment among these school leavers indicates the seriousness of their labor market difficulties. Nevertheless, a tracer study—particularly one conducted by mail—is not a reliable source for the overall rate of unemployment, because response bias probably exaggerates the unemployment percentage. The usefulness of the survey lies essentially in providing comparative data on the employed and the unemployed, and on groups within each class (provided, of course, that there are significantly large numbers in the subsamples).

The analysis which follows makes no distinction between those who are studying and those who are not, whether unemployed or employed. Since the school leavers reporting full-time study make up only a fraction of the sample, this aggregation will not make much difference to the major conclusions.

## Parental Background

Respondents were asked to report on their father's income, occupation, and educational attainment. Their responses suggest that a large proportion of the sample came from families of relatively low socioeconomic status. There were substantial differences in income reported among the three races and between metropolitan areas on the one hand and smaller towns on the other, as is shown by Table 15-2 which compares corresponding groups of male earners in the SLS and the 1970 Post-Enumeration Survey (PES). While the incomes of Malay school leavers' fathers appear to be somewhat lower than that of the population as a whole (a larger percentage falls into the bottom group earning less than M$100 a month), much more substantial variations exist within the distributions for the Chinese in both metropolitan and other urban

Table 15-2. Percentage Distribution of the Total Sample by Income Group

| Income (Malaysian dollars per month) | Malay | | Chinese | | Total | |
|---|---|---|---|---|---|---|
| | Metropolitan | Other urban | Metropolitan | Other urban | Metropolitan | Other urban |
| Father's income (SLS, 1973) | | | | | | |
| 1–99 | 16.7 | 40.4 | 3.6 | 4.9 | 10.9 | 31.4 |
| 100–149 | 18.6 | 19.6 | 10.2 | 11.4 | 16.0 | 18.1 |
| 150–199 | 18.8 | 15.1 | 16.9 | 19.5 | 18.3 | 16.1 |
| Subtotal | 54.1 | 75.0 | 30.7 | 35.8 | 45.2 | 65.6 |
| Individual male income (PES, 1970) | | | | | | |
| 1–99 | 10.6 | 31.7 | 18.5 | 23.2 | 16.9 | 26.1 |
| 100–149 | 19.6 | 18.0 | 16.0 | 17.2 | 18.4 | 18.2 |
| 150–199 | 18.8 | 15.3 | 15.7 | 15.7 | 16.7 | 15.6 |
| Subtotal | 48.4 | 65.0 | 50.2 | 56.1 | 52.0 | 59.9 |

Sources: SLS, 1973; PES, 1970.

288

areas.[2] Very few respondents of Chinese origin had fathers in the bottom income group, although this group accounted for a fifth of all Chinese income earners in the population as a whole. This important point should be borne in mind in interpreting the data, especially information about the different employment experiences of the two races. It is conceivable that Chinese students from poorer families go disproportionately to Chinese private schools not covered by the data.

It might be expected that those who completed only lower secondary schooling would have come from relatively poor family backgrounds. In fact, however, the parental income levels of the different streams of certificate holders did not vary significantly. School leavers with fathers whose income was reported to be less than M$100 made up 29 percent of the LCE sample, 23 percent of the MCE, and 29 percent of the MCVE sample. The fact that Malay upper school vocational certificate holders seem to come from an income group somewhat *higher* than the Malay upper school academic certificate holders is of particular interest. This conclusion is not due to aggregation—more than 50 percent of the sample are in small towns under 75,000 in which the same pattern holds. Only in Kuala Lumpur is there some suggestion that the parental income of the vocational stream is somewhat lower than that of the academic one.

The occupations of respondents' fathers can sometimes be a better guide to the family's socioeconomic background than income levels (see Table 15-3). There are large differences among the races—many more Chinese, for example, come from sales and services than from an agricultural background. But differences among the three streams of certificate holders are minor for each race. Generally, except for the Indians, most school leavers have a blue-collar background.

## Declared Factors in Job Selection

School leavers were asked to rank, in order of importance, ten factors which influenced their choice of job. Two points need to be taken into account in evaluating the responses to this question: the number of respondents who included a particular factor in their lists of major

---

2. The metropolitan areas, as defined in the PES, are Johore Bahru, Malacca, Kuala Lumpur, Klang, Ipoh, and Georgetown. Other urban areas are those with a population of more than 10,000.

Table 15-3. Percentage Distribution of Father's Occupation by School Leaver's Certificate and Race

| Father's occupation | LCE | | | | MCE | | | | MCVE | | | |
|---|---|---|---|---|---|---|---|---|---|---|---|---|
| | Malay | Chinese | Indian | Total | Malay | Chinese | Indian | Total | Malay | Chinese | Indian | Total |
| Administrative and clerical | 8.3 | 12.4 | 17.4 | 10.2 | 10.8 | 17.0 | 35.6 | 14.3 | 15.1 | 11.6 | 23.5 | 14.4 |
| Sales and services | 17.1 | 33.0 | 14.0 | 19.1 | 18.0 | 36.4 | 22.1 | 23.2 | 17.9 | 40.6 | 35.3 | 25.3 |
| Production workers | 38.2 | 42.6 | 45.5 | 39.7 | 30.9 | 34.8 | 27.9 | 31.7 | 31.3 | 31.8 | 19.6 | 30.8 |
| Agriculture | 36.4 | 12.0 | 23.0 | 31.1 | 40.4 | 11.9 | 14.4 | 30.8 | 35.7 | 16.0 | 21.6 | 29.4 |
| Number | 1,011 | 209 | 178 | 1,404 | 1,743 | 707 | 208 | 2,672 | 722 | 318 | 51 | 1,094 |

Source: SLS, 1973.

criteria, and the rank assigned by respondents to each factor mentioned. Both these elements are incorporated into the calculations of rank scores for each of the ten factors presented in Table 15-4.[3]

Table 15-4. Rank Scores of Job Selection Factors by Certificate and Race

| Factor | Certificate | | | Race | | |
|--------|-----|-----|------|-------|---------|--------|
|        | LCE | MCE | MCVE | Malay | Chinese | Indian |
| Monthly earnings | 3.6 | 3.5 | 3.3 | 3.5 | 3.3 | 3.2 |
| Future earnings | 3.2 | 3.5 | 3.4 | 3.3 | 3.8 | 2.7 |
| Urban location | 1.9 | 1.4 | 1.3 | 1.4 | 1.6 | 1.7 |
| Rural location | 1.0 | 0.9 | 0.7 | 1.0 | 0.5 | 0.7 |
| White-collar job | 0.5 | 1.0 | 0.7 | 0.7 | 1.1 | 1.0 |
| Blue-collar job | 1.1 | 0.7 | 1.4 | 0.7 | 1.3 | 1.4 |
| Occupation of firm | 0.9 | 0.9 | 1.0 | 0.6 | 1.5 | 0.8 |
| Government job | 3.8 | 3.5 | 3.6 | 3.7 | 2.7 | 4.1 |
| Private job | 0.8 | 0.9 | 1.0 | 0.9 | 1.0 | 0.7 |
| Other | 0.1 | 0.4 | 0.3 | 0.2 | 0.5 | 0.2 |

Source: SLS, 1973.

The factors considered to be most important by the school leavers in their choice of jobs are government employment, monthly earnings, and future earnings. With only minor differences, this is true for all certificate and race groups. (The special value placed on government employment is an important element in the labor market scene in Malaysia, for reasons discussed earlier.) None of the other seven factors tested appears to have had a strong influence on job selection. White-collar employment appears not to be nearly so desirable to respondents as is sometimes supposed; it ranks even lower than location, which is itself of only secondary importance.

3. To calculate the rank score each factor was given a rank scale ($\gamma_i$) from 1 to 5 (lowest to highest). The number of respondents ($n_{ij}$) who gave rank $\gamma_i$ to each factor varies by each type of certificate and racial group, and $N_j$ represents the highest number of respondents to a particular factor for any race and certificate group. The formula for the rank score is thus:

$$R_j = \sum_{i=1}^{5} \frac{\gamma_i\, n_{ij}}{N_j}.$$

## Search for Employment

The channels most frequently used by school leavers searching for jobs seem to be newspaper advertisements and direct contacts with employers by visit or by letter. As Table 15-5 illustrates, school leavers in all certificate, sex, and race groups rely mostly on direct visits or letters. Newspaper advertisements seem to be particularly popular among male and female Malays—in the case of the former, more so for MCE/MCVE graduates. Employment offices were of relatively minor importance in the minds of the sample—even though a sizable part of it was made up of employment office registrants. The employment office channel was used to a significant degree only by male LCE graduates.

Table 15-5. Percentage Distribution of Employment Channels Used to Obtain First Job by Certificate, Sex, and Race

| Employment channel | LCE | | | MCE and MCVE | | |
|---|---|---|---|---|---|---|
| | Malay | Chinese | Indian | Malay | Chinese | Indian |
| *Male* | | | | | | |
| Employment office | 23.2 | 15.2 | 23.6 | 6.5 | 11.9 | 7.5 |
| Newspaper ads | 29.2 | 10.9 | 10.6 | 45.7 | 16.2 | 23.9 |
| Family | 4.4 | 4.3 | 2.4 | 1.8 | 4.4 | 2.5 |
| Friends | 9.2 | 32.6 | 13.0 | 6.8 | 22.7 | 9.4 |
| School | 0.7 | . . . | 0.8 | 4.0 | 3.1 | 1.3 |
| Directly writing or visiting employer | 32.6 | 37.0 | 49.6 | 34.5 | 41.0 | 52.8 |
| Other | 0.7 | . . . | . . . | 0.7 | 0.8 | 2.5 |
| Number | 568 | 46 | 123 | 1,213 | 388 | 159 |
| *Female* | | | | | | |
| Employment office | 12.1 | 7.2 | 24.8 | 3.7 | 2.6 | 6.6 |
| Newspaper ads | 42.4 | 11.4 | 10.7 | 47.5 | 20.6 | 20.4 |
| Family | 7.2 | 13.8 | 7.4 | 3.7 | 8.5 | 6.6 |
| Friends | 10.3 | 47.9 | 15.7 | 8.2 | 23.3 | 12.3 |
| School | 1.7 | . . . | . . . | 4.7 | 5.0 | 1.9 |
| Directly writing or visiting employer | 24.1 | 19.8 | 40.5 | 30.8 | 37.5 | 47.4 |
| Others | 1.3 | . . . | 0.8 | 1.3 | 1.0 | 1.9 |
| Number | 526 | 167 | 121 | 1,542 | 873 | 211 |

. . . Zero or negligible.
*Source:* SLS, 1973.

There is no significant difference between the various categories of the sample by certificate, sex, and race in the locations in which they looked for jobs. The largest proportions of respondents made their searches relatively close to home; Table 15-6 shows that 25.6 percent of the sample looked only in their hometown, and 26.1 percent only in their home state. A significantly smaller proportion (15.1 percent) looked for jobs in other states, and 13.3 percent looked in all three places.

## Mobility

To obtain some idea of the extent and pattern of mobility among school leavers, data were collected on their towns of birth and the towns in which they were currently living (see Table 15-7).

The figures along the diagonal of the matrix represent the percentages of school leavers who were still living in their places of birth. The figures show that upward of 80 percent of the school leavers in the metropolitan areas had *not* moved. Mobility among school leavers in the smaller towns—Ipoh, the towns with populations of 10,000–75,000, and towns of more than 75,000 outside the metropolitan areas—is moderately high, with 25 to 30 percent of school leavers moving. Even among those who were born in very small towns of less than 10,000, only about half the sample seems to have moved. It should, however, be

Table 15-6. Locations in Which the Employed Looked for Jobs

| Location | Employed school leavers (percent) |
| --- | --- |
| Hometown only | 25.6 |
| Home state only | 26.1 |
| Other states only | 15.1 |
| Singapore only | 0.6 |
| Other | 1.2 |
| Hometown and home state | 8.1 |
| Hometown and other states | 3.2 |
| Home state and other states | 6.8 |
| Hometown, home state, and other states | 13.3 |
| Total | 100.0 |
| Number | 2,476 |

*Source:* SLS, 1973.

Table 15-7. Mobility: Movement from Town of Birth to Town of Present Residence

| Town of birth | Present residence | | | | | | | Total | Percentage of grand total |
|---|---|---|---|---|---|---|---|---|---|
| | 75,000 or more | Kuala Lumpur | Georgetown | Ipoh | Johore | 10,000–75,000 | Less than 10,000 | | |
| 75,000 or more | 68.4 | 16.9 | 0.7 | 0.7 | 1.7 | 4.0 | 7.6 | 100.0 | 4.7 |
| Kuala Lumpur | 1.3 | 85.9 | 1.3 | 0.6 | 1.1 | 6.0 | 3.8 | 100.0 | 8.3 |
| Georgetown | 0.2 | 4.9 | 85.5 | 0.8 | ... | 5.1 | 3.5 | 100.0 | 9.4 |
| Ipoh | 1.9 | 13.7 | 2.4 | 67.0 | 0.5 | 7.5 | 7.1 | 100.0 | 3.3 |
| Johore | 1.0 | 9.6 | ... | 1.0 | 80.4 | 2.9 | 5.3 | 100.0 | 3.3 |
| 10,000–75,000 | 1.2 | 10.7 | 1.3 | 1.7 | 2.6 | 75.1 | 7.4 | 100.0 | 41.5 |
| Less than 10,000 | 2.4 | 18.4 | 2.0 | 3.9 | 2.1 | 16.3 | 54.8 | 100.0 | 31.1 |
| Percentage of grand total | 4.7 | 19.2 | 8.2 | 4.3 | 4.5 | 37.6 | 21.5 | 100.0 | 100.0 |

... Zero or negligible.
Source: SLS, 1973.

remembered that the data are likely to underestimate overall mobility because smaller towns have been aggregated by size groups; movement among towns within a given size group is not recorded in the table.

Some idea of the relative importance of recipient areas can be found by comparing the percentages of the last row of the matrix with those of the last column. Kuala Lumpur is clearly the largest net gainer from movement from areas of origin; the main losers were the small towns. This is the expected pattern of mobility, but the relatively small amount of net movement is somewhat surprising. Even the small towns of less than 10,000 (which would in fact be classified as rural areas in the Malaysian census definition) lost less than a quarter of their population through migration to the metropolitan areas, and their percentage share of the total sample fell by just under 10 percentage points (from 31.1 to 21.5 percent).

## Conclusions

This brief look at the descriptive material from the SLS is preliminary to a full analysis of the factors affecting the employment experience of different classes of secondary school leavers. The major findings that have a bearing on the subsequent analysis are summarized here.

1. The secondary school leavers from the lower income group (father's income of less than M$200 a month) accounted for about the same percentage of the total in the sample as the proportion of low-income earners in the population of urban Malaysia. Only the Chinese in the sample had a disproportionately smaller representation in the very lowest income group (less than M$100 per month). There was no significant difference in parental economic status between the lower and upper secondary school leavers or between the vocational and academic streams of the middle secondary schools.

2. Jobs were found through employment exchanges by only 10 to 25 percent of the LCE group and 6 to 12 percent of the middle secondary sample. Individual contacts or newspaper advertisements were the most important channels.

3. Government jobs came highest in the school leavers' hierarchy of preferences, but white-collar jobs ranked lower in the order of preference than jobs with high forecast of future earnings (though of course these better paid jobs might easily be of the white-collar type).

4. There is some evidence for the traditional view that school leavers migrate from small to larger towns in search of employment, but the

magnitude of such movement was not very high. Small towns of less than 10,000 people lost no more than a quarter of their school leavers through migration to the metropolitan areas.

Chapter 17 analyzes in detail the determinants of employment rates of the sample to throw some light on differences in the employability of various groups. Before this analysis is undertaken, however, the following question needs to be considered: Given the very high levels of unemployment among the new entrants to the labor market, particularly among those with secondary schooling, what pressures toward adjustment can be detected in the Malaysian labor market? This question is discussed in Chapter 16 with regard to occupational and earnings patterns among school leavers.

## Appendix: Description of the SLS

The survey questionnaire was administered to three major groups during the summer of 1973. The first group was drawn from the public secondary schools of three types: academic, technical, and vocational. The second group was taken from the twenty employment offices located in various parts of Peninsular Malaysia. The third group was made up of apprentices at the Industrial Training Institutes (ITI) in Kuala Lumpur and Prai.

### Selection of the Sample

Out of a total of 376 general secondary schools in seven states, twenty-five were selected and stratified by language of instruction (Bahasa Malaysia and English). Four states were excluded from the survey; Perlis and Trengganu because they have very few schools from which students graduate at the MCE level, and Malacca and Negri Sembilan because their characteristics are very similar to those of other states included in the survey, such as Selangor and Johore. The survey schools were selected on the basis of average student performance, typical socioeconomic background, and urban location. At each participating school, a 20 percent sample of form III (LCE) graduates was taken from the 1968 and 1969 cohorts. To ensure that this sample fully represented nine-year school leavers, a teacher at every school helped survey administrators select only those LCE holders who did not proceed to form IV. In the case of the form V (MCE) leavers, a 25 percent sample was randomly selected from the 1970 and 1971 cohorts.

Thus, the survey data can be used to trace and compare the youths who left the education system after nine years and those who continued for two additional years.

In 1973 there were only three technical secondary schools in Malaysia, located in Kuala Lumpur, Georgetown, and Kuantan. All those who left these schools in 1970 and 1971 were sampled. In addition, all school leavers from four vocational secondary schools (out of a total of seven) at Georgetown, Kota Bharu, Kuantan, and Johore Bahru were included. Overall, the questionnaires were mailed to 4,707 academic, 1,222 technical, and 1,571 vocational secondary school leavers.

The second major subpopulation of the sample comes from the twenty employment offices in different parts of Peninsular Malaysia. Of the total of 4,649 persons sampled, 63 percent were registered at the employment offices in April 1973. The other 37 percent was made up of those who had been placed by the offices between June 1972 and April 1973. All respondents held certificates of general, technical, or vocational secondary education.

The ITI are the responsibility of the Ministry of Labor and Manpower, assisted by ILO experts. The questionnaires were administered in the classrooms to 487 students who had obtained either the form III or form V certificate.

The total sample is representative of the secondary school population in Peninsular Malaysia, as is shown by Table 15-8, which gives comparative data on the percentage enrollment by states of form III and form V students for the country as a whole and the distribution of school leavers in the sample by certificate held and state of residence.

*Response Rates*

Since the survey was conducted with the approval and assistance of the Malaysian government, it was possible to obtain an overall response rate of 52 percent. The rates varied among the different subsamples, with 54 percent responding in the employment office group, compared with 47 percent from the schools group. In the case of the ITI, the questionnaires were administered in the classroom so that all 487 handed out were returned. Table 15-9 summarizes the number of questionnaires sent and responses received from all sources. There was a significant difference between the response rates of the nine-year and the eleven-year school leavers: 36 percent and 52 percent respectively from the schools, and 30 percent and 81 percent respectively from the employment offices.

Table 15-8.  Enrollment in Secondary Schools and Distribution
of School Leavers by State of Current Residence
(percent)

| State | Enrollment in 1971[a] | | Distribution of school leavers in sample | | |
|---|---|---|---|---|---|
| | Form III | Form V | LCE | MCE | MCVE |
| Johore | 14.9 | 13.7 | 14.9 | 10.9 | 23.0 |
| Kedah | 9.1 | 9.2 | 10.3 | 11.0 | 2.4 |
| Kelantan | 6.7 | 6.3 | 6.6 | 7.2 | 15.8 |
| Malacca | 5.4 | 6.2 | 2.4 | 4.8 | 3.8 |
| Negri Sembilan | 6.1 | 5.7 | 1.6 | 3.2 | 2.5 |
| Pahang | 5.1 | 5.7 | 5.5 | 6.6 | 16.3 |
| Penang and Wellesley Province | 9.9 | 11.9 | 15.7 | 13.4 | 11.6 |
| Perak | 18.3 | 17.9 | 14.9 | 14.1 | 4.3 |
| Perlis | 1.4 | 1.0 | 0.5 | 0.4 | 0.3 |
| Selangor | 19.4 | 19.0 | 25.1 | 24.2 | 14.9 |
| Trengganu | 3.7 | 3.3 | 1.6 | 2.9 | 2.9 |
| Total | 100.0 | 100.0 | 100.0 | 100.0 | 100.0 |
| Number | 102,878 | 42,938 | 1,633 | 3,081 | 1,193 |

a. Assisted secondary schools.
Source: Calculated from Ministry of Education, *Educational Statistics of Malaysia, 1971*, pp. 148–58.

## Demographic and Other Features of the Sample

Of the total sample of 6,520 school leavers, 74.4 percent were males and 25.6 percent were females. A comparison of these figures with the overall enrollment for 1971 by gender in assisted general secondary schools at the form III and form V levels (58.4 percent males and 41.6 percent females) suggests that females are underrepresented in the survey sample.[4] Two reasons for the bias toward males in the survey sample are that it includes those holding technical and vocational certificates (who are in most cases male students), and the ITI subgroup consists almost entirely of males.

Malays constitute 64 percent of the sample, the Chinese 25 percent, and Indians 11 percent.

Because the survey covered form III and form V school leavers, the respondents were of young working age, ranging from seventeen to

4. Ministry of Education, *Educational Statistics of Malaysia, 1971*.

Table 15-9. Response Rates for the School Leavers Survey

| Sample group | Questionnaires sent (number) | Responses (number) | Response rates (percent) |
|---|---|---|---|
| Schools[a] | | | |
| Academic | | | |
| LCE (1968 and 1969) | 2,362 | 844 | 35.7 |
| MCE (1970 and 1971) | 2,345 | | |
| Technical | | | |
| MCE (1970 and 1971) | 1,222 | | |
| MCE academic and MCE technical | (3,567) | 1,676 | 47.0 |
| Vocational | | | |
| MCVE (1970 and 1971) | 1,571 | 997 | 63.5 |
| Total | 7,500 | 3,517 | 46.9 |
| Employment office | | | |
| LCE | 2,469 | 744 | 30.1 |
| MCE | 1,686 | | |
| MCE (technical) | 71 | | |
| MCE academic and MCE technical | (1,757) | 1,465 | 83.4 |
| MCVE | 423 | 307 | 72.6 |
| Total | 4,649 | 2,516 | 54.0 |
| Industrial Training Institutes | | | |
| LCE | 274 | 274 | 100.0 |
| MCE academic and MCE technical | 184 | 184 | 100.0 |
| MCVE | 29 | 29 | 100.0 |
| Total | 487 | 487 | 100.0 |
| Total sample | 12,636 | 6,520 | 51.6 |

a. Twenty-five academic, three technical, and four vocational schools were selected.
Source: SLS, 1973.

twenty-six years. Table 15-10 gives the distribution of the sample group by age and certificate. Although the age of school leavers from the employment office subgroup vary slightly more than those from the schools, nineteen- and twenty-year-olds made up the largest single age groups in both this subgroup and the sample as a whole.

Of all nine-year school leavers, 58.2 percent left school in 1968 or 1969. It was possible to select for the school group those students who had received their LCE in those years, but in the case of the employment offices and ITI the questionnaires were sent to form III certificate holders irrespective of the year in which they had actually left school. Thus, 81 percent of the LCE holders from the school sample left school in

Table 15-10. Percentage Distribution of Sample Group by Age and Certificate

| Sample group | 17 or under | 18 | 19 | 20 | 21 | 22 | 23 | 24 | 25 | 26 or more | Total | Number |
|---|---|---|---|---|---|---|---|---|---|---|---|---|
| Industrial Training Institutes | | | | | | | | | | | | |
| LCE | 16.1 | 11.3 | 16.4 | 16.1 | 11.3 | 14.2 | 9.9 | 3.3 | 0.4 | 1.1 | 100.0 | 274 |
| MCE | 1.6 | 4.9 | 16.3 | 15.8 | 21.7 | 22.3 | 13.6 | 2.2 | 1.1 | 0.5 | 100.0 | 184 |
| MCVE | ... | 13.8 | 17.2 | 10.3 | 20.7 | 20.7 | 13.8 | ... | 3.4 | ... | 100.0 | 29 |
| Employment office | | | | | | | | | | | | |
| LCE | 10.8 | 14.0 | 18.7 | 19.0 | 12.1 | 6.7 | 5.8 | 4.2 | 3.0 | 5.9 | 100.0 | 744 |
| MCE | 3.5 | 12.4 | 22.5 | 22.5 | 16.9 | 8.8 | 5.2 | 3.6 | 1.8 | 2.7 | 100.0 | 1,465 |
| MCVE | 2.3 | 19.2 | 35.2 | 21.8 | 12.1 | 5.2 | 2.9 | 1.0 | ... | 0.3 | 100.0 | 307 |
| Secondary schools | | | | | | | | | | | | |
| LCE | 4.6 | 4.7 | 34.7 | 42.9 | 10.3 | 1.2 | 0.8 | 0.2 | 0.2 | 0.2 | 100.0 | 844 |
| MCE | 3.0 | 5.2 | 30.8 | 40.2 | 17.1 | 3.3 | 0.2 | 0.2 | ... | ... | 100.0 | 1,676 |
| MCVE | 2.7 | 4.6 | 35.6 | 39.1 | 16.0 | 1.7 | 0.1 | ... | ... | 0.1 | 100.0 | 997 |
| Total | | | | | | | | | | | | |
| LCE | 8.8 | 9.4 | 25.6 | 29.4 | 11.2 | 5.3 | 4.1 | 2.3 | 1.3 | 2.6 | 100.0 | 1,862 |
| MCE | 3.2 | 8.4 | 26.3 | 31.1 | 17.3 | 6.8 | 3.1 | 1.8 | 0.9 | 1.2 | 100.0 | 3,325 |
| MCVE | 2.6 | 8.2 | 35.1 | 34.5 | 15.2 | 2.9 | 1.1 | 0.2 | 0.1 | 0.2 | 100.0 | 1,333 |

... Zero or negligible.
Source: SLS, 1973.

1968 or 1969 compared with 39.8 percent from the employment office and 37.2 percent from the ITI.

Of all eleven-year school leavers, 68.4 percent left school in 1970 or 1971. The breakdown by sample subgroups, however, shows a pattern similar to that for the nine-year leavers: 84.5 percent of form V school leavers graduated in 1970 or 1971, as opposed to 48.1 percent from the employment office subgroup and 33.8 percent from the ITI.

Forty-seven percent of all school leavers in the sample were taught in Malay, while 53 percent went to English language schools. Because the school sample was stratified by language of instruction, this sub-sample gives a fair representation of the type of instruction received by the student population in Malaysia as a whole. The race of the school leavers is the main factor in determining the language of instruction in school. The percentage distribution by race and language of instruction is:

|         | Malay instruction | English instruction | Total |
|---------|-------------------|---------------------|-------|
| Malay   | 71.1              | 28.9                | 4,272 |
| Chinese | 3.3               | 96.4                | 1,767 |
| Indian  | 5.1               | 94.8                | 727   |

In addition, 0.3 percent of the Chinese were taught in Chinese, and 0.2 percent of the Indians were taught in Tamil.

The distribution of school leavers by the towns in which they now live does not differ significantly among the three samples. In total, 37.5 percent live in towns with populations of 10,000–75,000; 21.5 percent in towns of less than 10,000; 19.3 percent in the greater Kuala Lumpur area, and 8.2 percent in the Georgetown area. The rest are distributed evenly between larger towns of 75,000 or more, Ipoh and Johore Bahru.

CHAPTER 16

# The Process of Labor Market Adjustment

THE PECULIARITY OF THE MALAYSIAN SITUATION is that the mean length of time of waiting before the first job is inordinately long, leading to an excess stock of youths looking for work. The market can be expected to adjust itself to this excess supply of school leavers in two ways. First, through the phenomenon of "bumping," employers raise the educational requirements for jobs so that secondary schooling may be demanded in occupations which previously needed only primary school qualifications. Alternatively, school leavers themselves may revise downward their expectations for the jobs and the earnings they consider acceptable. Both these processes of adjustment can take place even if, for some reason, wage rates are rigidly fixed over a significant range of jobs.

This chapter reviews the data on occupations and earnings for the school leaver population group. In each case the actual experience of school leavers is contrasted with their expectations.

## Occupational Pattern and Expectations

Has the rapid recent growth in secondary education enrollments had an impact on the occupational distribution of school leavers? This section examines the interaction between educational attainments and occupational categories in the Malaysian labor force; in particular, it tries to isolate any changes that have taken place in this interaction matrix in the recent past.

### The Education-Occupation Matrix

Three sources of information are available on the relation between education and occupational category in Malaysia. The first is the Post-

Enumeration Survey (PES) of 1970, the second the World Bank's 1975 Migration and Employment Survey (MES), and the third the Bank's 1973 School Leavers Survey (SLS). By far the largest data base is that of the PES, which covers the whole population, but valuable additional information is available from the two Bank surveys, and all three sources are used in the following analysis.

At this stage it is worth recapitulating the basis of the occupational classification used in the three surveys. The classification was prepared by the Ministry of Labor on the basis of the ILO's International Standard Classification of Occupations. The two-digit classification was used to subdivide the sales and service categories into upper and lower subgroups. The other five one-digit categories—professional and technical, administrative and managerial, clerical, agriculture, and production workers—were left intact. Chapter 7 has already dealt with the problems of classification arising from the fact that it was not possible to separate skilled production workers from the unskilled with any degree of clarity at the two-digit level.

Although it would be unrealistic to expect a perfect correlation between the level of educational attainment and the occupational category of a worker, it is reasonable to assume a relatively high correlation, not only on the demand side—because employers may try to find workers with certain educational qualifications for particular types of jobs—but also on the supply side, where education plays an important role in altering workers' preferences for different kinds of jobs. The final outcome constitutes the actual education-occupation matrix, which will, of course, depend on the interaction of these supply and demand functions in the market for different jobs. In a dynamic economy, preferences on both sides will be continuously modified in the light of changing labor market conditions.

### The PES Data

The PES data were used to get a complete percentage distribution among the occupational groups of males with different levels of schooling, broken down by race (see Table 16-1). Table 16-2 presents the same information for females, but without differentiation by race.

Both tables show a clear and expected correlation between educational attainment and occupational category. Workers shift from predominantly blue- to white-collar jobs not at one educational level, however, but over a band of educational levels that stretch from the

Table 16-1.  Education-Occupation Matrix for Males
(percentage of total in the schooling category)

| Years of schooling | Number | Professional, technical | Administra- tive, managerial | Clerical |
|---|---|---|---|---|
| No formal schooling | | | | |
| Malay | 163 | . . . | . . . | . . . |
| Chinese | 435 | . . . | . . . | . . . |
| 1–5 (incomplete primary) | | | | |
| Malay | 353 | . . . | . . . | . . . |
| Chinese | 1,369 | . . . | . . . | . . . |
| 6 (primary) | | | | |
| Malay | 567 | 6.5 | . . . | 7.2 |
| Chinese | 885 | . . . | . . . | . . . |
| 7–9 (incomplete LCE) | | | | |
| Malay | 200 | 7.5 | . . . | 24.5 |
| Chinese | 689 | . . . | . . . | 10.2 |
| 9 (LCE) | | | | |
| Malay | 131 | 13.7 | . . . | 30.5 |
| Chinese | 108 | 13.0 | . . . | 16.7 |
| 10–11 (incomplete MCE) | | | | |
| Malay | 117 | 23.1 | . . . | 33.4 |
| Chinese | 338 | 11.8 | 5.0 | 32.8 |
| 11, 12–13 (MCE and incomplete HSC) | | | | |
| Malay | 215 | 37.2 | . . . | 45.6 |
| Chinese | 426 | 35.7 | 6.1 | 33.8 |
| 13 (HSC) | | | | |
| Malay | 40 | 47.5 | 25.0 | 22.5 |
| Chinese | 77 | 57.1 | 13.0 | 14.3 |

. . . Less than 5 percent.
Source: PES, 1970.

post-primary to the incomplete MCE and correspond roughly to between seven and eleven years of education. Workers with primary education or less were almost entirely confined to the blue-collar jobs, and those who had advanced beyond the MCE level were employed almost entirely in white-collar jobs.

The PES data can also be used to answer another interesting question—has there been any substantial change in this pattern over time? It is reasonable to look for the bulk of such a change in the band of educational levels discussed above. The percentage of males aged under

| Sales | | Services | | | Production |
| Upper | Lower | Upper | Lower | Agriculture | worker |
|---|---|---|---|---|---|
| . . . | 8.0 | . . . | . . . | 54.6 | 26.4 |
| 7.6 | 19.1 | . . . | 9.7 | 10.1 | 45.7 |
| . . . | 5.4 | . . . | 18.1 | 21.5 | 41.6 |
| 7.3 | 21.9 | . . . | 8.0 | . . . | 52.5 |
| . . . | 6.5 | . . . | 32.8 | 10.6 | 29.5 |
| 5.1 | 20.5 | . . . | 8.0 | . . . | 54.8 |
| . . . | 8.0 | . . . | 23.5 | 6.0 | 23.5 |
| 7.0 | 21.6 | . . . | 6.7 | . . . | 47.5 |
| . . . | 6.9 | . . . | 22.1 | . . . | 16.8 |
| . . . | 18.5 | . . . | 9.3 | . . . | 28.7 |
| 6.0 | . . . | . . . | 19.7 | . . . | 12.8 |
| 7.1 | 16.3 | . . . | . . . | . . . | 18.3 |
| . . . | . . . | . . . | 9.3 | . . . | . . . |
| 5.2 | . . . | . . . | . . . | . . . | 7.5 |
| . . . | . . . | . . . | 5.0 | . . . | . . . |
| . . . | . . . | . . . | . . . | . . . | 6.5 |

twenty-five in these educational levels who are in white-collar jobs and the deviation of these percentages from the corresponding figures for males of all ages indicate the extent of the shift away from white-collar jobs among secondary school leavers in recent years:

| Schooling | Percentage in white-collar occupations | Deviation from percentage of all males |
|---|---|---|
| LCE | 29.4 | −11.6 |
| Incomplete MCE | 37.3 | −17.3 |
| MCE but incomplete HSC | 71.2 | −10.5 |

Table 16-2. Education-Occupation Matrix for Females
(percentage of total in the schooling category)

| Years of schooling | Number | Professional, technical | Administrative, managerial | Clerical |
|---|---|---|---|---|
| No formal schooling | 899 | ... | ... | ... |
| 1–5 (incomplete primary) | 621 | ... | ... | ... |
| 6 (primary) | 439 | 7.1 | ... | ... |
| 7–9 (incomplete LCE) | 255 | 13.7 | ... | 13.7 |
| 9 (LCE) | 92 | 35.9 | ... | 31.5 |
| 10–11 (incomplete MCE) | 166 | 27.7 | ... | 56.0 |
| 11, 12–13 (MCE and incomplete HSC) | 408 | 50.5 | ... | 42.4 |
| 13 (HSC) | 49 | 77.6 | ... | 18.4 |

... Less than 5 percent.
Source: PES, 1970.

*The School Leavers Survey* (SLS)

Since the SLS sample was confined to those with LCE and MCE/MCVE certificates and was limited to a rather narrow age group, it is reasonable to expect relatively few respondents in the senior occupational groups. In the analysis of survey data, therefore, groups have been compressed into three broad categories—white-collar occupations, sales and service (combining the senior and junior subgroups), and production workers.

Table 16-3 presents the percentage distribution of employed school leavers by the certificates they hold. The figures are tabulated separately for Malays and Chinese and for the two sexes. Although these results are not strictly comparable with those shown earlier, they strongly suggest a significant degree of occupational downgrading among secondary school leavers. White-collar employment is by no means the overwhelming choice of even the upper secondary school leavers; for those with lower secondary qualifications, production work is the predominant source of employment.

This is true of the sample as a whole, but there is a striking difference between the occupational distributions of the two streams of upper secondary school leavers. Those in the vocational stream—and particularly the males and the Chinese in this group—depend much less on white-collar jobs. The next subsection will examine whether the occu-

| Sales | | Services | | | Production |
| Upper | Lower | Upper | Lower | Agriculture | worker |
|-------|-------|-------|-------|-------------|--------|
| . . . | 13.5  | . . . | 39.5  | 21.0        | 19.9   |
| . . . | 9.2   | . . . | 41.9  | 11.9        | 31.9   |
| . . . | 6.2   | . . . | 34.4  | 7.1         | 42.6   |
| . . . | 17.3  | . . . | 22.7  | . . .       | 30.2   |
| . . . | 12.0  | . . . | . . . | . . .       | 14.1   |
| . . . | 6.0   | . . . | . . . | . . .       | 6.0    |
| . . . | . . . | . . . | . . . | . . .       | . . .  |
| . . . | . . . | . . . | . . . | . . .       | . . .  |

pational expectations of those who opt for vocational education also reflect this bias.

Another point of interest is the relatively small proportion of school leavers in sales and service. This suggests that school leavers in Malaysia show a preference for searching for jobs while being openly unemployed rather than accepting temporary employment in what is looked upon as a part of the informal labor market, open to anyone who wishes to join. This pattern is in keeping with other features of the school leavers' market—notably high unemployment rates and inflexible wage expectations—which are discussed extensively below.

The differential effects of secondary schooling on women in white-collar jobs are worth examining. The picture given in Table 16-3 may be misleading for females with LCE qualifications, because the sample in this subgroup is quite small. Percentages of females in white-collar jobs derived from MES data are:

| | Kuala Lumpur | | East Coast towns | |
| Schooling | All | Under 25 | All | Under 25 |
|-----------|-----|----------|-----|----------|
| Some secondary | 55.1 | 42.0 | 47.5 | 35.3 |
| MCE | 86.6 | 83.6 | 91.9 | 95.3 |

It should be remembered that the towns covered by the MES are relatively large. Nevertheless, for both levels of education shown, the per-

Table 16-3. Percentage Distribution of School Leavers
by Occupation

| Certificate | Number | White collar | Sales and services | Production workers[a] |
|---|---|---|---|---|
| Male | | | | |
| LCE | 392 | 16.6 | 18.4 | 62.0 |
| MCE | 797 | 40.4 | 15.3 | 42.3 |
| MCVE | 407 | 24.6 | 9.6 | 65.1 |
| Female | | | | |
| LCE | 80 | 17.5 | 22.5 | 60.0 |
| MCE | 303 | 66.3 | 9.6 | 23.8 |
| MCVE | 114 | 74.6 | 7.0 | 18.4 |
| Malay | | | | |
| LCE | 246 | 17.5 | 17.9 | 63.0 |
| MCE | 581 | 48.5 | 11.0 | 37.9 |
| MCVE | 263 | 41.8 | 6.1 | 51.3 |
| Chinese | | | | |
| LCE | 135 | 17.0 | 21.5 | 59.3 |
| MCE | 413 | 48.4 | 16.2 | 35.1 |
| MCVE | 231 | 28.6 | 11.7 | 59.3 |
| All | | | | |
| MCE (technical) | 172 | 52.9 | 11.6 | 33.1 |
| MCE (academic) | 974 | 46.2 | 13.8 | 38.5 |

a. The percentages in this group are inflated because the Malaysian occupation Code 99 includes both general laborers and those with an unspecified occupation.
Source: SLS, 1973.

centages of females in white-collar occupations are strikingly higher than those for males shown in Table 16-3. Further, the fall in the proportion of females in white-collar occupations for the younger age groups does not seem to be as great as that for males. A plausible hypothesis would be that there has been some substitution of females for males in white-collar jobs in recent years, because the females are paid less. This would be one way in which the market might adjust to an excess supply of school leavers in the face of a degree of rigidity in white-collar wages.

*Occupational Preferences*

Information on the occupational preferences of secondary school leavers makes it possible to judge how realistic these expectations are and to determine whether the government should attempt to alter them if they are partially responsible for high unemployment rates among secondary school leavers. The sLs asked the unemployed to list their three most preferred occupations. The degree of deviation of the actual occupational distribution of different groups of school leavers from their first and third preferences is illustrated in Table 16-4. The

Table 16-4. Deviation of First and Third Preferences
of Unemployed School Leavers from Actual Occupations
(percentage points)

| Certificate | White collar | Sales and services | Production workers |
|---|---|---|---|
| **All** | | | |
| LCE | | | |
| First preference | 38.0 | −13.3 | −25.1 |
| Third preference | 24.1 | −10.3 | −13.6 |
| MCE | | | |
| First preference | 32.1 | −9.6 | −22.8 |
| Third preference | 14.0 | −6.4 | −8.3 |
| MCVE | | | |
| First preference | 21.7 | −7.5 | −15.0 |
| Third preference | 15.6 | −2.8 | −13.2 |
| **Male** | | | |
| LCE | | | |
| First preference | 27.6 | −11.9 | −15.8 |
| Third preference | 22.5 | −10.7 | −11.9 |
| MCE | | | |
| First preference | 31.5 | −10.8 | −21.5 |
| Third preference | 16.2 | −7.2 | −10.2 |
| MCVE | | | |
| First preference | 21.5 | −7.6 | −14.7 |
| Third preference | 20.1 | −3.1 | −18.0 |
| **Malay** | | | |
| LCE | | | |
| First preference | 41.0 | −13.1 | −27.5 |
| Third preference | 22.5 | −8.1 | −14.9 |
| MCE | | | |
| First preference | 33.8 | −8.4 | −25.3 |
| Third preference | 10.6 | −4.2 | −6.8 |
| MCVE | | | |
| First preference | 16.0 | −4.1 | −12.6 |
| Third preference | 10.5 | 0.6 | −11.4 |

Source: sLs, 1973.

table shows that all groups had a high preference for white-collar jobs which they were not able to achieve. This is true for the third preference as well as the first, suggesting that the more modest level of expectation which this lower preference probably represents was still in excess of reality. The rigidity of the pattern of expectations is emphasized by the fact that the Socio-Economic Survey (SES) of 1967 (discussed in Chapter 14) found a similar bias toward white-collar jobs among the unemployed even though the SES sample included the entire population, not just secondary school leavers.[1] There does not seem to have been any significant change in preferences in the six years which elapsed between the two surveys.

Predictably, the vocational school leavers are least biased toward white-collar jobs both in actuality and in their expressed preferences. The excess of preferences for white-collar jobs over actual employment levels is also the lowest for the vocationally trained school leavers. The expectations of LCE level graduates in general and Malay LCE holders in particular seem to be the most conspicuously out of line with their actual occupational distribution. The data lead inexorably to the conclusion that, in spite of the evidence that secondary school leavers have begun to diversify their choice of occupations in recent years, their expectations remain unrealistically biased toward white-collar occupations. This state of affairs might reasonably be expected to contribute significantly to the high rates of unemployment experienced by secondary school leavers.

## Earnings of School Leavers: Actual and Expected

If the supply of secondary school leavers in the younger age groups is running ahead of demand, the relative earnings of this group should fall and the premium commanded by secondary schooling over primary education should be reduced. This type of adjustment will supplement the effects of bumping (the upward revision of educational standards) in certain jobs. Can the three available data sets confirm this prediction?

As illustrated by the age-earnings profiles for different educational levels in Figure 8-2, the profiles for successive grades diverge with age, at least up to the points of peak earnings. This finding is consistent

1. SES, 1967, p. 139.

with the supposition that the rate of return to education is falling over time, since the difference in return to higher education is relatively small for the younger age groups and increases with age. In fact, inspection of the profiles shows that for the 15–25 age group the earnings premium of secondary school leavers over those with primary education, and that of MCE graduates over those with some secondary schooling, are quite small compared with the differences observed at greater ages. Unfortunately, this piece of evidence is also consistent with an alternative hypothesis that the rate of growth of earnings with age is higher for higher educational grades (because, for example, employers are able to profit more from their employees' experience if they are better educated initially).

The basic problem in using available data to test the hypothesis proposed at the beginning of this section is, of course, that the data do not indicate what the earnings profiles of today's school leavers are likely to be in later life. It is possible to speak with certainty only about the starting wages of young school leavers.

### Earnings Data from the SLS

The information from the SLS is confined to the earnings of those who completed nine and eleven years of schooling, the LCE, and MCE/MCVE samples respectively, within a narrow age group. The distribution of earnings for the sample shows a striking degree of diversity of earnings among those with jobs (see Table 16-5). The coefficient of variation of

Table 16-5.  Earnings of Male and Female School Leavers
(Malaysian dollars per month)

| Certificate | Number | Mean | Standard deviation | Coefficient of variation |
|---|---|---|---|---|
| **Male** | | | | |
| LCE | 532 | 106.5 | 47.0 | 0.44 |
| MCE | 903 | 134.5 | 62.0 | 0.46 |
| MCVE | 436 | 128.5 | 55.5 | 0.43 |
| **Female** | | | | |
| LCE | 127 | 71.04 | 38.61 | 0.54 |
| MCE | 345 | 112.11 | 69.03 | 0.56 |
| MCVE | 126 | 117.01 | 59.96 | 0.51 |

Source: SLS, 1973.

earnings is much the same for the three groups; that is, the spread of earnings facing a job seeker is much the same in relation to the mean earnings of each educational group. A comparison of the data for males and females in Table 16-5 shows that monthly earnings for females with all types of certificates are lower than those for males—but the difference is much more apparent among the LCE graduates. The dispersion of earnings is generally greater for females.

The grouped distributions graphed in Figure 16-1 for male holders of the three certificates show that the majority of the sample is concentrated in the M$50–M$150 range. Among males nearly a third of MCE holders and a quarter of MCVE graduates earn more than M$150, however, while only about 15 percent of the LCE graduates have earnings at

Figure 16–1. Distribution of Males by Earnings Group

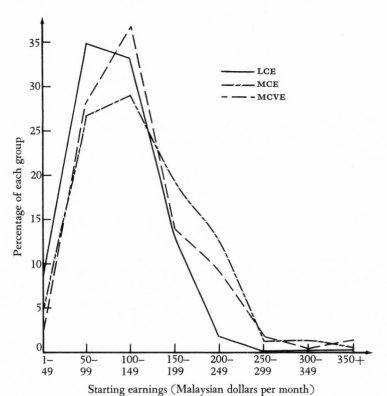

Starting earnings (Malaysian dollars per month)

Source: SLS, 1973.

this level. Although the grouped distributions for females are not shown, the difference between the percentages of LCE and MCE/MCVE certificate holders in the higher income groups is much greater for females than for males. The modal earnings group is M$50–M$99 for females with both LCE and MCE and less unequivocally so for those with MCVE.

### Race

The mean monthly earnings of Malays and Chinese by different certificate and sex groups are shown in Table 16-6. Contrary to expecta-

Table 16-6. Differences in the Mean Starting Monthly Earnings
of Malays and Chinese by Sex and Certificate
(Malaysian dollars per month)

| | Male | | | Female | | |
|---|---|---|---|---|---|---|
| Certificate | Malay | Chinese | t-value of difference of means | Malay | Chinese | t-value of difference of means |
| LCE | 110.5 | 103.5 | 1.52 | 67.23 | 87.32 | 2.03[b] |
| MCE | 145.5 | 127.0 | 3.94[a] | 116.06 | 106.72 | 1.39 |
| MCVE | 126.5 | 130.0 | 0.63 | 121.75 | 109.67 | 1.21 |

a. Significant at 0.01 level.
b. Significant at 0.05 level.
Source: SLS, 1973.

tions, the racial difference in mean earnings (t-value) is significant for only two out of the six subgroups shown. Male Malays with MCE qualifications have significantly higher mean earnings than their Chinese equivalents, whereas among the females, Chinese with LCE qualifications earn significantly more than Malays. The percentage difference seems to be substantial only for the female LCE graduates—the Chinese females earning about 30 percent more. The frequency distribution of earnings of the two races among MCE and MCVE graduates (not shown) confirms the impression given by the summary statistics that patterns of earnings by race are broadly similar. The only exception is that a larger proportion of Malay males with MCE certificates are in the higher earning group (above M$150)—which is what pulled up the average earnings for this group.

*The Government–Private Sector Wage Difference*

The difference between public and private sector wages is a major factor in the dispersion of earnings among school leavers. Figure 16-2 demonstrates that for males, in the case of both MCE and LCE certificate holders separately, the frequency distribution of earnings in government jobs lies markedly to the right of that for private sector employment. In the government sector, more than 30 percent of LCE holders earn more than M$150, while only 10 percent of those with the some qualification do so in the private sector. The discrepancy is even greater for MCE certificate holders, with 30 percent of males in government jobs having very high earnings (more than M$200), compared with only about 6 percent of those in private employment. The analysis in Chapter 9 suggested that public sector employment had only a limited influence on earnings for the sample as a whole; for the Malays, government employment did imply higher earnings, but this effect was removed once the human capital variables were taken into account. The current finding of a substantial difference in favor of the government sector may imply one or both of the following: (1) there may have been a substantial shift in the pay scale for people working for the government in recent years; (2) wages in the government sector substantially exceed those in the private sector at the beginning of a worker's career, but the gap is subsequently reduced. Whatever the relative importance of these two factors, the wage premium in the government sector must loom large in the minds of secondary school leavers.

*Multivariate Analysis of Earnings of School Leavers*

A multivariate analysis of the earnings data from the SLS may help to establish the quantitative importance of the different factors which seem to affect earnings. It is sometimes more meaningful to look at deviations in earnings, not in relation to the base of a particular variable—which the coefficients of the regression model with sets of dummy variables enables us to do—but as deviations from the overall mean. It is possible to provide this type of information by using multiple classification analysis (MCA). A second advantage of using the MCA is that deviations from the grand mean are additive for the different variables concerned, so that it is relatively easy to determine the combined effect of two or more variables. The present analysis includes only those variables which significantly affected earnings in a preliminary step-wise regression model.

Figure 16–2. Distribution of Earnings of Male LCE and MCE Certificate Holders in the Government and Private Sectors

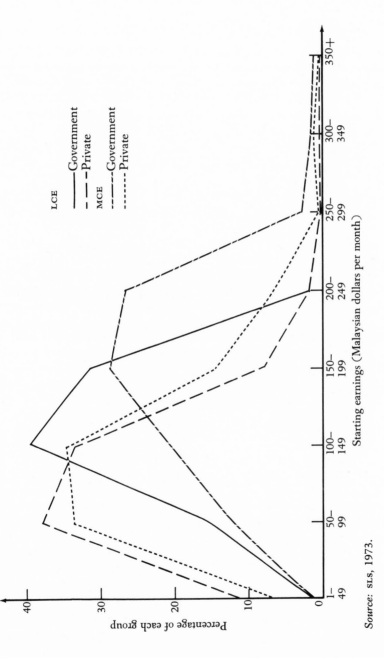

LCE
——— Government
— – – Private

MCE
—·—·— Government
········· Private

*Source:* SLS, 1973.

Starting earnings (Malaysian dollars per month)

Percentage of each group

315

The results of this exercise are presented in Table 16-7. It was decided to undertake the analysis separately for Malays and non-Malays, to have a better idea of the different effects of the variables on the earnings of the two racial groups. The gross effects give the deviations from the mean for each of the factors considered separately, while the net effects are the deviations adjusted for the other variables in the program. Generally, the program performs better for the non-Malays; the overall $R^2$ as well as the proportion of variance explained by the individual sets of variables ($\beta^2$) are higher for this group.

The occupational category of the worker's job and whether the job is in the government or the private sector stand out as important determinants of earnings for both racial groups—with relatively high $\beta^2$ as well as sizable coefficients. Being in a white-collar occupation has a noticeably greater effect on the earnings of the Malays, although more or less the same proportion of the two racial groups of the sample are in white-collar jobs. The difference in earnings between white-collar jobs and sales and services, for instance—controlling for other factors— is as much as M$60 for the Malays as against only M$30 for the non-Malays. Government employment, however, does not produce a higher differential for the Malays. A much higher proportion of Malays do get government jobs (36.5 percent against 12.9 percent among non-Malays), but the net difference between the private and government sectors is M$42 for Malays and M$47 for non-Malays—a premium of 42 and 45 percent respectively for a government job. The earnings differentials associated with both white-collar and government jobs represent an important element in the Malaysian labor market, probably accounting for much of the high earnings expectations of school leavers.

What is the effect of an additional two years of education after the LCE on the earnings of school leavers? Does this effect differ for those coming from the vocational and academic streams? The coefficients of net deviations of the certificate variable (with other variables held constant) show that incremental earnings over the amounts earned by an LCE holder are: for Malays with MCE 10.4, with MCVE 15.0; for non-Malays with MCE 25.1, with MCVE 34.2. In fact, however, the two major variables affecting earnings—white-collar and government jobs—are more easily obtained by holders of some certificates than others (see Table 16-8).

The figures in Table 16-8 can be taken to represent the probability of obtaining the particular category of job for each racial and certificate group. The higher probabilities of obtaining white-collar and government jobs for the MCE and MCVE holders compared with LCE graduates can then be multiplied by the corresponding coefficients of net deviation in Table 16-7 to obtain the additional earnings which school leavers with eleven years of education enjoy, over and above the *average* resulting from their better chances of obtaining white-collar and government jobs. When added to the "pure" differential attributable to holding particular certificates, they give some idea of the adjusted increased ·eturns to upper secondary education (see Table 16-9). Thus the positive incremental effect on earnings of two additional years of schooling is practically the same for MCE and MCVE holders, but it is significantly greater for the non-Malays: 24 percent for Malays and 37 percent for non-Malays.[2]

*The Earnings Expectations of School Leavers*

School leavers were asked how much they expected to earn after leaving school. In general, their reported expectations were well above the actual earnings of the group in the sample who were in fact employed. The percentage excesses of expected over actual earnings for the different groups are:

|      | Male | | Female | |
|------|-------|---------|-------|---------|
|      | Malay | Chinese | Malay | Chinese |
| LCE  | 49.8  | 97.1    | 132.2 | 82.1    |
| MCE  | 67.6  | 96.6    | 82.4  | 81.9    |
| MCVE | 61.7  | 77.5    | 61.1  | 57.1    |

Are these markedly higher levels of expected earnings due to the particularly unrealistic expectations of a minority of school leavers? The distributions of expected earnings for these three streams were graphed separately for sex and race (not shown). Single modes existed for all the distributions, but the distribution for five of the twelve groups studied had a prominent subsidiary mode. These subsidiary modes invariably occurred in an adjacent earnings class, and they did not suggest a particularly dispersed pattern of expectations among school leavers. (Table 16-10 gives the values of the expected and realized modal earnings of the different groups for easy comparison.) A sizable proportion of male school leavers have excessively high expectations; about a fifth of the Chinese LCE males and the same proportion of both Malay and Chinese MCE males had expected to earn in excess of

---

2. The mean monthly earnings of those with LCE (after controlling for the other variables) are M$109 for the Malays and M$87 for the others.

Table 16-7. Multiple Classification Analysis of Starting Monthly Earnings on Ten Sets of Explanatory Variables

| Variable | Percentage distribution | | Gross effect[a] | | Net effect[b] | |
|---|---|---|---|---|---|---|
| | Malay | Other | Malay | Other | Malay | Other |
| Sex | | | | | | |
| Male | 72.0 | 77.7 | 4.17 | 2.17 | 6.62 | 3.91 |
| Female | 28.0 | 22.3 | −10.70 | −7.58 | −16.99 | −13.67 |
| | | | $(\epsilon^2= 0.004)$ | $(\epsilon^2= 0.003)$ | $(\beta^2= 0.010)$ | $(\beta^2= 0.011)$ |
| Father's income | | | | | | |
| (Malaysian dollars per month) | | | | | | |
| Nothing | 5.5 | 9.6 | − 7.03 | − 2.79 | 2.43 | 4.13 |
| 1–79 | 15.3 | 1.9 | − 2.74 | −13.95 | − 5.95 | −11.11 |
| 80–129 | 20.4 | 10.2 | − 3.49 | −16.18 | − 5.23 | − 6.91 |
| 130–179 | 12.9 | 11.3 | − 6.77 | −10.42 | − 1.94 | − 5.08 |
| 180–279 | 18.0 | 22.4 | 2.03 | − 6.35 | 4.34 | − 4.65 |
| 280–349 | 5.8 | 9.8 | − 0.30 | 6.51 | 2.37 | 0.20 |
| 350 and over | 9.9 | 15.4 | 15.24 | 16.79 | 4.92 | 7.85 |
| Missing | 12.1 | 19.4 | 4.45 | 8.03 | 5.71 | 4.67 |
| | | | $(\epsilon^2= 0.004)$ | $(\epsilon^2= 0.023)$ | $(\beta^2= 0.002)$ | $(\beta^2= 0.006)$ |
| Town of residence | | | | | | |
| Missing | 0.4 | 0.8 | −32.43 | −28.31 | 6.62 | −20.30 |
| 75,000 and over | 5.1 | 6.8 | 12.68 | 11.45 | 19.50 | 5.06 |
| Kuala Lumpur | 26.3 | 26.9 | 3.72 | 12.52 | 7.66 | 8.90 |

| | | | | | | |
|---|---|---|---|---|---|---|
| Georgetown | 5.8 | 15.4 | −24.79 | −18.76 | −13.86 | −20.41 |
| Ipoh | 4.0 | 4.9 | −5.24 | −26.65 | −1.53 | −17.38 |
| Johore Bahru | 7.1 | 7.6 | 1.47 | 13.95 | 7.11 | 14.29 |
| 10,000–75,000 | 32.2 | 24.3 | 1.09 | 0.25 | −5.68 | 3.00 |
| Under 10,000 | 19.0 | 13.3 | −1.47 | −6.19 | −4.46 | −2.83 |
| | | | $(\epsilon^2 = 0.005)$ | $(\epsilon^2 = 0.035)$ | $(\beta^2 = 0.006)$ | $(\beta^2 = 0.026)$ |
| Certificate | | | | | | |
| Missing | ... | 0.6 | — | −7.04 | — | 9.22 |
| LCE | 26.1 | 21.5 | −28.73 | −31.85 | −9.87 | −25.50 |
| MCE | 49.0 | 47.3 | 9.06 | 2.52 | 0.27 | 0.42 |
| MCVE | 22.1 | 24.7 | 4.65 | 7.54 | 5.18 | 8.71 |
| HSC | 2.8 | 5.8 | 72.41 | 65.87 | 46.17 | 59.55 |
| | | | $(\epsilon^2 = 0.040)$ | $(\epsilon^2 = 0.102)$ | $(\beta^2 = 0.008)$ | $(\beta^2 = 0.076)$ |
| Grade secured | | | | | | |
| Missing | 14.4 | 15.1 | 0.99 | 19.14 | −7.10 | −12.38 |
| Grade I | 2.3 | 4.7 | −18.12 | 28.07 | −7.40 | 25.37 |
| Grade II | 4.9 | 14.3 | 24.31 | 12.32 | 18.38 | 3.91 |
| Grade III | 58.1 | 34.8 | 3.84 | −11.23 | 3.94 | 3.27 |
| Grade IV | 20.3 | 31.1 | −15.47 | −6.67 | −9.77 | −3.33 |
| | | | $(\epsilon^2 = 0.009)$ | $(\epsilon^2 = 0.036)$ | $(\beta^2 = 0.005)$ | $(\beta^2 = 0.013)$ |
| Employer | | | | | | |
| Missing | 11.0 | 7.9 | −13.98 | −21.60 | 4.42 | −8.03 |
| Government | 36.5 | 12.9 | 37.39 | 47.51 | 23.91 | 41.25 |
| Private | 52.4 | 79.2 | −23.11 | −5.55 | −17.59 | −5.90 |
| | | | $(\epsilon^2 = 0.075)$ | $(\epsilon^2 = 0.073)$ | $(\beta^2 = 0.034)$ | $(\beta^2 = 0.052)$ |

*(Table continues on the following page.)*

Table 16-7 (continued)

| Variable | Percentage distribution | | Gross effect[a] | | Net effect[b] | |
|---|---|---|---|---|---|---|
| | Malay | Other | Malay | Other | Malay | Other |
| **Occupation** | | | | | | |
| Missing, other | 21.0 | 10.0 | −32.84 | −29.15 | −27.51 | −12.83 |
| Professional, administrative, clerical | 35.0 | 36.1 | 47.39 | 25.13 | 33.62 | 13.68 |
| Sales, services | 9.2 | 15.6 | −29.98 | −27.22 | −25.99 | −16.24 |
| Production workers | 33.0 | 37.0 | −22.71 | − 4.62 | −12.62 | − 3.25 |
| Agriculture | 1.8 | 1.2 | 32.70 | −16.53 | 32.75 | 6.89 |
| | | | $(\epsilon^2= 0.119)$ | $(\epsilon^2= 0.092)$ | $(\beta^2= 0.064)$ | $(\beta^2= 0.027)$ |
| **Race and medium of instruction** | | | | | | |
| Malay and Malay | 63.2 | — | − 4.99 | — | − 0.73 | — |
| Malay and English | 36.8 | — | 8.59 | — | 1.26 | — |
| | | | $(\epsilon^2= 0.004)$ | | $(\beta^2= 0.00009)$ | |
| Other | — | 25.0 | — | −13.00 | — | − 1.89 |
| Chinese and English | — | 75.0 | — | 4.33 | — | 0.63 |
| | | | | $(\epsilon^2= 0.012)$ | | $(\beta^2= 0.0002)$ |
| **Terms of employment** | | | | | | |
| Missing | 7.8 | 5.1 | −11.43 | −22.31 | −15.01 | − 9.13 |
| Full time | 62.0 | 76.6 | 15.19 | 7.29 | 9.87 | 4.78 |
| Part time | 30.3 | 18.3 | −28.19 | −24.23 | −16.38 | −17.39 |
| | | | $(\epsilon^2= 0.036)$ | $(\epsilon^2= 0.036)$ | $(\beta^2= 0.015)$ | $(\beta^2= 0.016)$ |

Duration of first job (months)

| Duration of first job (months) | | | | | | |
|---|---|---|---|---|---|---|
| 0 | 2.4 | 2.5 | 25.25 | 1.21 | 9.28 | 2.64 |
| 1–3 | 18.9 | 18.9 | 5.09 | 2.54 | 1.90 | — 8.19 |
| 4–6 | 18.2 | 13.4 | — 1.40 | 1.55 | — 2.12 | — 4.22 |
| 7–12 | 22.7 | 23.0 | 3.50 | 8.01 | — 1.07 | 7.60 |
| 13–24 | 18.0 | 17.3 | — 2.45 | 6.23 | — 1.50 | 1.28 |
| 25–36 | 6.6 | 9.8 | — 12.72 | — 7.66 | — 6.53 | 1.19 |
| 37 and over | 4.4 | 6.0 | — 32.33 | — 15.15 | — 19.74 | 4.85 |
| Missing | 8.7 | 9.1 | 6.80 | — 11.16 | 18.53 | 1.07 |
| | | | $(\epsilon^2 = 0.008)$ | $(\epsilon^2 = 0.011)$ | $(\beta^2 = 0.005)$ | $(\beta^2 = 0.006)$ |

— Not applicable.
... Not significant.
Note: Malay: $R^2 = 0.174$; number in sample 1,352; mean starting monthly earnings 118.93; standard deviation 104.06.
Other: $R^2 = 0.245$; number in sample 1,096; mean starting monthly earnings 112.76; standard deviation 69.28.
a. Gross effect is the deviation in the starting monthly earnings of a particular category from the overall mean earnings.
b. Net effect is the deviation in the starting monthly earnings of a particular category from the overall mean after adjusting for effects of other predictors.
Source: SLS, 1973.

Table 16-8.  Percentage of Employed School Leavers in White-Collar
and Government Jobs by Race and Certificate

| Certificate | White collar | Government |
|---|---|---|
| Malay | | |
| LCE | 0.18 | 0.33 |
| MCE | 0.49 | 0.47 |
| MCVE | 0.42 | 0.33 |
| Other | | |
| LCE | 0.16 | 0.11 |
| MCE | 0.46 | 0.18 |
| MCVE | 0.29 | 0.07 |

Sources: SLS, 1973, and Table 16-7.

Table 16-9.  Adjusted Increased Returns to Upper Secondary Education
(Malaysian dollars per month)

| Item | For Malays | | For others | |
|---|---|---|---|---|
| | MCE | MCVE | MCE | MCVE |
| From white-collar jobs | 10.4 | 8.1 | 4.1 | 1.8 |
| From government jobs | 3.1 | . . . | 2.9 | −1.7 |
| From certificate | 10.4 | 15.0 | 25.1 | 34.2 |
| Total | 23.9 | 23.1 | 32.1 | 34.3 |

. . . Not significant.
Sources: SLS, 1973, and Table 16-7.

Table 16-10.  Modal Expected and Realized Earnings
by Certificate, Sex, and Race
(Malaysian dollars per month)

| Certificate | Malay | | Chinese | |
|---|---|---|---|---|
| | Expected | Realized | Expected | Realized |
| Male | | | | |
| LCE | 175 | 75 | 225 | 125 |
| MCE | 225 | 125 | 225 | 125 |
| MCVE | 225 | 75 | 175 | 125 |
| Female | | | | |
| LCE | 175 | 75 | 125 | 75 |
| MCE | 225 | 75 | 175 | 75 |
| MCVE | 225 | 75 | 175 | 125 |

Note: Values are midpoints of classes.
Source: SLS, 1973.

M$300. Interestingly, the MCVE group did not appear to include a subgroup with these very high expectations. The summary measures of the coefficient of variation of expected earnings for the different groups are:

|  | Male | | Female | |
|---|---|---|---|---|
|  | Malay | Chinese | Malay | Chinese |
| LCE | 0.46 | 0.34 | 0.49 | 0.37 |
| MCE | 0.59 | 0.63 | 0.53 | 0.47 |
| MCVE | 0.52 | 0.42 | 0.54 | 0.42 |

For males, the dispersion of actual earnings was broadly similar for the different streams, with a value of about 0.44, while females had a somewhat higher dispersion in the range 0.51–0.56. The dispersions for expectations are at comparable or lower levels for males and females, except in the case of MCE males of both races, who have markedly higher dispersion levels.

### Determinants of Expectations

To isolate some of the factors explaining the variations in expected earnings, regressions were computed for a series of explanatory variables. The best results obtained are shown in Tables 16-11 and 16-12 separately for Malays and non-Malays. The results of the regression analyses are disappointing. They have been able to explain only a small proportion of the variance in expected earnings—13 percent for the Malays and 11 percent for the non-Malays—and much of the explained variance is due to differences in gender and certificate held.

The increase in expected earnings associated with a certificate higher than LCE is markedly greater for the Malays than for the non-Malays. The constants (giving the earnings of the base category, LCE, and controlling for the other variables) are more or less the same for both groups. The additional expected earnings from an MCE qualification are 100 percent higher for the Malays; from an MCVE certificate they are nearly 75 percent greater. It will be recalled that the probability of obtaining white-collar or government jobs increased with upper secondary school qualifications much more significantly for the Malays in the sample than for the non-Malays. The higher earnings associated with these categories of jobs very probably contribute to the higher expectations of Malays from additional years of schooling. The evidence is thus consistent with the view that the public sector's salary structure influences the formation of high expectations among school leavers.

Table 16-11.  Regression Analysis of School Leavers' Expected Earnings after Leaving School: All Malays

| Variable | Beta value | Standard error | Percentage in each category | Step number |
|---|---|---|---|---|
| Certificate | | | | |
| LCE (base) | — | — | 34 | |
| MCE | 82.02 | 4.77 | 45 | 1 |
| MCVE | 59.97 | 6.02 | 19 | 4 |
| HSC | 156.77 | 14.78 | 02 | 2 |
| Grade secured | | | | |
| Grade 1 | 97.42 | 9.35 | 06 | 5 |
| Grade 2 | 72.08 | 8.85 | 06 | 6 |
| Grade 3 | 24.07 | 4.49 | 55 | 9 |
| Grade 4 (base) | — | — | 26 | |
| Sex | | | | |
| Male | 28.88 | 4.36 | 71 | 7 |
| Female (base) | — | — | 29 | |
| Medium of instruction | | | | |
| English | 19.54 | 4.48 | 29 | 10 |
| Not English (base) | — | — | 71 | |
| Employment status | | | | |
| Unemployed | −28.30 | 4.30 | 66 | 3 |
| Employed (base) | — | — | 34 | |
| Occupation | | | | |
| Production workers (base) | — | — | 40 | |
| Sales, services | −20.83 | 9.20 | 05 | 12 |
| Father's monthly income | | | | |
| Less than M$100 (base) | — | — | 53 | |
| M$200–M$299 | 13.94 | 5.85 | 13 | 11 |
| M$300 and over | 36.13 | 6.20 | 12 | 8 |
| Present residence | | | | |
| Towns of less than 10,000 (base) | — | — | 25 | |
| Kuala Lumpur | 12.07 | 5.38 | 16 | 13 |
| Year left school | | | | |
| 1969 (base) | — | — | 33 | |
| 1966 and earlier | 23.71 | 13.20 | 02 | 14 |
| Constant | 78.45 | 7.50 | | |
| $R^2 = 0.133$ | | | | |
| $F = 46.45$ | | | | |
| $N = 4,272$ | | | | |

Note: Within each category classes that were not significant in the regression model have been omitted.

Source: Data derived from SLS, 1973.

Table 16-12. Regression Analysis of School Leavers' Expected Earnings after Leaving School: Chinese and Others

| Variable | Beta value | Standard error | Percentage in each category | Step number |
|---|---|---|---|---|
| Certificate | | | | |
| LCE (base) | — | — | 29 | |
| MCE | 49.84 | 6.20 | 48 | 4 |
| MCVE | 18.85 | 8.10 | 17 | 8 |
| HSC | 65.68 | 11.91 | 06 | 6 |
| Grade secured | | | | |
| Grade 1 | 56.26 | 8.32 | 12 | 1 |
| Grade 4 (base) | — | — | 34 | |
| Sex | | | | |
| Male | 45.75 | 6.35 | 80 | 3 |
| Female (base) | — | — | 20 | |
| Race | | | | |
| Chinese | 29.91 | 5.86 | 70 | 2 |
| Other (base) | — | — | 30 | |
| Employment status | | | | |
| Unemployed | −10.91 | 5.16 | 51 | 9 |
| Employed (base) | — | — | 49 | |
| Father's monthly income | | | | |
| Less than M$100 (base) | — | — | 34 | |
| M$200–M$299 | 22.23 | 6.73 | 19 | 7 |
| M$300 and over | 37.58 | 6.12 | 26 | 5 |
| Present residence | | | | |
| Johore | 22.15 | 12.18 | 05 | 11 |
| Towns of 10,000–75,000 | 11.62 | 5.70 | 28 | 10 |
| Towns of less than 10,000 (base) | — | — | 16 | |
| Constant | 81.92 | 8.74 | | |
| $R^2 = 0.109$ | | | | |
| $F = 27.84$ | | | | |
| $N = 2,525$ | | | | |

Note: Within each category, classes that were not significant in the regression model have been omitted.
Source: Data derived from SLS, 1973.

As with possession of a certificate, the increase in expected earnings associated with higher grades (better examination scores) is much more pronounced for the Malays. For the non-Malays, in fact, only the highest grade (grade 1) has a significant coefficient. By contrast, Malay school leavers of all three grades above the base (grade 4) have significantly higher expectations: the additional expected earnings associated with grades 1 and 2 are spectacularly large. This result also reflects the expected institutional effect of a higher grade; like a higher certificate, it enhances the prospects of a Malay more than those of a non-Malay. The same point holds for school leavers who have had English as their language of instruction.

In the regression models for both racial groups, school leavers who were unemployed at the time of the survey reported significantly lower earnings expectations than the group who were in fact employed. No causal relationship should probably be attached to this finding. It is likely that the school leavers' expectations simply reflect attitudes based on their current employment status at the time of the survey.

### Revision of Expectations

It is possible that school leavers revise their earnings expectations in the course of their job search, but the process of revision is difficult to trace from available data. The questionnaire used in the survey asked the unemployed about the minimum wage they would be willing to accept and requested them to list three occupational choices in order of preference. Any revision of expectations that might have taken place during the school leavers' period of unemployment would be reflected in the ratio of the acceptable minimum wage for their first occupational preference (UMOG 1) to their expected earnings after leaving school. If the school leavers had unrealistic expectations, these would be reflected in a substantially lower minimum wage associated with their third preference (UMOG 3) relative to that recorded under their first preference.

In fact, the data show that the ratio between first preference wage and expected earnings on leaving school was biased somewhat toward a value above unity, suggesting that the unemployed school leavers had revised their expectations upward since leaving school. The percentage distribution of males by ratio illustrates this point:

| Certificate | Less than 0.6 | 0.6–0.8 | 0.8–1.0 | 1.0–1.5 | More than 1.5 |
|---|---|---|---|---|---|
| LCE | 3.1 | 10.1 | 43.0 | 25.7 | 18.2 |
| MCE | 4.9 | 10.9 | 49.1 | 23.5 | 11.6 |
| MCVE | 1.9 | 6.6 | 49.3 | 30.6 | 11.6 |

Essentially the same pattern holds true for all groups classified by race and sex.

By contrast, the ratio of third preference wage to first (UMOG 3/ UMOG 1) is, for all groups, normally distributed about the class 0.8–

1.0, which could be taken to include all those whose expectations have changed only marginally, if at all. For example, the percentage distribution of all school leavers with MCE was as follows:

| Less than 0.6 | 0.6–0.8 | 0.8–1.0 | 1.0–1.5 | More than 1.5 |
|---|---|---|---|---|
| 8.0 | 19.3 | 54.1 | 16.0 | 2.6 |

For the sample as a whole, school leavers expected as high earnings from their third preference as they did from their first.

The data suggest that the unemployed school leavers may have somewhat inflexible ideas about their expected earnings. Since these views are given in answer to hypothetical questions, they may not reflect respondents' reactions to actual situations, but neither can they be assumed to represent a consistently artificial and exaggerated estimate of earnings. A recent ILO study of urban Peru concluded that "the secondary students' earnings expectations are quite realistic and perhaps even on the low side compared to reality as far as the central tendency is concerned."[3]

## Conclusions

Examination of the education-occupation matrix for urban Malaysia shows that because the educational requirements for many jobs have been upgraded, a majority of the younger generation leaving school with qualifications lower than that of the completed MCE are no longer in white-collar jobs. In spite of the increased diversification of occupations among secondary school leavers in recent years, however, their expectations remain unrealistically biased toward white-collar employment.

The rate of return to postprimary education is lower for the younger age groups, but since this conclusion is based on cross-section data a falling rate of return to education cannot be conclusively demonstrated. In any event, it still pays most young people to pursue postprimary education.

The wide dispersion of earnings among younger school leavers should be the subject of further inquiry. The whole structure of earnings in the government sector is above that in the private sector, but diversity of earnings exists within each category of jobs. This dispersion in earn-

3. Jan Versluis, "Education, the Labor Market and Employment," World Employment Program, ILO Education and Employment Working Paper no. 4, December 1974, p. 17.

ings could significantly raise expectations about the private return to education, especially if school leavers attach a relatively low value to the risk of unemployment.

The earnings expectations of school leavers in all groups were found to be quite unrealistic, amounting to as much as twice the actual earnings of those who did get employment. There was also evidence that expectations were somewhat rigid: the minimum wage expected by those who were unemployed when surveyed was on the whole somewhat higher than that expected by the sample after leaving school.

Malay school leavers' earnings expectations increased with the possession of higher certificates and grades much more sharply than those of non-Malays. This finding may be related to the better opportunities for Malays to obtain more lucrative positions with better qualifications. It also suggests that there may be a link between the observed high earnings in the public sector and the formation of high expectations among school leavers.

# CHAPTER 17

# The Employment Rate and the Waiting Period in the Labor Market

DESPITE BOTH OCCUPATIONAL AND EARNINGS ADJUSTMENTS in the labor market in response to the excess supply of secondary school leavers, unemployment rates among this group were still very high and the period of waiting before obtaining employment was still inordinately long. Some groups in the SLS sample, however, tended to have higher unemployment rates or a longer period of waiting than others. The purpose of this chapter is to use statistical analyses to throw light on the factors influencing the rate of unemployment or the length of the waiting period. Since these factors are very closely linked, either could be used as the dependent variable to be "explained." The sample contains some respondents who have been absorbed into employment and others who were unemployed at the date of the survey. Because the waiting period is not yet complete for the latter group, the analyses which follow concentrate on the employment rate, although the statistical model used will make it possible to infer some of the variations in the periods of waiting experienced by different groups.

## The Period of Search

The rate of employment among school leavers can be considered in two ways—the proportion of school leavers of a particular cohort who find jobs after a certain period of time and the rate at which they leave the pool of the unemployed. If the rate of departure from the unemployed pool were uniform for all school leavers, the two sets of data would simply be different ways of referring to the same process. There is no reason to assume, however, that this rate is in fact constant. Thus the distribution of school leavers by the period of time spent in unemployment is of interest.

Those who were employed at the time of the survey were asked the length of time it took them to get their first job; those who were unemployed, how long they had been unemployed. The amount of time spent looking for the first job would not be affected by whether a particular school leaver had held a job since leaving school, but the length of unemployment would be affected. Only 13 percent of the unemployed had worked before, but there was some variation in the percentage between races, which is important to keep in mind in interpreting the data.

The sample is spread over several years of departure from school for both the LCE and the MCE/MCVE streams. The 1968 and 1969 cohorts were the important ones for the LCE group, however, and the cohorts of 1970, 1971, and 1972 were heavily represented in the MCE/MCVE sample. Table 17-1 presents information on employment and the duration of job searches and unemployment separately for the different cohorts and for the three races. The reported magnitudes are also influenced by a number of factors in addition to race and cohort, which will be examined with the help of multivariate analysis in subsequent sections. Certain broad results stand out at this stage.

School leavers differ substantially by race, both in the employment rate and the period of search. The Chinese, in particular, have a markedly higher employment rate, a shorter period of search for the first job, and a relatively brief spell of unemployment (in the case of those who were unemployed at the time of the survey). For the unemployed group the racial difference in the period of unemployment is greater for those who have never held a job, presumably because fewer unemployed Chinese fall into this category.

The sample contained two groups that were comparable in age. Since upper secondary school leavers (MCE/MCVE) spent two more years in school than lower secondary school graduates (LCE), the 1968 and 1969 cohorts of the LCE group are the same age as the 1970 and 1971 cohorts of the MCE group. Among the Chinese, those with an LCE have a predictably higher employment rate than those with an MCE because the former have had two extra years to look for a job. By contrast, the experience of the Malays is surprising; the MCE cohorts have a significantly higher rate of unemployment than the corresponding LCE cohorts of similar age. The finding suggests that upper secondary schooling is more important for the Malays than it is for the Chinese in obtaining acceptable employment. This point will be discussed further in a subsequent section.

An apparent paradox in the distributions of the length of unemployment by annual cohorts in Table 17-1 needs to be cleared up. Since the table includes only the unemployed who were still looking for their first jobs, it is difficult to understand why the length of unemployment varies among the unemployed from any given cohort. If those who left school in the same year entered the labor market in search of work at nearly the same time, there should be no variation in the observed length of unemployment among those who had never worked and were in the unemployed pool at the time of the survey. The large variations among school leavers from the same cohort mean that the period of nonparticipation in the labor market varies widely among school leavers. The determinants of nonparticipation will be examined later in the chapter in the light of survey data.

Table 17-1 shows that the time spent by the employed group in looking for their first jobs is considerably shorter than the length of unemployment of those who have not found work. To a large extent, this is as it should be. The first variable measures the elapsed time up to the point when a school leaver was absorbed into employment, while the length of unemployment refers to the entire period from his or her entry into the labor market right up to the date of the survey. But there is virtually no overlap between the values for the third quartile of the employed group and the first quartile of the unemployed—in spite of the considerable variation in the time of entry into the market for members of a particular cohort. This fact strongly suggests that the job seekers are split into two groups: those who are by ability or luck able to find gainful employment soon after they enter the labor market, and those who tend to be unemployable and therefore suffer very long periods of unemployment. If this is true, employability in the Malaysian labor market will have two dimensions: groups which have a greater probability of employment also tend to have a relatively short period of waiting before getting a job.

## Variations in the Employment Rate

The data in Table 17-1 generally indicated an inverse association in the Malaysian labor market between the rate of employment and the period of job search. The latter is an aspect of employability, but is not a causal variable explaining the employment rate. For the unemployed, the time unemployed is the total length of time a job seeker

Table 17-1. Employed School Leavers: Employment Rates and Length of Time Spent Looking for Work; and Length of Unemployment of School Leavers Who Have Never Worked

| | Race | Total in each group | Percentage employed | Length of unemployment (months) 1st quartile | Median | 3rd quartile | Time spent looking for jobs (months) 1st quartile | Median | 3rd quartile |
|---|---|---|---|---|---|---|---|---|---|
| **LCE** | | | | | | | | | |
| 1968 | Malay | 325 | 35.4 | 36.5 | 37+ | 37+ | 10.0 | 18.2 | 34.1 |
| | Chinese | 64 | 67.2 | 15.5 | 36.5 | 37+ | 3.6 | 6.8 | 13.4 |
| | Indian | 83 | 41.0 | 37+ | 37+ | 37+ | 7.4 | 11.6 | 21.2 |
| 1969 | Malay | 410 | 28.8 | 31.1 | 37+ | 37+ | 5.8 | 11.7 | 25.6 |
| | Chinese | 106 | 67.0 | 17.0 | 37+ | 37+ | 2.7 | 5.2 | 10.0 |
| | Indian | 92 | 42.4 | 21.0 | 37+ | 37+ | 4.7 | 11.0 | 21.9 |
| **MCE/MCVE** | | | | | | | | | |
| 1970 | Malay | 873 | 42.4 | 23.4 | 30.9 | 34.1 | 6.1 | 11.9 | 20.2 |
| | Chinese | 443 | 60.9 | 15.0 | 25.6 | 32.1 | 3.4 | 6.2 | 11.6 |
| | Indian | 106 | 40.6 | 12.5 | 21.1 | 31.5 | 5.1 | 9.5 | 18.5 |
| 1971 | Malay | 1,097 | 34.0 | 15.7 | 20.1 | 23.1 | 4.5 | 9.3 | 12.6 |
| | Chinese | 521 | 51.2 | 13.5 | 18.3 | 22.2 | 3.3 | 6.2 | 10.9 |
| | Indian | 138 | 36.2 | 12.9 | 18.6 | 22.5 | 5.0 | 9.5 | 15.8 |
| 1972 | Malay | 517 | 18.4 | 7.0 | 8.4 | 10.5 | 2.4 | 4.3 | 6.3 |
| | Chinese | 232 | 28.9 | 6.6 | 8.0 | 9.4 | 2.4 | 4.1 | 5.8 |
| | Indian | 82 | 15.9 | 5.4 | 7.5 | 9.1 | 4.9 | 6.3 | 14.0 |

*Note:* Those classified as unemployed are limited to school leavers who had not yet held a first job; the table excludes those who had found work initially but had become unemployed again by the time of the survey.
*Source:* SLS, 1973.

has been in the labor market at the time of the survey; for the employed, it represents only the time spent searching before getting a job—and does not take into account the time spent working in the current job. Since a person's employability will be affected by the time he has spent in getting his first job, it is necessary to control for this factor in examining the effects of other variables. A new variable, "time in job market," has therefore been included in the analysis which follows. For the unemployed, this variable is composed of the number of months of unemployment; for the employed, it is composed of the number of months of search before the first job, plus any period of unemployment between jobs, plus the number of months in employment (up to the time of the survey).[1]

The other variables included in the analysis are generally self-explanatory. Neither age nor year of leaving school was included, since both factors would undoubtedly be correlated with the amount of time spent in the labor market; of these three variables, the latter was considered the most useful for analytical purposes, since it excluded the period a job seeker might have spent outside the labor market after leaving school. Two of the variables combined different sets of information for the employed and unemployed: the earnings and occupation variables used *actual* values for the employed and *expected* values for the unemployed. The idea behind these hybrid variables is that the actual values for the employed represent a revision of the expectations still held by the unemployed at the time of the survey.

Experiments were made with some other variables which are not analyzed here. Gender did not seem to be important and was dropped. Two earnings variables were also tried: expected earnings after leaving school (for both the employed and the unemployed), and the ratio of actual (or minimum) earnings to expected earnings (as a measure of the revision of expectations). Neither worked.

The multiple classification analysis (MCA) presents the results in a particularly readable way when a large number of categoric variables is being used. The first column of the results presented in Table 17-2 for the entire sample gives the proportion of cases for each of the subgroups of the ten explanatory variables used. The gross effect gives the actual deviation of the employment rate for the particular class of a predictor from the mean employment rate for the sample. The value for

---

1. For the sake of simplicity, only those who had held one or two jobs (most of the employed population) were considered.

Table 17-2.  Multiple Classification Analysis of Employment Rates
on Ten Sets of Explanatory Variables

| Variable | Percentage distribution | Gross effect[a] | Net effect[b] |
|---|---|---|---|
| Father's income (Malaysian dollars per month) | | | |
| Nothing | 5.7 | 0.11 | 0.04 |
| 1–79 | 14.2 | −0.13 | −0.03 |
| 80–129 | 19.5 | −0.07 | −0.03 |
| 130–179 | 12.5 | −0.01 | −0.005 |
| 180–279 | 18.4 | 0.03 | 0.006 |
| 280–349 | 6.3 | 0.08 | 0.04 |
| 350 and over | 10.9 | 0.05 | 0.02 |
| Missing | 12.5 | 0.09 | −0.03 |
| | | $(\epsilon^2=0.026)$ | $(\beta^2=0.003)$ |
| Town of residence | | | |
| Missing | 0.6 | 0.03 | 0.06 |
| 75,000 and over | 4.7 | 0.09 | 0.04 |
| Kuala Lumpur | 18.4 | 0.17 | 0.08 |
| Georgetown | 8.2 | 0.09 | −0.04 |
| Ipoh | 4.3 | 0.01 | −0.03 |
| Johore Bahru | 4.7 | 0.21 | 0.06 |
| 10,000–75,000 | 37.8 | −0.09 | −0.03 |
| Less than 10,000 | 21.3 | −0.09 | −0.03 |
| | | $(\epsilon^2=0.058)$ | $(\beta^2=0.009)$ |
| Mobility index | | | |
| Missing | 1.2 | −0.06 | −0.07 |
| Not moved | 69.1 | −0.04 | −0.02 |
| Moved | 29.7 | 0.09 | 0.04 |
| | | $(\epsilon^2=0.016)$ | $(\beta^2=0.003)$ |
| Curriculum | | | |
| Other | 0.1 | 0.61 | 0.39 |
| Academic | 72.1 | −0.02 | −0.01 |
| Technical | 7.0 | 0.10 | 0.09 |
| Vocational | 20.8 | $(\epsilon^2=0.008)$ | $(\beta^2=0.003)$ |
| Certificate | | | |
| Missing | 0.2 | 0.08 | 0.008 |
| LCE | 25.2 | −0.02 | −0.09 |
| MCE/MCVE | 70.5 | 0.006 | 0.02 |
| HSC | 4.1 | $(\epsilon^2=0.0005)$ | $(\beta^2=0.02)$ |
| Occupation | | | |
| Missing, other | 12.7 | 0.10 | 0.17 |
| Professional, administrative, and clerical | 52.7 | −0.13 | −0.06 |

Table 17-2 (continued)

| Variable | Percentage distribution | Gross effect[a] | Net effect[b] |
|---|---|---|---|
| Occupation (continued) | | | |
| Sales, services | 6.8 | 0.30 | 0.09 |
| Production workers | 26.3 | 0.13 | 0.02 |
| Agriculture | 1.5 | −0.008 | 0.03 |
| | | $(\epsilon^2=0.09)$ | $(\beta^2=0.03)$ |
| Race and language of instruction | | | |
| Other | 11.7 | −0.02 | −0.03 |
| Malay and Malay | 45.9 | −0.09 | −0.03 |
| Malay and English | 17.3 | 0.07 | 0.06 |
| Chinese and English | 25.1 | 0.13 | 0.03 |
| | | $(\epsilon^2=0.038)$ | $(\beta^2=0.006)$ |
| Actual or expected earnings (Malaysian dollars per month) | | | |
| Nothing | 12.3 | −0.22 | −0.27 |
| 1–99 | 15.5 | 0.57 | 0.47 |
| 100–149 | 18.0 | 0.23 | 0.19 |
| 150–199 | 27.1 | −0.19 | −0.14 |
| 200–299 | 21.3 | −0.17 | −0.12 |
| 300 and over | 5.6 | −0.27 | −0.20 |
| Missing | 0.2 | 0.07 | −0.29 |
| | | $(\epsilon^2=0.361)$ | $(\beta^2=0.255)$ |
| Time in job market (months) | | | |
| 0 | 2.2 | −0.39 | −0.29 |
| 1–3 | 2.7 | −0.15 | −0.24 |
| 4–6 | 7.2 | −0.09 | −0.14 |
| 7–9 | 11.6 | −0.10 | −0.08 |
| 10–12 | 8.4 | −0.08 | −0.09 |
| 13–18 | 11.0 | 0.07 | 0.01 |
| 19–24 | 17.8 | −0.03 | 0.01 |
| 25–36 | 18.3 | 0.03 | 0.04 |
| 37 and over | 16.5 | 0.03 | 0.06 |
| Missing | 4.2 | 0.61 | 0.44 |
| | | $(\epsilon^2=0.097)$ | $(\beta^2=0.065)$ |
| Job history | | | |
| Yes | 23.9 | 0.23 | 0.12 |
| No | 76.1 | −0.08 | −0.04 |
| | | $(\epsilon^2=0.073)$ | $(\beta^2=0.019)$ |

Note: $R^2 = 0.498$; number of sample 6,307; mean rate of employment 38.91 percent; standard deviation 48.76.

a. Gross effect is the deviation in the percentage employment rate of a particular category from the overall mean percentage employment rate of 38.91.

b. Net effect is the deviation in the percentage employment rate of a particular category from the overall mean after adjusting for effects of other predictors.

Source: Data derived from SLS, 1973.

$\epsilon^2$ measures the variance in the dependent variable explained (in this case, the employment rate), taking each predictor by itself. The net effect gives the deviation from the overall mean after allowing for the other predictors included in the program, and $\beta^2$ is the variance explained by the particular predictor, after the effects of the other predictors are taken into account.[2]

The analysis is on the basis of ten predictors, but the earnings variable is by far the most important. The net variance explained by this variable is as much as 25.5 percent (compared with an overall $R^2$ of 0.498). The net deviations for the various classes of this predictor are also much more important than those of any other predictor. The deviations are of the expected orders of magnitude; the employment rate increases more for lower earnings classes and decreases more for higher classes. That many school leavers have very high expectations about their earnings levels must be one explanation of the high rate of unemployment. It is consistent with the evidence presented in Chapter 16 on the high incremental earnings from secondary school education in the Malaysian economy, and the wide diversity of earnings among school leavers, which leads many of them to hope for high earnings even though by no means all in fact do well.

Some doubts may nevertheless remain about the degree of importance of the earnings factor: Is it really as significant as the multivariate analysis suggests? It should be remembered that the earnings variable used is a hybrid, including purely subjective and hypothetical data for the unemployed on expected earnings, which are unrelated to any concrete situation such as the rejection of a job offer at a particular level of earnings. The number who had rejected job offers in the sample as a whole is too small to permit the use of this kind of more "real" earnings variable.

Table 17-3 therefore presents the MCA but omits the explanatory variable of actual or expected earnings. This exercise reduces the overall $R^2$ from 0.498 to 0.293. As might be expected, however, the explanatory power and the net deviations for most of the remaining predictors are increased.

Two factors which are basically control variables have a strong and predictable influence on the employment rate. These are *job history* and *time in the job market*. Predictably, those with previous job experience

---

2. The net effect thus corresponds to the regression coefficients of a multiple regression model, and $\beta^2$ to the partial correlation coefficient.

Table 17-3. Multiple Classification Analysis of Employment Rates
on Nine Sets of Explanatory Variables

| Variable | Percentage distribution | Gross effect[a] | Net effect[b] |
|---|---|---|---|
| Father's income | | | |
| (Malaysian dollars per month) | | | |
| Nothing | 5.7 | 0.11 | 0.04 |
| 1–79 | 14.2 | −0.13 | −0.03 |
| 80–129 | 19.5 | −0.07 | −0.04 |
| 130–179 | 12.5 | −0.009 | 0.003 |
| 180–279 | 18.4 | 0.03 | 0.01 |
| 280–349 | 6.3 | 0.08 | 0.04 |
| 350 and over | 10.9 | 0.05 | 0.003 |
| Missing | 12.5 | 0.09 | 0.03 |
| | | $(\epsilon^2=0.026)$ | $(\beta^2=0.003)$ |
| Town of residence | | | |
| Missing | 0.6 | 0.03 | 0.13 |
| 75,000 and over | 4.7 | 0.09 | 0.07 |
| Kuala Lumpur | 18.4 | 0.17 | 0.10 |
| Georgetown | 8.2 | 0.09 | 0.04 |
| Ipoh | 4.3 | 0.01 | −0.02 |
| Johore Bahru | 4.7 | 0.21 | 0.09 |
| 10,000–75,000 | 37.8 | −0.09 | −0.05 |
| Less than 10,000 | 21.3 | −0.09 | −0.05 |
| | | $(\epsilon^2=0.058)$ | $(\beta^2=0.017)$ |
| Mobility index | | | |
| Missing | 1.2 | −0.06 | −0.12 |
| Not moved | 69.1 | −0.04 | −0.02 |
| Moved | 29.7 | 0.10 | 0.05 |
| | | $(\epsilon^2=0.017)$ | $(\beta^2=0.005)$ |
| Curriculum | | | |
| Other | 0.1 | 0.61 | 0.42 |
| Academic | 72.1 | −0.02 | −0.002 |
| Technical | 7.0 | 0.10 | 0.03 |
| Vocational | 20.8 | 0.05 | −0.006 |
| | | $(\epsilon^2=0.008)$ | $(\beta^2=0.001)$ |
| Certificate | | | |
| Missing | 0.2 | 0.08 | −0.02 |
| LCE | 25.2 | −0.02 | −0.07 |
| MCE/MCVE | 70.5 | 0.005 | 0.02 |
| HSC | 4.1 | 0.008 | 0.12 |
| | | $(\epsilon^2=0.0005)$ | $(\beta^2=0.009)$ |

(Table continues on the following page.)

Table 17-3 (*continued*)

| Variable | Percentage distribution | Gross effect[a] | Net effect[b] |
|---|---|---|---|
| Occupation | | | |
| Missing, other | 12.7 | 0.10 | 0.09 |
| Professional, administrative, and clerical | 52.7 | −0.13 | −0.09 |
| Sales, services | 6.8 | 0.30 | 0.21 |
| Production workers | 26.3 | 0.13 | 0.09 |
| Agriculture | 1.5 | −0.008 | 0.05 |
| | | ($\epsilon^2$=0.085) | ($\beta^2$=0.046) |
| Race and language of instruction | | | |
| Other | 11.7 | −0.02 | −0.04 |
| Malay and Malay | 45.9 | −0.09 | −0.05 |
| Malay and English | 17.3 | 0.07 | 0.05 |
| Chinese and English | 25.1 | 0.13 | 0.07 |
| | | ($\epsilon^2$=0.038) | ($\beta^2$=0.012) |
| Time in job market (months) | | | |
| 0 | 2.2 | −0.39 | −0.43 |
| 1–3 | 2.7 | −0.15 | −0.34 |
| 4–6 | 7.2 | −0.09 | −0.22 |
| 7–9 | 11.6 | −0.10 | −0.10 |
| 10–12 | 8.4 | −0.08 | −0.13 |
| 13–18 | 11.0 | 0.07 | 0.03 |
| 19–24 | 17.8 | −0.03 | 0.02 |
| 25–36 | 18.3 | 0.03 | 0.07 |
| 37 and over | 16.5 | 0.03 | 0.10 |
| Missing | 4.2 | 0.61 | 0.54 |
| | | ($\epsilon^2$=0.098) | ($\beta^2$=0.119) |
| Job history | | | |
| Yes | 23.9 | 0.23 | 0.21 |
| No | 76.1 | −0.07 | −0.07 |
| | | ($\epsilon^2$=0.073) | ($\beta^2$=0.057) |

Note: $R^2$ = 0.293; number of sample 6,307; mean rate of employment 38.91 percent; standard deviation 48.76.

a. Gross effect is the deviation in the percentage employment rate of a particular category from the overall mean percentage employment rate of 38.91.

b. Net effect is the deviation in the percentage employment rate of a particular category from the overall mean after adjusting for effects of other predictors.

Source: Data derived from SLS, 1973.

had an employment rate more than 50 percent higher than the mean rate. Time in the job market explained 12 percent of the variation (in relation to the total explained of about 30 percent). The net deviations, after allowance is made for the effect of other variables, are generally larger than the gross deviations, and the ordering of the former over the range of class intervals of the predictor is more consistent. The mean rate of employment for the sample (39 percent) is attained only after a school leaver has been in the market for more than a year, and even for the sizable group (16.5 percent of the sample) whose participation in the labor market has been more than three years, the employment rate is just about 50 percent. Even if we discount somewhat for the bias in response rates which affects this group in particular, this finding is of serious significance for the Malaysian economy.

The fact that a fair proportion of the employed had had quite a short period of job search can be reconciled with the very small employment rate for those in the labor market less than three to six months. It merely means that those who were employed after a brief job search are not necessarily the recent entrants to the market, but have spent a sizable amount of time in their present job.

The other predictors can be arranged in order of the importance of both their contribution to the variance explained and the net deviation of employment rates within individual classes of the particular predictor.

*Occupation* is the strongest predictor after job history and time in the job market. The employment rate of those leaning to white-collar occupations is only three-quarters of the mean rate. All other occupational categories have equally striking positive net deviations. In particular, there is a very high net employment rate for those in sales and services, although only a small proportion of the sample is found in this class.

The analysis thus suggests that there is some truth in the presumption that the employment problem of school leavers is partly caused by their bias in favor of white-collar jobs. More significantly, their relative lack of interest in the typical informal sector job in sales and services helps explain their low employment rate.

*Town of residence* is an important explanatory variable and has a bearing on the confused state of theorizing in the literature. The employment rates in smaller towns (those in both the 10,000–75,000 and less than 10,000 population groups) are significantly below the mean rate, while the rates in the metropolitan areas of Kuala Lumpur, Johore Bahru, and Georgetown are substantially above the mean (even though the net effects are significantly lower than the gross deviations). This finding negates the suggestion sometimes made in the literature that unemployment—particularly of the more educated—is partly caused by urban drift to the larger cities. The point is verified by the fact that those who had migrated from their place of origin had higher employment rates.

Although the ordering of the four groups by employment probabilities is as expected, the degree of importance of *race and language of instruction* and the magnitudes of the net deviations are lower than is popularly believed. The gross deviation in employment rates (of opposite signs) for the Malays who were taught in Malay and the Chinese who were taught in English are cut by nearly half when other variables are taken into account. The Chinese who were taught in English do only a little better than the Malays who were taught in English.

The *certificate received* is a rather unusual predictor in that its explanatory power is greater when other variables are taken into account than when it stands by itself ($\beta^2$ is greater than $\epsilon^2$). Correspondingly, the net deviations of the individual classes of the predictor are much greater than the gross deviations. The substantially lower employment rate of LCE certificate holders and the substantially higher employment rate for HSC graduates are especially noteworthy.

According to the *mobility index,* those who had moved from their place of birth had an employment rate 7 percentage points (or about a fifth) higher than those who did nòt move. Unemployment apparently affects those school leavers who are unable to leave small towns much more severely than it does those who have moved out to the larger urban areas.

The gross deviations from the mean were quite substantial for school leavers of different streams or type of *curriculum.* In fact, since differentiation by streams affects only the MCE/MCVE sample (those with upper secondary qualifications), the variations in employment rates between the streams might have been reduced by including all school leavers in the sample. In the MCE group, however, the net deviations turned out to be small except in the case of the technical stream, which had roughly a 10 percent higher employment rate. The percentage of variation explained by this predictor was also very small.

The effect of *father's income* was in the expected direction. School leavers whose fathers' incomes were less than M$130 had relatively low employment rates. Here again, however, the net effects turned out to be very much smaller than the gross effects, indicating that low parental income was associated with other characteristics which had a more pronounced effect on the explanation of variations in employment rates.

## Multiple Step-wise Regression by Schooling Level

The MCA program is a helpful tool for presenting an overall picture of the determinants of the employment rate. A serious disadvantage, however, is that it is not easy to interpret the significance of the coefficients of the explanatory variables, and the order of importance of the different variables used is not given (as it is in a step-wise multiple regression model). Moreover, the inclusion of the level of schooling as one of the independent variables in a regression for all members of the sample implies that the coefficients obtained on the other explanatory variables are the same for all levels of schooling, because the coefficients of the schooling variables merely shift the fitted function and do not allow for changes in its slope. There is no a priori reason why the employment probability for the different schooling levels should, in fact, be subject to this uniformity of effect as far as the other explanatory variables are concerned.

It was therefore decided to run regressions separately on the LCE, MCE, and MCVE school leavers, restricting the analysis to males only and excluding the unemployed who had already held a job. Because the numbers left out were very small, the sample size was not seriously reduced. The results of the analysis are presented in Tables 17-4, 17-5, and 17-6 for the LCE, MCE, and MCVE samples, respectively. The overall picture of the factors increasing employability which the three regressions present is generally unchanged from the analysis in the previous section. Some important differences between the three subsamples do, however, emerge in the order of importance and the strength of the explanatory variables for each subgroup. The variables entering in the first three steps in the regression model for the three streams (in order of importance for each) are:

LCE: Time in the labor market (in excess of three years) and white-collar occupational preference

MCE: White-collar occupational preference, location in Kuala Lumpur, and the ratio of actual to expected earnings

MCVE: Malay with Malay language of instruction and the ratio of actual to expected earnings.

The difference in the values of the coefficients suggest the following main conclusions from the regressions:

1. Among the variables for *race and language of instruction,* Malays instructed in both Malay and English have lower employment rates than the Chinese taught in English, but this effect is strongest for those with the LCE, followed by those from the MCVE stream, and is least marked for the MCE group. In fact, for the MCE stream, Malays with English as their language of instruction are not at a significant disadvantage as they are in the other two streams.

Table 17-4.  Multiple Regression on Probability of Employment:
LCE Males
(dependent variable = 1 if employed, 0 otherwise)

| Explanatory variable | β | t-ratio | Step number | Percentage of sample |
|---|---|---|---|---|
| Race and language of instruction (base: Chinese and English) | | | | |
| Malay and Malay | −0.318 | −6.90 | 5 | 51 |
| Malay and English | −0.219 | −4.29 | 12 | 21 |
| Other | −0.241 | −4.54 | 13 | 17 |
| Residence (base: towns of 10,000–75,000) | | | | |
| Towns of 75,000 and over | 0.163 | 1.97 | 14 | 3 |
| Kuala Lumpur | 0.217 | 5.37 | 4 | 17 |
| Ipoh | 0.157 | 2.24 | 15 | 4 |
| Johore Bahru | 0.144 | 1.88 | 16 | 3 |
| Actual/expected earnings | −0.00067 | −4.19 | 6 | 147.07 |
| Actual/preferred occupation (base: blue collar) | | | | |
| White collar, professional | −0.143 | −4.17 | 3 | 29 |
| Sales, services | 0.165 | 3.09 | 9 | 8 |
| Time in labor market (months; base: 0–3 months) | | | | |
| 4–6 | 0.066 | 0.894 | — | 6 |
| 7–12 | 0.083 | 1.39 | 11 | 13 |
| 13–18 | 0.382 | 5.10 | 7 | 6 |
| 19–24 | 0.211 | 3.45 | 10 | 12 |
| 25–36 | 0.252 | 4.42 | 8 | 16 |
| 37–60 | 0.394 | 7.53 | 2 | 31 |
| 61 or more | 0.641 | 9.60 | 1 | 8 |
| Constant | 0.345 | 4.81 | — | — |

— Not applicable.
Note: $R^2 = 0.323$; $F = 16.92$; and $N = 1,081$ (except for actual/expected earnings where $N = 846$).
Source: Data derived from SLS, 1973.

2. The earnings effect is more or less of the same magnitude for the
LCE and MCE samples, but seems to be twice as strong for the vocational
graduates. It is reasonable to hypothesize that the bulk of the MCVE
graduates have relatively realistic earnings expectations and that those
who are out of line suffer heavily.

Table 17-5.  Multiple Regression on Probability of Employment:
MCE Males
(dependent variable = 1 if employed, 0 otherwise)

| Explanatory variable | β | t-ratio | Step number | Percentage of sample |
|---|---|---|---|---|
| Race and language of instruction (base: Chinese and English) | | | | |
| Malay and Malay | −0.158 | −5.15 | 5 | 46 |
| Other | −0.141 | −3.85 | 10 | 13 |
| Residence (base: towns of 10,000–75,000) | | | | |
| Kuala Lumpur | 0.206 | 6.62 | 2 | 17 |
| Ipoh | 0.099 | 1.94 | 12 | 5 |
| Actual/expected earnings | −0.0006 | −6.68 | 3 | 202.43 |
| Actual/preferred occupation (base: blue collar) | | | | |
| White collar, professional | −0.142 | −5.45 | 1 | 59 |
| Unknown, missing | 0.214 | 4.89 | 9 | 8 |
| Father's income (base: M$1–M$100) | | | | |
| 201–350 | 0.071 | 2.12 | 14 | 18 |
| 351 and over | 0.088 | 2.35 | 13 | 13 |
| Time in labor market (months; base: 0–3 months) | | | | |
| 4–6 | 0.015 | 0.30 | — | 9 |
| 7–12 | 0.064 | 1.47 | 15 | 19 |
| 13–18 | 0.139 | 2.95 | 11 | 12 |
| 19–24 | 0.210 | 4.75 | 8 | 19 |
| 25–36 | 0.323 | 7.34 | 6 | 20 |
| 37–60 | 0.431 | 8.51 | 4 | 10 |
| 61 and over | 0.618 | 6.41 | 7 | 1 |
| Constant | 0.328 | 5.72 | — | — |

— Not applicable.
Note: $R^2 = 0.298$; $F = 27.09$; and $N = 1,674$ (except for actual/expected earnings where $N = 1,475$).
Source: Data derived from SLS, 1973.

3.  White-collar occupational preference seriously reduces employ-ment rates for the LCE and the MCE streams, but this negative effect is only half as strong for those with vocational education certificates.

4.  Father's income is a significant variable only for those with an MCE, for whom it has the expected positive effect on employment prob-

Table 17-6.  Multiple Regression on Probability of Employment:
MCVE Males
(dependent variable = 1 if employed, 0 otherwise)

| Explanatory variable | β | t-ratio | Step number | Percentage of sample |
|---|---|---|---|---|
| Race and language of instruction (base: Chinese and English) | | | | |
| Malay and Malay | −0.267 | −5.76 | 1 | 46 |
| Malay and English | −0.129 | −2.59 | 12 | 24 |
| Other | −0.268 | −3.79 | 10 | 8 |
| Residence (base: towns of 10,000–75,000) | | | | |
| Towns of 75,000 and over | 0.216 | 2.04 | 14 | 3 |
| Kuala Lumpur | 0.231 | 4.36 | 4 | 14 |
| Johore Bahru | 0.271 | 4.07 | 5 | 8 |
| Actual/expected earnings | −0.0012 | −4.51 | 2 | 174.34 |
| Actual/preferred occupation (base: blue collar) | | | | |
| White collar, professional | −0.072 | −1.94 | 15 | 40 |
| Sales, services | 0.279 | 3.40 | 6 | 5 |
| Time in labor market (months; base: 0–3 months) | | | | |
| 4–6 | 0.076 | 0.72 | — | 5 |
| 7–12 | 0.046 | 0.59 | 3 | 20 |
| 13–18 | 0.166 | 1.99 | 16 | 13 |
| 19–24 | 0.273 | 3.61 | 9 | 28 |
| 25–36 | 0.335 | 4.31 | 8 | 22 |
| 37–60 | 0.459 | 4.73 | 7 | 6 |
| 61 and over | 0.822 | 3.10 | 11 | 0 |
| Constant | 0.458 | 4.74 | — | — |

— Not applicable.
Note: $R^2 = 0.33$; $F = 12.28$; and $N = 691$ (except for actual/expected
earnings where $N = 588$).
Source: Data derived from SLS, 1973.

ability. Even for this group, however, the coefficients are quite small
compared with the effects of some of the other variables in the model.

5. The definition of the last variable, time spent in the labor market,
and its relevance for the analysis, has already been discussed. The variable can reasonably be expected to be positively related to the probability of employment. The main point of interest is to establish the way

in which this probability changes as the time spent in the labor market increases, and whether the pattern of the variable's effect on employability is the same for the three educational groups.

To allow for the greatest possible degree of freedom in this pattern, time spent in the labor market was broken down into eight separate values which were included as dummy variables in the regression. The figures show that employment probability does indeed vary widely according to these different values for time in the labor market, and that the patterns for the three educational groups are by no means parallel. For ease of comparison, Figure 17-1 graphs the probability of employment against the time spent in the labor market for the three groups separately, after standardizing for all the other variables in the regressions. The graph shows that those with an LCE start out with the lowest probability of employment (0.02), whereas those with the MCE and

Figure 17–1. Probability of Employment as a Function of
Time Spent in the Labor Market for Males Only

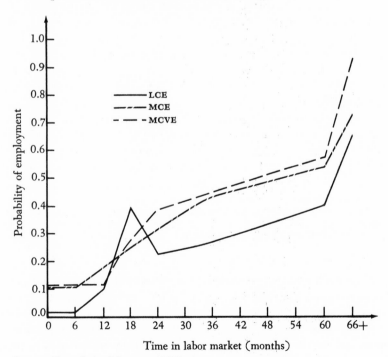

Time in labor market (months)

*Source:* Data derived from SLS, 1973.

MCVE have a higher initial probability of employment of 0.1. While the figure for the MCVE group remains more or less the same for values of up to twelve months in the labor market, both the LCE and the MCE groups experience an increase in their probability of employment after six months. The vocationally trained school leavers experience a substantial and sustained increase in their probability of employment after a year in the labor market, however, which gives them a higher probability value than both the MCE and the LCE groups before the twenty-four-month point—a lead that they maintain to the end of the set of observations. The other major point which emerges from the graph is that the profile for the LCE group lies substantially below those of the MCE and MCVE groups over nearly all the values for time in the labor market. The implications of this finding are discussed in the next section.

The explanatory power of the equations is roughly the same (about 0.31) for all the educational groups, but a brief comment is needed on the general validity of the method. The use of ordinary least squares (OLS) estimation for equations which have a binary dependent variable (one that takes a zero–one value) is subject to certain disadvantages. In particular, the estimates tend to be inefficient, and there is the possibility of predicting values outside the zero–one range. It has been shown, however, that the OLS estimates do not tend to cluster around either zero or one, and after a careful study of the costs and benefits associated with the use of alternative estimation procedures (such as the maximum likelihood estimation method) it was decided that the disadvantages of using OLS were outweighed by savings in both computer and project time, since the inefficiency in the estimates was, in any case, slight. Thus, although the estimates given in this section cannot be taken as expressing the exact values of the effects, they represent adequate estimates of the likely magnitudes.

## Age of Starting Work and the Waiting Period

Figure 17-1 showed that even after controlling for the major significant variables affecting employability, substantially different periods of time in the labor market were required for the three different schooling streams to attain a given rate of employment. For rates of employment in excess of 30 percent, a school leaver from the MCE stream would typically have to have been in the labor market for three to six months longer than one from the MCVE stream, but an LCE certificate holder would have had to have been in the market for a much more substantial period—something of the order of two and a half years longer (with the exception of the LCE school leavers forming the early peak at thirteen to eighteen months, who constituted just 6 percent of the LCE subgroup). Since the MCE and MCVE samples take their upper secondary school examination at roughly the same age, the difference in the amount of time the two groups spent in the labor market for an equivalent level of employment reflects a genuine employment advantage for the vocational stream. The LCE certificate holders, however, will have left school two years earlier than the upper secondary school leavers, and other things being equal, they will have been in the market two years longer. It is of some significance that this period is almost the same length as the extra time which LCE graduates need to spend in the labor market to attain the same rate of employment as the other two groups. It appears that the extra time available to this group as a result of leaving school earlier was simply used in waiting that much longer for a job. This rather surprising finding suggests a hypothesis about the way in which the labor market might work in Malaysia. There appears to be something like a minimum age at which school leavers can be accepted for employment in most sectors of the Malaysian economy. If such a minimum age exists, it must be set by conventions and unknown social factors, since no institutional reasons for it exist.[3] With such an age bias on the part of employers, leaving school at an earlier age will not be reflected in a higher probability of employment, but will only add to the time spent looking for work.

This hypothesis suggests that involuntary unemployment exists among school leavers. But two questions remain to be answered. First, how can the hypothesis be reconciled with the result of the multivariate analysis of the last section, which stressed the importance of the relatively high earnings expectation in reducing employability? Second, if the age bias on the part of employers affects employment in the formal sector, what prevents school leavers from getting absorbed in the self-employed sector or in small-scale wage employment?

As already mentioned, it is difficult to interpret accurately the significance of the expected earnings of the school leavers without any data on actual job offers which they have rejected. The direction of the cause and effect relationship is unclear. School leavers who have little hope of

---

3. Several employers alluded in personal interviews to their desire to hire only those new entrants to the labor market who had reached a certain age.

landing a job before a certain age will tend to report relatively high expected earnings; in other words, the sensitivity of job opportunity to the level of expected earnings would tend to be low. In Figure 17-1 the relationship between the probability of employment and time in the labor market was roughly parallel for the lower and upper secondary school streams over much of the field of observation—signifying a longer waiting period for the LCE holders about equal in length to their earlier departure from school. This result represented the net effect after allowance for the influence of the hybrid variable for actual-expected earnings on the mean values of each stream. It is possible to check whether the result would be different if the mean values of the actual (rather than actual-expected) earnings of each stream had been used. The effect would be to increase the constants of the employment probability function for each stream; the interesting question is whether they increase by different amounts. The relevant calculations are:

| | Mean of actual-expected earnings | Mean of actual earnings | Coefficient of earnings regression model | Increase in employment probability |
|---|---|---|---|---|
| LCE | 147.1 | 106.5 | −0.00067 | 0.027 |
| MCE | 202.4 | 134.5 | −0.0006 | 0.041 |
| MCVE | 174.3 | 128.5 | −0.0012 | 0.055 |

These figures suggest that in the regression model, with more realistic earnings expectations on the part of the school leavers, the employment probability graphs in Figure 17-1 would be shifted upward *more* for the MCE/MCVE streams than for the LCE group. Thus, for a given employment rate, the differences in the time spent in the labor market for the three streams would be greater than those in Figure 17-1. Holders of the LCE would have to wait rather more than two years longer than the MCE graduates. Thus, the difference in the waiting period between the LCE and the MCE/MCVE streams is *not* due to the former's relatively more unrealistic expectations about earnings.

With regard to the second question raised above, it has already been noted that very few of the employed school leavers in the sample were in the sales and service sector, or for that matter in family businesses, although a large proportion of them did accept employment in blue-collar production work. The evidence strongly suggests that while production is probably an acceptable second choice after white-collar employment in the school leavers' scheme of preferences, there is a great deal of reluctance to accept work in the private sales or service sector. In Malaysia a large part of the "free entry" informal sector is in fact accounted for by sales and services—small-scale production work has thus far been of less importance than in many other economies. By and large, school leavers operate in the formal sector, in which there is probably a certain amount of resistance to employing new workers below a certain age.

### Evidence from the Migration and Employment Survey

Further evidence is available from the Migration and Employment Survey (MES), which covered the entire adult male population of Kuala Lumpur and the East Coast towns and, unlike the SLS, included people of all ages and educational levels. The respondents were asked questions about the age at which they started looking for work, the age at which they left school, and the number of months it took them to get their first job after leaving school. The data on age of starting to look for work are of direct relevance to the hypothesis of a minimum employment age.

For the MES sample of the population as a whole, the school-leaving age is much higher than in most economies, whether advanced or less developed. The age at which respondents start to look for work will, of course, be directly influenced by the age at which they leave school. The differences between the two is the idle period during which the respondent was primarily unemployed (henceforth called IDLPD). Data from the MES show a relatively long IDLPD for much of the sample in spite of an exaggeratedly late school-leaving age given by many of the respondents. The reported time taken to get a first job, however, was quite short for the bulk of the sample. In other words, the MES respondents showed considerable evidence of passive unemployment, and only few signs of active unemployment before breaking into the labor market.

This phenomenon is not inconsistent with the evidence of active unemployment obtained from the SLS; it simply reflects the different character of the two samples and the contrasting methods used to obtain information from respondents. In the SLS school leavers from recent cohorts were specifically approached, and because the questionnaires were mailed by the Ministry of Labor they were encouraged to interpret their state of joblessness as active unemployment. Respondents to a household survey such as the MES, lacking such specific encouragement, would be more inclined to describe their unemployment in passive terms. In any event, the discussion which follows will present evidence of passive unemployment in the MES data which lends considerable support to the hypothesis of a relatively high minimum age of initial employment in the Malaysian labor market.

## School-Leaving Age

Table 17-7 sets out the percentage distribution of MES respondents who left school at various ages in the two regions, and also gives summary statistics. It is apparent that there is no strong modal school-leaving age in either region; respondents are spread all the way from age twelve to eighteen. The mean and median leaving ages are higher in Kuala Lumpur than in the East Coast—by about two years and one year, respectively—but this is almost entirely because of the substantially larger percentage of people with no schooling in the East Coast. Without this group, the mean age of leaving school would be 16.3 years in Kuala Lumpur and 15.8 in the East Coast—with a higher standard deviation in Kuala Lumpur (4.3 against 3.4 years).

Table 17-7. Percentage Distribution of Sample by School-Leaving Age

| Age | Kuala Lumpur | East Coast |
|---|---|---|
| 0 | 2.2 | 11.2 |
| 7–9 | 0.7 | 1.3 |
| 10–11 | 4.4 | 4.4 |
| 12 | 8.7 | 11.5 |
| 13 | 10.2 | 7.1 |
| 14 | 8.1 | 8.2 |
| 15 | 10.6 | 12.5 |
| 16 | 9.9 | 9.4 |
| 17 | 9.6 | 7.9 |
| 18 | 13.7 | 10.4 |
| 19 | 7.5 | 4.2 |
| 20 and over | 13.9 | 11.8 |
| Mean age | 15.899 | 13.988 |
| Median age | 15.973 | 15.005 |
| Standard deviation | 4.876 | 5.892 |

Source: MES, 1975.

Only a small proportion of the respondents in both regions said they had had work experience while still at school, although a substantial proportion came from rural or semirural areas. The percentages, broken down by place of employment, are:

| | Kuala Lumpur | East Coast |
|---|---|---|
| Family business | 12.8 | 8.7 |
| Family smallholding | 14.4 | 13.8 |
| Someone else's business | 6.6 | 3.5 |

Contrary to expectations, more of the respondents in Kuala Lumpur indicated that they had worked while still at school. This reflects the greater size of the Chinese population in this region, many of whose members come from families with small businesses. Nevertheless, the answers about the number of days worked and the earnings indicate that participation in economic activity while still at school was minimal.

### Age at Which Respondents Started Looking for Work

In spite of the fact that East Coast respondents reported a mean school-leaving age about two years younger than the mean reported for Kuala Lumpur, the difference in the age at which the two respondent groups started looking for work is only about six months. The summary statistics are:

|  | Kuala Lumpur | East Coast |
|---|---|---|
| Mean | 17.950 | 17.474 |
| Median | 17.843 | 17.333 |
| Standard deviation | 4.111 | 4.311 |

The fact that a substantially larger proportion of respondents in the East Coast had no schooling did not significantly reduce the mean age at which this group started looking for work. This point is confirmed by Table 17-8, which gives the percentage distribution of the sample by the ages at which respondents started looking. The modal age of start-

Table 17-8. Percentage Distribution of the Sample
by the Age of Starting to Look for Work

| Age | Kuala Lumpur | East Coast |
|---|---|---|
| 9–11 | 1.3 | 1.3 |
| 12 | 2.6 | 4.0 |
| 13 | 5.0 | 4.7 |
| 14 | 5.6 | 7.3 |
| 15 | 9.1 | 12.4 |
| 16 | 9.6 | 11.5 |
| 17 | 11.1 | 10.4 |
| 18 | _16.1_ | _16.5_ |
| 19 | 12.8 | 7.8 |
| 20 | 9.0 | 10.0 |
| 21 | 5.0 | 4.3 |
| 22 | 3.6 | 3.3 |
| 23 and over | 8.4 | 4.5 |

Source: MES, 1975.

ing to look for work is the same in the two regions—eighteen. In the East Coast 35 percent of respondents said they had started looking for work at the ages of seventeen to nineteen, against 40 percent in Kuala Lumpur.

The relatively late age of labor market entry in both regions—even in a population sample with different ages and schooling levels—is a peculiar and striking feature of the Malaysian labor market. In general, the age of labor market entry would be expected to be lower in a developing country than in an advanced economy, for at least three reasons: the lower level of schooling in developing countries; the greater need for children to contribute to the family income in economies with substantially lower standards of living; and the greater opportunities for obtaining gainful employment in the urban sectors of developing countries. This last reason is generally valid even if the availability of jobs in the modern sector is limited, because developing countries tend to have large informal urban sectors in which wages and earnings are flexible, and any legislation restricting the employment of young persons is not strictly applied.

All these factors would seem to exist in Malaysia. The typical age of finishing primary school is twelve, and although primary schooling is nearly universal in urban Malaysia today, the MES sample includes a large number of respondents from earlier generations who might well not have finished primary school. A sizable proportion of the younger generation in the current urban population would be likely to go on to secondary schools; however, even today only a small proportion could be expected to go beyond lower secondary schooling, which students typically finish at age fourteen or fifteen. Of course, many of them might not pass the school-leaving examinations at the appropriate age and might consequently be retaking their exams or continuing to study half-heartedly. The decision to continue this informal schooling is itself, however, a reflection of their inability or unwillingness to enter the labor market. In Table 17-8 as much as 21 percent of the sample in Kuala Lumpur and 16 percent in the East Coast said that they had left school at age nineteen or thereafter. It is reasonable to suppose that, for a fair proportion of this group, the continuation of schooling up to such a late age reflected a decision to postpone entry into the labor market.

### The Period of Idleness

Both the school-leaving age and the age of starting to look for work seems to have been surprisingly high in the two urban regions covered by the MES. There is, however, a gap between the mean age of leaving school and the mean age of starting to look for work in both regions. In other words, even though a large proportion of the sample identified the school-leaving age with the age of starting to look for work, a significant number also indicated a long period of idleness between leaving school and starting to look for work. Moreover, some late school leavers may not have reported the relevant ages correctly; if they had, the period of idleness might have been even higher.

Table 17-9. Percentage Distribution of Sample
by the Length of the Period of Idleness

| Years | Kuala Lumpur | East Coast |
|---|---|---|
| 0 | 48.1 | 50.6 |
| 1 | 15.6 | 12.4 |
| 2 | 10.0 | 10.1 |
| 3 | 7.4 | 5.9 |
| 4 | 4.3 | 6.1 |
| 5 | 4.9 | 4.6 |
| 6 | 3.7 | 2.2 |
| 7 | 1.9 | 3.4 |
| 8 | 1.0 | 1.5 |
| 9 | 1.2 | 1.0 |
| 10 | 1.1 | 0.8 |
| 11 and more | 0.9 | 1.4 |

Source: MES, 1975.

Table 17-9 gives the percentage distribution of the sample by the number of years of idleness after leaving school. About half the respondents in both regions indicated that there was no gap between their leaving school and entering the labor market. The period of idleness, however, is large in spite of the likely underestimation involved:

| | Kuala Lumpur | East Coast |
|---|---|---|
| Mean years of IDLPD | 1.672 | 1.916 |
| Standard deviation | 3.651 | 4.152 |

### Time Taken to Get Work

In sharp contrast to the reported sluggishness of their entry into the labor market, most respondents seemed to have taken only a short time to find jobs (see Table 17-10). It is somewhat surprising that the time

Table 17-10. Percentage Distribution of Sample
by Months Taken to Get First Job

| Months | Kuala Lumpur | East Coast |
|---|---|---|
| 0 | 44.5 | 71.2 |
| 1–5 | 10.2 | 8.7 |
| 6–11 | 9.4 | 2.1 |
| 12–17 | 13.9 | 3.5 |
| 18–23 | 2.2 | 0.3 |
| 24–35 | 5.4 | 4.3 |
| 36 and more | 6.4 | 5.3 |

Source: MES, 1975.

taken to get the first job was substantially lower in the East Coast than
in the metropolitan labor market of Kuala Lumpur. Possibly the relative
complexity of the latter market required job hunters to undertake a
more extended job search. In any event, the general finding that the
period of conscious search is normally short and the idle period before
looking for a job is normally long—and that the former is shorter in the
labor markets of the East Coast where the latter is longer—does suggest
a hypothesis about the nature of the responses to the question in the
survey. It may be that many respondents tended to identify job search
with the period spent *outside* the labor market. This would suggest
that searching for a job was a rather passive activity for most respondents.

### IDLPD and the Minimum Age of Employment

The survey findings as reported are perfectly compatible with the
hypothesis of a minimum age at which new entrants into the labor market are accepted for jobs in most sectors of the Malaysian economy. If
an age bias were generally recognized, many young school leavers
would feel there was not much point in searching for a job until a certain age had been reached, and this would explain the general persistence of idle periods after leaving school. If this hypothesis were true, a
specific relation would be expected between the age of starting to look
for work $(W)$ and the age of leaving school $(S)$.

This relation is best studied by examining the determinants of the
elapsed time between the two (IDLPD). If the hypothesis about the minimum age of employment is correct, there should be a significant
negative relation between IDLPD and the age of leaving school. The

strength of this relation—if it exists—and variations in it for the two urban labor markets covered by the MES are of interest, as is the effect on IDLPD of other variables such as race, the location of the respondent's last school, and father's education or occupation.

These variables, together with the square $(S^2)$ of the value for the school-leaving age $(S)$, were introduced step-wise into the regression model used to explain IDLPD so as to allow for nonlinearity. All respondents who gave their age of leaving school as zero were excluded to eliminate the exaggerated effect this cluster of observations would have had on the results. The equations are summarized in Table 17-11.

Table 17-11. Regression Equations Determining Elapsed Time between Leaving School and Looking for Work (IDLPD)

| Variable | Kuala Lumpur | | East Coast | |
|---|---|---|---|---|
| | $\beta$ | t-ratio | $\beta$ | t-ratio |
| Age left school $(S)$ | −0.081 | −2.56 | −1.594 | −5.53 |
| (Age left school)$^2$ $(S^2)$ | −0.008 | −17.62 | 0.034 | 4.07 |
| Race (base: Malay) | | | | |
| Chinese | −1.03 | −6.07 | ... | ... |
| Indian and other | −1.09 | −4.30 | ... | ... |
| Location of last school (base: rural) | | | | |
| Metropolitan area | −0.654 | −3.45 | ... | ... |
| Towns 75,000 and more | −1.008 | −3.09 | ... | ... |
| Towns 10,000–75,000 | −0.511 | −2.10 | ... | ... |
| Constant | 6.358 | 14.46 | 17.85 | 7.40 |
| $R^2$ | 0.58 | | 0.14 | |
| F | 220.16 | | 56.71 | |
| N | 1,105 | | 806 | |

... Not significant.
Source: Data derived from MES, 1975.

It is immediately apparent that the variance in the dependent variable explained by the regression is much higher for Kuala Lumpur. Several variables other than S and $S^2$ are significant for this region and not for the East Coast, but the difference in the performance of the regression model cannot be ascribed to this fact. $S^2$ alone, which came in at the first step of the model for Kuala Lumpur, explained 55 percentage points of the 58 percent of the total variance accounted for. One reason for the difference in performance is that the variance in the dependent variable to be explained, IDLPD, is about 30 percent higher in the East Coast.

As predicted by the hypothesis of the minimum employable age, there is a negative relation between IDLPD and S in both regions; the negative coefficient is much larger in the East Coast. Although the coefficient of $S^2$ is negative in Kuala Lumpur (suggesting an increasing rate of decline), the rate of decline of IDLPD with S slows down as S increases. A better idea of the relation between IDLPD and S can be obtained by looking at the predicted idle period for the two regions for different values of S. The respective values below take into account the other variables which are significant in Kuala Lumpur:

|  | IDLPD (years) | |
| --- | --- | --- |
| School-leaving age (S) | Kuala Lumpur | East Coast |
| 12 | 3.04 | 3.85 |
| 14 | 2.47 | 2.47 |
| 16 | 2.05 | 1.40 |
| 18 | 1.12 | 0.61 |
| 20 | 0.35 | 0.11 |

Additional schooling seems to reduce the idle period much more sharply in the East Coast than in Kuala Lumpur. Those who left school after age fourteen—the normal age for finishing lower secondary schooling—have lower absolute IDLPD values in the East Coast than in Kuala Lumpur; the rate of decline of IDLPD with additional schooling is also higher in the East Coast. Possibly in the long run the higher general quality of schooling in Kuala Lumpur induced school leavers to enter the labor market more slowly.

The predicted values of IDLPD do not suggest a rigid minimum age of employment in either region, but rather a gradual tendency for the IDLPD to decline as the age of twenty is approached. For most economies, this age of entry would be considerably lower.

## Conclusions

The evidence from the MES data lends support to the hypothesis that there tends to be a high minimum age of employment in Malaysia. This is not a rigid barrier to employment at younger ages, but the probability of getting a job is fairly low at these ages and gradually increases until the generally acceptable minimum age is reached. Lower and upper secondary school leavers, who typically leave school at ages substantially below this acceptable minimum, therefore tend to suffer long periods of active or passive unemployment. This conclusion is consistent with the pattern in Figure 17-1, which relates the employment probability of various groups of secondary school leavers to the amount of time they have spent in the labor market. Lower secondary school leavers who leave school two years earlier than the upper secondary graduates wait that much longer to attain the same rate of employment.

The sensitivity of the employment rate to expected earnings and the fact that school leavers were shown to have unrealistic expectations merit two comments. First, the direction of the causal relation in the observed association between expected earnings and the rate of employment cannot be established with absolute certainty. Second, even if it is assumed that high expectations *cause* low employment rates, the effect of more realistic expectations will be to shift the profiles in Figure 17-1 upward. The mean period of waiting to attain a reasonable rate of employment for the sample would still be exceptionally long by the standards of other countries.

It is tempting to speculate that both the acceptable age of first employment and the period of waiting will tend to fall as the labor market gets tighter with economic growth. The considerably steeper gradient of the function relating IDLPD to the school-leaving age for the East Coast towns compared with that for Kuala Lumpur might reflect the conditions of a more rapidly growing labor market in the East Coast.

While the analysis of employment rates among different streams of school leavers brings out the general importance of unrealistic expectations on the one hand, and the minimum age of employment on the other, some points also emerge about the special problems of subgroups in the sample.

The employment prospects of Malay school leavers in all streams were considerably worse than those of the Chinese, whether measured by the overall employment rate, the period of unemployment of those who had never had a job, or the time taken by the employed to get their first job (see Table 17-1). The multivariate analysis reported in Table 17-3 showed that the gross differences between the different race-language groups were reduced substantially when the influence of other factors on employment rates was taken into account. The spread between the gross employment rates of Malay-Malay and the Chinese-English was as much as 22 percentage points (around a grand mean of 39 percentage points). Evidently some variables which produced lower employment rates had a more than proportionate weighting of Malays. Among these variables location was important: Malays with Malay language of instruction were found more than other groups in small towns which generally had low employment rates. The separate regression equations by schooling levels in Tables 17-4 and 17-5 show that Malays have a worse employment experience than the Chinese—most markedly in the LCE stream, followed by the MCVE stream, and least in the MCE group. (Note the magnitudes of the negative coefficients of the Malay-Malay and Malay-English variables compared with the Chinese-English reference group.) In fact, among the MCE certificate holders, only the Malay-Malay have a significant negative coefficient; the employment rates of the Malay-English group and the Chinese-English are not significantly different. These differences in the employment rates for the race-language groups are net of other factors; that is, they persist after the influences of the remaining variables included in the regression, such as location, expectations, and time in the labor market, have been taken into account. Thus, the factors in the labor market suggested as the major causes of unemployment among school leavers appear to affect the Malays more than the Chinese, especially those with lower secondary qualifications. Nevertheless, the relatively greater pressure in the labor market accounted for by Malay school leavers had not led to any perceptible market adjustments by the time of the survey. The earnings of school leavers were more or less the same for the two races, and their occupational distribution between white- and blue-collar jobs was also similar (see Tables 16-6 and 16-3).

It was established in Chapter 16 that the returns to two extra years of education after lower secondary level were positive and were very similar for the academic and the vocational streams. It is also apparent that the employment rate of vocational school leavers is somewhat better than that of the academic group, when the time spent in the labor market and the other variables included in the regression models are taken into account. No strong policy conclusions can, however, be drawn from this result. It is possible that the better employment prospects apparently associated with vocational education are associated less with a direct improvement in their employability than with a prior tendency for those who drop out of the relatively intense competition for white-collar jobs to enroll in the vocational schools. In fact, the data show that, for both the Malays and the Chinese, the proportion of school leavers employed as production workers is much higher in the MCVE group than it is in the MCE (see Table 16-3). The question of the relative cost of providing vocational education would also need to be examined before coming to any policy conclusion about its social desirability.

Part IV

# Summary of Findings

THIS BOOK HAS ADDRESSED THE PROBLEM OF inequality in the urban
labor market in Malaysia. Since the analysis has concentrated on labor
earnings, the conclusions are more valid for the relatively poor, who
have little or no unearned income, than for the better-off. The starting
point of the analysis was a discussion of factors affecting household
income, based on a detailed examination of sample survey data; this
was followed by discussions of the determinants of personal earnings
and of unemployment.

Part I of the book assessed the quantitative importance of the dependency ratio on the one hand, and of low earnings on the other, in
the incidence of household poverty. Poor households do appear to
suffer from a relatively high burden of dependency, but even in absolute
terms this factor is *not* the principal cause of poverty. The percentage
of households in poverty increases monotonically with the number of
children in the household—and with the proportion of total income
contributed by the principal earner. Nevertheless, although 74 percent
of all households in which the principal earner is the sole breadwinner
and which have five or more dependent children suffer from poverty
(as against 30 percent for the entire sample examined), the total number of such families is not very large—about 13 percent of all poor
households. Of some general interest for students of urban income
levels in developing countries is the finding that, on balance, joint
households[1] help families to escape from poverty, because this type of
household structure seems to add more to earning strength than to
dependency. Joint families were found to be quite important in the
sample of households analyzed here; even on a fairly strict definition,
they accounted for about 40 percent of the full sample.

1. A joint household is one that contains members other than the household
head, his spouse, and his children or that supports dependent (nonearning)
relatives.

359

The weight of the dependency burden from which poor households suffer is significantly increased by adult as well as child dependency—not that poor households have a larger proportion of older people, nor are joint families more prevalent among the poor. Chapter 4 suggests the explanation: the proportion of earners among adults of working age is greater in households of higher economic status. This is contrary to much of the experience of developed countries and affects two groups of secondary earners in particular: married women and older men above forty-five years of age. Apparently the labor market offers gainful employment more easily to women from higher-income families and with more education; married women from richer families can probably also afford the cost of domestic help to look after the children when they go out to work. In the case of older men, retirement apparently occurs later in richer families.

While policies to improve female earning opportunities for the poorer households would clearly reduce adult dependency, the analysis in Chapter 5 indicates that the income of the principal earner is quantitatively much more important than the dependency ratio in accounting for differences in household income. First, the magnitude of the effect on household income levels of inequality in earnings per worker (as measured by its log-variance) is three times that of the dependency ratio. Very little of the inequality in the household income per head (YCON) is accounted for by the interaction between income per earner and the dependency ratio. Second, workers with equivalent personal resources (education and experience) seem to earn considerably more in high YCON families than in the poorer ones. The high YCON households no doubt have more workers with higher education, but it was shown that even if the returns to education (and experience) were the same across different YCON classes, the high YCON families would have a total income of a little less than three times that of the poor YCON class. Because of the less than average return to human capital for members of the poor families, and the higher than average return to these factors for workers in better-off households, the actual income ratio jumps to 6:1. When income per head is considered—that is, when differences in dependency ratios are included—the income imbalance between rich and poor households increases to 8:1.

In the light of the finding that the principal earner's income is the key determinant of household wealth or poverty, Part II of the book examines the factors which determine levels of personal income. The starting point of the analysis is an elaboration of the human capital model for urban Malaysia. Although it tends to overestimate the actual earnings of low-income employees and to underestimate those of high earners, the model performs remarkably well for what it does explain. Its overall explanatory power ($R^2$) is about 50 percent in urban Malaysia, compared with a level of around 30 percent in Britain and the United States; in other words, education and experience alone explain fully half the variance in personal earnings in Malaysia, but less than a third in the other two countries. Education in particular has much more explanatory power in Malaysia (40 percent) than in Britain and the United States, where length of schooling by itself explains no more than 6–7 percent of the variance in earnings. This difference—which is probably a fairly general point of contrast between developing and developed countries—is linked to two important features of developing economies. The number of years of schooling varies much more widely in developing countries, and the private rate of return to higher education is much higher. The latter phenomenon is related to the fact that the differences in earnings between different classes of occupations are significantly greater in developing than in developed countries. In Malaysia the professional or higher executive earns seven to eight times as much as the unskilled worker, while in Britain or the United States he probably earns only two to three times as much. Estimates presented in Chapter 7 suggest that the occupational skill differential may, if anything, be rather smaller in Malaysia than in other developing countries.

Public sector employment plays an influential role in Malaysia's urban labor market, as it does in many but not all developing countries, and it may contribute to the relatively high explanatory power of the human capital model of earnings. Although exact figures are not available, the public sector accounts for perhaps 40 percent of wage employment in Malaysia's urban economy. The public sector has also established standardized and relatively rigid pay scales based on formal education and seniority. The human capital model, which relies on precisely these two factors, might reasonably be expected to perform particularly well in explaining earnings in this sector; in fact, Chapter 8 shows that the model accounts for an astonishing 67 percent of the variance in male employees' earnings in the public sector. To the extent that public sector pay levels and criteria influence other sectors of the labor market, the model will also have a high degree of explanatory power for the economy as a whole.

The influence of the public sector, with its emphasis on formal qualifications, suggests the hypothesis that the observed association between education and earnings is a result of credentialism rather than the higher marginal productivity of educated labor. There is independent evidence—or at least some indication—that the role of credentialism might be strong in Malaysia. The analysis of the 1970 earnings data from the Post-Enumeration Survey showed that for each stage of the education process, success in obtaining the certificate appropriate to that stage resulted in substantially higher earnings than an incomplete performance. If credentialism is in fact an important feature of Malaysia's wage structure, then high private rates of return to education may coexist with a situation in which the supply of educated labor is seriously out of balance with the demand for it. This leads into the general issue of the high level of unemployment of educated labor, which is analyzed in Part III.

One of the purposes of the analysis of individual earnings in Part II was to assess the quantitative importance in urban Malaysia of labor market segmentation, which occurs when labor of equivalent quality earns different amounts in different parts of the market. The very existence of credentialism in the hiring of educated labor could be interpreted as an aspect of segmentation, since the phenomenon implies that educated workers get a premium for their certificates, irrespective of the quality of their effort or their output. A narrower definition of segmentation would be that labor with the same levels of education and experience tends to have different wage levels in different sectors. It was shown that enterprise size was an institutional factor leading to this kind of situation in the Malaysian labor market, but that the net quantitative effect of the size variable on earnings was probably smaller in Malaysia than in many other developing country labor markets (for example, that of Bombay). When other factors are taken into account, the overall difference in wages between the largest and the smallest enterprise size groups (those employing more than 100 and less than 10 employees) appears to be around 30 percent. Returns to education were higher in the larger enterprises, but this factor was offset to some extent by higher returns to experience in the smaller ones. The hypothesis that workers on the lower rungs of the labor market ladder—whether in unskilled occupations or small firms—tend to have generally flat age-earnings profiles was unambiguously refuted.

Various views advanced in the current literature about the relation between "excessive" rural-urban migration or particular types of migration on the one hand, and low earnings in certain sectors of the urban labor market on the other, were also found to be inapplicable in the Malaysian case. All three cities for which survey material was available (Kuala Lumpur and the two largest towns on the East Coast) had experienced rapid population growth as a result of migration, but recent migrants seemed to obtain jobs in disproportionate numbers, not in the small-scale informal sector, but in large enterprises employing 100 or more workers—perhaps in the public sector. Migrants generally performed better than natives, when allowance was made for the influence of factors other than migration itself on earnings.

The pattern of migration in Malaysia has distinctive features which differentiate it from the stereotype of rural-urban migration. A great deal of migration to the cities surveyed was from smaller urban centers; those coming from rural or agricultural backgrounds were by no means the overwhelming majority, as they are in the stereotype. A substantial proportion of migrants, moreover, turned out to have been stage migrants, who had made one or more intermediate stops before arriving in the city in which they currently lived. Migrants of this kind, who look for economic opportunities as they travel, can be expected to perform well in the economy. There was very little evidence of the temporary migration of such importance in some African and Asian cities, such as Bombay. One survey provided evidence that unemployment among secondary school leavers was *not* a consequence of the drift to the larger cities—rates of unemployment were actually higher in smaller towns than in Kuala Lumpur or other major metropolitan areas.

It has sometimes been maintained that job mobility within the urban labor markets of developing countries is probably not very great, and that workers who are unlucky enough to enter the market in the low-wage sector can become "trapped" there. In urban Malaysia the small-scale wage-earning sector appears to be the one in which wage levels tend generally to be low. The extreme hypothesis of a flat lifetime earnings profile for those who stay in the sector is refuted by the evidence, on the basis of cross-section data. Nevertheless, those who move out of the sector might have a higher growth rate of earnings than those who stay, as the analysis in Chapter 12 indicates. Those who have moved to larger enterprises over their working lifetimes have added significantly to their earnings, when other factors are taken into account. Education, however, still remains the principal determinant of earnings. Lifetime earnings are affected much more by the education of the respondent than by any other factor (including age). Those with the higher school certificate (HSC) or more advanced educational qualifications have the greatest lifetime increases in earnings, net of other effects.

The data also show substantial levels of mobility of labor from the small-scale to the other sectors. As much as 30 percent of the sample had started their careers in the small-scale sector; at the time of the survey about four-fifths of them had moved either to larger enterprises or to self-employment. For the sample as a whole, wage earners who made moves of this kind amounted to as much as 52 percent of the total. Thirty-seven percent did not change their sector of employment, while 11 percent shifted to an enterprise in a smaller size group. The self-employed sector attracted a net inflow of workers from the wage-earning sectors, especially the small-scale one, and this type of move seemed to have led to a greater net increase in lifetime earnings than other types. On balance, the analysis of individual earnings indicates that initial employment in the small-scale sector of Malaysia's urban labor market does not necessarily lead to low earnings, either at a point in time or over a worker's lifetime. The stereotype of the self-employed sector as one used by job seekers early in their career as a jumping-off point for a better job in the wage employment sector obviously needs revision in the Malaysian case.

Other findings derived from the data indicate the influence of race as a determinant of income. The simple human capital model (based on age and education factors) predicted that 22 percent of male Malay employees would earn less than M$150 per month, as against 14 percent of Chinese males. The actual percentages were found to be 31 and 19, respectively. The economically disadvantaged race does suffer from low levels of income to a greater extent than is predicted by the difference in educational attainments, but education remains important in accounting for the different proportions of Malay and Chinese who are low earners. The returns to education are, however, higher for the Malays at the lower end of the scale, so that the government's policy of extending postprimary education more widely is (together with public sector hiring policies) an effective tool for the reduction of the racial earnings gap for low earners. At the opposite end of the scale, returns to university level education are also higher for the Malays (there is little difference between the rates of return to education in the middle range for the two races). These higher overall rates of return to human capital factors for the disadvantaged race reveal a basic difference between Malaysia and, for example, the United States—where policies to reduce the racial earnings gap by encouraging human capital formation among the blacks have been partly frustrated by the lower marginal returns to human capital for this group.

Unemployment is a major cause of poverty in developed and developing countries alike. The unemployment rate is surprisingly high in

Malaysia, given the relatively rapid rate of growth of the economy compared with that in many other developing countries. The problem, however, is not so much one of unemployment of household heads, or of frequent spells of unemployment among prime-age workers; rather, it is an extreme case of youth unemployment. In most countries rates of unemployment among younger age groups tend to be higher than the average, and youth unemployment rates as high as those in urban Malaysia are not uncommon in several developing countries. The Malaysian situation, however, is distinguished by the extraordinarily long period of waiting before the new entrant into the labor market gets his first job. The problem has been particularly acute for secondary school leavers; a new entrant with a lower secondary school certificate may have had to suffer a period of active unemployment of two years or more before getting his first job. This state of affairs represents a substantial waste of human resources and could lead to serious social problems. It would be useful to know of comparable examples of inordinately long waiting periods. One similar case discussed in the literature is that of Sri Lanka,[2] where the problem has been particularly acute for job seekers with secondary school qualifications. A similar problem exists among college graduates in India, but because the absolute numbers involved are small, it does not show up in the overall unemployment rate for the urban economy as a whole.[3]

Survey data used here showed that Malay secondary school leavers had fathers whose incomes were somewhat lower than those of the population as a whole; a large percentage had parental monthly incomes less than M$100, and the vast majority came from families at the lower end of the income scale. The Chinese, by contrast, appeared to come from better-off families. It is possible that this finding may reflect a tendency for the poorer Chinese to go to Chinese private schools (which were not covered by the survey); or the racial difference in family socioeconomic status may have some connection with the survey finding that Chinese secondary school leavers had a lower rate of unemployment and a shorter waiting period than their Malay equivalents.

Explanation of the persistence of unemployment has been a central problem in the history of economics, and it would be overambitious to

2. See Peter Richards, "Job Mobility and Unemployment in the Ceylon Urban Labor Market," *Oxford Bulletin of Economics and Statistics*, vol. 35, no. 1 (February 1973).

3. See Mark Blaug, Richard Layard, and Maureen Woodhall, *The Causes of Graduate Unemployment in India* (London: Allen Lane, 1969).

expect to arrive at a comprehensive diagnosis at this stage for a special case of unemployment of the kind represented by the Malaysian situation. Nevertheless, the comprehensive analysis in Part III of this book has made it possible to identify several components of the problem in urban Malaysia with some clarity.

It was firmly established that school leavers' expectations at the time of the surveys were seriously out of line with reality. There was a very large gap between the proportion of respondents who wanted white-collar jobs, especially in the public sector, and the proportion who actually got them. Expected earnings were well above the actual earnings of those who did get jobs. The occupational sectors in which the school leavers were particularly interested tend to have relatively rigid wage structures characterized by credentialism. Faced with an excess supply of labor wishing to enter these sectors, the market has had to work around these rigidities through a dual process of educational upgrading of jobs and downward revision of the expectations of school leavers. The review of the evidence in Chapter 16 demonstrated quite clearly that such adjustments were taking place in the urban labor market in Malaysia. The education-occupation matrix for the younger age groups showed a significant number of secondary school leavers finding jobs as production workers rather than as clerks.

The persistence of unemployment and long periods of waiting, despite this process of market adjustment, requires three comments. First, there are obviously dynamic lags in the process; a more or less adequate restructuring of the market will take some time to achieve. Second, the dispersion of earnings, and especially of starting pay, during these adjustments will tend to increase the returns to job search and thus lengthen the period of waiting which school leavers believe to be ultimately profitable. Third, the upgrading of jobs and the dilution of the educational system might feed on each other to some extent, so that a shift in the demand curve of educated labor may induce at least some compensatory shift in the supply curve.

In contemporary discussions of the ways in which labor markets operate, it is often stated that a minimum—and perhaps rising—standard of education is the principal criterion used for hiring employees in the formal sector. Evidence presented in Part III of this book suggests that an equally important criterion seems to be operating in the Malaysian case: a minimum *age* of employment. Obviously, both of these selection criteria can persist in a situation which combines excess supply of labor with inability on the part of hiring units to cut costs by lowering entry wages. The role of the public sector wage policy in maintaining relatively high entry wages in Malaysia becomes very important in this context. Institutionalized high wages in the public sector—particularly at the lower end of the scale—together with a policy of preferential hiring may be socially beneficial by helping redress the economic imbalance against the Malays; available evidence makes it clear that this mix of policies has in fact reduced racial differences in earnings for those with secondary education. The other side of the coin, however, is represented by high unemployment rates among young school leavers and unnaturally long periods of idleness before entering employment.

Why do school leavers not seek employment in the informal sector? The answer must lie partly in the relatively low productivity of this sector in urban Malaysia. A further problem may be that the informal sector—particularly sales—is dominated by the Chinese. Given the degree of racial segregation of private sector employees noted in Part II of the text, the employment opportunities for Malay youths in this sector may be somewhat limited.

An expansion of overall demand for labor would obviously reduce youth unemployment by creating tighter labor market conditions and lowering employers' requirements for minimum education and age. The point made in the previous paragraph, however, suggests that policies to encourage the relative growth of small-scale enterprises or the informal sector might also be helpful in increasing employment levels among secondary school leavers.

The issues discussed in this book have included many of the major topics of concern in the urban labor markets of developing countries. Because empirical work in sufficient detail is very scarce, however, it is not possible to be precise at this point about the applicability of some of the findings in this book to other developing countries. The main conclusions of Part I of the book—the relatively minor importance of dependency ratios relative to the earnings of the principal worker in determining family income, and the fall in both adult and child dependency with increases in household income—are probably of fairly general validity. The structure of earnings in Malaysia, discussed in Part II, is substantially determined by the basic human capital factors of age and education; formal education is likely to be equally important in the urban economies of most developing countries. In those in which the public sector plays as significant a role in urban employment as it does in Malaysia, credentialism will also be a major factor in the determination of earnings.

Other findings in Part II and Part III of this book are more likely to be specific to Malaysia or to a relatively small number of similar special cases. For example, earnings differences—after allowance is made for human capital factors—were of minor importance in Malaysia, unlike the situation in other urban labor markets in developing countries. The relatively small size and importance of the nonformal sector may be another special feature of the Malaysian economy; it has been suggested that this factor may partially account for yet a third peculiarity of the Malaysian labor market, the long pre-employment waiting periods and high levels of open unemployment among school leavers. In the final analysis, it will be possible to test these and other generalizations only when accurate information is available about other urban labor markets in different types of economies. This implies the need for more case studies, probably in as much detail as this one for Malaysia.

# Index

Dipak Mazumdar is a senior economist with the Development Economics Department of the World Bank.

•